HISTORY OF CIVILIZATION
VOLUME II: SINCE 1648
by
Paul Bernstein and **Robert**

About the Authors

<u>Professor Bernstein</u>:

1. Present Position: Dean, College Of General Studies, Rochester Institute of Technology, Rochester (N.Y.)
2. Publications: "The Rhine Frontier in 1859," *Lock Haven Bulletin,* Vol. I, No. 1 (1959); "The Economic Aspect of Napoleon III's Rhine Policy," *French Historical Studies,* Vol. I, No. 3 (May, 1960). Received a research grant from the American Philosophical Society of Philadelphia to complete a study entitled *Biarritz, 1865.*

<u>Professor Green</u>:

1. Present Position: Associate Professor of European History, The Pennsylvania State University. Formerly taught at the State University of Iowa.
2. Publications: *Protestantism and Capitalism: the Weber Thesis and Its Critics* (Boston: D. C. Heath, 1959). Presently in preparation is a study of Louis XIV.

About the Book

1. Material has been arranged in outline form.
2. Important facts, documents, and names have been underlined so that important information can be seen easily.
3. Thirteen maps have been included to clarify the geographical aspects of world history.
4. A list of scholarly references for further reading can be found at the end of each chapter.
5. Appropriate emphasis has been given to India, Southeast Asia, and the Far East in addition to western civilization.

HISTORY OF
CIVILIZATION
VOLUME II: SINCE 1648

By

Paul Bernstein
Dean, College of General Studies,
Rochester Institute of Technology

Robert W. Green
Associate Professor of European History
The Pennsylvania State University

1976

LITTLEFIELD, ADAMS & CO.
Totowa, New Jersey

ACKNOWLEDGMENTS

The map appearing on pages 4-5, has been reproduced from *A History of Civilization, Vol. I,* by Crane Brinton, John B. Christopher, and Robert Lee Wolff. Map by Vaughn Gray. Copyrighted 1955 by Prentice-Hall, Inc., Englewood Cliffs, New Jersey. Used by permission of the publisher.

The maps appearing on pages 62, 108, and 487 have been reproduced from *A History of Civilization, Vol. II, 1715 to the Present,* Second Edition, by Crane Brinton, John B. Christopher, and Robert Lee Wolff. Maps by Vaughn Gray. Copyrighted 1955, 1960 by Prentice-Hall, Inc., Englewood Cliffs, New Jersey. Used by permission of the publisher.

The maps appearing on pages 66, 147A and 147B, 234A, 234B, 337A and 337B, 347A and 347B, 355, 428, 452-453, have been reproduced from *Modern Civilization: A History of the Last Five Centuries,* by Crane Brinton, John B. Christopher, and Robert Lee Wolff. Maps by Vaughn Gray. Copyrighted 1957 by Prentice-Hall, Inc., Englewood Cliffs, New Jersey. Used by permission of the publisher.

PREFACE

A systematic study of history is the best way to explore the byways of the past. Such an organization of historical data can help the student appreciate his heritage, focus attention on important questions of interpretation, and make evident the importance of this information with regard to an understanding of the present. It is the purpose of *History of Civilization*, Vols. I and II, to accomplish these objectives.

Within these outlines considerable emphasis has been placed on the culture and affairs of India, Southeast Asia, and the Far East. This is not only recognition of the growing importance of these areas in the twentieth century, but it is designed to point up the great accomplishments of Asia during antiquity. In addition, a full treatment of the Prehistoric period has been included in Vol. I, along with some of the leading theories on the creation of the universe.

Considerable space has been devoted to the analysis of human cultural accomplishment. Particular attention has been given to the fields of literature, architecture, art, science, mathematics, and music. It might be noted that Vol. II was designed to begin around the year 1648, although some material may date from the beginning of the sixteenth century. This will enable the student to continue from the point where the first volume of this set left off.

This outline on the *History of Civilization* is offered as a guide to systematic study. It is not a substitute for a textbook, and does not preclude the need for reading source materials, secondary works, and monographic studies. Used in a careful manner, this outline can help the student master and understand the mass of data he will inevitably encounter.

CONTENTS

Maps

HISTORY OF CIVILIZATION
VOLUME II: SINCE 1648

Chapter 1

WESTERN EUROPE IN THE SEVENTEENTH AND EIGHTEENTH CENTURIES

I. England During the Reign of James I (1603–1625)

A. James I, already King James VI of Scotland, was chosen to succeed Queen Elizabeth I (ruled 1558–1603).

    1. James was the great-great grandson of Henry VII of England, the grandfather of Elizabeth I.

    2. Though James' mother was Mary Queen of Scots, a rival to Elizabeth I, he was nevertheless the closest living relative of Elizabeth.

B. James vigorously advocated strengthening royal power; and his policies soon entangled him in serious religious, political, financial, and foreign policy controversies with Parliament.

    1. James enunciated a theory of the "Divine Right of Kings," which was unsuited for conditions in England during his reign.

        a. According to James, kings were "God's lieutenants on earth" and needed to account to no mortal man for their actions or policies.

        b. James repeatedly asserted that "The king is from God, and law is from the king."

        c. James insisted the church should be ruled by bishops appointed and controlled by the king. Bishops, in turn, controlled the clergy below them (episcopal system of church government).

    2. James soon clashed with the Puritans who wished to "purify" the church of England, making its liturgy more like the Calvinist church in Scotland and governing the church by elders (presbyters) rather than bishops.

        a. The Puritans had hoped James would be sympathetic

1

to their views because he had been raised in Presbyterian Scotland.

   b. James, however, openly opposed the Puritans as subversive of his monarchial power and tried to make them conform to the Church of England.

   c. The Puritans were a minority, but they were vocal and influential in Parliament and became resolutely opposed to James.

3. James tried to meet increasing costs of government by relying on revenues over which Parliament had no control.

   a. He sold titles and monopolies, squeezed as much revenue as possible from customs duties, and collected forced loans from individuals.

   b. When an individual appealed to the law courts for protection and the crown lost the case, James dismissed the Chief Justice, Sir Edward Coke (Bates case, 1606).

   c. These policies called public attention to James' attempts to extend royal authority over all government affairs and to exclude Parliament from its traditional political role.

4. James' foreign policy was no more popular than his domestic programs.

   a. James tried to arrange a marriage for his son with a Spanish princess, and the English hated Spain.

   b. When the Spanish marriage proposal failed, Prince Charles married a Roman Catholic French princess, a match hardly more welcome to the Protestant English.

   c. James' policies relative to the Thirty Years' War (1618–1648) were indecisive and only reaped criticism at home.

C. As his reign drew to a close, James had utterly failed to increase royal power in England.

   1. His policies had alienated one group after another, and he had clashed with Parliament repeatedly.

   2. More serious, the various groups offended by James' policies gradually began to unite in firm opposition to any extension of royal authority.

II. The Reign of Charles I and the Civil War (1625–1649)

A. Charles I was as firm a believer as his father in the Divine Right of Kings and just as determined to prevent Parliament from restraining royal authority.

B. From his first Parliament Charles demanded money for war against Spain.

   1. Parliament granted funds, but Charles used the money for other purposes.

   2. Parliament refused to provide additional money and urged the king to remove his favorite minister, the Duke of Buckingham.

C. Charles then tried to raise money by demanding forced loans from his subjects and quartering his troops in private homes at the householder's expense.

D. In 1628 Parliament forced Charles I to agree to the "Petition of Right" before it would vote the funds he needed. The "Petition of Right" was one of the most important steps in the development of constitutional government and it declared illegal:

   1. The quartering of troops in private homes;

   2. The levy of forced loans or other taxes without consent of Parliament;

   3. The imprisonment of any person without bringing a specific charge against him;

   4. The declaration of martial law in time of peace.

E. From 1629 to 1640, Charles ruled without Parliament.

   1. He collected tariff duties in spite of Parliament's protests and imprisoned some individuals who refused to pay.

   2. He revived old taxes and dues, among them the "ship money" tax, which originally was paid only by seaport towns to maintain the fleet.

      a. Charles doubled the ship money tax rate and collected it from inland towns as well as seaports.

      b. When this tax was contested by John Hampden, the crown won the law case; but public attention was focused on Charles' tax policies.

   3. Financially, Charles was reasonably successful but his policies were bitterly resented and paved the way for revolution.

EUROPE IN 1648

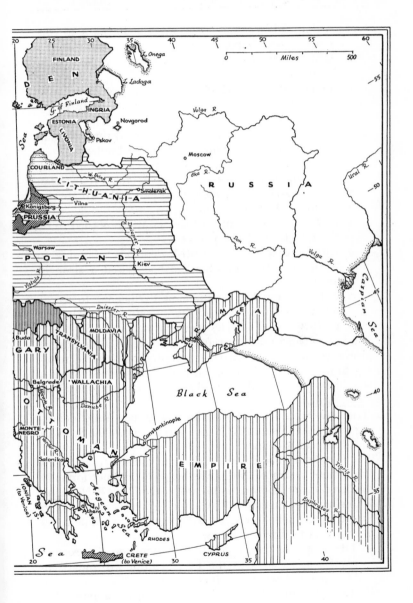

FINLAND

L. Onega

L. Ladoga

G. of Finland

DEN

D

ESTONIA

INGRIA

LIVONIA

Novgorod

Pskov

Volga R.

Moscow

R U S S I A

Oka R.

Ural R.

Sea

COURLAND

W. Dvina R.

L I T H U A N I A

Smolensk

Königsberg

Vilna

PRUSSIA

Don R.

Volga R.

Warsaw

P O L A N D

Vistula R.

Kiev

Dnieper R.

Caspian Sea

Dniester R.

C R I M E A

GARY

TRANSYLVANIA

MOLDAVIA

Buda

Belgrade

WALLACHIA

Danube R.

Morava R.

Black Sea

MONTE-NEGRO

O T T O M A N

Constantinople

Danube R.

Salonika

E M P I R E

IONIAN IS. (to Venice)

Aegean Sea

Athens

Tigris R.

Euphrates R.

RHODES

Sea

CRETE (to Venice)

CYPRUS

Miles

0   500

F. Charles' religious policies were hardly more popular than his taxes.
  1. The king did his utmost to force the Puritans to conform with the Church of England.
     a. Arbitrary royal courts were revived to persecute the Puritans.
     b. Thousands of Puritans and other non-conformists fled from England and established colonies in North America.
  2. Charles also relaxed the restrictions against Roman Catholics, a highly unpopular policy in England.
  3. In 1637 Charles and his Archbishop of Canterbury, William Laud, tried to force Charles' Scotch Presbyterian subjects to accept the episcopal system of church government and the Anglican ritual.
     a. In 1638 the Scots joined together and promised to resist Charles by force if necessary.
     b. Charles gave way to Scottish demands, planning to break his promises when he had raised a stronger army.
     c. But the king had to summon Parliament to secure money for an army, and the assembly of Parliament in 1640 ended Charles' personal rule.
G. When Parliament met, it refused funds until a long list of grievances were met. Charles promptly dissolved it, refusing to meet their demands, but not getting funds. Since it was in session only three weeks, it is known as the Short Parliament.
H. Then the Scots attacked Charles' inadequate army, defeating it in a skirmish; and Charles agreed to pay the Scots an indemnity to withdraw.
I. The king again had to call Parliament to raise funds. This Parliament, assembled in November 1640, was not formally dissolved until 1660 and is known as the Long Parliament.
J. Knowing Charles had to have funds to meet the Scottish threat, Parliament forced the king to accept a whole series of measures to limit royal power.
  1. The king was forced to dismiss, imprison, or execute royal officials such as the Earl of Strafford and Archbishop Laud whom Parliament opposed.
  2. The Triennial Act, requiring the king to summon Parliament at least once every three years, was passed.

    3. All arbitrary royal law courts, such as the Court of Star Chamber, were abolished.

    4. Ship money and other forms of unparliamentary taxation were forbidden.

    5. Another act prevented Charles from dissolving the Long Parliament without its own consent.

K. In 1642, King Charles tried to prevent further parliamentary action by ordering the arrest of five of the leaders of the opposition to him in the House of Commons.

    1. When this plan failed, Charles went to Nottingham in northern England and summoned all loyal citizens to join him and form an army.

    2. Parliament's response was to prepare for war by voting to raise an army of ten thousand men.

L. The Civil War opened with a royalist offensive directed toward London late in 1642. The king's forces were initially successful because of superior cavalry but failed to move on London before new defenses could be established, and the king withdrew to Oxford.

    1. The Royalist forces were strongest in northern and western England; Parliament kept control of the south and east, including London, the major seaports, and the navy.

    2. While persons of every class were found in both camps, the nobility generally supported the king, and the royalist forces were called "Cavaliers."

    3. The bulk of Parliament's forces were composed of merchants, tradesmen, and small farmers. Because they wore their hair close-cropped, they were called "Roundheads."

    4. The decisive element bringing victory to Parliament's forces was the creation of a new, highly organized and disciplined cavalry force, the "Ironsides," under the leadership of a previously obscure member of Parliament, Oliver Cromwell.

       a. At Marston Moor (1644) the Ironsides won a sweeping victory over the royalist cavalry.

       b. Cromwell then persuaded Parliament to reorganize its remaining forces on the pattern of the Ironsides, and in 1645 the "New Model Army" was created.

       c. The New Model Army shattered the royalist forces at Naseby (1645) and Longport (1645).

    d. King Charles I surrendered himself to the Scots in 1646. They turned him over to Parliament in 1647 for £400,000 back pay.

M. In 1647 Parliament's members were in bitter disagreement over how to establish a new government.

    1. The majority of Parliament was Presbyterian and was willing to put Charles back on his throne if he would make the Church of England Presbyterian.

    2. The New Model Army was dominated by Independents who wanted all types of Puritanism tolerated. Cromwell was an Independent, and tried hard but unsuccessfully to bring about an agreement between Parliament and the army.

    3. The king escaped, fled to Scotland, and promised the Scots to establish the Presbyterian Church in England if they would help him invade England.

    4. At <u>Preston (1648)</u> Cromwell and the New Model Army smashed the Scots and royalists, taking Charles prisoner.

    5. Returning to London, Cromwell excluded the Presbyterians from Parliament <u>(Pride's Purge, 1648)</u>. The remaining members, later called <u>"the Rump,"</u> consisted of fifty-three Independents.

    6. The Independents formed a special High Court of Justice and condemned Charles I as "a tyrant, a traitor, murderer, and public enemy to the good people of this nation."

    7. Charles I was executed January 30, 1649.

    8. Cromwell had firmly opposed earlier attempts to try Charles I; only when Cromwell became convinced the king was completely untrustworthy did he join those demanding Charles' death.

III. The Commonwealth, the Protectorate, and the Interregnum (1649–1660)

A. So long as Charles I was in power, the revolutionaries were united in opposing him; when he was defeated and executed, the revolutionaries could not agree on the establishment of a new order to replace the old.

B. Shortly after Charles' execution, the Rump declared England a free <u>Commonwealth.</u>

    1. The monarchy and the House of Lords were abolished.

    2. The executive power was supposed to be vested in a forty-one member council of state; but, in fact, the power of the state rested on the army.

    3. As the master of the army, Cromwell was the real ruler of England.

C. Because Cromwell and the Independents favored religious toleration, an enormous proliferation of religious sects were permitted to exist. Baptists and Quakers were protected by Cromwell; and Jews, excluded from England since 1290, were permitted to enter freely.

    1. These religious sects advocated many different economic and political programs.

       a. Some groups were politically conservative, but others favored ideas which were radical for the time. The Levellers, for example, favored such practices as universal manhood suffrage and progressive taxation.

       b. Even more radical were some groups, such as the Diggers, who favored communal property. Other radical groups preached the imminence of the Second Coming of Christ and believed in the immediate establishment of some earthly utopia.

    2. In the face of these divided views, it proved impossible to find a parliamentary solution which could govern England and satisfy all the divergent views.

D. These religious, economic, and political divisions practically forced Cromwell, whatever his personal desires might have been, to govern as a dictator to avoid chaos in England.

    1. Cromwell clashed repeatedly with the Rump and arbitrarily increased its membership to represent Scotland and Ireland (Barebone's Parliament).

    2. Barebone's Parliament, well-intentioned but impractical, was dissolved in 1653; the Commonwealth came to an end.

E. Only four days later the army promulgated a written constitution, the "Instrument of Government," which established the Protectorate.

    1. A new single chamber Parliament of four hundred sixty members representing England, Scotland, and Ireland was to hold legislative power.

    2. Executive power was vested in one man, the Lord Protector, Oliver Cromwell.

3. <u>The Protector and the Parliament soon clashed</u> over the division of power between them, and Cromwell resorted to military force to rule the realm.

F. In ruling England by military power, Cromwell used many of the tyrannical methods for which he had earlier attacked Charles I; by no stretch of the imagination could Parliament be said to have directed the government during the period 1649–1658.

G. While he ruled England, Cromwell carried out a vigorous and largely successful foreign policy.

1. <u>In 1649, the Scots proclaimed the son of Charles I king.</u> The Irish rose in favor of the young Charles II; but Cromwell crushed the Irish revolt, confiscated the property of Catholic rebels, and gave it to his Protestant supporters. English-Irish relations became more embittered than ever.

2. <u>In 1650, the Scots, led by Charles II, invaded England.</u> Though he was greatly outnumbered, Cromwell completely routed the royalists in a brilliant series of victories, and Charles II fled to France.

3. <u>In 1652, a trade war with the Dutch began.</u> By 1654 this war had been successfully concluded by the English.

4. From 1656 to 1659, the English were at war with Spain. The English gained the valuable continental port of Dunkirk, the colony of Jamaica, and shattered the Spanish fleet.

5. Cromwell arranged trade treaties, which were highly advantageous to England, with Sweden and Denmark.

6. The European powers had the greatest scorn for the actions of the English revolutionaries, but they quickly came to respect England as a great power while Cromwell ruled.

H. The period from Cromwell's death (September 3, 1658) to Parliament's proclamation of Charles II as king (May 8, 1660) was known as the <u>Interregnum.</u>

1. When Oliver Cromwell died, his son, Richard, was made Lord Protector; but a dispute between Parliament and the army led to his resignation.

2. <u>General Monk</u> led his army from Scotland to London, seized control and called together all the surviving members of the Long Parliament of 1640.

3. When Charles II proclaimed a general amnesty for all

persons not exempted by Parliament and promised liberty of conscience to all (Declaration of Breda), the Long Parliament initiated the steps which proclaimed him king.

IV. The Restoration Era (1660–1688)

A. The Restoration period takes its name from the fact that a member of the Stuart family (Charles II) again occupied the throne. The age was characterized by reaction against the strict Puritan "blue laws" and by intermittent clashes between Parliament and the crown over religious and financial issues. These clashes culminated in the Revolution of 1688.

B. The Church of England was restored as it had existed during the reign of Charles I. A series of laws (Clarendon Code, 1661–1665) was passed to enforce religious conformity.

  1. The Clarendon Code imposed many restrictions on Roman Catholics and "Dissenters"—Protestants who were not members of the Church of England.

  2. Charles II (ruled 1660–1685) viewed the French royal absolutism of Louis XIV as a political ideal and was sympathetic to Roman Catholics in England.

    a. In 1672 he issued a Declaration of Indulgence to remove all disabilities against Roman Catholics and Protestant Dissenters.

    b. In response to the king's action Parliament passed the Test Act of 1673 providing that all officials of the government must receive the sacrament according the rites of the Church of England and must repudiate the Roman Catholic doctrine of transubstantiation.

  3. Although severe penalties were provided for violators of these laws, many persons escaped punishment via legal loopholes and casual enforcement of the laws.

C. Though Charles II was most discreet about his hopes for increasing the authority of the crown, Parliament carefully limited the funds granted to the king.

  1. Unknown to Parliament, however, Charles II was secretly receiving subsidies from Louis XIV of France (Treaty of Dover, 1670).

    a. The English were to aid the French against the Dutch.

   b. Charles II was publicly to declare himself a Roman
      Catholic at the opportune time.
   2. The opinion was widespread that war against the Dutch
      was just a pretense to enable Charles to establish a
      standing army, and Charles yielded to demands for
      peace in 1674.
D. Charles II had no children and the crown passed to his
   brother, James II (ruled 1685–1688), a declared Roman
   Catholic.
   1. In 1685, James II had no sons. The English assumed
      James II would be succeeded by his Protestant daughter,
      Mary, and her husband William of Orange.
   2. James II soon angered Parliament by clearly indicating
      his intention to re-establish the Roman Catholic Church
      in England and to rule as an absolute monarch.
      a. James refused to dismiss an army which had been
         raised to quell Monmouth's rebellion (1685). Parlia-
         ment was alarmed by the presence of a royal stand-
         ing army near London.
      b. He established a new religious court and demanded
         Parliament repeal the Test Act and the Habeas
         Corpus Act. Parliament refused.
      c. James violated the Test Act in making appointments
         and, in 1687, issued the Declaration of Indulgence
         suspending all penal laws against Catholics and
         Dissenters.
      d. The Declaration of Indulgence embittered the dis-
         pute concerning whether a king, issuing decrees as he
         chose, could simply ignore Parliament.
      e. While the Declaration of Indulgence appeared to be
         a step toward religious liberty, most Englishmen re-
         garded the Roman Catholic faith as a threat to Eng-
         land, just as they had thought of it in the days of the
         Spanish Armada.
   3. In 1688 a son, who would be a Roman Catholic, was
      born to James II. This meant James would be succeeded
      by a Roman Catholic ruler.

V. The Revolution of 1688 and Its Settlement

A. The Revolution of 1688 grew from the unpopularity of
   James II and from a desire to prevent a Roman Catholic
   ruler from succeeding James II.

B. Some members of Parliament offered the crown to William and Mary, the elder Protestant daughter and son-in-law of James II.

1. <u>William, Stadholder of the United Provinces,</u> the outstanding Protestant leader of the Dutch struggle against France, could not refuse the opportunity to add England's strength to the Dutch resistance to Louis XIV.

2. William landed in England with a small force; and when James II found he could not rally sufficient forces to defend himself, he fled to France.

3. Because the Revolution of 1688 was comparatively bloodless, it is frequently called the "Glorious Revolution," the term the English usually prefer.

C. Early in 1689 Parliament formally offered the crown to William and Mary on terms soon enacted into law as the <u>Bill of Rights.</u>

1. The crown was forbidden to impose taxes without the consent of Parliament.

2. Elections to Parliament were to be free, and freedom of speech and debate was never to be impaired in Parliament.

3. No one who professed the Roman Catholic faith or who married a Roman Catholic could occupy the throne.

4. Parliament was to meet regularly and frequently.

5. A standing army could not be raised or maintained within the kingdom without consent of Parliament.

6. William was to share the crown with his wife, and the couple ruled as William III (1689–1702) and Mary II 1689–1694) .

D. Because William and Mary were childless, Parliament passed the <u>Act of Settlement in 1701</u> to regulate succession to the throne.

1. The crown was to go to Anne (ruled 1702–1714), younger sister of Mary.

2. If Anne died childless (which did occur) , the crown was to go to the Protestant Sophia of Hanover or her issue. Sophia was a grand-daughter of James I. The Roman Catholic son of James II was excluded from the succession.

3. In 1714, the crown passed to Sophia's son, who became George I (ruled 1714–1727) .

E. In Scotland the settlement of the Revolution of 1688 was more violent than in England.
   1. The Highlanders rose in favor of the son of James II. Initially the Scots were victorious over William's troops, but the Scottish leaders were killed and the revolt slowly collapsed.
   2. In 1707, the Act of Union was agreed upon by which Scotland and England were combined into the United Kingdom of Great Britain. Scotland thenceforth sent representatives to Parliament. One flag, the Union Jack, combining the crosses of St. Andrew and St. George symbolized the new kingdom.

F. In Ireland developments took a less fortunate turn.
   1. Since most of the Irish were Roman Catholic, they warmly supported James II and rose against William.
   2. Not until 1690, when King William himself smashed the Irish in the Battle of Boyne, did armed resistance cease.
   3. William tried a moderate settlement in Ireland, permitting the Irish Roman Catholics the privileges they had had under Charles II.
   4. The English government, however, only a year later excluded Roman Catholics from government positions and later provided other restrictions as well. The bitter relationships between Ireland and England continued.

VI. The Development of Cabinet Government in England

A. The extension of Parliament's authority by the Revolution of 1688 and the lack of familiarity with the English government characteristic of the occupants of the throne following the revolution provided an opportunity for the development of new procedures in government.
   1. While the king was supposed to be the chief executive who governed from day to day, the final authority in the government rested with Parliament.
   2. The most used line of communication between the king and Parliament was the employment of members of Parliament to act as advisors (ministers) to the king.
   3. William III (1689–1702) gradually realized his relations with Parliament were most satisfactory when his cabinet ministers were chosen from the majority party in the House of Commons.

    a. During the reign of Charles II, the members of Parliament divided into two groups.

    b. One group, critical of the Stuarts and somewhat representative of Puritan views, was termed <u>Whigs.</u>

    c. The other, more sympathetic to the Cavaliers, was called <u>Tory.</u>

    d. The Whigs, who had been the leaders of the Revolution of 1688 and continued to oppose any Stuart restoration, naturally enjoyed the favor of the kings following the revolution.

4. The reigns of George I (ruled 1714–1727) and George II (ruled 1727–1760) provided excellent opportunities for the cabinet ministers to assume more and more of the kings' executive functions.

    a. Neither George I nor George II regularly attended cabinet meetings. This permitted the cabinet members to settle their differences privately and present the king with recommendations supported by the entire cabinet.

    b. The leadership in discussion among cabinet members was usually assumed by one man; he became the prime minister.

5. <u>During the period 1721–1742, the leading role in cabinet affairs was played by Sir Robert Walpole.</u>

    a. Walpole was the most influential Whig leader and also served as First Lord of the Treasury.

    b. Walpole's policy was to promote domestic prosperity and to avoid war.

    c. On the whole, Walpole was remarkably successful; but soon after the English entered the War of Jenkin's Ear against Spain in 1739 and the War of the Austrian Succession (1740–1748), he resigned.

6. <u>The next outstanding cabinet leader to appear was William Pitt, "the Elder," (the Earl of Chatham),</u> who assumed leadership from 1757 to 1762.

    a. Walpole's pacifist policies had left the British unprepared for war, and the early years of the Seven Years' War (1756–1763) provided only defeat and disaster for the British.

    b. Pitt devised and carried out vigorous policies, turning defeat into victory, gaining for the British the rule of North America east of the Mississippi from the Gulf of Mexico to the polar regions (Peace of Paris, 1763).

   c. The British destroyed French control of India during the Seven Years' War and could have gained even more in the peace settlement if George III had supported Pitt's policies.

B. George III (ruled 1760–1820) tried to restore royal control of government administration.

   1. George III did not claim authority over Parliament but sought to control the appointment of cabinet ministers and to make them responsible to him.

   2. This led to the resignation of William Pitt (1762) and the gradual reduction of the domination of the House of Commons by the Whig party.

   3. From 1770 to 1782, Lord North was prime minister. During his ministry, the cabinet followed the king's direction and was, in effect, responsible to the king. The disaster of the American Revolution and the growing power of the king seriously alarmed Parliament and the British people.

   4. The situation was prevented from becoming far more serious by the king's appointment of William Pitt the Younger as prime minister in 1783. The Younger Pitt served as prime minister almost continuously until his death in 1806.

     a. Pitt restored the government's finances and pushed through the Act of Union (1800), merging the parliaments of Great Britain and Ireland. He arranged an unusually profitable trade treaty with France in 1787; he advocated parliamentary reform, the abolition of slavery, and the removal of restrictions on Roman Catholics.

     b. The long and successful ministry of William Pitt the Younger did much to restore parliamentary control of the cabinet and of the executive power of government.

VII. English Economic and Cultural Development in the Seventeenth and Eighteenth Centuries

A. The English greatly increased their wealth during this period though the process was interrupted by revolution at home and war abroad.

1. Colonies established, generally by trading companies, in the seventeenth century gradually became commercially important.

2. In addition to colonial development in North America and the West Indies, English trading companies established themselves in India and the East Indies.

B. The wealth gained in colonial and commercial activity provided the capital needed for the beginnings of the Industrial Revolution (see Chapter VII).

C. At the same time new developments in agricultural techniques were increasing English wealth. These developments, most of which occurred in the eighteenth century, are sometimes called the "Agrarian Revolution."

1. New methods of tillage were introduced.

   a. The outstanding pioneer in this work was Jethro Tull, who advocated repeated cultivation of crops during their growth.

   b. Tull devised new machines for planting, harrowing, and raking to facilitate cultivation.

2. Methods were devised to enable farmers to feed their livestock through the winter instead of slaughtering most of it each fall.

   a. Winter feed was provided by sowing turnips, clover, and artificial grasses, which also replenished the soil for other summer crops.

   b. Lord Townshend, known as "Turnip" Townshend, was the leading pioneer in this work. His introduction of new crop rotation systems made it no longer necessary to let fields be fallow; and, therefore, the available amount of arable land was increased by nearly a third.

3. Robert Bakewell was the great eighteenth century pioneer of selective breeding of livestock. Bakewell's experiments in breeding sheep and horses were so successful that others soon utilized his methods for selective breeding of cattle.

4. These new agricultural techniques doomed the old open field system which allotted scattered strips to individual peasant cultivators.

   a. Open fields and common pastures were divided by fences and hedgerows to permit use of new agricultural methods.

     b. The poorer farmers were the usual victims of these reforms since they lacked the funds to adapt the new methods.

     c. Forced to sell, many of the poorer farmers and rural laborers moved to the factory towns, furnishing labor for the beginning Industrial Revolution.

D. During the seventeenth and eighteenth centuries, English life and social customs varied from one extreme of rigorous Puritan sobriety to the other, characterized by the notorious profligacy of the Restoration period.

  1. During the Commonwealth and the Protectorate, social life reflected the habitual seriousness of the Puritans.

     a. Their literature was permeated by a religious earnestness and reflected reverence and simple tastes.

     b. Puritans passed a law in 1642 closing the theaters because they regarded pageantry and comedy as unwarranted distractions from the serious purposes of life.

     c. The Puritans are well-known for their restrictions on recreation and social life and the proliferation of "blue laws," which they enacted and enforced.

  2. The Restoration Era witnessed a reaction to Puritan standards of behavior.

     a. The reopened theaters offered biting satire, wit, and flagrant indecency.

     b. Many Restoration literary works were presented in coarse and profane language and bowed to the tastes of the era by including liberal measures of obscenity.

     c. The royal court during the reign of Charles II was openly immoral and set a standard of licentiousness the population seemed happy to follow.

  3. In the eighteenth century, English social leaders prided themselves on refined manners and publicly rejected the profligacy of the Restoration. Beneath the surface refinement, however, ignorance, squalid poverty, and drunkenness were rampant.

     a. Most of the population received no education and were illiterate; institutions of higher learning were poorly attended—in 1750, only three hundred seventeen freshmen matriculated in all England.

     b. Most of the population in the cities occupied crowded, filthy, disease-ridden slums.

     c. Alcoholism became common as the upper classes

consumed tremendous quantities of port wine, but the less fortunate drank gin. It is estimated that in 1736 every twenty-fifth house in London was a gin shop, most of which posted signs promising to make the customer "drunk for a penny, dead drunk for two-pence."

E. The outstanding religious development in eighteenth century England was the appearance of the Methodist denomination.

1. In reaction to the fierce theological disputes of seventeenth century England, rational religion became more widely accepted.

   a. Rational religion emphasized a rational interpretation of the relationships between man and God.

   b. Advocates of rational religion denounced religious emotionalism, considered religious fervor or enthusiasm a delusion, and were particularly influential in the Church of England.

   c. The Anglican rational religion, however, apparently failed to satisfy the religious desires of many of the English.

2. In 1729 at Oxford University a group of students led by John Wesley (1703–1791) formed a "Holy Club" to cultivate personal piety and to do benevolent deeds.

   a. These students instructed children of the poor, visited hospitals and prisons, fasted twice weekly, and received Holy Communion weekly.

   b. Because of the methodical regularity of their lives, the members of the Holy Club were dubbed "Methodists" by other students.

   c. Among the members of the Holy Club were Charles Wesley, later famous as a hymn writer, and George Whitefield, who became an eminent preacher.

   d. The club members had no desire to establish a new sect; all were Anglicans who wished to keep their faith alive and preach the gospel to those who had not heard it.

3. In 1735 John and Charles Wesley went to the newly founded colony of Georgia to convert the Indians, but their mission was a failure, and they returned to England in 1738.

4. In 1738 George Whitefield and John Wesley began preaching "the glad tidings of salvation" in England.

   a. Wesley and Whitefield preached no new doctrines but performed with such fervent zeal that they attracted immense crowds.

   b. The clergy of the Church of England, however, considered Whitefield and Wesley insane preachers of seditious doctrines. The aristocracy was not willing to accept a doctrine of the universal brotherhood of man on earth.

   c. Denied the pulpits of the Anglican church, the Methodists began preaching outdoors. John Wesley, furthermore, organized societies to give lasting effect to his preaching.

   d. The Church of England would not supply Wesley with ministers, so he ordained lay preachers.

   e. John Wesley never left the Church of England; but soon after his death, his followers established an independent denomination.

5. By the time of Wesley's death in 1791, his followers, led by nearly five hundred preachers in England and United States, numbered almost one hundred twenty thousand. In United States the Methodists became the largest Protestant denomination.

F. English literature and the theater continued to flourish in spite of the turbulence of the seventeenth and eighteenth centuries.

   1. The translation of the Bible known as the King James' version, published in 1611, was probably the outstanding literary work of the reign of James I. The translation was made from the original Greek and Hebrew by fifty-four scholars.

   2. Ben Johnson (1573–1637), actor and writer of tragedies, did much to sustain the excellence of the English theater during the reigns of James I and Charles I. Jonson's writings were frequently revived for the Restoration theater.

   3. The Cavalier poets, Robert Herrick (1591–1674), John Suckling (1609–1642), Thomas Carew (1598?–1639?), and Richard Lovelace (1618–1658), are best known as love poets.

a. These writers were more interested in perfection of form than in the content of their writings.

b. The Cavalier poets largely ignored the political and religious controversies surrounding them.

4. John Donne (1573–1631) is the best known among a group called the metaphysical poets; their writings presented an intellectual, introspective, and mystical interpretation of life.

5. John Milton (1608–1674) was probably the greatest English poet of the seventeenth century.

a. Milton's masterpiece was *Paradise Lost,* an epic poem that described God's creation of man and man's subsequent fall.

b. Milton actively supported Cromwell and was an accomplished prose writer. Probably his greatest work is *Areopagitica,* a plea to Parliament to abolish censorship laws and to permit a free press.

6. John Bunyan (1628–1688), a Puritan preacher, wrote *Pilgrim's Progress,* considered by some the greatest allegory in English literature. *Pilgrim's Progress* was written to instruct the reader in Puritan morals and was used to train children for many generations.

7. When the Restoration reopened the theaters, French classical influence was very strong. Restoration dramatists and audiences considered Elizabethan drama crude and corrupt in form.

a. John Dryden (1631–1700) was one of the few Restoration dramatists to rise above the usual refined scurrility of his contemporaries. His *All for Love* was a new version of Shakespeare's *Anthony and Cleopatra.* Dryden also aided in directing the development of English literature by his work as a critic and essayist.

b. A reaction to the cynical Restoration comedies took the form of sentimental and moralistic dramas by Colly Cibber and Richard Steele.

8. The eighteenth century theater gradually restored the balance between sentimental and cynical comedy.

a. John Gay's *Beggar's Opera,* first appearing in 1728, was a burlesque on the current theatrical tastes and was an immediate success.

b. Oliver Goldsmith's *She Stoops to Conquer* (1773) and Richard Brinsley Sheridan's *The Rivals* (1775)

and *School for Scandal* (1777) are considered greatly
superior to earlier Restoration dramas.

9. The diarists <u>Samuel Pepys (1633–1703)</u> and John Eve-
lyn (1620–1706) provide posterity with a remarkable
record of seventeenth century life. Often brutally honest, these diaries are unusually enlightening eyewitness
accounts of events during the Restoration era.

10. <u>Alexander Pope (1688–1744)</u> blended the classical ideals
and style of the seventeenth century with many of the
concepts of the eighteenth century enlightenment.
   a. Pope's *Rape of the Lock* (1712) is a satire on the
   frivolities of the fashionable set.
   b. Many consider Pope's *Essay on Man* (1733) his greatest work. In rhymed couplets he discusses man's relations to Providence, nature, and society.

11. Newspapers and literary journals began to appear in
the eighteenth century.
   a. The *Daily Courant* first appeared in 1702. The *Spec-
   tator,* published by <u>Joseph Addison (1672–1719)</u> and
   <u>Richard Steele (1672–1729)</u>, first appeared in 1711.
   b. The *Morning Post* began publication in 1772 and
   the *London Times* in 1788.

12. One of the greatest satirists of the eighteenth century
was <u>Jonathan Swift (1667–1745)</u>. His greatest work,
Gulliver's Travels (1726) was an immediate success.

13. The best known literary arbiter of eighteenth century
England was <u>Samuel Johnson (1709–1784)</u>. His *Dic-
tionary* (1755) was the first adequate catalogue of the
English language.
   a. Johnson's best literary work is his *Lives of the Poets,*
   a series of biographical and critical sketches of English poets.
   b. <u>James Boswell</u> wrote *The Life of Samuel Johnson*
   (1791), considered by some the finest biography in
   the English language.

14. Two more great writers of English prose literature were
<u>Edmund Burke (1730–1797)</u> and <u>Edward Gibbon
(1737–1794)</u>.
   a. Burke is justly famous for his writing on the American Revolution, but his greatest work is probably
   Reflections on the French Revolution (1790), a con-

servative protest against developments across the channel.

    b. Gibbon's *Decline and Fall of the Roman Empire* remains a great literary and historical work though some of its conclusions have since been proven unsound.

15. The rise of the modern English novel also occurred in the eighteenth century.

    a. Daniel Defoe (1660–1731) cast *Robinson Crusoe* (1719) in novel form.

    b. Samuel Richardson's *Pamela: or Virtue Rewarded* (1740) quite possibly was the first to use the world of ordinary life and feelings as a subject for fiction. His *Clarissa, or the History of a Young Lady* (1748) presented more of the sufferings of the female heart. Its sticky sentimentality was relieved, however, by considerable psychological insight.

    c. Henry Fielding (1707–1754) wrote *Joseph Andrews* (1742) as an "antidote" to *Pamela,* and his *Tom Jones* (1749) is still considered one of the most perfect novels in the English language.

    d. Tobias Smollett (1721–1771) introduced a third kind of novel, neither sentimental like Richardson nor realistic like Fielding. *Roderick Random* (1748) is a study of eccentrics, stressing their differences from the normal world.

    e. Laurence Sterne's *The Life and Opinions of Tristram Shandy* (1759) was another variation, a series of episodes combined into an amusing character study.

    f. Oliver Goldsmith's *Vicar of Wakefield* (1766) is probably more widely read today than any other novel of that period. Many of the eighteenth century novels were written about the increasingly prosperous middle class, and most of the novels proved very popular.

16. While most of the eighteenth century writers appeal to reason and emphasize form and elegance in their works, the beginnings of Romanticism appeared in the latter part of the century. The love of nature and sentiment so characteristic of the Romantics was emphasized in the poetry of Thomas Gray (1716–1771), author of *Elegy in a Country Churchyard.*

VIII. France During the Reign of Louis XIV (1643–1715)

A. France in this period was the most powerful single nation in Europe, replacing Spain as the predominant power. In addition, France was the cultural leader of Europe at this time, setting the styles in fine arts, architecture, drama, manners, dress, and language. The French developed new techniques of military organization, diplomatic procedure, and government organization. Both these new techniques and many aspects of French culture were adopted by other nations during the seventeenth and succeeding centuries.

B. <u>French internal development from 1648 to 1715.</u>

    1. The population of France at this time is estimated to have been about twenty million. This was about twice the population of Spain and approximately four times the English population. France had more manpower than any other European nation except Russia and, therefore, possessed the population resources necessary for the erection of a powerful state.

    2. <u>The French economy</u> was based on both a flourishing agriculture and a comparatively large number of commercially prosperous cities. Many historians consider France to have been the wealthiest nation in Europe at this time.

    3. <u>The French monarchy,</u> however, was seriously handicapped in its attempts to utilize these resources efficiently.

        a. About three hundred different local areas had their own systems of law *(droit coutumier)*. This prevented the uniform execution of royal edicts, since the crown frequently had to arrange special provisions with individual communities or provinces.

        b. <u>French commerce</u> was hindered by many internal tariffs and tolls. Ordinarily, the royal government could abolish these tolls only by purchasing the privilege of collecting them from the person who held it and forsaking the revenue produced by the tolls.

        c. <u>The French tax structure</u> and revenue system was inequitable and inefficient. The most important tax was the *taille,* a tax based on income from real estate. The clergy and nobility were exempt from the *taille,* however. The French were also burdened by an astounding variety of excise taxes; the *gabelle,* a tax on salt, was probably the most notorious excise tax. Excise taxes, however, were often difficult to collect and may have often harmed the economy.

4. Early in the reign of Louis XIV the political situation and economic conditions created serious dissatisfaction.

   a. Since Louis was but five years old when his reign began in 1643, the government was in the hands of his mother, Anne, acting as regent. The chief minister of the government was Cardinal Mazarin, and the regent ordinarily acted upon his advice.

   b. Cardinal Mazarin continued the same oppressive taxes as his predecessor, Cardinal Richelieu, had, and, like Richelieu, continued to extend the authority of the crown, often at the expense of the nobility.

   c. Taxes were particularly heavy in France because of the costs of the Thirty Years' War (1618–1648). France won the war, but the sacrifices involved caused much dissatisfaction.

5. Growing out of these conditions, the uprising known as the Fronde (1648–1652) threatened the power of the French monarchy.

   a. The uprising was begun by the Parlement of Paris. The Parlement of Paris was not a representative institution; it was an assembly of judicial magistrates who had bought or inherited their positions. The Parlement maintained no royal edict had the force of law unless the Parlement agreed to enter it in the official register of laws.

   b. The Parlement of Paris, apparently encouraged by the example of the English Parliament, presented a charter demanding, among other things, that no new taxes be levied without its permission.

   c. Cardinal Mazarin, in reply, ordered the arrest of the leaders of the Parlement, and the people of Paris rose in revolt against Mazarin.

   d. The revolt spread erratically into other parts of France, and for four years the government was nearly paralyzed by intrigue and intermittent civil war.

   e. Gradually the people of France realized the nobility, who had taken over the leadership of the uprising, and the members of Parlement were only interested

in extending their own privileges. Led by the skilled
general <u>Turenne,</u> the royal forces gradually regained
control and restored order.

f. Mazarin remained in power and the Parlement was
forbidden to take part in affairs of state. More important, the people of France were convinced the
crown offered them the best hopes for good government and improved conditions. The Fronde thus
backfired in favor of the king.

6. <u>In 1661, Cardinal Mazarin died, and Louis XIV began
to rule in his own right.</u> Louis kept control of the government in his own hands, never permitting anyone to
become a chief minister like Richelieu or Mazarin.

7. <u>Louis XIV made a determined attempt to reorganize the
archaic French government.</u> He was by no means completely successful though he did more to reorganize the
government than any other ruler before the French
Revolution of 1789. His most effective reforms affected
the upper levels of the central government. Louis
organized the work of the central government around
four councils.

a. <u>The Council of State</u> (or High Council) was pri-
marily concerned with problems of foreign policy.

b. <u>The Council of Dispatches</u> was concerned with all
internal affairs except finances.

c. <u>The Council of Finances</u> dealt with such problems as
taxation, tariffs, and keeping track of revenues and
expenditures.

d. <u>The Privy Council</u> was responsible for the administration of justice.

e. Louis met regularly (usually at least once a week)
with each council except the Privy Council; he seldom interfered with the work of the law courts and
expected the Privy Council to administer the judicial
machinery. The ministers of the other councils
gathered information and offered advice; Louis, however, made the decisions and took the responsibility.

f. Louis XIV was particularly successful in finding ministers of outstanding ability. A minister like <u>Colbert</u>
might serve on several councils, but he was kept completely subordinate to the king. Few rulers in history
have been served by ministers so capable as Col-

bert (finance), <u>Le Tellier</u> (foreign affairs,) <u>Louvois</u> (war), and <u>Vauban</u> (military engineering).

8. <u>The use of intendants,</u> officials who were responsible for implementing royal policies in the various provinces, was extended and systematized by Louis XIV. Each intendant supervised the administration of justice, tax collection, and military administration in his district, called a "généralité." Unlike many government positions, the office of an intendant could not be purchased. An intendant could be appointed, transferred, or dismissed at the king's will.

9. <u>In spite of his reforms, financial matters were a constant problem for the government of Louis XIV.</u>
   a. The clergy and nobility were exempt from the most important tax, the *taille,* a tax on income from real estate.
   b. While the king managed to collect a few taxes from the clergy and the nobility, these two groups did not carry their fair share of the tax burden.
   c. <u>Colbert, the minister of finance,</u> put a vigorous mercantilist program into effect. He adjusted tariffs to exclude foreign goods, began new industries, eliminated many internal tariff barriers and tolls, cut the interest rates on government debts, and controlled wages and prices of many articles.
   d. Colbert's programs greatly increased the government's revenue, but expenditure, especially for war, increased even more rapidly.
   e. To meet the rising deficit, the king resorted to many financial expedients such as selling government positions and titles of nobility and experimenting with various inflationary schemes. Such expedients usually provided no more than temporary relief.

10. With the help of Louvois, his minister of war, Louis XIV initiated a series of military practices and reforms which were soon copied by almost all the European powers.
   a. The king's purpose was to assure his own complete control of the armed forces. He destroyed the nobility's power to dominate the military machine by virtue of commissions they had purchased.
   b. Louis systematized military ranks, reorganized the

chain of command and created a whole series of
ranks which could be obtained only by merit.

c. The government took over control of recruiting,
housing, and provisioning troops. Systematic inspec-
tions were begun to cut down corruption in military
administration. The Inspector General of Infantry,
Colonel Martinet, was so zealous his name has become a synonym for strict military discipline.

d. Literally dozens of other innovations of every sort
were introduced into the French army. Among these
were a system of supply depots enabling the army to
operate in any season of the year, rudimentary field
hospitals, probably the first veterans' hospital (Hotel
des Invalides), and an officers' reserve system which
made it possible to expand the army quickly when
war threatened.

e. The host of military reforms introduced by Louis and
Louvois made it possible to organize, supply and
command an army which at one time totalled about
four hundred thousand men. This was not only the
most powerful army in Europe but was nearly ten
times the size of the armies operating during the
Thirty Years' War. It is hardly surprising that most
European powers hastened to copy Louis' military reforms or adapt them for their own purposes.

11. The reign of Louis XIV was marked by three major developments in religious policies. All three tend to indicate the growing dominance of the state in affairs of the
Gallican Church (the Roman Catholic Church in
France).

a. The Huguenots (French Calvinists) were a minority
of about one million five hundred thousand persons
early in Louis' reign. By the Edict of Nantes (1598),
the French crown had granted the Huguenots the
privilege of practicing their own religion in the communities where they were a majority of the population. They had the same opportunities to hold public
office or to pursue other activities as any other
Frenchman.

b. The Edict of Nantes had been modified in 1629, but
the legal and religious privileges of the Huguenots
had remained unchanged.

c. Early in the reign of Louis XIV, the crown began putting pressure on the Huguenots to convert them to Catholicism. The Edict of Nantes was interpreted as narrowly as possible to restrict their privileges; bribes were offered to Huguenots to become Catholics; and troops were frequently quartered in Huguenot homes to harass the Huguenots into joining the Gallican Church.

d. In 1685, after hearing reports of many conversions and being advised there were no remaining Huguenots, Louis XIV revoked the Edict of Nantes.

e. Following the revocation of the edict, about two hundred thousand Huguenots (the exact number is unknown) fled from France. Many of the refugees were skilled artisans and tradesmen, and they took their wealth and skills to England, Holland, Brandenburg, and America.

f. Within France, the revocation was very popular and widely approved, but elsewhere it caused Louis to be viewed as a religious bigot. Some controversy exists as to how much it hurt France economically, but surely the revocation did not help the French economy.

g. Louis XIV also became entangled in a dispute with the papacy over the administration of church offices during the time following the death of the incumbent clergyman and preceding the appointment of a successor (right of *régale*). Louis called the clergy together to consider the problem (Assembly of the Gallican Clergy, 1682), and the clergy supported the crown. The issue was a matter of prestige or status, not revenue; and the king finally achieved his goal although the controversy (Gallican Crisis) dragged on for several years. The state thus extended its control over one more part of church administration.

h. The controversy between the Jesuits and Jansenists also reached its height during Louis' reign. The Jansenists were Catholics who wished to reform the church from within. Their name is derived from their interest in the writings of Cornelius Jansen, Bishop of Ypres (1585–1638). The Jesuits, concerned about the Jansenists' growing influence, finally convinced the papacy that the Jansenists were heretical.

i. Louis XIV apparently did not understand the theological issues involved, but he was concerned because some of the followers of the Jansenists had played important roles in the Fronde (notably De Retz, Cardinal Archbishop of Paris). Louis XIV hated Frondeurs and turned the power of the state against the Jansenists.

j. Louis ordered the destruction of the Jansenist convent at Port Royal and the dispersion of its members. He persuaded Pope Clement XI to issue the bull _Unigenitus_ (1713) to anathematize many of the Jansenists' teachings.

k. The conduct of the Jansenists had been so exemplary and their following so widespread, however, that Jansenism continued its existence in France until the nineteenth century. Louis XIV may have extended royal authority over more of the affairs of the Gallican Church, but he probably did so only by destroying a significant part of its vitality.

C. French foreign policy from 1648 to 1715.

1. The long range objective of French foreign policy during the reign of Louis XIV was to achieve what he called the "natural frontiers" of France: the Pyrenees, the Alps, and the Rhine river.

a. Areas already under control of the French crown reached the Pyrenees and the Alps. To extend French power to the Rhine, however, involved acquiring territories ruled by German princes plus the conquest of the Spanish Netherlands (modern Belgium) and the United Provinces (now the Kingdom of the Netherlands).

b. The French attempt to conquer the territories west of the Rhine involved France in four wars, each more serious than its predecessor. France opposed the European balance of power in each war.

2. The War of Devolution (1667–1668) takes its name from Louis' contention that territories in the Spanish Netherlands belonged to his wife by the custom of "devolution," a practice by which the property of a man married more than once went to the children of the first marriage. Louis' wife, Maria Theresa, was a half-sister

of the king of Spain, a daughter of Philip IV and his first wife.

a. French armies invaded Flanders and Franche-Comté. England, the United Provinces, and Sweden, alarmed by French power, formed the "Triple Alliance" to counterbalance France.

b. Louis, wishing to avoid a prolonged war against a coalition, arranged a compromise treaty, the Peace of Aix-la-Chapelle, by which the French abandoned Franche-Comté but kept eleven border towns in the Spanish Netherlands.

3. The Dutch War (1672–1678) followed Dutch boasting that they had defeated and humbled Louis XIV by the Triple Alliance. Louis first isolated the Dutch diplomatically by bribing the English to desert the Triple Alliance (secret Treaty of Dover, 1670) and arranging Swedish neutrality by similar means.

a. The Dutch were divided internally by a serious debate over whether the United Provinces should be a decentralized republic led by John DeWitt or a centralized hereditary monarchy ruled by William of Orange.

b. Just as Dutch internal affairs neared a state of chaos, the French armies invaded the United Provinces. The Dutch reaction was to murder John DeWitt and entrust the defense of the country to William of Orange. William ordered the dikes cut to slow the French invasion.

c. Again the French invaded Flanders and Franche-Comté, and again the European powers formed an alliance to check the French. This time the Holy Roman Empire, Denmark, Spain, and the Electorate of Brandenburg formed the anti-French combination. In 1677 William of Orange married Mary, the daughter of James II of England. Louis XIV thought this marriage would draw England into the war against France; so peace negotiations were begun.

d. The Treaty of Nimwegen ended the war with the French receiving all Franche-Comté and more border towns in the Spanish Netherlands. The French were glad to gain these territories from Spain but were chagrined that the territories of the Dutch remained intact.

4. <u>The War of the League of Augsburg (1688–1697)</u>

a. The inexact terminology of earlier peace treaties left the control of various territories in the vicinity of the Rhine in doubt. Taking advantage of this situation, Louis XIV established a series of special tribunals, <u>"chambers of reunion,"</u> to investigate land titles and enlarge his claims.

b. This procedure was most successful for the French, who took possession of all Alsace and Luxembourg. But French success spurred the creation of another anti-French alliance, the League of Augsburg (1686), which included the Holy Roman Empire, Spain, Sweden, and several of the German states. When the English revolution of 1688 placed William of Orange on the English throne, England and the United Provinces joined the League.

c. Meanwhile, the French invaded the Rhenish Palatinate; and the military action spread to the Netherlands, Italy, the high seas and North America. In America French and English colonists and their Indian allies became engaged in what is known as King William's War.

d. The French were initially successful, but the French navy could not match the combined English and Dutch fleets. The allies could not, however, muster the strength necessary to invade France. <u>The Peace of Ryswick (1697) resulted from this stalemate.</u>

e. The Peace of Ryswick changed little. The French relinquished the territories they had seized since the Treaties of Nimwegen except Alsace and its capital city, Strasbourg; the French also granted some commercial concessions to the Dutch and recognized William of Orange as King of England. Colonial conquests of the French, English and Dutch were all restored to their pre-war status.

5. <u>The War of the Spanish Succession (1702–1713)</u>

a. During the last few years of the seventeenth century it became clear that the mentally unbalanced Charles II of Spain would die without heirs. Almost every dynastic family of Europe hoped to place one of its members on the Spanish throne, and the great powers studied Spain and its possessions with greedy and hopeful eyes.

b. <u>The leading contenders in the dynastic struggle were the Austrian Hapsburgs and the French Bourbons.</u> Prolonged diplomatic negotiations and intrigues, complicated by English and Dutch designs on the Spanish empire, ensued. In 1700 Charles II died, willing Spain and all its possessions to the grandson of Louis XIV, who was to become Philip V of Spain.

c. Louis XIV knew war would follow if his grandson became king of Spain. If he refused the crown, however, France would risk being surrounded by Hapsburg territories as it had been in the dangerous times of Holy Roman Emperor Charles V, because the second choice in the will was the Austrian Archduke Charles.

d. In this war France had only the slender aid provided by Spain and Bavaria to oppose the Grand Alliance of England, the United Provinces, the Holy Roman Empire, the Electorate of Brandenburg, and Portugal. The Grand Alliance not only had superior naval power but also had the most capable generals, notably John Churchill, Duke of Marlborough (ancestor of Sir Winston Churchill) and Prince Eugene of Savoy. The most able French generals had died of old age or had been killed in the earlier wars.

e. From 1702 until 1709 the French suffered one defeat after another; but when Louis asked for peace terms, the allies' provisions were so harsh that the French and Spanish carried on. In 1711, Archduke Charles became Holy Roman Emperor Charles VI, and the English and Dutch did not want one man to occupy both the imperial and the Spanish thrones as Charles V had done. In England the peace-minded Tory party replaced the Whig war party. Allied disunity made it possible for Louis XIV to negotiate an acceptable peace settlement.

f. <u>The Treaties of Utrecht (1713) and Rastadt (1714) ended the war.</u> The English gained the most: Gibraltar, Minorca, Newfoundland, Nova Scotia (Acadia), the Hudson Bay territory, and the *Asiento* (the con-

tract to supply Spanish colonies with African slaves).
Austria received the Spanish Netherlands, the Kingdom of Naples, the Duchy of Milan, and the island
of Sardinia. The Elector of Brandenburg was recognized as King *in* Prussia. The Duke of Savoy was
recognized as King of Savoy and given the island of
Sicily which was exchanged for Sardinia in 1720. The
Dutch received the control over the border fortresses
between France and the Netherlands. Philip V was
recognized as King of Spain, but it was provided that
the same person was never to occupy both the Spanish and French thrones.

6. The War of the Spanish Succession ended French pre-
dominance in Europe. France was still a great power,
but only one of several great powers. The foreign policy
of Louis XIV achieved approximately the modern
boundaries of France by the acquisition of Franche-
Comté, Alsace, and portions of the Netherlands; but a
high price was paid for these territories. France was
contained, not destroyed; but its resources were strained
by the wars, which also created a large public debt.
Equally serious was the lack of firm royal political leadership after the death of Louis XIV in 1715. The inability or disinclination of Louis' successors to rule effectively contributed heavily to the French Revolution
of 1789.

D. French cultural development during the reign of Louis
XIV.

1. French culture enjoyed a golden age during this period.
Classical culture, introduced into France in the sixteenth
century French Renaissance was patronized by the crown
and reached its height in France during Louis' reign.
The literature and architecture of the time are characterized by order, harmony, dignity, and grandeur.
The highest excellence was probably attained in drama,
which established the theatrical practices still most frequently followed by dramatists of the western world.

2. *Cid*, a tragedy whose first appearance in 1636 is often
considered to have begun the Augustan age of French
culture, was written by Pierre Corneille (1606–1684).
His other best known works are *Horace, Polyeucte,* and
Cinna, the last frequently considered his greatest.

    a. Corneille was usually more interested in portraying human character than in the narration of a plot.

    b. Corneille idealized the virtues of his heroes and eloquently praised patriotism and national glory. Love of country must take precedence over personal love; death is preferable to dishonor.

3. Jean Racine (1639–1699) had his first triumph with the presentation of *Andromaque* (1667). Outstanding among his other tragedies were *Bajazet* (1672) and *Phèdre* (1677). Two Biblical dramas, *Esther* (1689) and *Athalie* (1691), reinforced his fame.

    a. Racine's work is characterized by dramatic force and exquisite beauty of language; but he was, above all, a master in the analysis of human passions.

    b. Racine usually portrays his characters as nearly helpless victims of their own passions. Uncontrolled human emotion is the enemy of human society destroying the orderly, dignified grandeur of the classical ideal.

4. Jean Poquelin (1622–1673), better known by his theatrical name, Molière, is famous for his comedies. His first great comedy was *Les Précieuses Ridicules* (1658), which ridiculed the affected language and pretentious manners of the times. *Tartuffe* (1664) was a daring attack on religious superstition and clerical hypocrisy. *Le Misanthrope* (1666), often considered his masterpiece, portrays the hard lot of the upright man in a frivolous and false society.

    a. Molière's many comedies satirize the follies of people of every class; he ridicules pedantry, avarice, jealousy, vanity, and impudence wherever he finds them. He exalts honor, sincerity, and resolution.

    b. Molière's skill created universal types still with us today: social climbers, misanthropes, hypocrites, and misers.

5. La Fontaine (1621–1695), another major literary figure of the period, is remembered for his *Fables*. Many of his plots were borrowed from earlier writers, but La Fontaine's penetrating observations and reflections and his keen sense of humor make the *Fables* a burning commentary on the weaknesses and vices of the whole human race.

6. The classical patterns followed by the writers of the pe-

riod were profoundly influenced by the most skilled critic of the period, Nicolas Boileau (1636–1711).

7. French literary versatility produced many remarkable works in addition to those already mentioned.

    a. Madame de Sévigné (1626–1696) was one of the great letter writers of all time. Her letters not only demonstrate literary skill but also provide an invaluable collection of testimony on life in the seventeenth century.

    b. One of the most amazing records of life at Versailles is provided by the *Memoirs* of Saint-Simon (1675–1755). Presenting a lively picture of events from 1691 to 1723, the complete published edition of the *Memoirs* fills forty volumes.

8. French classical literature was widely read elsewhere in Europe and influenced the literary development of other countries. Like Greek drama, it concerned itself largely with human emotions and problems common to almost all human society. This quality of universality gave it widespread appeal even beyond that provided by its linguistic beauty and precision. Louis XIV systematically subsidized writers in an attempt to add to French grandeur, and he was remarkably successful.

9. The reign of Louis XIV was also notable for its architectural accomplishments.

    a. The palace of Versailles, still a major tourist attraction, was built to provide an impressive setting for the royal court.

    b. Magnificent salons, culminating in the Hall of Mirrors eighty yards long, were marveled at by visiting diplomats and aristocracy.

    c. The elaborate gardens with their many fountains were no less impressive. A "Grand Canal" two hundred feet wide and a mile long was used to stage mock naval battles to supplement the pageantry of the court.

    d. Versailles achieved its intended purpose, but it was extremely expensive. Louis also spent money on several other palaces, but the French could hardly afford these luxuries while paying for the wars growing out of Louis' foreign policy.

10. Louis XIV also paid the king's musician, Lully, to com-

pose operas and classic ballet for the court. Painting, architecture, music, literature—all were guided by the classical standard. All were supported by the state to contribute to its dignity and order and grandeur.

IX. France from the Death of Louis XIV to the Revolution of 1789

A. When Louis XIV died (1715), he was succeeded by his great grandson, Louis XV, who was then six years old.

1. In the early part of the reign of Louis XV, the government was run by an ineffective regency led by the Duke of Orleans.

2. The Duke of Orleans had good intentions and tried to institute needed reforms, but he lacked the resolution to carry out his plans.

3. In 1723 Louis XV was declared ruler at the age of thirteen. He was very able but almost completely indifferent to affairs of state.

4. In 1729 Louis made Cardinal Fleury chief minister. Fleury's regime was characterized by peace and prosperity; he actually balanced the budget by avoiding war. However, he could not prevail against those advocating French entry into the War of the Polish Succession (1733–1738) and the War of the Austrian Succession (1740–1748). The Polish war gained France Lorraine, but the Austrian war had unfortunate long range consequences and damaged French finances.

5. After Fleury's death in 1743, Louis permitted the control of the government to fall into the hands of favorites such as his notorious mistress, the Marquise de Pompadour. Intrigue at court and lack of co-ordination became the chief characteristics of the French government.

6. In 1771 Louis began to reassert his royal power and with the aid of his chief minister, Maupeou, instituted judicial reforms. Judgeships could no longer be purchased, and judges were forbidden to accept fees from persons whose cases they judged.

7. Before Louis XV could carry his reforms further or counterbalance the bad effects of his reign, he died of smallpox in 1774.

B. <u>Louis XVI, grandson of Louis XV, bore little resemblance to his predecessor.</u>

1. He was simple, kind, honest, religious without fanatical intolerance, economical in personal expenses, and untouched by the immorality of the court. Probably few rulers were so concerned for the welfare of their subjects.

2. But Louis XVI lacked initiative, was slow to comprehend, and was almost completely without self-confidence. Usually echoing the opinion of the last person with whom he had conversed, he was unable to resist the influence of the people who surrounded him at Versailles and opposed reform.

3. <u>Marie Antoinette,</u> the queen, was attractive and gracious; but she was extravagant and indiscreet and attracted popular criticism. More serious was her interference in government policies and her opposition to needed reforms which prejudiced the careers of her favorites.

4. In an early attempt at economic reforms Louis XVI appointed <u>Jacques Turgot</u> minister of finance. Turgot abolished many useless offices, reformed tax collection, encouraged agrarian production, and restored the government's credit. When he proposed to abolish feudal dues and end the privileged tax exemptions of the nobility, the court party prevailed, and he was dismissed from office (1776).

5. Louis then appointed the Swiss banker <u>Jacques Necker</u> as his finance minister. Necker tried to introduce reforms more slowly, but he had to borrow money to support the American Revolution. When he tried to cut expenditures at court, Marie Antoinette and the courtiers demanded his dismissal. Necker resigned in 1781, leaving the finances in worse condition than when he took office in 1776.

6. In 1783 <u>Charles Calonne</u> became minister of finances. Calonne was an early pump-primer who tried to create the appearance of prosperity by lavish spending of borrowed money. He did well until 1786 when the government found it could not borrow additional funds. In an attempt to get funds, Calonne proposed tax reforms asking the king to convoke the Assembly of Notables to consider tax proposals.

7. The Assembly of Notables, meeting at Versailles in 1787, refused tax reforms and advised Louis to dismiss Calonne. Louis sacked him.

8. Louis now appointed Loménie de Brienne finance minister, but his proposals for tax reform were blocked by the Parlement of Paris. Louis recalled Necker in 1788 who insisted the Estates-General be called. Louis issued the order for the convocation of the Estates-General in May of 1789. It was part of this body that declared itself a National Assembly, committed itself to the task of writing a constitution, and began the French Revolution in June 1789.

9. During the reigns of Louis XV and Louis XVI the government was also exposed to constant criticism by the writers of the movement known as the "Enlightenment" (see Chapter IV). A brief discussion of other conditions contributing to the outbreak of the French Revolution will be found in Chapter V.

BIBLIOGRAPHY

Clark, G. N., *The seventeenth century* (Oxford: Clarendon, 1947).

———, *The later Stuarts, 1660–1714* (Oxford: Clarendon, 1949).

Davies, G., *The early Stuarts, 1603–1660* (Oxford: Clarendon, 1949).

Doolin, P. R., *The Fronde* (Cambridge: Harvard University Press, 1935).

Firth, C. H., *Oliver Cromwell and the rule of the Puritans in England* (New York: Putnam's, 1900).

Friedrich, C. J., *The age of the baroque, 1610–1660* (New York: Harper, 1952).

Gershoy, L., *From despotism to revolution, 1763–1789* (New York: Harper, 1944).

Gooch, G. P., *Louis XV* (London: Longmans, Green, 1956).

Heaton, H., *Economic history of Europe,* revised edition (New York: Harper, 1948).

Lewis, W. H., *The splendid century* (New York: Sloane, 1954).

Ogg, D., *Europe in the seventeenth century* (London: Black, 1952).

Packard, L. B., *The age of Louis XIV* (New York: Holt, 1929).

Plumb, J. H., *The first four Georges* (New York: Macmillan, 1957).

Roberts, P., *The quest for security, 1715–1740* (New York: Harper, 1947).

Wolf, J. B., *The emergence of the great powers, 1685–1715* (New York: Harper, 1951).

Chapter 2

CENTRAL AND EASTERN EUROPE IN THE SEVENTEENTH AND EIGHTEENTH CENTURIES

I. Russia from the Mongols' Destruction of Kiev (1240) to the Death of Tsar Ivan IV (1584)

A. The collapse of the Kievan Russian state left Russia divided and subject to a variety of political, religious, and social influences. (For an account of the Kiev state, see Vol. I, pp. 152–154).

 1. In western Russia, along the Polish and Lithuanian borders, political organization was along feudal lines. This area was Roman Catholic, however, rather than Greek or Russian Orthodox.

 2. In the north, in the vicinity of the city of Novgorod, political power was in the hands of a commercial oligarchy. Novgorod suffered serious internal strife, however, and its nearly sterile soil made it dependent on the Moscow region for grain.

 3. The region around Moscow not only profited from its competitors' liabilities, but it also had assets of its own.
  a. Moscow was located far from the borders of the lands occupied by the Slavic peoples. This central location was more easily defended from invasion than a city like Kiev.
  b. Moscow lay near the watershed from which the rivers flow northwest to the Baltic or south to the Black Sea. Russian rivers were the main trade routes and provided Moscow with a good commercial location.

B. The rulers of Moscow were exceptionally able and laid the foundations for a powerful, centralized state.

 1. The grand dukes of Moscow very early established the

practice of primogeniture. This avoided many quarrels over succession to the throne following the death of each prince.

2. The leaders of Moscow acted as agents of the Mongols who had conquered Russia. The rulers of Moscow were able to make use of Mongol support to weaken or destroy some of Moscow's rivals.

    a. Acting as Mongol agents gave the grand dukes of Moscow an opportunity to observe conditions at the Tartar ruler's court. When the Tartars appeared weakened, the rulers of Moscow led the Russians against the Mongols.

    b. In a series of hard fought battles, Grand Duke Dimitri (1359–1389) led the Russians to victory over the Mongols. It took nearly a century more to destroy completely Tartar power in Russia, but the Muscovite dukes could justly claim to be the leaders of Russian liberation.

3. Moscow and its leaders enjoyed the vitally important support of the Russian Orthodox Church. Early in the fourteenth century the Metropolitan Archbishop made Moscow the ecclesiastical capital of Russia.

    a. When the Turks captured Constantinople in 1453, Moscow replaced the old Byzantine capital as the center of the Greek Orthodox (or Greek Catholic) Church.

    b. Enlarging on the claim of Constantinople to be a "new Rome," the Russian clergy claimed Moscow was the "Third Rome."

    c. Later (1547), when Ivan IV, Grand Duke of Moscow was proclaimed "Tsar of all the Russias," the Russian clergy provided the tsar (Russian term for Caesar) with an imaginary ancestry going back to the Roman Emperor Augustus.

4. Hand in hand with the Byzantine religious tradition was the imperial political theory of the Byzantine Empire.

    a. Grand Duke Ivan III (1462–1505) married the niece of the last Byzantine emperor and adopted as many of the imperial customs as he dared.

    b. Ivan III no longer consulted his nobility but reserved to himself the power to make all important decisions.

    c. Adopting the Byzantine double eagle as his standard, Ivan III employed Italian architects to build the Kremlin, an enormous fortress palace, setting himself apart from his followers like a Byzantine emperor.

    d. Ivan III was instrumental in creating a new class of nobility, the service gentry, who owed everything to the tsar. They held their titles and estates only so long as they served the tsar.

    e. Since estates were worthless without labor, the government later helped the service gentry to keep the peasants on their estates. This also made it easier for the government to collect taxes and recruit men for military service. Binding the peasants to their lands introduced serfdom which finally became almost universal in Russia.

C. Grand Duke Ivan IV (the Terrible) began his reign as a child in 1533. At first unable to prevent the nobility from humiliating him, by 1547 Ivan was strong enough to escape control of the nobility and make himself tsar.

    1. From 1547 to 1560 Ivan IV carried out institutional reforms and governed well.

        a. He repressed corruption in imperial administration of the provinces.

        b. He convoked the first *zemski sobor* (land assembly) representing the towns, the clergy, and the nobility. This body was advisory only, however, and met only once during his reign.

    2. Later, when Ivan fell ill, the nobility refused to swear allegiance to his son. Ivan sought revenge by creating the *oprichnina* (separate realm).

        a. Ivan declared everything in the *oprichnina* belonged to him personally while the rest of Russia, the *zemschchina*, was to be administered as before.

        b. The men whom Ivan appointed to administer the *oprichnina* were directed to terrorize the leading nobility of the *zemschchina*.

        c. These terrorists, the *oprichniks,* were the forerunners of the grim secret police forces which have long characterized Russian society.

        d. The *oprichniks* waged a relentless war on the nobility, confiscating their estates, driving them into exile or killing them.

    e. The tsar's authority was extended as the nobility was beaten down.

3. Ivan IV carried on a vigorous foreign policy at the same time he fought the nobility within his realm.

    a. The conquest of Kazan to the east opened the way for Russian penetration and conquest of Siberia.

    b. The conquest of Astrakhan extended his domains to the Caspian Sea and threatened the one remaining Tartar state in European Russia, the Khanate of Crimea.

    c. Attempts to gain a port on the Baltic Sea and to gain territories from Poland to the west were unsuccessful.

4. Constant warfare with their neighbors helped to convince the Russians of the necessity of a strong centralized state whose powers were concentrated in the hands of one ruler.

II. Russia from the Death of Ivan IV (1584) to the Accession of Peter the Great (1682)

A. Theodore, son of Ivan IV, was mentally incompetent and unable to carry on the autocratic rule established by Ivan III and Ivan IV. With the death of Theodore in 1598, the dynasty died out.

B. A complicated power struggle for control of Russia opened the "Time of Troubles" (1598–1613).

1. Rival cliques among the nobility tried to gain power although most of the nobility did not wish to see another tsar so strong as Ivan IV had been.

2. Peasant revolts against the nobility were frequent during the Time of Troubles as the peasants tried to improve their deplorable situation.

3. Both Poland and Sweden attacked Russia during the Time of Troubles.

    a. Sweden extended its power on the eastern shores of the Baltic Sea.

    b. The Poles invaded Russia, trying to place a Polish prince upon the Russian throne.

4. Among the rival factions of the nobility, Boris Godunov,

brother-in-law of Tsar Theodore, was the first to place himself on the throne.

  a. Boris Godunov brought some degree of order to affairs, but he died in 1605; and anarchy followed.

  b. Another faction placed Basil Shuisky on the throne from 1606 to 1610.

5. Polish and Swedish invasions followed Shuisky's fall until Russian militia drove the Poles from Moscow.

6. The *Zemski Sobor* met in 1613 and elected Michael Romanov, a grandnephew of Ivan IV, tsar of Russia.

  a. Michael Romanov began a dynasty which lasted until all the surviving members of the family were executed by the Communists in 1917.

  b. Michael Romanov (ruled 1613–1645) extended serfdom and subjugated the *Zemski Sobor* to please the nobility. During his reign Russian explorers first reached the Pacific Ocean (1637).

C. In 1653 a serious schism developed in the Russian Orthodox Church as a result of the purification of the ritual by Nikon, the Patriarch of Moscow.

1. The changes introduced actually were a restoration of the ritual as it had been performed in Byzantine Constantinople, but many Russians objected to any change in the ritual to which they had become accustomed.

2. Tsar Alexis I (ruled 1645–1676) supported Patriarch Nikon for political and diplomatic reasons.

  a. Tsar Alexis hoped to incorporate Kiev and the eastern Ukraine into the Russian empire.

  b. The inhabitants of those areas followed the older Greek ritual and the tsar hoped to make the Russian ritual acceptable to these new subjects.

3. Patriarch Nikon put through his reforms but only at the cost of driving out of the church the "Old Believers" who would not accept the changed ritual.

  a. The "Old Believers" were vigorously persecuted, and Russia experienced a wave of mass suicides and executions.

  b. "Old Believers" were declared non-Christian by the law and their children were legally illegitimate.

4. Patriarch Nikon asserted his authority was above the tsar's.

    a. Tsar Alexis I turned against the patriarch and forced him out of office.

    b. The tsar then managed the church himself and the state controlled the church to a greater degree than ever before.

III. The Reign of Peter the Great (1682–1725)

A. As a youngster Peter had little formal education. He was barely literate, but he was intelligent and particularly interested in technical matters.

  1. Peter experienced a particularly turbulent youth.

    a. Peter's father, Tsar Alexis, had married twice. Peter's mother was the tsar's second wife, and Ivan, eldest surviving son of the first wife had a better claim to the throne than Peter.

    b. Ivan, however, was mentally retarded and his older sister, Sophia, was made regent. Sophia was to rule until Ivan and Peter reached maturity.

    c. Factionalism and intrigue flourished in this situation, and Peter witnessed the murder of members of his mother's family in a palace revolt inspired by Sophia.

  2. Peter, meanwhile, had been building a personal following which he used to usurp Sophia's power in 1689.

    a. Sophia was placed in a convent.

    b. Until his death in 1796, Ivan shared the throne with Peter, but Ivan never exercised any real authority.

B. Peter's interest in western technology and his desire to gain western aid against the Turks led to his tour of western Europe (1697–1698).

  1. Peter failed to get support for a crusade against the Turks but did get the Poles to join him in an alliance against Sweden.

  2. Peter studied shipbuilding in Holland and England and gunnery in Prussia. He was deeply impressed by western social customs and dress.

  3. Peter's western travels were ended by the news that the Streltsi (the royal palace guards) were in revolt.

    a. Peter rushed home, suspecting Sophia and his wife of inspiring the revolt to seize control in his absence.

    b. Mass tortures and executions followed Peter's return to Moscow. The Streltsi was liquidated; and Peter put his wife in a convent.

C. Once the revolt was crushed, Peter gave his attention to re-organizing the army and navy.

1. Peter apparently borrowed his military reforms from the French and the Prussians.

2. The naval program was only a modest beginning by western standards, but Peter's fleet later defeated the Swedish and Turkish fleets.

D. Peter's concern with military organization was geared to the objectives of his foreign policy: to secure seaports on the Black Sea in the south and the Baltic in the northwest.

1. The Turks barred Russia from the Black Sea, and the Poles and the Swedish blocked the access to the Baltic Sea.

2. Peter's foreign policy resulted in the Great Northern War (1700–1721).

   a. In this war Russia was allied with Denmark and Poland against Sweden.

   b. Sweden was ruled by Charles XII, only eighteen years old when the war began. The allies thought the time was ripe to seize Sweden's holdings which nearly surrounded the Baltic.

   c. The allies seriously misjudged Charles XII, a ruler who loved war and was an extremely capable military leader.

   d. Charles seized the initiative, invaded Denmark, and forced King Frederick IV to come to terms.

   e. Charles XII then crossed the Baltic and routed the Russian army at Narva (1700). He captured almost all of Peter's new artillery but did not pursue and destroy the Russian army which outnumbered his forces five to one.

   f. Poland was Charles' next conquest. He deposed the king and placed his own candidate on the throne.

   g. In 1708, Charles tried to invade Russia and seize Moscow; but Peter adopted a scorched-earth policy and Charles, suffering from the climate and supply shortages, was forced to withdraw.

   h. In 1709, as Charles again attempted invasion, his army was destroyed by the Russians at Poltava. This defeat ended the Swedish capability to prevent Russian expansion in the Baltic area.

   i. The war ended with the Treaties of Stockholm

(1720) and the <u>Treaty of Nystadt (1721)</u>. Sweden lost all her possessions in Germany except a small portion of West Pomerania. Sweden ceded Estonia, Livonia, Ingria, the Karelian isthmus and the fortress of Viborg to Russia. The Polish king was restored to his throne and Denmark occupied Holstein.

j. Sweden was finished as a great Baltic power, and the western powers became deeply concerned over Russian influence in that area.

3. Twice Peter I tried to drive the Turks from the Black Sea, but he was defeated. His policy, however, was continued by his successors. Both tsars and Communists have never ceased to exert pressure on the Turks who bar Russian access to the Mediterranean Sea.

E. <u>Peter the Great attempted to carry out sweeping internal reforms at the same time he carried on his aggressive foreign policy.</u>

1. Peter continued his predecessors' policy of extending serfdom. It was easier to collect taxes and recruit soldiers and forced labor from serfs than free men. At the end of Peter's reign, there were few free peasants in Russia except in the Ukraine.

2. In 1718, the tsar reorganized the internal administration of the government.

a. Ten colleges (departments) of government were established: war, navy, revenue, foreign affairs, etc.

b. To handle local government, Peter divided Russia into eight provinces, each with a governor and a council drawn from the nobility.

c. A Russian Academy of Sciences was begun, and Peter planned a school system.

d. Almost all Peter's domestic programs suffered from the allocation of available revenues for military expenditures and the shortage of trained administrators and teachers.

e. In an effort to build up the economy and supply the army, Peter adopted a mercantilist program. Russian exports had consisted largely of raw materials before Peter's reign. He had considerable success in building up the iron industry, but his successors did not actively encourage industrial development, and Russian industry lagged far behind the west.

3. Peter I carried on the autocratic tradition of acquiring more and more control over the church.

    a. Peter abolished the highest clerical office, the position of patriarch.

    b. The patriarch was replaced by the Holy Synod, a committee of bishops supervised by a procurator.

    c. The procurator was a layman appointed by the tsar.

4. Symbolizing Peter's fascination with the westernization of Russia was the construction of his new capital, St. Petersburg, the "window to the west."

    a. St. Petersburg was begun in 1703 in the swamps along the Neva river. Piling to support buildings and streets had to be driven in the whole area to be occupied by the city.

    b. St. Petersburg was built at a tremendous cost, both in money and human life. Thousands of workers died of fever, but serfs were forcibly recruited to replace the workers who perished.

    c. This city remained the capital of Russia from Peter's time until the Russian revolution of 1917. Then it was named Petrograd, and the capital returned to Moscow. Following Lenin's death in 1924, it was renamed Leningrad.

5. Peter I tried to force western social customs on the Russians.

    a. Peter forced the Russians around him to adopt western dress, shave off their long beards, and end the isolation of women from society. The nobility were expected to take up ballroom dancing and smoking.

    b. So long as Peter lived, the nobility around him practiced western social customs. The vast majority of the Russian people were untouched by Peter's social reforms.

F. Peter the Great was not so much an innovator as an accelerator of processes already begun. It was the technology, more than any other aspect of western civilization, that Peter I forced upon Russia.

IV. Russia from the Death of Peter the Great (1725) to the Accession of Catherine II (1762)

A. None of the six rulers who tried to govern Russia during

this period possessed the combination of abilities and interests necessary for the task.

1. Recognizing the weakness of the rulers, the nobility were able to throw off many of their obligations to the state. In the absence of strong tsars like Ivan IV and Peter I, the nobility ceased to be a service gentry who enjoyed their privileges only so long as they served the tsar.

2. The struggle between those favoring westernization and persons favoring the Russian culture continued to rage.

   a. Those favoring westernization were referred to as "Westernizers."

   b. "Slavophils" feared western influences were corrupting and would destroy Russian culture and institutions.

   c. Western, especially French, social customs were becoming common among the Russian nobility at this time. French dress, manners, and language were frequently adopted by the Russian nobility.

   d. The University of Moscow was founded in 1755.

B. The Russians maintained an aggressive foreign policy and interfered increasingly in European affairs in spite of weak rulers.

1. In 1739 Russia once more gained Azov from the Turks after three years of war.

2. The Treaty of Abo (1743) awarded Russia more Finnish territory following a brief conflict with Sweden.

3. Russia gained nothing from the Seven Years' War (1756–1763) because of her premature withdrawal from the conflict, but she played a major role in the war.

4. Seeking closer ties to Prussia, Empress Elizabeth (ruled 1741–1762) arranged for the marriage of her successor, Peter III, to a German princess, Sophia Augusta Frederica of Anhalt-Zerbst.

   a. Princess Sophia adopted the Russian Orthodox religion, learned the Russian language, and adopted a Russian name, Catherine.

   b. Catherine's husband, Tsar Peter III, was not quite bright. He humiliated his queen publicly and alienated the palace guard.

   c. Catherine, with the help of the Orlov brothers, carried out a palace revolution which deposed Peter III and made her empress. A few days later, the deposed

Peter was killed, or murdered, in a brawl with his jailers.

V. The Reign of Catherine II, the Great (1762–1796)

A. <u>Internal Russian affairs during Catherine's reign.</u>
1. Catherine II was intelligent and energetic. With a shrewd sense of the importance of public opinion, she carried on a voluminous correspondence with the leading publicists of the Enlightenment in western Europe, notably Diderot and Voltaire. She never went so far as to offend the Russian church by any reforms, however, and was very cautious in the application of any theoretical reforms to practical problems.
   a. Catherine convoked a <u>Legislative Commission</u> which met in 1767 and 1768 to codify Russia's laws.
   b. The Legislative Commission represented all Russian classes except the serfs.
   c. The discussions of the Commission revealed more dissatisfaction with local officials and administration than with the autocracy itself.
   d. Not until 1775 did Catherine II make some changes in local administration. She made no other attempt to codify the law or put the recommendations of the Legislative Commission into effect.
2. <u>During the years 1773–1775 occurred the Pugachev rebellion,</u> one of the most serious peasant revolts in Russia's history.
   a. Pugachev, a Cossack, led the peasants of southeastern Russia. He promised to free the serfs and hang the landlords.
   b. The Pugachev rebellion was put down by the Russian army, but only with great difficulty.
   c. Whatever genuine ardor for reform Catherine possessed disappeared with the Pugachev rebellion.
   d. By 1790, after the French Revolution had begun, Catherine proposed burning the books written during the Enlightenment, jailed the manager of the Moscow University Press, and exiled to Siberia some of the writers who criticized serfdom and some of the abuses in her regime.
3. Catherine did not dare to offend the nobility because of

the way she had come to the throne. To please the nobility she guaranteed their privileges by the <u>Charter of Nobility (1785)</u>.

   a. The Charter of Nobility gave the nobles the exclusive right to own serfs.

   b. Nobles could now legally buy and sell serfs, with or without their lands.

   c. The nobility as a class was exempted from almost all taxes, from military service, from confiscation of their lands, and from loss of their titles of nobility.

  4. Russia's trade with western Europe increased rapidly during Catherine's reign.

   a. England was Russia's best customer.

   b. Russians sold raw materials, especially naval stores, to the English and received manufactured goods and colonial products (particularly coffee, sugar, and spices) from the English.

B. <u>Russian foreign policy during the reign of Catherine II.</u>

  1. Catherine carried on Peter the Great's drive to the south and west. Catherine's targets were the Ottoman Empire and Poland.

  2. From 1768 to 1774 the Russians fought the Turks. The <u>Treaty of Kuchuk-Kainarji</u> gained concessions for the Russians.

   a. The Russians were granted free access to the Black Sea.

   b. The Turks ceded to Russia the district of Kabarda just north of the Caucasus mountains.

   c. The Russians were given the right to protect Christians living within the Ottoman Empire. This provision provided the Russians an excuse to intervene in internal affairs of the Turks' domains.

  3. Since her first war against the Turks had been profitable, Catherine planned another which, she hoped, would lead to a partition of the Ottoman Empire.

   a. Such a project was too ambitious to carry out alone; so Catherine II drew Joseph II of Austria into her plans for partition of the Turkish empire.

   b. In 1783, Russian troops occupied the Crimea to provoke the Turks. The Turks proved to be stronger than Catherine anticipated; and the Austrians, hampered by rebellion in the Austrian Netherlands, did not provide the expected aid.

c. To make matters worse, the Prussians encouraged Sweden to attack the Russians in Finland, and the British aided the Turks.

d. Catherine II came to terms in the <u>Treaty of Jassy (1792)</u>. She got the sultan to recognize Russian occupation of the Crimea and to cede to Russia the territory between the Bug and Dniester Rivers.

4. At the same time the Russians pressed the Turks in the south, Catherine II carried on an aggressive and profitable policy at the expense of Poland to the west.

VI. The Reign of Paul I (1796–1801)

A. Though Paul was probably the best educated tsar to accede to the throne up to that time, Catherine had deliberately kept him uninformed about affairs of state.

1. Catherine II always feared that conspirators were trying to depose her and put Paul in her place.

2. Paul seemed determined to reverse all his mother's policies.

B. When Paul I became tsar, he tried to reform local government and improve the condition of the serfs by giving them state lands and limiting the number of days per week a serf was required to work for his lord.

1. Paul restored compulsory service by the nobility. He also forced the nobility to pay new taxes.

2. The new tsar wished to impose Prussian military discipline upon the turbulent palace guard.

C. Paul's tough policy toward the nobility and the palace guard was his undoing. He was murdered in 1801 by a group of conspirators from the palace guard. His son, Alexander I, was placed on the throne.

VII. Brandenburg-Prussia (1415–1740)

A. The development of Brandenburg into the Kingdom of Prussia and Prussia's key role in the unification of Germany and the creation of the German Empire was carried out under the leadership of the Hohenzollern family.

1. <u>In 1415 the Hohenzollern family was given the rule of the Electorate of Brandenburg.</u>

    a. The territory of Brandenburg was located in north central Germany and included the city of Berlin.

    b. Its designation as an electorate meant its ruler was one of the seven men who elected the Holy Roman Emperor and one of the leading princes of Germany.

2. In 1609, the Hohenzollern family inherited the territories of Cleves, Mark, and Ravensburg in northwestern Germany.

3. In 1618, the Hohenzollerns received East Prussia as a fief of the Polish crown.

    a. The status of East Prussia as a fief meant the Hohenzollerns were expected to give loyal support to the King of Poland so long as they ruled East Prussia.

    b. East Prussia, surrounding its capital city of Konigsburg, lay far to the east of Berlin.

4. One long-range objective of Hohenzollern policy thus became the unification into one centralized state of these territories scattered from the Rhine River to the eastern shore of the Baltic Sea.

B. In 1640 Frederick William, the Great Elector of Brandenburg, began his rule.

1. The Thirty Years' War (1618–1648) was raging in Germany, and Brandenburg had been ravaged by the opposing armies.

    a. Frederick William, the Great Elector, nevertheless began training a small army, believing military power would be his major asset in preserving Brandenburg and gaining territory in the peace settlement.

    b. The elector was skilled in diplomacy and took advantage of the French desire to build up Brandenburg as a counter-balance to Hapsburg power in southern Germany.

2. The Peace of Westphalia (1648), which ended the Thirty Years' War, brought more territory to the Hohenzollerns.

    a. Eastern Pomerania and the bishoprics of Halberstadt, Minden, Camin, and Magdeburg were awarded to the elector.

    b. These territories were all in central Germany near, or adjacent to, Brandenburg.

3. Frederick William the Great Elector next intervened in a war between Sweden and Poland (1655–1660). The

Treaty of Oliva (1660) granted the Hohenzollerns full
and independent sovereignty over East Prussia.

4. At the same time the Great Elector was working hard
to build up Brandenburg's economy. Only a prosperous state could support a powerful army.

   a. His internal economic policies were characteristic of
   mercantilism. High tariffs were used to protect
   domestic industries.

   b. State subsidies were supplied to begin new industries. Roads and canals were constructed, and a postal
   system was established.

   c. The Great Elector attracted colonists to his territories
   by offering free land, special exemptions from taxes,
   and religious toleration. Many Huguenots fleeing
   France following the revocation of the Edict of Nantes
   settled in Brandenburg.

   d. Little was done to improve the condition of the peasants. The nobility were permitted to control the peasants so long as they did not contest the policies of the
   elector's government.

C. When Frederick William the Great Elector died in 1688,
he was succeeded by Elector Frederick III who became
Prussia's first king in 1701.

   1. As the War of the Spanish Succession approached, the
   Hapsburgs sought Hohenzollern military aid.

   2. Elector Frederick III refused military assistance unless
   he received a royal title.

      a. The Hapsburg emperor could hardly recognize a
      kingdom within the boundaries of the Holy Roman
      Empire.

      b. Since East Prussia was outside the boundaries of the
      Holy Roman Empire, it was arranged that Elector
      Frederick III bear the title, Frederick I, King *in*
      Prussia.

      c. Subsequently the rulers of Brandenburg were kings
      of Prussia, and all the Hohenzollern possessions were
      referred to as the Kingdom of Prussia.

D. The second King of Prussia was Frederick William I
(ruled 1713–1740). He completed the internal development
of the kingdom.

   1. King Frederick William I carried on and intensified the
   mercantilist policies of his predecessors.

2. Frederick William I imposed obligations to the state on each class in the Prussian social structure.
   a. The nobility were expected to serve as officers in the army or as officials of the government and to supervise their landed estates. The nobility had the exclusive right to own large landed estates.
   b. The middle class was expected to carry on the commercial and industrial activity of the kingdom, to staff the Prussian civil service, and to pay taxes. Ordinarily they were forbidden to own farm lands and were not permitted to serve in the army.
   c. The peasants tilled the fields of the nobility, paid taxes, and served as the enlisted men in the army.
3. Frederick William I was an eccentric autocrat, but he was energetic and efficient.
   a. During his reign Prussia's army became Europe's most highly trained military force.
   b. His son, who became Frederick II (the Great), tried to flee from the kingdom to escape the stern rule of Frederick William I.
   c. The king imprisoned Prince Frederick and forced him to serve in the army and the civil service. The prince was forced to acquire a thorough knowledge of the kingdom and its government.
   d. Frederick William I also created the General Directory, which supervised the administration of the government in a manner somewhat similar to the councils established to govern France during the reign of Louis XIV. The General Directory, however, also supervised local government.
   e. When Frederick William I died in 1740, he left the Kingdom of Prussia well-organized, peaceful, and prosperous. His son, however, was anxious to use Prussia's excellent army to gain glory and territory.

VIII. The Austrian Empire (1648–1740)

A. Hapsburg rule in the seventeenth century.
   1. The Hapsburg family had two branches.
      a. One ruled in Spain until the line died out in 1700 and was replaced by members of the Bourbon (French) family following the War of the Spanish Succession (1702–1713).

    b. The other branch of the Hapsburg family ruled in Vienna and controlled Austria, Styria, Carinthia, the Tyrol, Bohemia, and part of Hungary.

    c. The Austrian Hapsburgs occupied the throne of the Holy Roman Emperor and had hoped to centralize and consolidate their control of the Holy Roman Empire.

2. The Austrian Hapsburgs had been decisively defeated in the Thirty Years' War (1618–1648).

    a. The Peace of Westphalia confirmed the power of each local German ruler over his lands within the Holy Roman Empire.

    b. The French supported the individual German princes against the Holy Roman Emperor and supported Brandenburg as a rival to the Hapsburgs.

    c. The title of Holy Roman Emperor conferred prestige, but little more, after 1648.

    d. The remaining areas ruled by the Hapsburgs (Austria, Styria, Carinthia, the Tyrol, Bohemia, and part of Hungary) composed the Austrian Empire and were sufficient to make it a major European power.

    e. Since the Hapsburgs failed to centralize their control of the Holy Roman Empire during the Thirty Years' War, they hoped to extend their holdings by expanding south and east, taking more of Hungary and the Balkan peninsula.

3. Hapsburg expansion to the southeast brought them into conflict with the Turks.

    a. During the reign of Sultan Suleiman II (the Magnificent) (1520–1566), the Turks had conquered a large part of Hungary.

    b. After the Spanish naval victory at Lepanto (1571), the Turks abandoned their aggressive policies.

    c. The Grand Vizier Mohammed Kiuprili (1656–1661) and his son, Ahmed Kiuprili (1661–1678) carried out a series of internal reforms in the Ottoman Empire and resumed the military offensive against Christian Europe.

    d. After a series of victories, the Turks laid seige to Vienna in 1683. The Hapsburg capital was saved only by an alliance of Poland, Venice, and Russia.

    e. In 1699 the Treaty of Karlowitz gained most of Hungary for the Hapsburgs. 1699 marks a turning point in the history of the Balkans. No longer did the Moslems threaten Europe; instead, the European powers expanded at the expense of the Ottoman Empire.

B. The War of the Spanish Succession (1702–1713) brought additional territories to the Austrian Hapsburgs.
   1. From Spain, Austria received the Spanish Netherlands (modern Belgium), Naples, Milan, and Sardinia.
   2. In 1720, by the Treaty of London, Austria ceded Sardinia to the Duke of Savoy who gave the Austrians Sicily in exchange.

C. Emperor Charles VI and the Austrian Succession Problem.
   1. Charles VI (ruled 1711–1740) had no son and feared the European rulers would refuse to recognize his daughter, Maria Theresa, as ruler of the Austrian Empire.
   2. In an attempt to prevent a war which might cost the Austrian Empire territory, he got the rulers of Europe to sign the Pragmatic Sanction, a document designating Maria Theresa heiress and ruler of the Austrian Empire.
   3. Charles' advisors tried in vain to convince him that a strong army would be a much greater asset to Maria Theresa than the Pragmatic Sanction.

IX. The War of the Austrian Succession (1740–1748)

A. Among the signers of the Pragmatic Sanction was Frederick William I of Prussia.
   1. Frederick William died in May, 1740 and Emperor Charles VI died the following October.
   2. Frederick II of Prussia chose to ignore his father's commitment and sent his army to seize and occupy the rich Hapsburg province of Silesia. This action began the War of the Austrian Succession.

B. Other European powers, eager to profit from any Hapsburg losses, joined the fray.
   1. France, Spain, Saxony, and Bavaria joined Prussia against the Austrian Empire.
   2. The British, most concerned about gaining colonial territories and privileges from Spain and France, supported Austria.

     a. The British struggle with the Spanish is known as the <u>War of Jenkin's Ear.</u>

     b. The British-French colonial struggle is known as King George's War.

C. The Treaty of Aix-la-Chapelle (1748) ended the war.

    1. Prussia retained Silesia, but no other significant changes were made on the European continent.

    2. Colonial possessions were restored to their pre-war status.

     a. The British returned to the French the conquests made in North America.

     b. In India, the French returned Madras to the British.

X. The Seven Years' War (1756–1763)

A. <u>Maria Theresa hoped to recover Silesia and check the rising power of Prussia.</u> To achieve these aims, she tried to isolate Prussia diplomatically.

    1. With the help of her adviser, Count Kaunitz, Maria Theresa persuaded the French, the Russians, Sweden, Saxony, and some of the smaller German states to join the Austrian Empire in an alliance against Prussia.

    2. The British could not be drawn into the alliance.

     a. The British still hoped to acquire French and Spanish colonies, and the French were members of the alliance.

     b. The English king was still elector and ruler of the German state of Hanover.

     c. The British were fearful the French might conquer Hanover, and Prussia was willing to defend Hanover in return for subsidies and other support.

    3. The creation of a formidable alliance supporting Austria rather than Prussia and the British switch from Austria to Prussia is frequently referred to as the "Diplomatic Revolution."

B. <u>Frederick II decided to strike first before the allies had time to mobilize and coordinate their superior resources.</u>

    1. In 1756, therefore, Frederick's armies suddenly overran Saxony and invaded Bohemia. During the first two years of the war, the Prussians were surprisingly successful.

    2. The superior numbers of the allies began to swing the balance, however.

       a. Constant pressure, especially from the Austrians and the Russians, forced Frederick to take the defensive.

       b. The British ceased to subsidize Prussia in 1760 when George III became king.

       c. Frederick II repeatedly demonstrated great military skill, but his situation was desperate by late 1761.

    3. The Prussians were saved only by the death of Empress Elizabeth of Russia on January 5, 1762.

       a. Elizabeth's successor, the mentally unstable Peter III, was a great admirer of Frederick.

       b. Peter III withdrew Russia from the alliance against Prussia.

    4. The Austrians realized, following several Prussian victories, that decisive defeat of Prussia and recovery of Silesia was hopeless.

    5. The European conflict ended in 1763 by the Treaty of Hubertusburg, which confirmed Prussia's possession of Silesia.

C. During the Seven Years' War in Europe the colonial struggle between Britain and France was intensified in India and North America.

    1. In India the French were led by Joseph Dupleix and the British by Robert Clive (see Chapter III).

    2. The British established their rule not only in India but in Bengal, as well. The French were decisively defeated.

    3. In North America the French and Indian War raged from 1754 to 1763.

       a. The French were initially successful, capturing the vital junction of the Monongahela and the Allegheny Rivers and building Fort Duquesne at the present site of Pittsburgh. In 1755 the French inflicted a costly defeat on the British force led by General Braddock.

       b. Not until 1758 did the reforms and energetic leadership of William Pitt the Elder bring victory on the battlefield. In 1758, the British captured Fort Duquesne (renaming it Fort Pitt); and in 1759 conquered Ticonderoga, Crown Point, and Quebec. The British Navy seized Guadeloupe and Martinique in the West Indies and Senegal and Goree in West Africa.

4. <u>The Peace of Paris (1763) confirmed the British colonial victory.</u>

   a. France ceded to Britain practically all her claims in North America. The British were considered to rule the continent east of the Mississippi River.

   b. The British returned Guadeloupe and Martinique to France along with French West African trading posts.

   c. The British returned Havana and Manila to Spain, and Spain ceded Florida to the English.

   d. The French ceded New Orleans to Spain along with the territory west of the Mississippi known as Louisiana.

   e. In India, the French abandoned all territorial claims, but the English returned the French trading posts.

   f. The Peace of Paris confirmed Britain's emergence as the world's strongest colonial power—a position it maintained for at least 150 years.

XI. Poland in the Seventeenth and Eighteenth Centuries

A. <u>Ethnic, religious, and geographic factors in Polish development.</u>

   1. About half the population was Polish; the remainder was composed of Lithuanians, Russians, Germans, and Jews.

      a. The variety and size of foreign groups probably retarded development of Polish national feeling.

      b. German and Russian minorities, in particular, supported interventionist policies of Prussia and Russia.

   2. The Roman Catholic religion was the official faith in Poland.

      a. Most of the Russians and many Lithuanians were members of the Russian or Greek Orthodox church.

      b. Many of the Germans were Lutheran.

      c. At one time the Polish government maintained religious toleration, but the Jesuits persuaded the government to pass and enforce discriminatory religious laws in the eighteenth century.

      d. The Protestants' and Greek Orthodox Catholics' loyalty to the government was weakened by religious persecution.

3. Poland lay almost entirely in the north European plain without natural defenses to the east or west.

   a. No geographic barrier hindered invasion by either Russia or Prussia.

   b. The Polish nobility, constantly trying to weaken the king, reduced the size of the army so that Poland was practically defenseless.

B. Economic and social factors contributing to Polish decline.

   1. The shifting of commerce to the all-water routes to India reduced the traffic on overland routes which passed through Poland.

   2. Turkish conquests in the Black Sea area cut Poland's trade routes to the Black Sea and the Mediterranean.

   3. The Polish nobility, anxious to reduce commercial interests to a servile status, limited commercial profits by law.

   4. Poland was ravaged by the Black Death once in the seventeenth century and again in the eighteenth. Historians generally consider Poland's economic condition in the eighteenth century worse than it had been in the thirteenth.

C. Polish political development probably contributed most to its decline.

   1. After the Jagiello dynasty died out in 1572, the Polish nobility, who had the power to appoint the king, usually placed foreign princes on the throne.

   a. Augustus II and, later, Augustus III, who ruled between 1697 and 1763, were particularly unfortunate choices.

   b. These two rulers were Saxons and exploited their positions for personal rather than national interests.

   2. The Polish nobility, who enjoyed almost complete control of all local government, devoted most of its efforts to weakening the Central Diet.

   a. In 1652 the nobility initiated the use of the *liberum veto* (free veto) in the proceedings of the Central Diet.

   b. The *liberum veto* enabled any one member to veto any measure before the assembly.

   c. Later extensions of the *liberum veto* provided that any one member could dissolve the entire session of the

assembly by his dissenting vote. During the entire
reign of Augustus III (1734–1763), not one Diet served
its full term of office.

3. The last Polish king to exercise effective personal rule
was <u>John Sobieski (1674–1696)</u>. His successors were for
the most part weak or puppets of foreign powers.

D. The Partitions of Poland

1. Following the death of Augustus III in 1763, the Russians succeeded in placing Stanislaus Poniatowski on the
Polish throne; he took his orders from the Russian
ambassador.

2. Neither Frederick the Great of Prussia nor Maria Theresa of Austria was willing to permit Russian expansion into Poland without territorial compensation for his own realm.

3. The Polish Diet was powerless to resist the demands of Russia, Prussia, and Austria and surrendered about one third of Poland's territory occupied by about one half of its population in the First Partition of Poland in 1772.

   a. Russia took the lion's share: White Russia and all Polish territory east of the Dvina and Dnieper Rivers.

   b. Prussia took West Prussia which was bounded by East Prussia on one side and Brandenburg on the other.

   c. Austria took Galicia and other smaller areas just north of the Hungarian portion of the Austrian Empire.

4. The shock of the First Partition was so severe it even impressed the Polish nobility, and the Poles made a desperate attempt to reform the state between 1772 and 1792.

   a. A political reform movement produced a new constitution providing a hereditary monarch, a representative bicameral legislature, and abolition of the *liberum veto*.

   b. Polish commerce experienced a revival and the universities at Vilna and Cracow began to stir with national literature.

5. But the Russians had made significant gains against the Turks (Treaty of Jassy, 1792) and their armies were freed for use against Poland.

   a. The revolutionaries in France declared war on the Kingdom of Prussia and the Austrian Empire in April 1792.

   b. Prussia and Austria, threatened in the west by France, could not hope to prevent any acquisition of Polish territory by Russia.

   c. The Poles organized an army of about fifty thousand men led by Thaddeus Kosciusko (1746–1817). The Poles fought desperately but were overwhelmed by the superior numbers of the Russian army.

   d. The result was the Second Partition of Poland (1793). Russia again took the largest share: most of Lithuania, the West Ukraine, and East Podolia. These areas included a population of about three million.

   e. Prussia took "Great Poland," an area south of West Prussia and east of Silesia populated by about a million inhabitants. Austria, somewhat betrayed by Prussia, received nothing.

6. Russia now intervened in the government of what remained of Poland. The old unworkable constitution with the *liberum veto* was restored.

7. In a desperate struggle against impossible odds, Kosciusko led the Polish Rebellion of 1794 against the Russians.

   a. For a few months the Poles held their own against the Russian army.

   b. Kosciusko was injured and taken prisoner by the Russians whose superior strength inevitably crushed the Polish forces.

8. The Third Partition of Poland (1795) wiped Poland off the map of Europe until it was restored in 1919.

   a. Russia took what remained of Polish Lithuania, Courland, and the Ukraine.

   b. Prussia took the area between the Vistula and Niemen Rivers, including the city of Warsaw.

   c. Austria took Cracow and additional territory in the south.

BIBLIOGRAPHY

Ergang, R. R., *The Potsdam Führer* (New York: Columbia University Press, 1941).

Fay, S. B., *The rise of Brandenburg-Prussia to 1786* (New York: Holt, 1937).

Florinsky, M., *Russia: a history and an interpretation,* vol. I (New York: Macmillan, 1953).

Gaxotte, P., *Frederick the Great* (New Haven: Yale University Press, 1942).

Graham, S., *Boris Godunof* (New Haven: Yale University Press, 1933).

Kliuchevskii, V. O., *A history of Russia,* 5 vols. (London: J. M. Dent & Sons, Ltd., 1911–1931).

Padover, S., *The revolutionary emperor: Joseph the Second, 1741–1790* (New York: Robert O. Ballou, 1934).

Schevill, F., *The Great Elector* (Chicago: University of Chicago Press, 1947).

Sumner, B. H., *Peter the Great and the emergence of Russia* (New York: Macmillan, 1951).

Chapter 3

EARLY MODERN ASIA

I. India During the Early Modern Era

A. <u>Decline of the Mogul Empire</u>
   1. After the death of <u>Aurangzeb (1658–1707)</u> the Mogul dynasty produced no monarchs of ability.
      a. The numerous campaigns of this ruthless ruler drained the treasury.
      b. Aurangzeb's anti-Hindu policy alienated most of his subjects.
      c. The Mogul government was thoroughly corrupt.
      d. Both the Marathas and Sikhs fought the weak Moguls after 1707.
   2. Marauders from Persia under Nadir Shah burst into India and wrecked Delhi in 1739. Afghan raiders repeated this act in 1757.

B. <u>The Anglo-French struggle for India.</u>
   1. Although the Portuguese had reached India as early as 1498 under <u>Vasco da Gama,</u> their power began to wane during the seventeenth century.
      a. Under men like <u>Almeida,</u> Portugal dominated the foreign trade of India to 1600.
      b. In 1600 the <u>English East India Company</u> was chartered by Elizabeth I. This new commercial firm plus the Dutch East India Company (1602) meant competition for the Portuguese. By the end of the seventeenth century British enterprise and power had broken Portuguese and Dutch resistance, but France loomed as a new threat.
      c. The English established trading centers at Surat (1612) and Madras (1639). The acquisition of Bom-

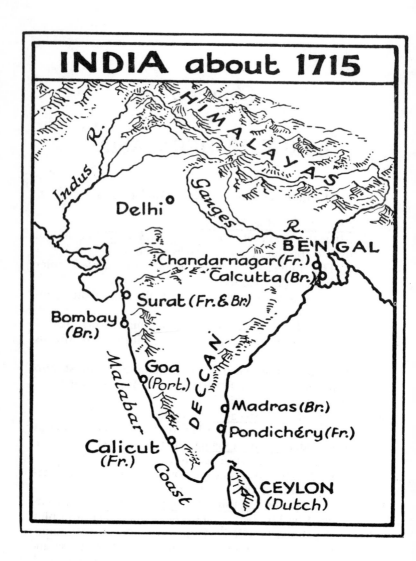

INDIA about 1715

HIMALAYAS

Indus R.

Ganges R.

Delhi

BENGAL

Chandarnagar (Fr.)

Calcutta (Br.)

Surat (Fr. & Br.)

Bombay (Br.)

DECCAN

Goa (Port.)

Madras (Br.)

Pondichéry (Fr.)

Malabar Coast

Calicut (Fr.)

CEYLON (Dutch)

bay from Portugal in 1661 caused the trading post at Surat to decline. In 1698 the English East India Company was given the right to establish a trading post at Fort William (Calcutta). Here the English were permitted to collect taxes for the Mogul government, an office called the *zamindari*.

2. The English East India Company was a joint-stock company with headquarters in London.

    a. Its authority was based on royal charters, the laws of England, and its position as *zamindar*.

    b. The charter of the company was renewed again and again until private traders began to challenge their position. These trade rivals agreed to merge with the English East India Company in 1708 under a new name, but the organization still retained its old name with people at large.

    c. Permanent trading posts of the company were called factories or presidencies.

    d. For protection and tax purposes, the company acquired some territory near each trading post, but such acquisitions were not extensive during the seventeenth century. During this century the Mogul monarchs were still able to check European penetration.

3. The French challenge

    a. Although France was the last European power to show a significant interest in India, her challenge was a serious threat to the English East India Company.

    b. Anglo-French rivalry was already manifested in the War of Spanish Succession (1702–1713) and the War of Austrian Succession (1740–1748).

    c. In addition, the French East India Company *(Compagnie des Indes Orientales)* had been founded in 1664. Numerous factories had been opened, particularly at Pondichery, Karikal, Mahé, and Chandernagor.

    d. Under the energetic and able Joseph Dupleix, the French seized Madras (1746) during the War of Austrian Succession. The peace of Aix-la-Chapelle restored Madras to the English East India Company, but French influence in southern India (Deccan and Carnatic) was great until the recall of Dupleix in 1754.

4. The Seven Years' War (1756–1763)
   a. The English war effort in India was directed by an ex-clerk named Robert Clive.
   b. Under Clive, the British retook Calcutta from the Nawab of Bengal and seized the French post at Chandernagor (1757). Clive then smashed the French and their Indian allies at Plassey (1757). This battle foreshadowed the destruction of French power in India despite Lally's later attempt to seize Madras (1758–1759).
   c. The Treaty of Paris (1763) left France with a few trading posts such as Pondichery and Chandernagor, but they could not be fortified.
   d. In 1769 the poor French position in India compelled them to dissolve the *Compagnie des Indes Orientales.*
   e. Still another threat to English hegemony disappeared at this time: the powerful Marathas were seriously weakened by an Afghan invasion force under Ahmed Shah Durrani (Battle of Panipat, 1761).
   f. By the elimination of the French and this serious blow to the Marathas, the English were able to win a position of supremacy in India.

C. A century of rule by the East India Company (1763–1858)
   1. Despite the great British victory over the French during the Seven Years' War, the East India Company faced disaster within a decade.
      a. The company won the right to collect taxes in Bengal for the Mogul emperor. As collector of revenue *(diwan),* the company permitted agents to do the work, and then sent the emperor a smaller amount.
      b. In addition to this practice of tax-farming, the East India Company permitted Hindu businessmen to exploit the populace (usury).
      c. In the south the British had to tolerate the powerful Hyder Ali who had seized Mysore from the Nizam of Hyderabad. The Marathas had recovered by the late 1760's and took Delhi.
      d. These wars plus a declining revenue brought the company to the brink of bankruptcy in 1772.
   2. Warren Hastings (1772–1785)
      a. Upon taking office as governor of Bengal, Hastings reformed the tax system. This increased the com-

pany's revenue and curbed the abuses of the *zamin-dars*. An efficient and equitable system of justice was another accomplishment.

b. Rumors of wrongdoing reached London, however, and impelled Parliament to pass the Regulating Act of 1774: all of British India was to be administered by a governor-general (Hastings) and a council.

c. Despite opposition on the council, Hastings smashed the united forces of the French, the Marathas, Hyder Ali, and the Nizam of Hyderabad (1779–1785).

d. Jealous colleagues like Philip Francis led to the downfall of Hastings.

e. The demand for reform caused Parliament to intervene in Indian affairs once again.

3. Pitt's India Act of 1784

a. The East India Company was allowed to continue its business activities.

b. Intervention in Indian politics was forbidden, a pious declaration which the British almost immediately had to abandon in self-defense (Wars with Tipu Sahib).

c. A Board of Control in England was established to regulate the activities of the East India Company. Its President was made a Cabinet member.

4. The Charter Act of 1814 permitted any British subject to trade in India, but the East India Company retained its monopoly in the Far East.

a. By 1834 the East India Company lost all trading privileges in the Orient, but it continued to function as an agency of the British government until 1858.

5. The First Afghan War (1839–1842)

a. After initial successes against Dost Mohammed, the British seized Kabul.

b. A successful Afghan uprising annihilated the British invasion force by 1842.

c. Under Sir Charles Napier, the British had greater success to the south. Sind was seized in 1843, to be followed by the Punjab in 1849.

6. By 1850 the British had annexed or cowed every Indian state capable of serious resistance.

a. Lord Dalhousie, governor-general from 1848 to 1856, used the "doctrine of lapse" to add seven additional political units to British India.

    b. This policy permitted annexation of a territory that had no heir from the ruling dynasty.

    c. The Second Burmese War led to annexation of Lower Burma (Pegu), including Rangoon and the eastern coast of the Bay of Bengal (1852).

  7. The Sepoy Mutiny (1857–1858)

    a. The initial revolt was among the native troops (sepoys) who claimed that cartridges issued to them were smeared with cow and pig fat. Moslems regarded the pig as unclean, while Hindus felt the cow was sacred.

    b. The basic causes included the aggressive annexations of Lord Dalhousie, the Moslem hope of rebuilding the Mogul Empire, and the Maratha hope of reemerging as a powerful Hindu state. Indian nationalism was also a factor.

    c. Most of the Indian princes and people were aloof.

    d. Horrible atrocities were committed on both sides.

    e. The end of the rebellion saw the British banish the last Mogul ruler and take all political authority away from the East India Company.

D. Liberalization of British rule (1858–1919)

  1. Beginning in 1861 the governor-general ruled along with a legislative as well as an executive council. Indians were appointed to these councils.

  2. After 1880 Indians were permitted to seek government positions. While the bulk of the intermediate and lower positions were soon filled by efficient Indian civil servants, the good pay caused most of them to support the British rather than join the growing band of nationalists.

  3. The British reorganized the army along tribal or sectarian lines to forestall any feeling of Indian nationalism. They refrained from aggressive annexations (Dalhousie), and preferred to dominate the native princes by individual treaties.

  4. Improvements were made in farming, sanitation, famine prevention, and medical facilities. Internal warfare, infanticide, and *suttee* were outlawed. The British also introduced paper money and an income tax. An excellent railway system was built.

  5. The development of Indian nationalism

a. By 1880 Indian nationalist feeling was a force of considerable importance.

b. The nationalist movement was led by Banerji, Gokhale, and Tilak.

c. The Indian National Congress was formed in Bombay in 1885. It received considerable encouragement from Lord Dufferin, the governor-general, plus other sympathetic Englishmen (Hume). Only two Moslems attended, an indication of future communal trouble with the Hindus.

d. Indian national feeling was quickened by the Ethiopian victory over an Italian army at Adowa (1896), plus the Nipponese victory in the Russo-Japanese War of 1904–1905. The prestige of the white man was lowered in India.

e. But the Indian nationalists were divided: the moderates under Gokhale wished to achieve representative government gradually, while the extremists under Tilak desired complete independence at once (Congress of 1907).

f. A further division in the ranks of the Indian nationalists occurred when the Moslem League was organized at Dacca in 1906. The Moslems preferred a continuation of British rule to a Hindu-dominated India.

g. The Morley-Minto reforms (1907–1909) placated the moderate Indian nationalists, although the extremists continued to demand independence *(swaraj)*. The reforms resulted in elected native majorities in the provincial legislatures, but the legislature of the central government remained under British control. One Indian sat in the Viceroy's executive council.

h. During World War I India remained loyal to Great Britain. Her manpower and resources were of substantial help in France, Africa, and the Middle East.

i. In August 1917 the Secretary of State for India, Montague, promised the "gradual extension of self-government" to India.

j. The Government of India Act of 1919 which followed was a disappointment: the governor-general retained complete control over the central government, but in the provinces some of the ministries were "transferred" to India officials. These "transferred" ministries were responsible to provincial legislatures, but the British-appointed governor could veto their acts. Provincial governors retained "reserved" powers over police, courts, and prisons. This division of authority in the provinces was called dyarchy. Only a few Indian property owners could vote, and separate constituencies were established for Hindus, Moslems, and other groups.

k. Severe crop failures and an influenza epidemic added to the tension. Many serious riots occurred which led to the repressive Rowlatt Acts of March 1919: rioters could be held without a trial, and judges could handle cases without a jury.

l. Gandhi now embarked on a program of passive resistance *(satyagraha)* against the Rowlatt Acts. This however, was supplemented by riots in Calcutta and the Punjab.

m. The Amritsar massacre of April 13, 1919 by General Dyer's troops further inflamed Indian opinion against Great Britain.

II. China Under the Manchus (1644–1911)

A. The Manchu (Ch'ing) Dynasty was the second foreign line to rule China.

1. After moving south from the Amur River area, the Manchus occupied Peking in 1644.

2. At first the Manchus controlled only northern China, and forty years of fighting was needed to bring southern China (Yünnan, 1681) and Formosa (1683) under their sway.

3. The great Manchu empire included Mongolia, Sinkiang, and Manchuria. Even Tibet was made a protectorate, while Burma, Nepal, Korea, Annam, and Laos paid tribute to Peking.

4. The Manchus forced the Chinese to wear their hair-do (queue) and dress as a sign of submission. Manchus were given the best government positions, but they continued the civil service tests and paid homage to Confucian ideals. Over the centuries the Manchus became thoroughly Chinese.

5. K'ang Hsi (1661–1722)

    a. This great ruler ended resistance to the regime in southern China and Formosa. From 1681 to 1712 peace was the rule.

    b. Portuguese penetration was limited to Macao, while the Russians were held at bay by the Treaty of Nerchinsk (1689).

    c. Prosperity was the rule in China. The population grew.

    d. The greatest literary accomplishment of the reign was the 44,000 character *K'ang Hsi Dictionary*. Also noteworthy was the *Ming History* and the *Complete T'ang Poetry*.

6. Ch'ien Lung (1736–1796)

    a. Chinese authority was extended far into central Asia during this reign. Turkestan, Tibet, and Burma could ignore Peking only at their peril.

    b. Foreign commercial intercourse was restricted to Canton despite the efforts of Flint and the Earl of Macartney.

    c. Corruption among the civil servants under Ho Shen and a series of revolts plagued the last two decades of Ch'ien Lung's reign.

    d. Under imperial auspices, a select library of over 3400 works was put together under the title *Complete Work of the Four Treasuries*. The *General Catalogue* contained notices of 6700 additional works. This fine piece of work was used by Ch'ien Lung to destroy all printed matter critical of the regime.

7. Ch'ia Ching (1796–1820)

    a. Revolts against the Manchus became more frequent, particularly by such groups as the White Lotus Society and the Heavenly Reason Society.

    b. Southern China was the greatest source of revolutionary activity, since the populace here regarded the Manchus as foreigners. The individuality and aggressiveness of the southern Chinese plus their dissatisfaction with the share of government positions they received made them a dangerous element for the Manchus.

    c. The problem of trade with Europeans became even more pressing after 1800. The Chinese had long limited trade contacts to a few Hong merchants in Canton: they did not permit the European traders to have broad contacts with the Chinese. In addition, the Chinese did not permit diplomatic relations with the West to exist on a basis of equality: China was the center of civilization, and all Westerners were inferior. With the tremendous increase of British power after 1750 (because of the Industrial Revolution), the old relationship could no longer be continued. Furthermore, the introduction of opium into China by the British hurt many Chinese physically, and altered the balance of payments in favor of Great Britain.

B. The Western impact on China
  1. The Opium War (1839–1842)
    a. The new Manchu ruler, Tao Kuang (1821–1851), made several vain attempts to end the traffic in opium.
    b. When the imperial commissioner Lin Tse-hsü burned a large quantity of British opium at Canton, war ensued (November, 1839).
    c. The British seizure of several coastal ports forced the Chinese to conclude peace. The Treaty of Nanking (August, 1842) forced the Manchus to open five key seaports to Western merchants. In addition, the Chinese had to pay an indemnity of £21,000,000 and end the monopolistic system of confining trade to Canton.
    d. The British were also given Hong Kong.
    e. The import-export tariff rate was set at 5% *ad valorem,* and was not to be changed except by mutual consent. This unequal treaty provision prevented the Chinese from setting their own tariffs until 1930.
    f. All diplomatic correspondence was now to be written as between equals. No longer would Great Britain, or other western states, accept the haughty Chinese attitude of superiority.
  2. Further Chinese concessions
    a. In a Supplementary Treaty of October, 1843 the British included a most-favored-nation clause because of American pressure. This extended to all states having a most-favored-nation clause in their treaties with China concessions the Manchus had already made to the British.

     b. In 1844 <u>Caleb Cushing</u> secured several advantages for the United States in the <u>Treaty of Wanghsia.</u> All Americans (in time all foreigners) were immune from Manchu authority in China. They were to be tried in American courts under American law. This humiliating concession deprived the Chinese of considerable sovereignty within their own country.

     c. The <u>Treaty of Whampoa (1844)</u> with France won toleration for Roman Catholicism in China. Protestant denominations won similar recognition in 1845.

3. The T'ai P'ing rebellion (1850–1864)

     a. This revolt was inaugurated by Hung Hsiu-ch'üah, a mystic who hoped to found the "Heavenly Kingdom of Great Peace."

     b. Hung's revolt was both a religious crusade and an anti-Manchu rebellion. He combined elements of Christianity with the worship of Shang Ti, the ancient Chinese deity of pre-Chou times. His followers desecrated Buddhist, Taoist, and Confucian shrines.

     c. The T'ai P'ing failed to win over the important class of Chinese intellectuals despite their advocacy of land redistribution and opposition to the use of opium, arranged marriage, and footbinding. They argued that the sexes were equal.

     d. When the T'ai P'ing became more dangerous to the Western powers than the decadent Manchus, they gave the tottering Peking regime support. The "Ever Victorious Army" of <u>F. T. Ward</u> and <u>C. G. Gordon</u> was instrumental in crushing the T'ai P'ing.

     e. Western aid thus saved the declining Manchu government, but the rebellion caused enormous physical damage.

4. <u>The Second Opium War (1856–1860)</u>

     a. Hostilities began when the Chinese seized the *Arrow*, a ship flying the British flag but boasting a Chinese crew.

     b. Canton was seized by an Anglo-French force. In June, 1858 the Chinese were compelled to sign the humiliating Treaties of Tientsin with Great Britain, France, Russia, and the United States.

     c. These treaties permitted foreign envoys to live in Peking, opened ten additional ports to Western commerce, and legalized the opium trade. Through non-cooperation and occasional violence the Chinese attempted to check further Western inroads. They did not appreciate the threat of Western military and industrial might.

5. The real power in China from 1861 to 1908 was the Empress Dowager, T'zu Hsi.
   a. The "Old Buddha" dominated weak emperors like T'ung Chih (1862–1874) and Kuang Hsü (1875–1908).
   b. Not even T'zu Hsi understood the nature of the Western threat. Foreigners, for example, completely controlled the Chinese customs.
   c. Inefficiency and corruption was the rule within the Manchu administration.
   d. Military weakness cost China control over several valuable areas: The Russians acquired the entire Pacific coast north of Korea (1860), while France won control over Indo-China by 1885. Britain annexed Upper Burma in 1886, and the Japanese took the Ryukyu islands. Portugal was allowed to annex Macao (1887).
   e. In addition, the Western powers divided China into "spheres of influence." Control of a "sphere of influence" gave a foreign power the most valuable economic concessions in a specified area.

6. The Sino-Japanese War (1894–1895)
   a. This conflict was the result of a decade of trouble over Korea.
   b. Newly-westernized Japan easily defeated the poor Manchu armies.
   c. The Treaty of Shimonoseki (April, 1895) forced China to recognize Korean independence, gave the Japanese Formosa (Taiwan) and the Pescadores, and provided for payment of an indemnity.
   d. Russia, Germany, and France did not permit Japan to annex the Liaotung peninsula and Port Arthur. Russia herself took this area in 1898.

7. The Hundred Days of Reform
   a. The defeat by the despised Japanese and the European scramble for concessions caused many Chinese to seek reforms.
   b. The reformers were led by two scholars from southern China, Kang Yu-wei and Liang Ch'i-ch'ao.

    c. They convinced the young emperor that drastic changes had to be inaugurated at once, and for one hundred momentous days in 1898 China appeared on the road to becoming a modern state.

    d. T'zu Hsi and the Confucian-minded officialdom opposed Westernization. Through moral reform rather than industrialization China could rewin her old position of eminence.

    e. A palace revolution saw the emperor imprisoned and the reformers routed (September 22, 1898).

  8. The Boxer Rebellion (1899–1900)

    a. The basic suspicion of foreigners, the aggressive conduct of the West, and the attitude and actions of the missionaries and their converts helped bring on this outburst.

    b. The Boxers (Society of Harmonious Fists) were a revolutionary group in Shantung and southern Chihli provinces. Their persecution of missionaries and Christian converts was encouraged by the governor of Shantung.

    c. The anti-foreign elements in Peking continued to encourage the Boxers after they were driven from Shantung (December, 1899). The Manchus sought their aid in expelling Westerners.

    d. The Boxer uprising was particularly severe in Shantung, but its effects went beyond that area. After the murder of many Christians and the siege of foreign embassies in Peking, an international relief force seized the Chinese capital (August, 1900).

    e. The Chinese were forced to pay an indemnity of $738 million, establish a foreign ministry, and accept foreign control of Chinese customs offices.

C. Conservative reform and revolution

  1. Even conservatives like T'zu Hsi now embarked on a program of reform, though in a half-hearted manner.

  2. A ministry of education was formed, and thousands of Chinese students flocked to Japan for an education.

  3. The army was improved and some new railroads were constructed.

  4. The 1905 boycott of American goods because of the further exclusion of Chinese from the United States in-

dicated the development of a nationalistic feeling, a sense of identity as Chinese.

5. Some political reform was allowed with the establishment of provincial assemblies in 1909. Although the Manchus expected these assemblies to be harmless political outlets, they proved to be so vocal that a National Assembly was convoked in 1910.

6. The Chinese Revolution broke out on October 10, 1911.

   a. The immediate cause was the government's decision to nationalize the new railways. Chinese provincial investors were further angered when they learned their railway stock would not be redeemed at face value.

   b. The rebellion started when a bomb explosion in Hankow accidentally exposed the headquarters of a revolutionary group. The revolutionaries were joined by Colonel Li Yüan-hung who agreed to lead the group.

   c. Yuan Shih-k'ai was named Prime Minister by the National Assembly (November 8, 1911), while Sun Yat-sen was named President by a revolutionary assembly in Nanking (December 30, 1911).

   d. Sun Yat-sen soon resigned his office for the sake of national unity, and permitted Yuan Shih-k'ai to become President (February 15, 1912).

   e. Because the president quickly came into conflict with the newly-elected legislature, opposition parties formed. The most important was Sun Yat-sen's Kuominatang (Nationalist) party.

   f. The dictatorial Yuan Shih-k'ai died in 1916 and was succeeded by Li Yüan-hung.

III. The Emergence of Japan (1568–1919)

A. Japan's "Christian century"

   1. By the sixteenth century the prestige of the Ashikaga shoguns reached a new low. The real power was in the hands of great feudal barons (*daimyo*) and their military retainers (*samurai*).

   2. It was at this time (1542) that the Portuguese came to Japan.

      a. During the period 1549–1551 Xavier introduced the Christian faith into Japan.

b. The Jesuits of Xavier were followed by Franciscans, Augustinians, and Dominicans.

c. Christianity won numerous adherents. The dress of the Catholic priests was like that of their Zen Buddhist counterparts. In addition, Christianity was associated with the military and commercial power of the new Western traders. Some Japanese even looked upon Christianity as a political counterweight to Buddhism.

d. But the missionaries soon became unpopular because of their political intrigue, intolerance, and forcible conversions.

e. In addition, Dutch and English Protestant traders told the Japanese how Catholics had been treated in their lands.

f. In 1587 <u>Toyotomi Hideyoshi</u> issued a decree ordering the missionaries to leave Japan. Although this decree was not enforced, persecution of Christians became increasingly effective under Tokugawa Ieyasu (1606). By 1637 the Christian communities were physically wiped out. To eliminate contact with foreigners, Japanese were not permitted to go abroad. Foreign trade was limited to a tiny Dutch factory on the island of Deshima near Nagasaki. It remained Japan's only important link with the West until Perry's visit in 1854.

B. <u>Tokugawa Japan (1600–1868)</u>
1. <u>Oda Nobunaga (1534–1582)</u>
   a. His capture of the capital at Kyoto in 1568 made Nobunaga master of central Japan.
   b. He broke the power of the monasteries in central Japan with the capture of the temple-castle of the True Pure Land Sect in Osaka.
   c. Nobunaga was assassinated by a vassal in 1582.
2. <u>Toyotomi Hideyoshi (1537–1598)</u>
   a. With the help of Ieyasu, Hideyoshi won control over central Japan.
   b. The seizure of the Hojo stronghold of Odawara (1590) gave Hideyoshi control of northern and eastern Japan.
   c. Ieyasu, the great vassal of Hideyoshi, moved his military and administrative headquarters to Edo (Tokyo).

From Edo the great eastern plain of Japan could be dominated.

d. Because of numerous *samurai* with little to do, Hideyoshi began an invasion of China in 1592. Korean and Chinese resistance stopped the attack, and after Hideyoshi's death in 1598, Japanese troops were recalled from southern Korea.

3. Tokugawa Ieyasu (1543–1616)

a. After defeating a coalition of rivals at Sekigahara (1600), Ieyasu won virtual control of Japan. He became shogun three years later.

b. Ieyasu moved the military capital to Tokyo. The city soon became the cultural and economic center of Japan as well.

c. Permanent political stability became the foremost goal of Ieyasu. Feudalism remained, but it was made to serve the interests of the Tokugawa in Tokyo.

d. The key areas of eastern and central Japan were placed under control of the "hereditary *daimyo*," those who had supported Ieyasu before Sekigahara (1600). The lords who acknowledged Ieyasu after Sekigahara, the "outer *daimyo*," were placed in the more remote areas. Secret police *(metsuke)* watched both groups. The *daimyo* were not generally permitted to construct new castles, and had to live part of each year at Tokyo. Residence here would weaken the hold they had on their domains. In addition, family hostages had to remain in Tokyo when they returned to their estates.

e. The *daimyo* were generally free to run their domains as they pleased.

f. The emperor and his retinue were dominated by the Tokugawa shoguns.

g. This totalitarian state continued to function for 250 years after Ieyasu's death. So well was the central government organized at Tokyo, that it continued to rule effectively even when the shogun was weak.

4. Tokugawa civilization

a. Taking a leaf from the Confucian tradition of China, the Tokugawa established four distinct social classes: the warrior-administrator, the farmer, the artisan, and the merchant. Unlike China where the warrior was in the lowest social class, the Japanese *samurai* was given the greatest social distinction.

b. Despite the increasing importance of the merchants, particularly in the cities, the rigid Tokugawa social stratification placed them in a position of little prestige. Merchants were among the intellectual leaders of Japanese society.

c. The peace and prosperity of the Tokugawa era saw the population reach thirty million. A money economy replaced the traditional reliance on rice.

d. The Tokugawa period witnessed three important dramatic forms: the *No* plays (solemn pantomimic dances on Shinto themes), the *Ayatsuri* (puppet theatre), and the *Kabuki*. Starting around 1650, the Kabuki performed either dramas based on contemporary problems or historical novels.

e. Buddhism declined, but Confucian ethics remained an important element of Japanese thinking. Confucianism influenced the code of the *samurai,* the well-known *Bushido* ("way of the warrior").

f. Shinto, the "way of the gods," was revived in the middle of the seventeenth century. It was both a popular religion and a nationalistic philosophy.

g. Prior to 1700 the *wagakusha* (students of Japanese antiquity) school developed. Under Mitsukuni (1622–1700) a great history known as the *Dai Nihon Shi* was begun. It asserted that the emperor, not the Tokugawa shogun, was the legitimate head of the state. This school blamed the prevalence of Chinese customs and thought for the poor position of the emperor. Mabuchi (1697–1769) and Motoori Norinaga (1730–1801) went even further: they believed Japan to be superior to all other states, and that the emperor was a divinity. After 1800 these ideas began to win support among the *daimyos* (Choshu and Satsuma) and the large educated middle class.

5. Downfall of the Tokugawa shogunate

a. The shogunate of Ienari (1793–1837) indicated the depth of Tokugawa decadence: inefficiency coupled with the breakdown of the traditional policy of isolation spelled trouble. Military weakness before the great *daimyos* was also apparent.

b. The revival of Shinto had given great impetus to the imperial cause.

c. Many *daimyos* and *samurai* became impoverished because of the inflation that accompanied the new money economy.

d. The intellectual and cultural leadership had passed into the hands of the urban middle class, a group that was dissatisfied because of its meagre political power. Some merchants did purchase titles, however.

e. The visits of Perry in 1853 and 1854 threw Japan open to western influence. The treaty of Kanagawa (1854) with the United States opened two ports to American trade, and permitted commercial relations under specified conditions. Treaties with other Western powers soon followed.

f. At first foreign trade proved harmful: it brought about inflation, and was resented because of the terrible conduct of the Westerners. The new trade treaties were used to discredit the Tokugawa shogun.

g. An anti-foreign group, led by the Choshu, Satsuma, and Tosa clans, also agitated for the restoration of the emperor as the supreme authority. Many foreigners and Japanese who favored concessions to the West were murdered by the pro-imperial forces in the 1860's. Among them was Ii Naosuke.

h. Various Western fleets bombarded Kagoshima (1863) and Shimonoseki (1863 and 1864) and thereby broke the anti-foreign resistance in Japan. More Japanese realized that they had to stand together and learn from the West until such time as they could be rid of foreign pressure.

i. In 1866 the inept Tokugawa shogun, Iemochi, died. The anti-foreign emperor at Kyoto, Komei, also died soon thereafter.

j. Because of vigorous clan opposition and the need for national unity in the face of Western incursions, the new shogun resigned and left the leadership solely in the hands of the young emperor, Meiji (November 1867).

k. The Tokugawa forces were defeated at Ueno (July 1868) after a short civil war. Only now could the Emperor Meiji (1868–1912) issue his renowned Charter

Oath of Five Articles: this promised a popular assembly and an end to feudal practices which were outmoded. The capital was moved from Kyoto to Tokyo.

C. Meiji Japan (1868–1912)

1. The imperial party dropped its anti-foreign policy once it was in control.

2. In 1871 a cabinet system was instituted. Sanjo was named prime minister, while representatives of the powerful Satsuma, Choshu, Tosa, and Hizen clans filled important cabinet posts.

3. The new government struck an important blow for centralized political control by smashing the old feudal structure.

   a. The *daimyos* were compensated for their domains.

   b. The clans were abolished and their lands divided into prefectures.

   c. The *samurai* were now freed from their allegiance to the *daimyos,* but they were without income or occupation. To pacify this group, they were given pensions (half in cash and half in bonds.) Many entered the business and industrial world.

4. Universal military service on the German model was introduced (1872). With British assistance the navy was reorganized (1873).

   a. So good was the new national army that it was able to crush a *samurai*-led force during the Satsuma Rebellion of 1877.

5. Industrialization proceeded under government leadership.

   a. There was little surplus capital in private hands.

   b. The government founded new industries in cooperation with the commercial families that had financed the Meiji Restoration.

   c. The new industries were often given to these families for a small sum.

   d. The lack of purchasing power in Japan forced the Japanese to seek foreign markets, sometimes by force.

6. A ministry of education was organized in 1871. Its goal was education for all Japanese.

7. The Gregorian calendar replaced the lunar calendar in 1873.

8. In 1889 a new constitution was put into effect.
   a. Agitation for representative government had been led by Itagaki.
   b. The new constitution reserved many powers for the emperor: the right to declare war and make peace, and the authority to issue ordinances having the effect of law.
   c. Militarism and strong central government persisted in spite of the new constitution. Only generals and admirals, for example, could fill the naval and war ministries, this having been established by a pre-constitutional decree.
   d. In addition, the new constitution made no mention of the *genro,* the elder statesmen who really directed the affairs of state during the Restoration. These clan representatives were unable to keep the military in check.

9. Japanese foreign policy
   a. During the Meiji era the Japanese became increasingly aggressive in eastern Asia. This was a radical change from the peaceful Tokugawa policy.
   b. The Sino-Japanese commercial treaty of 1871 was a treaty between equals, but the Japanese had additional aspirations in China. An expedition was sent to Formosa in 1874 to punish those guilty of mistreating shipwrecked Japanese sailors. In reality, this was done to keep the restless military busy until Japanese industrialization could be completed.
   c. Friction over Korea in the 1880's and 1890's led to a conflict between China and Japan, the Sino-Japanese War of 1894–1895. An easy Japanese victory forced the Chinese to sign the Treaty of Shimonoseki (April 17, 1895); China recognized the independence of Korea, paid Japan an indemnity, and gave Japan Formosa, the Pescadores, and the Liaotung peninsula. In November, 1895 Russia, Germany, and France forced the Japanese to restore the Liaotung peninsula to China.
   d. Russia and Japan now became rivals in Korea and Manchuria. Russia's seizure of the Liaotung peninsula in 1898 and her failure to completely evacuate

Manchuria after the Boxer Rebellion, led to the Anglo-Japanese Alliance of 1902.

e. The Japanese offered to permit Manchuria to remain as a Russian sphere of interest if the czarist government did not contest their position in Korea (1903). Russia refused to cooperate, and this led to the Russo-Japanese War of 1904–1905.

f. The Treaty of Portsmouth (1905) gave Japan the southern half of Sakhalin, the Liaotung peninsula, and a promise that Korea would be a Japanese sphere. Russia agreed to evacuate Manchuria and restore that area to China.

g. A secret Russo-Japanese convention of 1907 recognized Japan's recently acquired sphere in southern Manchuria. Russian interests in Outer Mongolia and northern Manchuria were admitted.

h. Japan now felt ready to annex Korea and did so in August, 1910.

i. In 1915, when most of the great powers were occupied with World War I, the Japanese issued the obnoxious Twenty-One Demands. Complete acceptance would have made China a Japanese sphere. Japan won important concessions in Shantung and southern Manchuria, but her demands for advisers in the Chinese government were set aside as a result of American pressure.

BIBLIOGRAPHY

Anstey, Vera, *The economic development of India* (3rd ed., New York: Longmans, Green, 1936).

Bolitho, H., *Jinnah: creator of Pakistan* (New York: Macmillan, 1955).

Boxer, C. F., *The Christian century in Japan, 1549–1650* (Berkeley: University of California Press, 1951).

Callard, K., *Pakistan: a political study* (New York: Macmillan, 1957).

Chiang, Siang-Tseh, *The Nien rebellion* (Seattle: University of Washington Press, 1954).

Eckel, Paul E., *The Far East since 1500* (New York: Harcourt, Brace, 1947).

Ennis, T. E., *Eastern Asia* (Chicago: Lippincott, 1948).

Feverwerker, A., *China's early industrialization, 1884–1916* (Cambridge: Harvard University Press, 1959).

Fleming, Peter, *The siege at Peking* (New York: Harper, 1959).

James, D. H., *The rise and fall of the Japanese empire* (New York: Macmillan, 1951).

Latourette, K. S., *The Chinese: their history and culture* (2nd ed., New York: Macmillan, 1934).

Latourette, K. S., *The history of Japan* (New York: Macmillan, 1957).

Majumdar, R. C. *et al, An advanced history of India* (1st ed., London: Macmillan, 1951).

Morse, H. B. and MacNair, H. F., *Far eastern international relations* (Boston: Houghton-Mifflin, 1931).

Murdoch, J. A., *A history of Japan,* 3 vols. (London: Routledge, 1949).

Reischauer, Edwin O., *Japan past and present* (London: Duckworth, 1947).

Roberts, P. E. and Spear, T. G. P., *History of British India under the Company and the Crown* (London: Oxford University Press, 1952).

Smith, T. C., *The agrarian origins of modern Japan* (Stanford: Stanford University Press, 1959).

Thompson, E. and Garratt, G. T., *Rise and fulfillment of British rule in India* (London: Macmillan, 1934).

Varg, P. A., *Missionaries, Chinese, and diplomats* (Princeton: Princeton University Press, 1958).

Waley, A., *The Opium War through Chinese eyes* (New York: Macmillan, 1959).

Wilson, Robert A., *Genesis of Meiji government in Japan, 1868–1871* (Berkeley: University of California Press, 1957).

Wright, A. F., *Buddhism in Chinese history* (Stanford: Stanford University Press, 1959).

Yanaga, C., *Japan since Perry* (New York: McGraw-Hill, 1958).

Chapter 4

THE DEVELOPMENT OF SCIENCE AND THE ENLIGHTENMENT

I. The Scientific Legacy of the Middle Ages and the Renaissance

A. During the Middle Ages some of the monasteries and universities preserved part of the knowledge of natural science inherited from the ancient world.

B. Medieval scholars studied Greek philosophy and knowledge of the natural world.

    1. Additional knowledge of mathematics and science were derived from contact with the Moors.

    2. Medieval philosophers tried to integrate much of the philosophy and knowledge of the ancient world into their own Christian philosophy.

C. Medieval scholars considered truth to be a product of the application of human reason to divine revelation (the Scriptures).

    1. Medieval thinkers were willing to make use of observations of the natural world to support their theories.

    2. Observed phenomena, however, were frequently disregarded if the data disagreed with the accepted authorities such as the Scripture or Aristotle.

D. Renaissance scholars were probably even more fascinated by Greek and Roman civilization than medieval writers had been.

    1. Renaissance artists and technicians added to the technological developments of the Middle Ages.

    2. Renaissance men like Leonardo da Vinci were careful observers of natural phenomena; but they lacked a scien-

tific method to systematize their knowledge (see Vol. 1, pp. 268–269).

E. <u>During the Middle Ages and the Renaissance the Ptolemaic view of the universe was accepted.</u>

   1. The Ptolemaic system (named for the Greek astronomer Ptolemy) maintained the earth was at the center of the universe.

      a. The sun was thought to move around the earth in a circular orbit at uniform speed.

      b. The planets were said to move in epicycles in relation to the earth.

   2. The universe was considered finite, and the Ptolemaic theory actually explained the position of the planets which could be seen with the naked eye.

II. Nicholas Copernicus (1473–1543)

A. Copernicus was a Polish scholar who studied in Italy at the University of Bologna.

   1. While at Bologna, Copernicus heard the Ptolemaic theory seriously questioned by his professor of astronomy, Domenico di Novara (1454–1504).

   2. The Ptolemaic system was particularly criticized for its complexity; it required seventy-nine epicycles to account for the observed motions of the planets.

B. Returning to Poland, Copernicus continued his studies for over thirty years finally stating his conclusions in a treatise, *Concerning the Revolutions of Heavenly Bodies* (1543).

   1. Copernicus proposed that the earth rotated around the sun in a circular orbit at uniform speed.

   2. He maintained the earth rotated upon its own axis.

   3. Copernicus' system was less complicated than the Ptolemaic, requiring only thirty-four epicycles rather than seventy-nine.

C. Copernicus' work provoked strong reactions.

   1. Both Roman Catholic and Protestant theologians opposed it on the grounds that it was in conflict with established religious belief.

   2. No formal action was taken against Copernicus' treatise until <u>Giordano Bruno (1549–1600)</u> made it the basis of his philosophy.

      a. Condemned as a heretic by the Roman Inquisition, Bruno was burned at the stake.

      b. Copernicus' treatise was placed on the *Index of Prohibited Literature* in 1616 where it remained until 1835.

   3. Astronomers, mathematicians, and other scholars of the sixteenth century seemed no more eager to accept Copernicus' view than the theologians.

III. Tycho Brahe (1546–1601) and Johann Kepler (1571–1630)

A. Brahe was a Danish nobleman who was fascinated by precise astronomical observation.

   1. Brahe designed and built instruments accurate within one-tenth of a minute (one-six hundredth of a degree). Copernicus had to rely on observations made with instruments accurate only to the nearest ten minutes (one-sixth of a degree).

   2. For over twenty years Brahe made observations and collected data on the positions of the planets in their orbits.

B. Kepler was a mathematician interested in Copernicus' theory. He became an assistant to Brahe and continued to work with Brahe's observations after Brahe's death.

   1. Kepler found the circular orbits and uniform velocities of the planets assigned to them by Copernicus did not precisely conform to the positions of the planets observed by Brahe.

   2. After many years spent in calculation, Kepler concluded:

      a. The planets moved at different velocities in proportion to their distances from the sun.

      b. The speed of a planet moving along its orbit varied in a mathematically predictable pattern.

      c. The planets moving around the sun traveled in elliptical, not circular, orbits.

   3. In 1616, Kepler's conclusions were published in a book, the *Epitome of Copernican Astronomy*. This work was placed on the *Index of Prohibited Literature* in 1633 and remained there until 1835.

IV. Galileo Galilei (1564–1642)

A. <u>Galileo began his career as a mathematician and apparently discovered the law of the pendulum and the uniform acceleration of falling bodies before he was twenty.</u>
   1. The telescope had been invented shortly after 1600 and Galileo began using it for astronomy.
   2. His observations of the moon, of sun spots, and his discovery of four satellites of Jupiter confirmed by observation the theories set forward by Copernicus and modified by Kepler.
   3. Galileo's subsequent support of the Copernican system brought him into difficulty with the Inquisition, which, in 1615, ordered him to cease advocating any heliocentric theory.
   4. In 1632, however, Galileo published his *Dialogue Concerning the Two Chief Systems of the World,* supporting the Copernican theory. Galileo was summoned before the Inquisition and forced to recant the portions of the book declared to be contrary to the Scriptures.

B. <u>Galileo also made many contributions to the study of dynamics.</u> *Discourses and Mathematical Demonstrations Concerning Two New Sciences* (1638) contains his conclusions.
   1. Aristotle, the accepted authority, maintained force must be continuously applied to a body to keep it in motion.
   2. Galileo denied Aristotle's view, maintaining a body will continue in a given direction at uniform velocity unless force is applied to change the direction or velocity.
   3. This principle of inertia set forward by Galileo became Newton's First Law of Motion.

C. <u>Probably Galileo's most important contribution was to develop a scientific method.</u> He was trying to find a way to convince those who were skeptical about his discoveries and never asserted he had worked out a scientific method.
   1. The first step was to establish a hypothesis. The hypothesis was usually arrived at by logical deduction or mathematical calculation.
   2. The second step was to devise an experiment which would make it possible to demonstrate and observe the hypothesis.
   3. The third step was to accept or modify or reject the hypothesis according to the results of the experiment.

4. The tremendous significance of this process was that men looked upon it as a new way to establish truth. It was no longer necessary to argue on the basis of the authority of the Scriptures or the Greeks. Experiment and observation were the new authorities.

V. René Descartes (1596–1650)

A. Descartes was a Frenchman who believed mathematics was *the* tool to explain the mysteries of the universe.

1. Descartes invented analytic geometry to synthesize algebra and geometry.
2. Descartes believed that if one could discover basic self-evident truths, a philosophic system could be built upon them just as geometric theorems are derived from basic axioms.
3. For Descartes, then, the problems was to discover the basic self-evident truths.
   a. Descartes began by rejecting all beliefs of whose truth there could be the slightest doubt.
   b. Descartes was skilled at doubting, and he finally reached the point where he could doubt everything but the fact that he was doubting.
   c. To doubt required thought, and therefore Descartes argued that he who thinks must exist. This is expressed in his famous motto: *"Cogito ergo sum"* (I think, therefore I am).
4. Descartes explained this process in his most famous work, *Discourse on Method* (1637). He went on to construct a philosophic system but relied so heavily on deduction that many of his conclusions could not be supported by observation.

B. Probably Descartes' encouragement of careful skepticism about many previously accepted ideas was his greatest contribution.

VI. Isaac Newton (1642–1727)

A. In the years 1665 and 1666 Newton, a young English mathematician of humble origins, made three enormous contributions to the development of science.

1. He invented what he called the "calculus of fluxions."

      a. Newtonian calculus became the basis of most modern mathematics.

      b. A German philosopher, Gottfried Wilhelm Leibnitz, independently discovered calculus ten years later. The methods of notation devised by Leibnitz are most widely used today.

   2. <u>Newton discovered the composition of light and began the scientific study of optics.</u>

   3. <u>In this same two-year period he formulated his first ideas concerning gravitation.</u> Not published until 1687, Newton's theory of gravitation was presented in *The Mathematical Principles of Natural Knowledge.*

      a. Many scholars and philosophers before Newton had speculated about gravity. They were particularly curious as to why the planets stayed in orbit. Newton was the first to produce a mathematical explanation of the observed phenomena.

      b. Newton's theory states that between any two bodies there exists an attraction directly proportional to the product of their masses and inversely proportional to the square of the distance between them.

      c. This theory provided an explanation of why planets stayed in orbit and of the ebb and flow of the tides.

B. <u>Newton also formulated additional laws of motion,</u> did some very useful work in metallurgy, served as Warden of the Mint, was a member of Parliament for two terms, a professor of mathematics at Cambridge, and served as President of the Royal Society for twenty-four years.

VII. The Development of Scientific Tools and Academies

A. During the seventeenth century scholars devised some of the tools necessary for exact observation and calculation.

   1. A Scotsman, <u>John Napier,</u> invented logarithms and published the results of his studies in 1614.

      a. About a decade later, the first slide rules appeared.

      b. Descartes set the precedent for using the first letters of the alphabet for given quantities and the last letters for unknown quantities.

      c. During the same century decimal notations for fractions came into general use, and signs for addition, subtraction, multiplication, and division were standardized.

2. The telescope first appeared about 1608, although its originator is unknown. <u>Johann Lippershey,</u> a Dutchman, was one of the first to make and sell a considerable number of telescopes.

3. Another Dutchman, <u>Zacharias Jansen,</u> constructed a compound microscope about 1590.

4. Although Galileo had established the law of the pendulum, it was not until 1656 that a reasonably accurate pendulum clock was developed. Its maker was a Dutchman, <u>Christian Huygens.</u>

5. In 1648 a French mathematician, <u>Blaise Pascal,</u> developed a mercury barometer to measure air pressure.

6. Reasonably accurate thermometers appeared only in the eighteenth century.

    a. In 1721 <u>Daniel Fahrenheit,</u> a German scientist developed the temperature scale which bears his name.

    b. In 1742 a Swede, <u>Anders Celsius,</u> began using a tempperature scale of 100 degrees; this became the Centigrade scale.

B. These instruments were crucial to the advancement of science. Earlier scientists had to rely largely on sensory impressions which did not provide sufficiently accurate measurement. All these instruments were refined by later technicians who devised additional new and useful tools.

C. <u>Scientific academies</u> grew out of the need for and utility of meetings where scientists could discuss matters of mutual interest and exchange information.

1. The universities, with the exception of medical faculties, were hesitant about many of the new discoveries. Many of the universities were sponsored or controlled by churches less than enthusiastic about the theories of Copernicus, Kepler, and Galileo.

2. A number of small academies were established in Italy in the early decades of the seventeenth century.

3. The two most important academies were the Royal Society of England and the French Academy of Sciences.

    a. The French Academy of Sciences began meeting informally about 1631; it was formally recognized by the government in 1666.

    b. The Royal Society of England began meeting in 1645,

but met only irregularly due to the interruptions of the civil war and domestic turbulence. In 1662 it received a charter from Charles II as The Royal Society of London for Promoting Natural Knowledge.

4. The scientific academies published journals and sponsored meetings to facilitate the exchange of ideas. They raised money for research and tried to apply the results of research to practical problems.

VIII. Physiology and Medicine

A. Medieval physicians relied heavily on the ancient Greek doctors Hippocrates and Galen. During the sixteenth century a few courageous physicians risked their reputations challenging the ancient authorities.

1. Two Italian professors, Eustachio and Falloppio, made additional discoveries in the study of anatomy, bequeathing their names to modern physiology. The Spaniard, Servetus, described pulmonary circulation of the blood.

2. Paracelsus (1493–1541), a Swiss physician, attacked Galen's work and insisted medicine was an experimental science and emphasized the close relationship between chemistry and medicine.

3. Andreas Vesalius (1514–1564), a Dutch physician serving as a professor of medicine in the Italian university of Padua, was a major contributor to the study of anatomy.

   a. Vesalius noticed, as he dissected bodies, various errors in Galen's work and resolved to rely on his own observation rather than Galen's authority.

   b. In 1543 he published *On the Structure of the Human Anatomy,* a milestone in the history of medicine.

   c. Vesalius was so severely criticized by his contemporaries that he gave up teaching to become personal physician to Emperor Charles V.

B. The challenge of these sixteenth century physicians to the ancient authorities helped clear the way for further advances in the seventeenth and eighteenth centuries.

1. William Harvey (1578–1650), an English physician who studied at Padua under Falloppio, published in 1628 his findings on circulation of blood.

   a. Servetus had discovered the heart pumped blood

through the lungs, but Harvey was the first to assert that blood flowed from the heart to the arteries and then returned to the heart via the veins.

b. Harvey's *Anatomical Exercise on the Motion of the Heart and Blood in Animals* aroused widespread opposition.

c. Harvey's theory was confirmed, however, by the work of Marcello Malpighi (1628–1694), a professor at the University of Bologna. Using the new compound microscopes, Malpighi discovered capillary circulation of the blood, explaining how the blood got from the arteries to the veins.

d. Malpighi made other important contributions by microscopic study. He studied silkworms, human nerve tissue, the human skin (one layer of which is still called the "Malpighian layer"), and plant life. The study of plant anatomy was founded on Malpighi's research.

2. Robert Whytt (1714–1766) discovered reflex action and began the study of neurology.

3. Preventive medicine received a great stimulus by the introduction from Turkey of the practice of inoculation for smallpox.

a. A Boston physician, Zabdiel Boylston (1679–1766) was possibly the first among western doctors to try inoculation.

b. The more effective and less dangerous cow pox vaccination against smallpox was developed in the early nineteenth century by Edward Jenner.

IX. Chemistry and Physics

A. The pseudo-science of alchemy was so firmly established in Europe that the development of chemistry as a science was slow to begin.

1. Alchemists' primary goal was to find a way to change base metals into gold. They followed no scientific method and disagreed among themselves about the composition of matter.

2. Philosophers, too, had puzzled over the composition of matter.

a. The Aristotelian view, accepted by some philosophers

and alchemists, was that there were four basic elements: air, earth, fire, and water.

b. Another view, held by a considerable group of alchemists known as Spagyrists, maintained there were three elements from which all matter was composed: salt, mercury, and sulfur.

3. It was an English chemist, <u>Robert Boyle (1627–1691)</u>, who took the first major step in demolishing these views.

    a. In *The Sceptical Chymist* (1661), Boyle attacked the alchemists for failure to base their views on careful observation of natural phenomena.

    b. Boyle characterized an element as a pure substance which could not be broken down into anything simpler.

    c. He maintained none of the Aristotelian elements could pass this test.

    d. Boyle was the first to describe a chemical compound as the result of the combination of two or more constituents possessing peculiar qualities not found in any one constituent alone.

    e. He also predicted the discovery of many more elements.

    f. He is famous, too, for his scientific law. Boyle's law says the volume of a given quantity of gas varies inversely with its pressure.

B. Later chemists carried on Boyle's initial steps to make chemistry a science.

1. In 1766 <u>Sir Henry Cavendish</u> announced the discovery of hydrogen, which he called "inflammable air."

2. In 1774 <u>Joseph Priestley</u> in England and <u>Carl Scheele</u>, a Swede, independently discovered oxygen.

3. It was a Frenchman, <u>Antoine Lavoisier (1743–1794)</u>, who first described the oxygen theory of combustion, which is still accepted today.

    a. Lavoisier demonstrated the increase in weight occurring when a substance is burned is the simple chemical addition of oxygen.

    b. He showed, also, that the total weight of all the chemical compounds involved in any instance of combustion is the same at the end of the reaction as at the beginning. This is the law of conservation of matter.

    c. Lavoisier's experiments destroyed the phlogiston theory previously accepted. This theory held that all combustible substances possess one common component which escapes in the act of burning.

    d. In his *Elementary Treatise on Chemistry* (1789), Lavoisier listed thirty-three chemical elements, twenty-three of which are still recognized as such.

    e. Many consider Lavoisier as the father of modern chemistry. In a tragic parody of justice, he was sent to the guillotine by a revolutionary tribunal because he had been a tax collector during the Old Regime. No proof of mis-conduct was presented, and his service to France in standardizing its weights and measures was ignored.

C. Physics developed slowly and steadily upon the foundations laid by Galileo and Newton and other pioneers. During the eighteenth century the study of electricity became particularly significant.

    1. William Gilbert (1540–1603), a physician to Queen Elizabeth, reawakened interest in magnetism in the early modern era.

        a. Gilbert demonstrated that the earth itself had magnetic properties and that iron could be magnetized.

        b. Repeating the old experiment of rubbing amber on fur and observing it would attract objects such as straw and hair, he named this phenomena of attraction "electric" from the Greek word for amber (*elektron*).

    2. Many experimented with electricity in the seventeenth century, but little advance was made until 1729 when an Englishman, Stephen Gray, discovered certain substances would conduct electricity and others would not.

    3. About 1745 the Leyden jar was devised. Its importance was that it provided a useful electrical charge for experiments.

    4. In 1752 Benjamin Franklin demonstrated that lightning was electricity and used this knowledge to devise the lightning rod.

    5. In 1799, Alessandro Volta, the Italian physician after whom the volt is named, invented the voltaic pile or battery.

        a. Volta's discovery made possible a steady flow of elec-

tricity for experimental or practical application.
  b. Before 1799, the experimenter could work with electricity only in fitful flashes.
  6. The work of early physicists with electricity paved the way for its tremendous development by scientists and technicians of the nineteenth century (see Chapters VII and VIII).
D. Concurrently with the development of science, Europeans made steady advances in technology. Significant technological innovation was characteristic of the Middle Ages and continued through the early modern era accelerating rapidly in the Industrial Revolution which began in the eighteenth century (see Chapter VII).

X. The Enlightenment

A. The Enlightenment generally refers to the political, economic, and social thought of a period beginning early in the eighteenth century and ending around 1789 with the beginning of the French Revolution.
B. To a very considerable degree, the Enlightenment represents the impact of the development of science upon political, economic, religious, and social thought of the time.
  1. Many scientists, such as Newton, made no claim that their theories could or should be applied to political, economic, or social problems.
  2. Other thinkers and writers, however, were tremendously impressed by scientific discovery, especially Newton's theory of gravitation.
    a. These thinkers believed that all events were governed by "laws of nature" or "natural laws," as they called them.
    b. They argued that the theory of gravity was a natural law which had always operated on all things everywhere.
    c. They believed that if Newton could discover such a law of nature, then other natural laws governing political, economic, and social affairs could also be discovered by man.
  3. These writers and thinkers of the eighteenth century are referred to as *philosophes.* This is a French word for which there is no exact English equivalent. Probably

the English word whose meaning is closest to *philosophe* is "publicist."

   a. Most of the *philosophes* were not outstanding as original thinkers or philosophers.

   b. The major activity of the *philosophes* was to circulate and popularize ideas or combinations of ideas borrowed from earlier thinkers.

   c. The *philosophes* hoped to uncover natural laws covering all human concerns and reform society so it would conform with those natural laws.

   d. Many *philosophes* considered human reason the best means for discovering the laws of nature and the best guide for reforming society.

   e. They considered those aspects of society desirable which they called "reasonable," or "natural."

   f. Generally, the *philosophes* were scornful of traditional values or institutions. They considered many older institutions as "unenlightened" results of unreasonable customs.

   g. The *philosophes* were very optimistic about making a paradise of human society. They were confident that man, whom they considered good, would quickly reform and adjust his society once enlightened reason showed him the way.

4. The optimism of the *philosophes* and their contemporaries was heightened by the writings of John Locke late in the seventeenth century.

   a. In addition to Locke's political treatises defending constitutionalism, representative government, and revolution against tyranny, he wrote a philosophical treatise, *Essay Concerning Human Understanding* (1690).

   b. In this work Locke insisted that humans were born with a perfectly blank mind *(tabula rasa),* lacking preconceived notions or innate tendencies.

   c. Therefore, Locke argued, all human knowledge was the result of experience. Experience was composed of sensations and reflections upon sensations.

   d. As a result, Locke asserts, whatever a man becomes depends upon his environment, which produces his experience.

5. Some *philosophes* believed, therefore, that it would be

possible to improve man's nature by improving his environment. His environment would be greatly improved by reforming society to conform with the laws of
nature they expected to discover.

6. The optimism of the *philosophes* spread the idea of
   progress in the eighteenth century.

   a. Earlier thinkers viewed the ideal society as static. A
      perfect society would be stable and unchanging.

   b. In addition to those *philosophes* inspired by the
      theories already mentioned, others were persuaded by
      the seventeenth century literary controversy between
      two groups known as the "ancients" and "moderns."

   c. The "ancients" insisted the classic civilization of
      Greece and Rome transcended all other ages.

   d. The "moderns" maintained contemporary man was
      superior to the Greek or Roman because he could add
      to classic thought the achievements, especially in sci-
      ence, of man since that time.

   e. By the eighteenth century, most *philosophes* sided
      with the "moderns," convinced that man was pro-
      gressing toward a better world.

   f. The idea of progress, first widely accepted in the eight-
      eenth century, became an essential part of western
      ideology in the nineteenth and twentieth centuries.

C. The "Enlightenment" had a profound effect upon religious
   thought, spreading deism, on the one hand, and popular
   religious revivalism, on the other.

   1. Many varieties of deism appeared in the seventeenth and
      eighteenth centuries, but most of them shared several
      basic tenets.

      a. God's most important role in the universe was as the
         Creator (many deists referred to God as the First
         Cause).

      b. God created the universe subject to natural laws He
         established and did not intervene in its operation
         thereafter.

      c. Since the universe was bound to operate by natural
         laws established when it was created, there was no
         need for prayer nor any hope for divine intercession
         in human affairs.

      d. The only use for any church was that it would en-

courage virtue and morality. Organized and institu-
tionalized religion was reduced to moral philosophy.

e. Most deists denied that the Scriptures were divinely
ordained or inspired. Man was to be guided by "natural reason." Man's observation of the natural universe combined with his reason would tell him what
was good or bad.

f. Some deists were not sure that reason was a sufficient
guide to virtue, but they expected that universal, natural laws of morality would be discovered and would
guide man.

g. Some deists believed man had an immortal soul, and
some did not.

2. Deism appeared in seventeenth century England where
it was advocated by such men as Lord Herbert of Cher-
bury (1583–1648), Matthew Tindal (1657–1733), William
Wollaston (1659–1724), Junius Toland (1670–1722), and
Viscount Bolingbroke (1678–1751). It spread to France
in the eighteenth century and was adopted by many of
the *philosophes.*

3. A few of the *philosophes* went beyond deism, accepting
agnosticism or atheism. Baron d'Holbach (1723–1789),
a French *philosophe,* was a complete atheist and materialist, asserting the entire universe was nothing but
matter in spontaneous motion.

4. While the *philosophes* were concerned with various deis-
tic philosophies, many more Europeans were attracted
by the religious reform movements such as Pietism and
Methodism.

a. In Lutheran Germany, Pietism developed from the
writings of Philip Spener (1635–1705).

b. Unlike the cold materialism of the Enlightenment,
Pietism stressed religious devotion and daily emula-
tion of the life of Christ.

c. The Pietists and Methodists emphasized a highly personal and emotional relationship between man and
God.

d. George Fox (1624–1691), an English contemporary of
Spener, also preached on the theme of the close relationship between man and God.

e. Fox traveled through England, the Netherlands,

North America and the West Indies advocating that man live a life of moderation and be guided by his "inner light" religion.

f. Simplicity and pacifism were characteristic of the Society of Friends (Quakers) which Fox founded.

g. Concerning the origins and development of Methodism, see Chapter 1, part VII.

h. During the eighteenth century, Pietism, Methodism, and the Quaker movement spread rapidly.

D. The thought of the *philosophes* was never synthesized into a system. An outline of the thought of some of the major *philosophes* will provide an illustration of the variety of concerns and opinions.

1. Baron Charles-Louis de Montesquieu (1689–1755) was a member of the French aristocracy and was particularly interested in political liberty.

a. Montesquieu's best known work is *The Spirit of the Laws* (1748). In this lengthy work Montesquieu studied the government and laws of all human society searching for the simple underlying spirit of all law.

b. Montesquieu concluded that the ideal form of government for any society is determined to a large degree by such conditions as the climate and the size of the realm to be governed.

c. Montesquieu asserted that in France political power should be divided between the king and various "corporate bodies," such as the nobility, the church, and provincial assemblies.

d. Consistent with his opposition to the concentration of political power in the hands of the French king was Montesquieu's advocacy of "separation of powers," a doctrine which he emphasized and which profoundly influenced the writers of the constitution of the United States.

e. Montesquieu was no democrat, and he had little concern for freedom of expression or religion.

2. François-Marie Arouet, better known as Voltaire (1694–1778) came from a French lawyer's family. Voltaire's works, totaling over one hundred volumes in their modern version, demonstrate his great literary skill; logical and easily read, they show how skillfully Voltaire used wit and sarcasm to present his arguments.

a. Unlike Montesquieu, Voltaire was most concerned for freedom of the press and of religion.

b. He was little concerned with the form of government so long as it was enlightened. An enlightened government, in Voltaire's view, would promote the arts and sciences, recognize no state church, enforce religious toleration, and advance material and technical progress.

c. Voltaire thought the best hope for progress was through the rule of an enlightened monarch surrounded by enlightened advisors, under whose control enlightenment would filter down to the masses. To Montesquieu, Louis XIV was a villain; to Voltaire, he was a hero.

d. Voltaire was a deist who attacked religious dogma. He asserted man's reason enabled him to tell good from evil. A church was socially useful to preach virtuous behavior to the ignorant and credulous mass of mankind but nothing more.

e. Voltaire held a low opinion of the human race as a whole, and his views have been summarized as a belief in "liberty for the intelligent." He was far more effective as a critic than as the author of constructive proposals for reform.

3. Jean-Jacques Rousseau (1712–1728), born in Geneva and spending his youth in poverty, became one of the most enigmatic but influential of the *philosophes*.

a. Rousseau considered man naturally good but corrupted by society. The best traits of human character, such as kindness, honesty, and unselfishness, he insisted were products of nature.

b. Rousseau considered reason a false guide if followed alone. Following intuition, conscience, or spontaneous feeling was more likely to lead the individual to true happiness than his reason.

c. Rousseau's major political work was *The Social Contract* (1762) in which he introduced a concept he called the "General Will," which still causes controversy among scholars of the Enlightenment.

d. Rousseau never defined the General Will, but he characterized it as "absolute," "sacred," and "inviolable." The social contract was an agreement among the people by which all individuals surrendered their natural liberty to each other, fusing their individual wills into a combined General Will, and agreed to accept the rulings of the General Will as final.

e. Rousseau regarded all officials of the government as nothing but delegates of the General Will. Rousseau did not describe the organization of government and had little admiration for parliamentary institutions.

f. Rousseau desired a commonwealth in which every person could feel he belonged; he wanted every citizen to have a sense of participation and membership.

g. Many writers maintain Rousseau's concept of the General Will evolved into the idea of nationality. His emphasis on the importance of emotion and intuition, rather than reason, made him a forerunner of the Romanticist movement of the nineteenth century.

4. Another group of *philosophes* were known as the "Encyclopedists" because they contributed in some way to the *Encyclopédie* of Denis Diderot (1713–1784).

a. The Encyclopedists relied more on experience and less on reason than many of the *philosophes*.

b. The *Encyclopédie,* whose first volume appeared in 1751, was intended to include all human knowledge up to that time.

c. Many of its articles were written to support rationalistic and materialistic views. In spite of prolonged difficulties with the censors, the seventeen volume *Encyclopédie* enjoyed wide sales.

5. A group of *philosophes* particularly concerned with economic questions were the Physiocrats, who believed in applying physiocracy, "the rule of nature," to economic problems.

a. Probably the best known Physiocrats were François Quesnay (1694–1774) and Dupont de Nemours (1739–1817), founder of the family who gained fame in United States as leaders in the chemical industry.

b. The Physiocrats considered agriculture the source of all wealth. They considered the most fundamental natural law of economics to be the desirability of permitting the free circulation of wealth produced by agriculture.

c. Since the Physiocrats wanted free circulation of wealth, they vigorously attacked the mercantilist policies of the government because of the controls imposed on the economy in the application of mercantilism.

6. The outstanding figure in eighteenth century economic thought was the Scot, Adam Smith (1723–1790). Though he was probably influenced by the Physiocrats, he did not share their belief in the primacy of agriculture.

a. Smith's great work was *The Wealth of Nations* (1776). This study went much further than any of its predecessors in making a systematic description of economic activity.

b. Smith's descriptions of such phenomena as the "law of supply and demand" and the "law of diminishing returns" exercised a tremendous influence on his contemporaries and upon the subsequent development of economic thought.

c. Smith insisted the wisest economic policy of a government was *laissez faire* (the government should interfere as little as possible with private enterprise).

d. Naturally enough, Smith joined the Physiocrats in attacking mercantilist policies of the period.

7. In spite of the variations in the ideas of the *philosophes,* the thought of the Enlightenment was almost always characterized by cosmopolitanism and secularism.

a. Enlightened thought was cosmopolitan in that the *philosophes* expected their ideas would apply to all men in all places at all times. If the law of gravity applied equally to a citizen of Paris and a Chinese coolie, then, they reasoned, the laws of nature they hoped to discover would be equally universal.

b. Their thought was secular in that their concern was for this world, not the next. The value of any institution or custom was determined by their judgment of its social utility. Even if God was reduced to a First Cause who could not intervene further in human affairs, the church was acceptable if it helped keep people virtuous by its preaching.

XI. Music in the Eighteenth Century

A. The development of music in the eighteenth century has little direct connection with the beginnings of science or the Enlightenment, but it overshadowed the progress of the other arts.

B. In a fashion somewhat similar to the broadening philosophical concepts and the appearance of scientific systems, Bach and Handel broadened the scope of music and amplified the constructive devices and the breadth of expression of their art.

  1. Johann Sebastian Bach (1685–1750) was probably the leading German composer of the eighteenth century.

    a. Bach composed every form of music except opera, which was unpopular at that time.

    b. He was particularly interested in religious music and composed some of the most impressive religious music ever written, such as his *B Minor Mass* and his *Passion According to St. John.*

    c. He borrowed the contrapuntal form from the sixteenth century and wove it into the rich complexity of his compositions.

    d. Bach's Brandenburg concertos, along with his fugues and cantatas, are highly sophisticated and abstract compositions; and they exercised a great influence on his successors.

  2. George Handel (1685–1759) was born in Germany, studied in Italy, and followed the Hanoverian kings to England where he remained.

    a. Handel employed an elaborate system of tonality in his music. Some musicians assert his tonal system was later employed by Beethoven and Brahms.

    b. Handel strove for emotional effects which forced him to subordinate the usual classical form in music.

    c. Handel was a prolific composer; his complete works fill one hundred volumes. Probably his most famous composition is his *Messiah* (1742).

  3. Franz Joseph Haydn (1732–1809) was an Austrian who improved the form of the sonata.

    a. Haydn provided an innovation in symphonic composition by using a strong melodic theme heightened or diminished by orchestral effects utilizing striking changes in volume.

b. Haydn was an innovator in choosing the precise instruments he desired to convey a particular musical mood.

4. Wolfgang Amadeus Mozart (1756–1791) wrote over 600 musical compositions in his brief lifetime. He wrote in every known musical form. Mozart perfected the classic forms of the symphony and the concerto.

5. Ludwig von Beethoven (1770–1827) was born in Bonn, Germany, but he spent most of his life studying and composing in Vienna.

   a. Beethoven's musical technique was essentially classical in form; but his technique and construction were particularly original, enabling him to produce music of amazing emotional power and beauty.

   b. Beethoven wrote thirty-two piano sonatas, nine symphonies, and many pieces composed for chamber music. His works have an unusual appeal in that they please both the musical elite and the general public.

XII. Enlightened Despotism

A. Enlightened despotism refers to the attempts made to apply some of the ideas of the *philosophes* to actual political, economic, and social conditions.

   1. In France no sustained and serious effort at enlightened rule occurred. Louis XV was able but hardly conscientious. Louis XVI was sincere but lacking in ability (see Chapter 1, part IX).

   2. In Russia, the reign of Catherine II presented an enlightened façade masking the misery of millions of serfs (see Chapter 2, part V).

B. The Kingdom of Prussia under Frederick II (the Great) was probably the most efficient European government at that time. Frederick proudly referred to himself as the "First Servant of the State."

   1. Frederick the Great was very familiar with the ideas of the *philosophes*.

      a. He believed, as many of them did, that the main instrument of reform and progress was the state. In the

Kingdom of Prussia, it was the crown that provided leadership in reform.

b. He endorsed and practiced the secular, anti-ultramontane views of the *philosophes*. In Prussia, religious toleration was maintained.

c. Frederick II was also successful in beginning and maintaining a system to stabilize grain prices in Prussia. This program was probably beneficial to the kingdom.

2. Frederick II, however, diverged from the ideals of most *philosophes* in other respects.

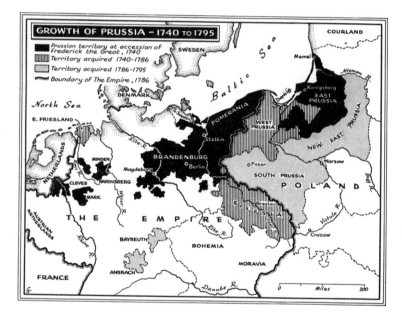

GROWTH OF PRUSSIA — 1740 TO 1795

■ Prussian territory at accession of Frederick the Great, 1740
▧ Territory acquired 1740-1786
▨ Territory acquired 1786-1795
⌐ Boundary of The Empire, 1786

a. Prussia maintained a vigorous mercantilist policy; *laissez-faire* did not fit the Prussian scheme of mobilizing the economic life of Prussia to support the army.

b. Frederick II ruled from 1740 to 1786. For almost a third of that time Prussia was at war.

c. Frederick's seizure of Silesia, which began the War of the Austrian Succession and contributed to the Seven Years' War, may have been smart power politics, but it was hardly enlightened.

d. The same judgment probably applies to Prussia's role in the partitions of Poland.

e. Frederick II followed enlightened policies just so long as they harmonized with his political or economic plans. If he had to choose between enlightened methods and reason of state, the enlightened methods were sacrificed.

C. Of all the rulers of Europe, Joseph II, Emperor of Austria from 1780 to 1790, probably made the most sincere and energetic effort to put the ideals of the Enlightenment into practice. With all his good intentions, Joseph II seemed to be a poor judge of the forces opposing reform.

1. Joseph II took steps to equalize taxes and provide all his subjects with equal civic rights, abolishing serfdom at the same time.

2. Joseph II freed the press and ordered toleration for all religions.

   a. He clashed with the papacy over control of the church in Austria.

   b. Joseph II suppressed many monasteries in the empire using their property to finance secular hospitals in Vienna, thus laying the foundations of Viennese excellence as a medical center.

3. Opposition to Joseph's reforms led him to create a secret police.

   a. The secret police reported to Joseph II on government officials' performance of their duties or on the activities of any suspected troublemaker.

   b. Some historians maintain Joseph II was the first ruler to establish a systematic police state, even if it was created as an instrument of enlightenment and reform.

4. Joseph II actually anticipated many reforms later carried out by revolutionaries in France.

   a. However, Joseph II tried to change too much too quickly.

   b. When he died, the Austrian Netherlands and Hungary were on the verge of revolt. The nobles opposed his reforms, and the peasants were bewildered and restive.

c. Joseph's reign probably illustrates the limitations of reform from the top and suggests that drastic and abrupt reform requires a wave of public opinion to initiate it and sustain it effectively.

BIBLIOGRAPHY

Becker, C., *The heavenly city of the eighteenth century philosophers* (New Haven: Yale University Press, 1932).

Brunn, G., *The enlightened despots* (New York: Holt, 1929).

Bury, J. B., *The idea of progress: an inquiry into its origins and growth* (New York: Dover, 1955).

Cassirer, E., *The philosophy of the Enlightenment* (Princeton: Princeton University Press, 1951).

Clark, G. N., *Science and social welfare in the age of Newton* (Oxford: Clarendon, 1937).

Cobban, A., *Rousseau and the modern state* (London: Allen & Unwin, 1934).

Hazard, P., *European thought in the eighteenth century* (London: Hollis & Carter, 1954).

Morely, J., *Diderot and the Encyclopaedists,* revised edition (London: Macmillan, 1923).

Nussbaum, F. L., *The triumph of science and reason, 1660–1685* (New York: Harper, 1953).

Palmer, R. R., *Catholics and unbelievers in eighteenth century France* (Princeton: Princeton University Press, 1939).

Sullivan, J., *Isaac Newton, 1642–1727* (New York: Macmillan, 1938).

Torrey, N., *The spirit of Voltaire* (New York: Columbia University Press, 1938).

Chapter 5

THE FRENCH REVOLUTION AND THE NAPOLEONIC ERA

I. The Controversial Nature of the Revolution

A. The French Revolution and its subsequent impact on the development of western civilization are so important and so complex that they are still highly controversial. The revolution not only overthrew a monarchy and established a republic which became a military dictatorship, but it also substantially altered economic and social conditions and affected cultural patterns as well.

B. Whether its goals were good or bad and whether the goals justified the violence of the revolution are questions which continue to lead to varying appraisals of the revolution as a whole.

II. Conditions in France on the Eve of the Revolution

A. The attempts of the government to adopt reforms to meet its most serious problems are described in Chapter 1, part IX. The nobility blocked most of the proposals for reform and forced Louis XVI to summon the Estates-General who were to meet in May 1789.

  1. The Estates-General took its name from the fact that it represented three estates or classes.

    a. The first estate was the clergy. Many of its members, particularly among the higher clergy, were members of the nobility.

    b. The second estate was the nobility, which had constantly increased its power and influence in France after the death of Louis XIV in 1715.

      c. The third estate was, simply, everyone not in the first or second estates. Within the third estate the commercial and industrial leaders were the most influential and articulate.

  2. The Estates-General was supposed to operate somewhat like a three-chambered legislature. Whatever was proposed and passed by one estate had to be accepted by the other two.

      a. Each estate could always veto the proposal passed by another.

      b. In a joint session, the first two estates ordinarily had a sufficient number of votes to defeat the third.

B. The class structure in France created discontent.

  1. The privileges of the clergy applied only to archbishops, bishops, and abbots.

      a. These members of the clergy derived sizable incomes from the tithes the Church received from the income from real estate.

      b. Revenues from Church property were considerable. According to some estimates the Church owned about one-tenth of the land in France.

      c. The Church was exempt from royal taxation, though it usually made a contribution to the government each year.

      d. Church revenues paid the salaries of the clergy and also supported hospitals, schools, and charity.

      e. The parish priests, unlike the higher clergy, frequently shared the views of the third estate from which they usually came.

  2. The nobility also occupied a favored position.

      a. The major source of the nobility's income was landed wealth. The nobility apparently owned about one-fifth of the land of France.

      b. Members of the higher nobility held most of the important offices in the government. Many received pensions from the crown.

      c. The nobility was exempt from most direct taxation and enjoyed special rights before the law.

      d. The exalted social status of the nobility was a source of irritation to wealthier members of the third estate.

      e. Some of the provincial nobility in the rural areas were, however, practically bankrupt.

    f. While the clergy and the nobility paid some revenues to the crown, they did not pay their fair share.

    g. It is estimated that the clergy and nobility together composed about three per cent of the population.

3. <u>The upper level of the third estate was composed of men of industrial and commercial wealth and professional men.</u>

    a. In addition to the possession of most of the commerce and industry of France, these men are thought to have owned almost as much land as the nobility.

    b. This group was articulate and vocal. It was familiar with the works of the *philosophes*. It opposed mercantilist interference with the economy.

    c. The tax burden imposed no financial hardship on this group. But they resented the exclusive status and privileges of the nobility.

4. <u>A second group within the third estate were the shopkeepers, craftsmen, and unskilled wage earners.</u>

    a. These people lived a marginal existence and faced serious economic hardship during any financial depression or interruption of commerce.

    b. Smaller in number than the peasants, this group was influential in the development of the revolution because they concentrated in the cities, especially Paris.

5. <u>The peasants, who owned about two-fifths of the land, comprised the largest group within the third estate.</u>

    a. Conditions among the peasantry varied widely. A peasant who owned his land was frequently well situated.

    b. Peasants who owned too little land to feed themselves from it usually supplemented their incomes by working for the nobility.

    c. Peasants who owned no land ordinarily eked out an existence by working the lands of the nobility. They were poorly paid and risked starvation whenever a crop failure occurred.

    d. Conditions varied widely from one area of France to another.

    e. Taken as a whole, however, the peasants of France were often considered to have been among the most fortunate in Europe. Only the English peasant was as well- or better situated than the French. Prussian and Russian agricultural labor endured much less satisfactory conditions and Poland was known as the "peasants' hell."

   f. The peasants' chief grievances were the tax burden, payments and services to the nobility, and land ownership. Landless peasants wanted land; those who owned land wanted more.

C. <u>The most critical problem facing the government was financial.</u> The War of the Austrian Succession, the Seven Years' War, and French support of the American Revolution had increased the government debt.

   1. The debt was not disproportionately large for a nation as wealthy as France.

   2. The crux of the problem was that revenues constantly failed to meet expenditures because tax collection was reduced by excessive exemptions and inefficiency.

   3. Every attempt to reform the revenue system failed, largely as a result of the action of the nobility, who insisted the Estates-General be summoned to solve the problem.

   4. When the king agreed to summon the Estates-General, the third estate was fearful that the nobility would gain control of the government through their control of the representatives of the first and second estates.

      a. The third estate demanded, therefore, that it be given as many representatives as the first two estates combined.

      b. The king finally agreed to this demand. The first and second estates were to have three hundred delegates each, and the third was to have six hundred.

      c. Meanwhile, however, the Parlement of Paris, functioning as a law court dominated by the nobility, ruled that the estates would meet and vote separately. This procedure, voting "by order," would maintain the nobility's control.

      d. The third estate wanted all estates to meet jointly and vote "by head." Voting "by head" would give the third estate a chance to overrule the first two estates.

   5. By the spring of 1789, even before the Estates-General met or the financial problem was considered, class an-

tagonism was jeopardizing the chances for cooperation and peaceful reform.

III. The Estates-General and the National Assembly

A. The Estates-General met as planned in May 1789, but immediately a struggle over voting "by order" or "by head" deadlocked the meetings.

   1. On June 13, the third estate declared itself a "National Assembly." The king, urged on by the nobility, responded by closing the hall where the third estate met.

   2. On June 20, 1789, the third estate moved its meeting to an indoor tennis court and its members swore and signed the Oath of the Tennis Court.

      a. This oath stated that wherever its signers gathered, the National Assembly existed.

      b. It further provided that its members would not disband until they had drafted a constitution.

      c. The Oath of the Tennis Court began the French Revolution because its signers had no authority to write a constitution but took upon themselves the sovereign power to do so.

   3. The king ordered the three estates to meet separately but failed to enforce his commands. The National Assembly continued to meet.

   4. With the government paralyzed at Versailles, France began to drift toward anarchy. Food was scarce, prices were high, and unemployment was rising. Peasants refused to pay taxes, law enforcement ceased, and armed mobs roamed through the rural areas. Rumors of every sort drove the people to the verge of panic.

B. In Paris, these conditions led to the fall of the Bastille on July 14, 1789.

   1. A Parisian mob, apparently excited by rumors, demanded that the governor of the old prison furnish them arms.

   2. Misunderstandings and vehement agitation led to a mob assault upon the Bastille. The mob seized the prison, murdered the governor of the Bastille and the mayor of Paris.

   3. Louis XVI did not know what to do; so he recognized

a citizens' committee, which had been formed in Paris, as the new municipal government.

   a. The king sent away the troops that he had summoned to Versailles and ordered the remaining representatives of the first two estates to join the National Assembly.

   b. The Parisian middle class, wishing to protect themselves and their property from mob rule, formed a militia, which became the National Guard.

   c. The Marquis de Lafayette was placed in command of the National Guard.

   d. The people of Paris had unwittingly saved the National Assembly. The king's acceptance of the situation in Paris, his recognition of the National Assembly, and its protection by the militia put Louis XVI in a position from which he could hardly turn back.

C. The events in Paris encouraged further disorder in the rural areas. During July 1789 a panic known as the "Great Fear" swept over most of France.

   1. One aspect of the complex psychological phenomenon of the "Great Fear" was a general agrarian insurrection. The peasants' objective was to destroy manorial archives which held the records of peasant obligations to the nobility.

   2. The National Assembly could restore order in the country only by meeting the peasants' demands.

      a. In an evening session on August 4, 1789, the National Assembly voted to end serfdom and most of the feudal privileges.

      b. Peasants, however, still had to pay all arrears in rents as compensation to the lords.

      c. Only in 1793, during the radical phase of the revolution, were the peasants freed from paying compensation in any form.

D. As its first step in planning the new order, the National Assembly issued on August 26, 1789, the Declaration of the Rights of Man and Citizen.

   1. This document declared "men are born and remain free and equal in rights." Man's natural rights were held to be "liberty, property, security, and resistance to oppression."

2. Freedom of thought and religion were guaranteed along with equality before the law. No one could be arrested or punished except by due process of law.

3. The only sovereign was the nation itself, and all public officials and armed forces acted solely in its name. Taxation was to be only by common consent. The powers of government were to be separated among different branches.

4. This declaration was a philosophical descendant of similar bills of rights of American state constitutions, of the English Bill of Rights (1689), and of the ideas of the *philosophes.*

   a. Thousands of copies of the declaration were circulated in France and became part of the ideology of the revolution.

   b. The declaration was spread through other parts of Europe, as well, and excited popular interest abroad.

E. The task of solving other problems divided the National Assembly. The question of the role to be played by the king in a new government was particularly explosive.

   1. Once again it was suspicion and fear of the aristocracy that proved decisive.

      a. By October, 1789 Louis XVI had still not approved either the August 4th decrees nor the Declaration of Rights. He was thought to be trying to protect the nobility.

      b. The Parisian mob, jobless, hungry, and dissatisfied, marched on Versailles. On October 5, they forced the royal family to move to Paris.

      c. Soon the National Assembly moved to Paris. This move was very important because it greatly increased the influence of the Paris workers in the development of the revolution.

      d. The assembly was afraid any troops it would assemble might turn against it. Therefore, it frequently had to rely on the people of Paris if force was required.

   2. In December, 1789, the assembly passed laws to reorganize the government administration of France.

      a. The old provinces were replaced by eighty-three departments.

      b. Municipal governments, elected by a restricted franchise were given powers to levy and collect taxes and keep order.

c. Reacting against the crown's seven centuries of effort to centralize the government, the assembly failed to provide any means to collect taxes for the central government.

F. Revolution had not solved the financial problems of 1789. These the assembly tried to meet by confiscating the lands of the Church.

1. The government seized the Church lands and issued *assignats,* interest bearing notes secured by the confiscated property.

   a. It was not long until the government issued too many notes against the property it had seized, and the value of the *assignats* began to drop below their face value.

   b. While *assignats* could be transferred from one holder to another, they were not sufficiently flexible to be as useful as a sound currency.

2. The confiscation of Church lands left the clergy without income and its educational and charitable functions lacking support. To meet these problems the assembly passed the Civil Constitution of the Clergy in July, 1790.

   a. This law provided clergy were to be elected like civil officials rather than appointed from above.

   b. Bishops were instructed merely to notify the papacy of their election. Bishops were forbidden to acknowledge any papal decree.

   c. No papal letter or decree could be published in France without permission of the government.

   d. Apparently the assembly's intent was not to separate the church and state but to develop the church as an arm of the state.

   e. In the spring of 1791 the Pope condemned not only the Civil Constitution of the Clergy but also the revolution and all its works.

   f. The assembly retaliated by requiring all French clergy to swear an oath of loyalty to the government and the Civil Constitution of the Clergy.

   g. About half the clergy, later called the "juring" clergy, took the oath. The remainder, later known as the "non-juring" or "refractory" clergy, refused. Only seven bishops in all France took the oath.

h. The Civil Constitution of the Clergy has been called "the greatest tactical blunder of the revolution." It put the Church in resolute opposition to the revolution and divided the people of France. To accept the new clergy was to defy the Pope; to remain loyal to the non-juring clergy was to support a group which opposed the revolution. Louis XVI himself personally used the services of non-juring priests.

G. The Constitution of 1791 was proclaimed in September. For two years the National Assembly had governed the country while simultaneously working to devise the constitution. It was put into effect immediately. The National Assembly, by 1791 called the Constituent, disbanded.

1. The new government was to be a constitutional monarchy with the supreme power vested in a unicameral Legislative Assembly.

2. In spite of the ideals of its writers, the Constitution of 1791 was more notable for its weaknesses than its strength.

   a. The government was excessively decentralized by the excessive powers given to local governments which enforced national legislation only if they wished.

   b. The Constitution of 1791 was hardly democratic. The French were divided into "active" and "passive" citizens; only the former could vote. Whether a citizen was "active" depended on how much tax he paid.

   c. The tax qualification for "active" citizenship was so high that only about half of the adult males could vote.

   d. In addition, voters only elected members of electoral colleges who, in turn, elected members to the Legislative Assembly.

   e. Membership in the electoral college was also determined by tax qualifications, which were so high that only about fifty thousand persons could qualify as electors or candidates for office.

3. In dealing with pressing current problems both the National Assembly and the Legislative Assembly had to make compromises and provisional arrangements, which frequently caused complaint.

   a. The public debt was still unpaid. The debt was not repudiated because a large part of it was owed to the men who sat in the National Assembly and the Legislative Assembly.

    b. A *laissez-faire* economic policy was adopted. Gilds were abolished, and laws against the *compagnonnages* were passed. The *compagnonnages* were unions of workers who did not belong to gilds.

    c. These policies did little to ease labor trouble existing in 1789. Business declined during the strife of the revolution, and there was a wave of strikes in 1791.

H. <u>The chances that a constitutional monarchy would survive were weakened by the role played by Louis XVI.</u>

    1. The actions of the king made it appear that he opposed the course of the revolution and either supported the aristocracy or was their tool. Whenever Louis supported the revolutionary government, he was so slow to give his approval that he appeared only to be giving in to a force he could not oppose.

    2. In April, 1791 Louis XVI tried to escape from France. Accompanied by his family, he got as far as Varennes where they were arrested, returned to Paris, and virtually, but not technically, imprisoned.

        a. This episode, known as the "flight to Varennes," displayed how ineffective Louis could be in a crisis. Had he asserted himself, the royal family would probably have escaped safely.

        b. It was, at best, a strange sort of constitutional monarchy which the titualar head of the government was caught trying to flee the country.

        c. Naturally, Louis' attempted escape greatly encouraged distrust of the king.

    3. Another condition weakening the new government was the fact that the members of the National Assembly ruled that no member of the National Assembly could sit in the new Legislative Assembly.

        a. The Legislative Assembly lacked the political experience gained by the National Assembly.

        b. Many members of the National Assembly joined political clubs. Some political clubs were more radical and some more conservative than the National Assembly as a whole.

        c. The most famous of these political clubs was the Jacobin club. Its members were radical by comparison to the assembly, and they often used the club to plan their strategy for assembly meetings.

d. By the time the Legislative Assembly took over, the Jacobin club included some of its members, as well. In addition, the Jacobins became affiliated with similar clubs all over France.

e. The Jacobins, as a result, formed a strong revolutionary organization outside official government agencies somewhat like the Communist Party in Soviet Russia.

f. It was the Girondins, a faction of the Jacobin club, that led France into war.

I. The war in which the Constitutional Monarchy became involved was the shock it could not stand.

1. From the beginning of the revolution, people had constantly fled from France. These people were known as *émigrés*.

a. Many *émigrés* were members of the nobility. Some had been members of the National Assembly and fled because they thought the revolution was going too far.

b. The *émigrés* tried to get other rulers in Europe to intervene in France, stop the revolution, restore their properties and privileges, and save the royal family.

c. The French revolutionaries were always fearful the *émigrés* would return and destroy the work of the revolution and the revolutionaries as well.

2. The rulers of Europe, however, had problems of their own; and none was anxious to abandon his plans and go to war with the French.

a. Catherine II of Russia hoped the Western European governments would invade France so that she would have a free hand to clutch all the eastern European territories.

b. In England, William Pitt ("the Younger") wanted no war to interfere with his plans for the reform of Parliament.

c. The Austrian emperor, Leopold II, occupied the key position because Marie Antoinette was his sister. Leopold II wanted to avoid war, however, so that he could profit in any partition of Poland.

d. The Prussians were also interested in Polish partition rather than becoming involved in France.

3. But the revolutionary government in France was making

a habit of unilateral action. It had annexed the papal territory of Avignon and the territory of Alsace without the consent of the papacy or the German princes concerned. The flight to Varennes made it clear Louis XVI was a prisoner.

4. In August 1791 Emperor Leopold II met with Frederick William II (ruled 1786–1797) of Prussia, and the two rulers issued the Declaration of Pillnitz.

    a. This declaration said Emperor Leopold II and King Frederick William II would take military action to restore order in France *if* all the other powers would join them.

    b. Leopold II was sure all the other powers would never join him, but the declaration would get rid of tiresome requests from the *émigrés*.

5. In France, the Declaration of Pillnitz produced a mixture of fear, frenzy, and defiance.

    a. Pressure for war in France came from all sides. The Girondin faction of the Jacobin club declared the revolution would never be secure in France until it had spread to the rest of the world.

    b. Others who had already gained from the revolution favored war to prevent the return of the nobility.

    c. Many conservatives in France thought war would restore the king's prestige and prevent the revolution from going further inside France.

    d. The French apparently completely overlooked the crucial *if* in the Declaration of Pillnitz.

    e. On April 20, 1792 the Legislative Assembly declared war against "the king of Hungary and Bohemia."

IV. The "Second Revolution" and the Convention

A. The French declaration of war was followed by increasing internal turmoil. Prices were rising, the value of the *assignats* was falling because the government's future was uncertain, and peasants were hoarding.

1. Another wave of fear and uncertainty swept through France in the early summer of 1792. People were afraid the *émigrés* would return; fear and distrust of the king grew. Troops gathering in Paris feared they might be betrayed at home while fighting at the front.

2. The poor of the cities suffered most from the economic conditions. Joining the troops recruited for the war, the Parisian mob rose and forced the Legislative Assembly to abrogate the Constitution of 1791.

3. This uprising on August 10, 1792 is often called the "Second Revolution." The immediate results of this uprising were:

   a. The king was suspended from office.

   b. The Legislative Assembly was to be replaced by the Constitutional Convention (later referred to as the National Convention), which was to be elected by universal manhood suffrage.

   c. A revolutionary municipal government, the Paris Commune, was established in Paris.

   d. Hysteria and anarchy prevailed in Paris. A small group of radicals spread the belief that it would be too dangerous to leave counter-revolutionaries in Parisian prisons while the army was at the front.

   e. Consequently, from September second to the sixth, about two thousand prisoners were killed in Paris. This slaughter is known as the "September Massacres."

B. The National Convention met for the first time September 20, 1792. The Convention ruled France until the summer of 1795. This government was the most radical phase of the revolution. Characteristic of the confidence that they were the architects of a new order were the changes the members of the Convention made in the calendar. They proclaimed the Year One, changed the names of all the months, and threw out the seven day week in favor of a new ten day week (workers in the new order would have fewer days of rest).

1. The same day the Convention first met, the French won the Battle of Valmy. This victory stopped the enemy advance toward Paris.

2. The French then launched a military offensive, and succeeded in annexing Nice, Savoy, Basel, and the area of modern Belgium.

3. The British, the Dutch, the Prussians, and the Austrians were alarmed by French successes. When the four powers began to confer about measures to be taken, the French declared war on all four on February 1, 1793.

4. Within the Convention, the Jacobins were the leaders; but the Jacobins were split into two major factions.

   a. One faction was the Girondins. Most of its members were from the provinces, and they wanted less rapid change than the other Jacobins.

   b. The Girondins tried to delay the treason trial of the deposed king, but the Convention tried him and found him guilty.

   c. Then the Girondins tried to delay the execution of the king, but the order for his immediate execution was carried by a vote of 361 to 360. On January 21, 1793 Louis XVI met his death with courage and dignity.

   d. After Louis' death, the Girondins were considered counter-revolutionary by the majority of the Convention.

   e. The other Jacobin faction was called the "Mountain" because they occupied the highest tiers of seats in the meeting hall.

   f. Most members of the Mountain were Parisians. It was this faction that sent Louis to the guillotine, making themselves regicides.

   g. There was no turning back for the Mountain. As regicides, they knew their lives would be forfeit if the revolution failed. All those who wanted the revolution to go further or feared any turning back to 1789, looked to the Mountain to protect their interests.

5. During the spring of 1793, the allies drove the French out of Belgium and threatened again to invade France.

   a. The radicals in Paris were terrified. They rose in revolt demanding a regulated economy (price controls, rationing, currency controls) to win the war.

   b. This group of radicals was called the *enragés*. The Girondins considered the *enragés* anarchists, but the Mountain was willing to work with them.

   c. On May 31, 1793, the *enragés,* supported by the Paris Commune and part of the National Guard, invaded the Convention and forced the arrest of the Girondist leaders.

   d. Some of the Girondins fled to the provinces; almost all those who did not flee were sent to the guillotine. The Mountain then controlled the Convention.

6. The problems facing the Convention in June, 1793 were staggering.
    a. The country was threatened by foreign invasion.
    b. Peasants were in open revolt against military conscription in many parts of France.
    c. Many leading cities in France refused to cooperate with the central government.
    d. So-called "Revolutionary Groups" of radicals were roaming the countryside, seizing food and looting.
7. To meet these problems the Convention's program was to repress anarchy and civil strife, to win the war, and to introduce democracy without going to the extremes desired by the Paris Commune.
8. The Convention's method was to expand the powers of the Committee of Public Safety, which had first been appointed in April, and to create two new agencies.
    a. One agency was the Committee of General Security, which was a sort of supreme political police.
    b. The other agency was the Revolutionary Tribunals, which were a short step above the lynch law procedures of the September massacres.
    c. Under the general direction of the Convention and the Committee of Public Safety, these two new agencies carried out the Terror.
    d. About forty thousand people in all France were executed during the Terror, which lasted from June, 1793 to July, 1794. In Paris, two thousand six hundred thirty-nine were executed.
    e. The Terror was not a class war. Only eight per cent of its victims were members of the nobility, and about seventy per cent of those executed were peasants and laborers.
9. The Committee of Public Safety functioned as the executive branch of the government during the period the Convention was in power. It was composed of twelve members of the Convention, who were reelected every month.
    a. In practice, the Committee of Public Safety became a joint dictatorship and war cabinet. It prepared and guided legislation through the Convention.
    b. Probably the most famous member of the Committee

of Public Safety was <u>Maximilian Robespierre,</u> who
was the committee's political expert.

c. Another famous member of the committee was <u>Lazare
Carnot, the "organizer of victory."</u> Carnot, an ex-
army officer, functioned brilliantly as a minister of
war. By the spring of 1794, the French had fourteen
armies equipped and in the field largely as a result of
Carnot's planning and organizing.

10. <u>The Committee of Public Safety was ruthless and effective in meeting many of the most serious problems facing
the Convention.</u>

a. The trend toward decentralization of the government
was abruptly reversed. Rural rebellions were crushed
by "representatives on mission." These were members of the Convention sent into the provinces and
accompanied by military units.

b. Administration was centralized by the replacement
of locally elected officials by "national agents" named
by the Committee of Public Safety.

c. The foreign invasion was met by forces raised by the
<u>"levée en masse."</u> This military conscription program
required all able-bodied men to serve the government.

d. By the spring of 1794, the French had eight hundred
thousand men in arms. This was the biggest armed
force in Europe, and its members' devotion to revolutionary ideals made it stronger still.

e. The Committee of Public Safety imposed economic
controls on the country to support the military effort.
Gold, silver, and foreign currency were confiscated;
prices and wages were controlled; military supplies
were requisitioned.

11. <u>The Committee of Public Safety also found time to write
the Constitution of 1793, which the Convention
adopted.</u>

a. This constitution provided for a republican government elected by universal manhood suffrage.

b. It was never put into effect because the Convention
declared the government would remain "revolutionary until the peace." As it turned out, the Convention disappeared before a peace treaty was signed.

c. The Committee of Public Safety wiped out any debts

     still owed by peasants trying to pay off old manorial or feudal obligations.

    d. The Committee of Public Safety also had social legislation passed abolishing slavery and providing schools for boys of all classes. The educational program achieved little because funds and personnel were lacking.

12. The Committee of Public Safety took a dim view of any individual or group which advocated any policies different from its own.

    a. The most extreme revolutionary party were called Hébertists (the term came from the name, Hébert, an officer of the Paris Commune). This was the party of extreme Terror, the foremost proponents of dechristianization and the revolutionary calendar.

    b. The Hébertists were a large and ill-defined group, which included many members of the Convention. They denounced the merchants and bourgeoisie and supported extremely radical measures of every sort.

    c. The Committee of Public Safety regarded the Hébertists as trouble-makers who were disrupting the execution of the committee's program. In the autumn of 1793, the Committee of Public Safety began relentlessly crushing the Hébertists. By the spring of 1794, its leaders had been sent to the guillotine and the movement suppressed.

    d. The revolutionary Paris Commune was also destroyed, and the municipal government of Paris was taken over by officials appointed by Robespierre.

    e. Robespierre had personally opposed the suppression of the Hébertists, fearing the Committee would lose the support of the workers. His judgment turned out to be correct, but he was overruled by the remainder of the committee.

    f. The new government of Paris opposed strikes and tried to keep wages down by the plea of military necessity, but it never regained the support of the leaders of the Paris workers, who denounced the revolution as a bourgeois movement.

    g. In a desperate effort to regain support of the radicals the committee turned against the most conservative element in the Mountain, Danton and his followers.

   h. Sending the Dantonists to the "national razor" alienated conservative support for the Committee of Public Safety, but it did not win back the radicals.

13. To a considerable degree, the success of the Committee of Public Safety was its undoing.

   a. In the spring of 1794, the French armies drove out the invaders and conquered the Low Countries. The allies were again divided by their interests in the next partition of Poland.

   b. With the fear of invasion gone, the French were less willing to submit to the dictatorial policies of the Committee of Public Safety.

   c. Members of the Convention were afraid. After the execution of Hébertists and Dantonists, who would be the next victims of the Terror?

   d. On July 27, 1794 the Convention voted to "outlaw" Robespierre. He and several of his associates were sent to the guillotine the next day, and the Terror began to subside.

   e. The Convention reduced the powers of the Committee of Public Safety, closed the Jacobin club, and removed most of the economic regulations earlier imposed.

   f. The decline of the committee and the execution of Robespierre began what is often referred to as the "Thermidorian reaction," because the revolution began shifting to a more conservative policy during the month of Thermidor on the revolutionary calendar.

14. When the unpopular economic regulations of the Committee of Public Safety were removed, inflation and speculation followed.

   a. Those who suffered most from inflation and economic disorder were the workers in the cities, who expressed their discontent in sporadic mob violence.

   b. In May, 1795, a Parisian mob almost succeeded in dispersing the Convention. The Convention called troops to Paris and crushed the insurrection (the "Prairial" uprising).

   c. It was the men of commerce and industry, the bourgeoisie, whose control now became evident. They had dominated the Constituent Assembly and had survived the Convention.

d. This bourgeois group still had faith in the revolution. They approved of equality before the law and of a written constitution. Democracy, however, meant mob rule and terror to them.

e. The bourgeoisie, now in control of the Convention, set aside the Constitution of 1793 (which had never been put into effect) and wrote another, the Constitution of 1795 or of the Year III).

f. The Constitution of 1795 established the French government known as the Directory.

V. The Directory (1795–1799)

A. The conservative Constitution of 1795 gave the vote to almost every literate Frenchman, but he voted only for an "elector."

1. Electors were persons who owned real estate, and they had to own so much that only twenty thousand people in all France could qualify as electors.

2. The electors, in turn, voted for the members of the bicameral legislature, composed of the lower chamber, the Council of Five Hundred, and the upper house, the Council of Ancients, with two hundred and fifty members.

3. The two legislative chambers chose the Directory, which was composed of five Directors.

4. The Constitution of 1795 was to apply to the Belgian area as well as France. Other European powers had not recognized this French conquest, and their determination to drive the French out committed the Directory to a war policy.

B. The Directory's existence was threatened almost from the beginning from both the right and the left.

1. On the right were those who favored restoration of a monarchy. The army contained many royalists. The regicide survivors of the Convention could not afford to have a Bourbon ruler return.

2. On the left were the workers from the cities, the surviving radicals of 1793.

a. Probably the most serious radical threat to the Directory was the secret Conspiracy of Equals led by

Babeuf. Babeuf favored the abolition of both private property and parliamentary government and the establishment of a planned society.

b. In 1796 and 1797, the Directory arrested Babeuf and many of his followers; some were executed, some deported, and the movement crushed.

c. Meanwhile, those workers who made no move toward following Babeuf continued to suffer from scarcity and inflation; but the government did nothing to help them.

C. In March, 1797, occurred the first really free election held in republican France. The vast majority of successful candidates favored a constitutional monarchy.

1. The establishment of a monarchy, especially if it involved restoration of the Bourbon family, was precisely what the regicide republican element could not risk, even if they had to continue the war and violate the constitution to avoid it.

2. Napoleon Bonaparte, by 1797 an ambitious and successful French general, also desired the opportunities continued war would provide him to further his career.

3. On September 4, 1797, the republicans, with the help of troops sent by Napoleon Bonaparte, carried out a *coup d'état* (*coup d'état* of Fructidor).

a. Protected by Napoleon's troops, the legislature annulled the election of many of the officials chosen in March, 1797.

b. Two Directors were dismissed, one of them, Carnot, the "organizer of victory"; he was exiled.

c. In carrying out the *coup* of Fructidor, the surviving republicans of the Convention maintained they were saving the revolution. Actually, they converted the Directory into a dictatorship dependent on the army.

D. The development of French foreign policy during the revolution provided many favorable opportunities for an ambitious militarist like Napoleon but revealed the ineffective leadership of the Directory.

1. The war which had developed from the Declaration of Pillnitz (1791) is often called the War of the First Coalition. The powers of coalition were divided by their ambitions; and the size, fervor, and leadership of the French armies brought success.

    a. The Austrians and Prussians kept their main forces in the east because of their interest in the partition of Poland.

    b. The French armies drove their invaders back and, by 1795, were on the offensive.

    c. The Prussians made a separate peace with the French, while the Spanish made an alliance with France to protect their empire and Mediterranean possessions from the British.

    d. In 1796, Napoleon Bonaparte was given command of a French army which was to attack the Austrians in Italy. The Directory did not supply his army adequately or pay his troops.

    e. Napoleon supplied his own army by local requisitions, drove the Austrians from Italy in a brilliant campaign, and even made the Directory dependent upon him by sending captured funds and booty to Paris.

2. Without serious consultation with the Directory, Napoleon dictated peace terms to the Austrians in the Treaty of Campo Formio (1797). This treaty ended the war of the First Coalition. Its major provisions were:

    a. The Cisalpine Republic, composed of the Duchy of Milan and part of the Papal States, was created.

    b. The Austrian Netherlands (modern Belgium) were ceded to France.

    c. In return, the Austrians were given Venetia.

    d. A large portion of the left bank of the Rhine was ceded to France; German princes dispossessed by this provision were to be compensated with Church lands east of the Rhine.

    e. The French took from Venetia the Ionian Islands off the coast of Greece as stepping stones to the east.

3. Following the *coup d'état* of Fructidor, the Directory gave Napoleon command of the army training to invade England, but he decided invasion was premature and resolved to strike at the British and India by the invasion of Egypt.

    a. In 1798, Napoleon led a French force which evaded the British Mediterranean fleet and landed near the estuary of the Nile.

    b. The Russians did not want the French to interfere

with Russian plans for expansion into the Near East;
so the Russians joined the Austrians and the British
in forming the Second Coalition.

c. In August, 1798, the British isolated Napoleon in
Egypt by destroying the French fleet in the Battle of
the Nile (also known as the Battle of Aboukir Bay).

d. To make matters worse, the British occupied the island of Malta and Russian forces, under Marshal
Suvorov, were operating as far west as Switzerland and northern Italy. The Cisalpine Republic
collapsed.

e. Once again the French were saved by division among
the allies. The Russians decided the British had
become a more serious threat to Russian hopes in the
Near East than the French were; so Marshal Suvorov's army was withdrawn.

f. Napoleon deserted the remains of his army in Egypt
and returned to France.

E. By 1799, when Napoleon returned from Egypt, the only
success in the Directory's foreign policy had been Napoleon's Italian campaign. The African attempt was described to the French as a success, but the credit went to
Napoleon rather than the Directory. The Directory's prestige also suffered by contrast to the energetic leadership
earlier provided by the Committee of Public Safety.

1. The Directory's domestic policy had been dictatorial
and unpopular. Uprisings by both radicals and conservatives had been forcefully crushed; more elections
had been quashed; most of the *assignats* and the public
debt had been repudiated.

2. Napoleon found that some of the civilians in the government were planning a change and needed military
support.

a. Napoleon and these civilians were willing to
cooperate.

b. On November 9, 1799, Napoleon's troops drove the
legislators from their chambers (*coup d'état* of Brumaire) and a new form of republic was established.

c. The *coup* of Brumaire, which destroyed the Directory, is usually considered to mark the end of the
French Revolution. For the next fifteen years, the

government of France was largely the institution-
alized expression of Napoleon's policies.

VI. French Internal Development Under Napoleon

A. The government which replaced the Directory was known
   as the Consulate. It lasted from 1799 to 1804.
   1. The Consulate took its name from its executive branch,
      which was composed of three Consuls. Naturally, the
      First Consul was Napoleon Bonaparte, who wrote the
      Constitution establishing the Consulate.
   2. The constitution provided universal male suffrage.
      a. The voters, however, only elected ten thousand
         "notables."
      b. From the ten thousand elected notables, the govern-
         ment appointed all its officials.
   3. A tricameral legislature was provided.
      a. The lower house, the Legislative Body, could vote on
         legislation but could not initiate legislation or
         discuss it.
      b. The upper house, the Tribunate, could discuss legis-
         lation but could not vote.
      c. Another body, the Senate, sanctioned or vetoed bills
         passed by the Legislative Body and appointed officials
         from the list of notables.
   4. Aside from the consuls themselves, the chief agency of
      the government was the Council of State. It prepared
      and initiated legislation and was presided over by
      Napoleon.
   5. To establish and maintain internal order Napoleon ap-
      pointed prefects to run each of the eighty-three depart-
      ments of France.
   6. A secret police force, directed by Joseph Fouché, former
      terrorist and Hébertist, helped keep order.
   7. Napoleon proclaimed a general amnesty permitting
      émigrés and deportees to return. Napoleon picked his
      assistants from every political spectrum requiring only
      that they be loyal to him and refrain from quarreling
      with each other.
B. Napoleon arranged the Concordat of 1801 to establish
   peace with the Church. The most important provisions of
   Napoleon's concordat with the papacy were:

1. The Pope could depose French bishops; this cleared the way to get rid of both the juring and non-juring clergy and begin anew;
2. All clergy were placed under the discipline of the Pope;
3. The Church relinquished all claims to former tithes or Church property;
4. Religious toleration remained;
5. Both Roman Catholic clergy and Protestant ministers received their salaries from the state.

C. Like the Concordat of 1801, many of Napoleon's legal and administrative reforms remained long after the fall of his Consulate and Empire.

1. Practically all public authority was placed in the hands of paid government officials; all citizens were under the legal authority of the state and in the same relation to it.
2. The Consulate effectively completed the work of the revolution by the abolition of all privileged estates, legal classes, local liberties, hereditary offices, gilds, and manors.
3. Tax collection and financial administration were greatly improved. The central government appointed collectors, who dealt with the individual taxpayer.
   a. No exemptions were permitted.
   b. As a result, the government could make a reasonable estimate of its income and plan its finances sensibly.
   c. The Consulate began its work free of debt because the Directory had repudiated its debts.
4. Possibly Napoleon's greatest and most durable contribution was the Code Napoleon.
   a. The Code Napoleon actually contained five law codes: a civil code, a code of civil procedure, a code of criminal procedure, a penal code, and a commercial code.
   b. All these codes emphasized equality before the law.
   c. The Code Napoleon carefully protected private property. It provided for all forms of contracts, leases, and business organizations.
   d. The Code Napoleon banned labor unions. In criminal cases, it helped the government more in detecting crime than it aided the individual to defend himself.
   e. The Code Napoleon recognized civil marriage and divorce.

f. The Code Napoleon is still the basis of French law and provides the fundamental law for many Latin American countries as well as the state of Louisiana in the U.S.A.

D. The government of the Consulate was established by the Constitution of 1800, which was overwhelmingly ratified by the French voters.

  1. The Constitution of 1800 fixed the term of office of the First Consul at ten years. In 1802, another plebiscite made him First Consul for life.

  2. In 1804, a new constitution, again ratified by plebiscite, declared that "the government of the republic is confided to an emperor."

    a. The Senate, at Napoleon's suggestion, appointed him emperor.

    b. The Consulate became the Empire, and First Consul Napoleon Bonaparte became Napoleon I, Emperor of the French.

    c. Pope Pius VII came to Paris to *assist* in the coronation. Napoleon, however, placed the crown on his own head.

E. The Empire, which lasted from 1804 to 1814, changed the First Consul into an Emperor, of course, but otherwise retained the major features of the internal organization of the Consulate.

  1. The Consulate and the Empire did not achieve the highest hopes of the revolution, but the worst evils of the Old Regime had been removed.

  2. What the third estate wanted in 1789 was largely accomplished except for parliamentary government, which, to the degree it existed under Napoleon, was a sham. After ten years of revolutionary turmoil, however, most of the French were satisfied with Napoleon's solutions to the problems of governing France.

VII. Napoleon's Conduct of French Foreign Affairs

A. In 1799, when Napoleon had returned to France from Africa to join in overthrowing the Directory, the War of the Second Coalition was still in progress, though the coalition was seriously weakened by Russia's withdrawal.

  1. In 1801, the Russians joined the so-called Armed Neu-

trals to protect their shipping from British search and seizure.

2. The Austrians dissolved the Second Coalition by signing the Treaty of Lunéville in 1801.

3. Left alone, the British signed the Peace of Amiens in 1802. The treaties of Lunéville and Amiens gave the French extremely advantageous peace terms.

   a. The Austrians again agreed to all the terms of Campo Formio.

   b. France retained the Austrian Netherlands (Belgium) and the left bank of the Rhine as integral parts of the French republic.

   c. The French received recognition of their ring of satellite states: the Batavian Republic (Holland), the Ligurian Republic (Genoa), the Helvetic Republic (Switzerland), and the Cisalpine Republic in the Po valley.

   d. The British agreed to withdraw from Malta, Trinidad, Minorca, Elba, and the French Caribbean islands.

B. The peace settlement was so prejudicial to British war aims that it probably would soon have been broken. Napoleon, however, pushed forward various aggressive schemes which made another war inevitable.

1. Napoleon "reorganized" the governments of the satellite states to give himself greater personal control in each one.

2. Within Germany, the princes, with Napoleon's blessing (and following the provisions of Campo Formio), were engaged in a mad scramble for Church lands.

   a. The larger states in Germany, particularly Prussia, Bavaria, Württemberg, and Baden, all enlarged their territories.

   b. Most of Germany's ecclesiastical principalities and forty-five of its fifty-one free cities were taken over by larger neighbors.

   c. The German Diet ratified these seizures in 1803, and the German states looked to the French to maintain their new position.

   d. The consolidation of German states led Holy Roman Emperor Francis II to promulgate the Austrian Empire because the new situation in Germany would lead to the election of a Protestant Holy Roman Emperor

3. In the New World Napoleon sent troops to Haiti to regain control of the rebellious colony and apparently planned to use the Louisiana Territory (ceded by Spain to France in 1800) to revive the French colonial empire in America.

4. The British were so concerned about Napoleon's actions that they refused to leave Malta. When Napoleon protested the British action, they declared war on France (1803).

5. Napoleon's attempt to subdue Haiti had failed; and, faced with war in Europe, he sold the Louisiana Territory to the United States in 1803.

C. In 1805, the Austrians and Russians allied with the British, and the war between England and France became the War of the Third Coalition.

1. From 1803 to 1805, Napoleon had been preparing to invade England; but during the summer of 1805, the Russians and Austrian armies moved westward.

2. To deal with the Austro-Russian threat, Napoleon moved seven army corps from the channel to the upper Danube and began one of his most brilliant campaigns.

3. At Ulm, on October 15, Napoleon's troops surrounded an Austrian force of fifty thousand men and forced it to surrender without resistance.

4. Only six days later, however, off Cape Trafalgar, Lord Nelson directed the British fleet in an engagement which resulted in the destruction of the major part of the combined Spanish and French fleets.

  a. Trafalgar clearly established British naval supremacy.

  b. That supremacy would last, however, only if Napoleon could be prevented from controlling the continent whose resources would enable him to build a bigger fleet than the British.

5. On December 2, 1805, Napoleon won another great victory at Austerlitz.

  a. The battle of Austerlitz forced the Russian army to withdraw into Poland, and the Austrians made peace (Treaty of Pressburg).

  b. Napoleon took Venetia from Austria and annexed it

      to his new Kingdom of Italy, which included most of Italy north of Rome.

    c. Austria ceded territories to Napoleon's German allies, Bavaria, Wurtemburg, and Baden. Bavaria and Wurtemburg were made kingdoms, and Baden became a grand duchy.

    d. The Holy Roman Empire was dissolved. In its place, Napoleon began to gather the German states into his new Confederation of the Rhine, of which he made himself "protector."

6. Prussia had not joined the Third Coalition because Napoleon had gained their neutrality by a whole series of promises. Fearful of Napoleon's plans for Germany, the Prussians, unaided, went to war with the French. It was a big mistake.

    a. In 1806, at the battles of Jena and Auerstadt, the French completely smashed the Prussian army.

    b. The Prussian government fled all the way to Königsberg, hoping the re-forming Russian army would protect them.

    c. But the terrible Frenchman pursued the Russians, too. In 1807, occurred the bloody-but-indecisive Russo-French battle of Eylau; and in June 1807, Napoleon shattered the Russians at Friedland.

7. Tsar Alexander I was ready to make peace. He feared a French invasion of Russia might produce a rebellion of serfs or nobility or both. He did not, furthermore, wish to be a pawn of British policy. The Third Coalition had gone the way of the two before it.

    a. The Emperor of the French and the Tsar of All the Russias met privately and drew up the Peace of Tilsit (1807).

    b. In effect, the Peace of Tilsit amounted to a mutual agreement that Napoleon would be the emperor of the west, and Tsar Alexander would be emperor of the east.

    c. Napoleon played upon Alexander's ambitions and implied that France would support Russian desires to conquer Turkey, Persia, Afghanistan, and India.

    d. Prussia was allowed to exist as a buffer between east and west, but the French occupied Berlin and took all Prussia's territory west of the Elbe river.

    e. Napoleon combined Hanover and the territory taken from Prussia into a new Kingdom of Westphalia, which he incorporated into his Confederation of the Rhine.

    f. Russia and France signed a joint alliance against England that was supposed to last five years.

D. Meanwhile, in 1806, Napoleon had given new impetus to the economic struggle against England by establishing the "Continental System."

    1. At Berlin, in 1806, Napoleon issued the "Berlin Decree," forbidding the importation of British goods into any part of Europe dependent upon or allied to France.

    2. The aim of the Continental System was to destroy British trade, cause a depression, and thereby destroy Britain's ability to support a war.

    3. The republicans of 1793 had tried the same tactics. Napoleon made these measures more systematic; and because he controlled so much more of Europe, his economic controls were a more serious threat to the English.

    4. Napoleon persuaded Russia to join the Continental System and required Austria and Prussia to do so.

    5. He then tried to extend it to neutral Denmark and Portugal. The British, fearing the Danes would join, bombarded Copenhagen and seized the Danish fleet. The enraged Danes gladly joined Napoleon.

    6. The Portuguese, old allies of the British, refused to join the Continental System. Napoleon occupied Portugal and forced them to cooperate, an action that entangled him in the problems of the Iberian peninsula.

E. By a series of deceptions Napoleon persuaded Charles IV of Spain and his son, Ferdinand, to abdicate the Spanish throne. In 1808, Napoleon made his brother, Joseph, King of Spain and supported him with a large army.

    1. The object of these moves was to control Spanish and Portuguese seaports.

    2. The Spanish, however, regarded the French army as a collection of godless villains who desecrated churches. They resisted by guerilla warfare. Soon the French were involved in a savage guerilla war in many parts of Spain.

    3. The British sent an expeditionary force, eventually commanded by the Duke of Wellington, to aid Portugal.

The Peninsular Campaign began in 1808 and lasted five years. On the whole, it went badly for the French.

F. While Napoleon struggled with his Spanish troubles, the Austrians proclaimed a war of liberation in 1809.

1. Napoleon had hoped for Russian help against Austria, but Tsar Alexander was concerned about Napoleon's desire to establish a Polish state, the Grand Duchy of Warsaw, and Napoleon's failure to support Russian expansion into the Balkans.

2. Napoleon moved his armies along the familiar route to Vienna and smashed the Austrians in the battle of Wagram (July, 1809). The Austrians made peace in October on Napoleon's terms (Treaty of Schönbruun or Vienna, 1809).

   a. Part of Austria's territory was used to create the Grand Duchy of Warsaw.

   b. Parts of Dalmatia, Slovenia, and Croatia, to the south, were used to create another French satellite, the Illyrian Provinces.

   c. Both these moves, enlarging Napoleon's interests in Poland and the Balkans, caused the emperor's relations with the tsar to deteriorate further.

3. In 1809, while Napoleon was occupied with Spanish and Austrian problems, the tsar seized the opportunity to overrun Finland.

G. By 1809, Napoleon was concerned because he had no heir. He determined to divorce Josephine and make a spectacular marriage, thereby forcing aristocratic Europe to bestow its recognition upon him.

1. French overtures to secure the tsar's sister as a bride for Napoleon were rebuffed. This action did not improve Russo-French relations.

2. Napoleon then arranged to marry Marie Louise, daughter of the Austrian emperor, niece of Marie Antoinette. They were married in 1810.

   a. In a year Marie Louise bore Napoleon a son, who was entitled King of Rome.

   b. Napoleon became more pompous. He created a new nobility, hoping that with the passage of time the new noble families would tie their fortunes to the Bonaparte dynasty.

H. In December, 1811, the Russians formally withdrew from

the Continental System, which was not working well for the French. <u>Napoleon then resolved to invade Russia and crush the Tsar.</u>

1. During the spring of 1812, Napoleon assembled an army of seven hundred thousand men in Germany and Poland. It was the biggest force mobilized up to that time for a single operation.

2. The invasion began in June, but Napoleon could not not carry out the short and decisive campaign he planned.

    a. The Russian army withdrew as fast as he advanced. The Russians destroyed everything as they retreated so that the invaders could not live off the land.

    b. Napoleon defeated the Russians at Borodino, but he was unable to destroy their army.

    c. The invading forces reached Moscow in September, but the city caught fire and hoped-for supplies were destroyed.

    d. When the tsar would not negotiate with him, Napoleon decided to retreat. The unusually severe Russian winter and Russian guerilla warfare destroyed his army; nearly five-sixths of the invaders lost their lives or were captured.

3. <u>In 1813, Prussia and Austria joined the Russians and the British to form the Fourth Coalition.</u> In June, the Duke of Wellington's forces crossed the Pyrenees and invaded France.

    a. Napoleon, meanwhile, had rushed back to France and raised another army.

    b. In October, 1813, Napoleon's forces were crushed in the <u>battle of Leipzig.</u> After Leipzig, Napoleon fought a brilliant campaign, but the odds were hopeless.

    c. On March 31, 1814, the armies of the Fourth Coalition entered Paris.

    d. Napoleon was exiled to the island of Elba, over which he was granted sovereignty, and the allies settled down to the problems of arranging a peace settlement at Vienna (see Chapter 6).

4. The allies at Vienna did not impose a harsh peace settlement on the French. Louis XVIII, the nearest surviving Bourbon relative of Louis XVI was placed on the French throne.

    a. Louis XVIII granted a constitution to the French which kept most of Napoleon's internal reforms intact and provided the people with personal liberty and a restricted share in the government.

    b. The coalition powers did not burden the French with a war indemnity nor with the costs of an army of occupation.

    c. Not vindictive himself, Louis XVIII was, however, accompanied by a swarm of overbearing and unreasonable *émigrés,* who did their best to persecute those who had driven them out.

    d. Louis XVIII made the mistake of replacing the tri-colored flag of the revolution and Napoleon with the old white Bourbon banner. Many French saw this as the symbol of the Old Regime.

    e. The French were suffering the dislocating effects of the demobilization of their armies.

5. <u>While the coalition powers bargained at the peace conference, Napoleon escaped from the island of Elba and landed in France March 1, 1815.</u>

    a. Adherents of the revolution flocked to Napoleon's standard, and Louis XVIII departed for the frontier.

    b. Napoleon reached Paris and plunged into preparations for war. In June he advanced into Belgium, hoping to defeat the British and the Prussians separately before their forces could unite.

    c. Near the village of Waterloo he met the British forces led by the Duke of Wellington. Napoleon took the offensive, but the Prussians arrived before Napoleon could defeat the British. The Anglo-Prussian force then attacked and destroyed the French army (June 18, 1815).

    d. Napoleon fled, hoping to escape to America. The British naval blockade frustrated this attempt, and he surrendered to the captain of a British frigate.

    e. The time from Napoleon's return from Elba to his surrender to the British (March 1–June 22, 1815) is often referred to as <u>"the Hundred Days."</u>

    f. After the Hundred Days, the coalition powers were less lenient with Napoleon and the French. Napoleon was sent to the south Atlantic island of St.

Helena where he was kept under close guard until he died of cancer of the stomach in 1821.

g. The allies reduced the territory of France to its boundaries of 1790. The French were required to pay a war indemnity and the costs of an army of occupation until the indemnity was paid.

VIII. The Impact of the Revolution and Napoleonic Era on the Internal Development of European States

A. Many of the changes brought to France during the period 1789–1814 spread to other nations in Europe.
  1. Reforms varied as they were applied in other states according to circumstances and desires.
  2. The ideology of the revolution began to spread soon after it appeared in France, and the military successes of the French enabled them to make or inspire the actual application of their ideas and reforms.
B. At the height of his power, Napoleon's domain consisted of three parts.
  1. At the center was the French Empire where he was in direct control.
  2. The second part was the impressive group of satellite states. These, together with France, composed the "Grand Empire." French control was exercised indirectly but effectively in the satellites.
  3. The third part was the "allied states," which remained under their traditional governments but frequently cooperated with the French. They were supposed to support the Continental System, but Napoleon exercised no direct influence upon their internal affairs.
C. In all the dependent satellite states the patterns of development were roughly similar.
  1. The first stage was conquest and occupation by the French forces.
  2. The second was the establishment of a native government supported by local citizens willing to cooperate with the French.
  3. Next a constitution was drafted and the relations of the new government with France were worked out.
D. Napoleon considered himself an enlightened reformer. In influencing the establishment of governments in the satel-

lite states, he made certain ideals and practices common to most of them.

1. He insisted the form of government should be the result of a rational plan rather than an institution growing out of a jumble of traditions.

2. <u>Napoleon was zealous in supporting the rule of law.</u> He transplanted the civil code of the Code Napoleon wherever possible and insisted on equality before the law.

3. He liquidated the manorial system wherever he could. Lords lost all legal jurisdiction over peasants who became subjects of the state. Peasants were given freedom to move about, marry, or bring suit in a court of law.

   a. In the satellite states, however, the peasants had to pay the lords compensation for release from the various feudal duties.

   b. East of the Rhine, especially in Poland, Napoleon had to compromise with the aristocracy because they were the only group who could give him effective support.

4. <u>Everywhere in the Grand Empire the church lost its position as a public authority alongside the state.</u>

   a. Church courts and tithes were abolished.

   b. Church property was confiscated and monastic orders dissolved or closely regulated.

   c. Religious toleration became the law; the same civil rights were extended to Catholics, Protestants, and Jews.

   d. In Spain, the Inquisition was outlawed. Napoleon's insistence on these policies in Spain is a measure of his sincerity. More than anything else, it was his religious policy which provoked such savage Spanish resistance.

5. <u>Within the Grand Empire gilds were abolished or reduced to mere formalities.</u> Ancient privileges of towns and provinces were revoked. Many internal tariffs were removed.

6. <u>Law courts were separated from administrative parts of the governments.</u> Offices were no longer sold nor were they permitted to become hereditary.

7. The one major principle of the revolution that Napoleon did not try to apply to the Grand Empire was self-government by elected legislatures.

E. Initially, there was much pro-Napoleonic feeling within the Grand Empire. This was especially true in Italy. To many observers, Napoleon seemed a true enlightened despot who conveyed the benefits of the revolution without its violence and disorder.

F. French imperialism, however, also created deep resentments.

1. Europeans naturally objected to the seizure of wealth and supplies by the French armies. They objected to contributions of money and manpower they were forced to make to Napoleon's war machine.

2. Resentment grew when the policies of the satellite states were obviously dictated by the French ambassadors or when the Continental System hurt their economies.

3. The most important manifestation of resentment against the French was the development of nationalism.

4. Nationalism developed in different ways in different areas, but in most places it grew as a reaction to the forced internationalism imposed by the French.

5. National spirit had fired the revolutionary and Napoleonic armies with a fervor previously unknown, but it reacted against Napoleon by inspiring the forces that opposed him.

6. In England, nationalism reacted against the reforms of the revolution and encouraged the English to forget their very considerable domestic problems in order to rally together against Bonaparte.

7. In Spain, national feeling focused on the restoration of the Bourbon rulers and the position of the Church.

8. In Poland, the nationalists favored Napoleon because he appeared to be their greatest hope against domination by Russia, Prussia, and Austria. The Poles, however, supported Napoleon for their own purposes rather than from any overwhelming admiration for France.

9. In Italy, the French occupation was popular. French control shattered the idea of loyalty to the various duchies, papal states, and foreign dynasties by which Italy had long been ruled. French occupation created conditions making the unification of Italy a reasonable aspiration.

10. The most momentous impact on national development occurred in the German area.

   a. The humiliating defeat of the Prussians at Jena and Auerstadt dramatized the need for reform.

   b. Under the leadership of Baron Stein, Prussia adopted many of the reforms concerning the peasants that the French advocated.

   c. In Prussia, however, peasants who remained on the land were liable for traditional fees in such a way that the nobility retained more of its importance.

   d. The nobility had to be preserved in Prussia because of their indispensable military role.

   e. Prussia's undeviating opposition to Napoleon freed it from any taint of collaboration with the French and made it the natural focus of anti-French feeling.

   f. During the Napoleonic era, German philosophers and publicists did much to develop a "cultural" nationalism which was, above all, anti-French.

   g. Cultural nationalism, as set forward by Herder and Fichte, not only reacted against the ascendancy of French civilization but also appealed to the German's fascination with political unity and national greatness.

   h. Probably the most critical period in the development of German nationalism came later in the nineteenth century, but German reaction to Napoleon's conquests gave it a vigorous initial boost.

BIBLIOGRAPHY

Brinton, C., *A decade of revolution, 1789–1799* (New York: Harper, 1934).

Brunn, G., *Europe and the French imperium, 1799–1814* (New York: Harper, 1938).

De Tocqueville, A., *The old regime and the revolution* (New York: Doubleday Anchor Books, 1955).

Ford, G., *Stein and the era of reform in Prussia, 1807–1815* (Princeton: Princeton University Press, 1922).

Fournier, A., *Napoleon the First: a biography* (New York: Henry Holt & Company, 1903).

Gershoy, L., *The French revolution and Napoleon* (New York Appleton-Century-Crofts, 1933).

Geyl, P., *Napoleon: for and against* (New Haven: Yale University Press, 1949).

Gottschalk, L., *The era of the French revolution* (Boston: Houghton Mifflin Company, 1929).

Guedalla, P., *The duke* (London: Hodder & Stoughton, Ltd., 1931).

Kircheisen, F. *Napoleon* (New York: Harcourt, Brace and Company, 1932).

Lefebvre, G., *The coming of the French revolution* (New York: Knopf, 1957. A Vintage Book).

Palmer, R. R., *Twelve who ruled* (Princeton: Princeton University Press, 1941).

Pundt, A. G., *Arndt and the nationalist awakening in Germany* (New York: Columbia University Press, 1935).

Tolstoy, L., *War and peace* (New York: Simon and Schuster, 1942).

EUROPE AFTER 1815

····· Boundary of the
        German Confederation

KINGDOM OF
NORWAY & SWEDEN

UNITED KINGDOM
OF GREAT BRITAIN
AND IRELAND

SCOTLAND

IRELAND

WALES

ENGLAND

London°

North
Sea

DENMARK

Atlantic Ocean

The
Hague°

NETHERLANDS

Brussels°

LUX.

°Aachen

Paris°

Seine R.

Marne R.

PRUSSIA

Berlin°

GERMAN

Wartburg°

°Frankfurt

°Hambach

CONFEDERATION

BOHEMIA

°Prague

Danube R.

AUSTRIA

Vienna°

OF

Loire R.

FRANCE

Garonne R.

SWITZERLAND

Rhone R.

TYROL

LOMBARDY

VENETIA

Turin°

Milan°

Par.

Venice

Mod.

KINGDOM OF SARDINIA

°Florence

TUSCANY

PAPAL

STATES

Rome°

Adriatic

PORTUGAL

Lisbon°

Tagus R.

Ebro R.

Madrid°

SPAIN

Barcelona°

Guadalquivir R.

Cadiz°

BALEARIC IS.

CORSICA
(to France)

Mediterranean

SARDINIA

Naples°

K. OF

THE

TWO

SICILIES

SICILY

Sea

MALTA°
(Br)

Abbreviations:
Par. = Parma;   Mod. = Modena

55

50

45

40

30

20   15   10   5   0   5   10   15

5   0   5   10   15

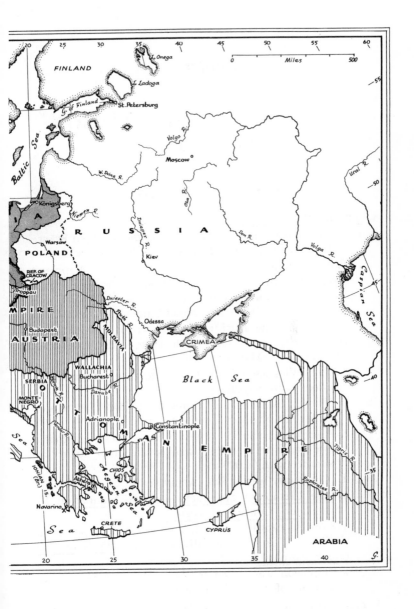

Chapter 6

REACTION AND REVOLUTION, 1815—1852

I. The Vienna Settlement

A. <u>The situation in 1814</u>

1. In the early months of 1814 allied armies invaded France from the Rhine valley, Belgium, and Switzerland.

2. With a small army of less than 90,000 men Napoleon fought a brilliant rear guard action in northern France against a combined force of Prussians, Austrians, and Russians. Dissension was evident among the allies.

3. Castlereagh, the British foreign secretary, hastened to the continent and persuaded the allies to sign the Treaty of Chaumont (March 9, 1814).

   a. The allies agreed not to engage in separate negotiations with Napoleon.

   b. The British promised a subsidy of £5,000,000 to support the war effort for the remainder of 1814.

   c. After the conclusion of peace, the allies agreed that if one was attacked the others would come to her assistance with 60,000 men.

   d. The treaty was to last twenty years.

   e. <u>The Chaumont agreement was the foundation for the later "Concert of Europe."</u>

4. The allied capture of Paris finally forced Napoleon to abdicate. This was formalized by the <u>Treaty of Fontainebleau (April, 1814).</u>

   a. Napoleon was exiled to the island of Elba with an annuity of two million francs a year.

B. <u>First Treaty of Paris (May 30, 1814)</u>

1. The allies gave France relatively generous terms. She was permitted to retain her 1792 frontiers.
   a. France retained Avignon, Comtat-Venaissin plus the strategically located towns of Saarbrücken, Saarlouis, and Landau. The French also kept Savoy.
   b. France was not compelled to pay an indemnity or endure an occupation army.
   c. France did have to give up the Rhine valley and Belgium after a twenty year occupation.

C. Second Treaty of Paris (November 20, 1815)
   1. The Hundred Days
      a. Dissatisfied with his fate on Elba, Napoleon made a daring return to France.
      b. He ejected the Bourbons and held control from March to June of 1815.
      c. His defeat by Wellington and Blücher at Waterloo led to exile on St. Helena.
   2. France was now subjected to a much more severe peace treaty.
      a. Her frontiers were reduced to those of 1790. This cost France Saarbrücken, Saarlouis, Landau, Savoy, Philippeville, and Marienburg.
      b. France had to pay an indemnity of 700 million francs, and agree to an army of occupation of her northeastern departments.
      c. But despite Prussian and Austrian demands, Castlereagh and Alexander I saw that France was humiliated no further.

D. The Congress of Vienna (1814–1815)
   1. Deliberations began at Vienna on September 15, 1814 and continued until the Final Act was drawn up on June 9, 1815. The "Big Five" dominated the sessions: Metternich of Austria, Hardenberg of Prussia, Castlereagh of Great Britain, Czar Alexander I of Russia, and Talleyrand of France. Because of Talleyrand's skill and his use of the idea of legitimacy, France had an important voice at Vienna. In particular, Talleyrand used the Polish-Saxon question to win an important place in the Vienna deliberations.
   2. The men of Vienna were determined to maintain the political status quo. Nationalism and liberalism, two of

the key movements of the nineteenth century, were vigorously opposed.

3. <u>The Vienna Final Act (June 9, 1815)</u>

   a. Holland was given the Austrian Netherlands (Belgium) and Luxemburg to compensate her for colonial losses to Great Britain. This new state kept Antwerp out of French hands, and erected a stronger than usual barrier to France on the north.

   b. Prussia was given the Rhine Valley in order to create an eastern barrier to French expansion. She also received three-fifths of Saxony.

   c. To erect a stronger barrier against the French along the Mediterranean, Piedmont was given part of Savoy and Genoa.

   d. As compensation for the loss of the Austrian Netherlands, the Hapsburgs received the Italian provinces of Lombardy and Venetia. This gave Austria a vantage point from which she could dominate Italy.

   e. In place of the Holy Roman Empire which Napoleon had ended in 1806, the men of Vienna created a Germanic Confederation (*Deutscher Bund*). Austria won the presidency and with it a certain dominance in German affairs until the emergence of Bismarck. This new confederation of 39 German states was bound together by a Diet and a mutual assistance agreement against outside (French) attack.

   f. Norway was taken from Denmark and given to Sweden.

   g. Sweden, in turn, ceded Finland to Russia.

   h. The neutrality and independence of Switzerland were guaranteed.

   i. Great Britain acquired a portion of South Africa, Guiana, Mauritius, Malta, the Ionian Islands, and some Caribbean islands.

   j. Russia gained a substantial part of Poland, and retained Bessarabia which she had gotten from Turkey in 1812. As has been noted, Russia kept Finland which she acquired in 1809.

   k. The Final Act was essentially a series of bargains and compromises. No one state was permitted to emerge with a preponderance of strength. The Final Act created what has been called a "chandelier" balance of power based on the principles of legitimacy and the political status quo.

II. The Congress System (1815–1833)

A. Holy Alliance
1. Metternich had a vital interest in maintaining the balance of power as embodied in the Vienna Final Act. Within Austria he was determined to maintain conservative government by playing one nationality off against another.
2. But Metternich's theory of conservatism extended beyond the Hapsburg domains. He believed that there was a connection between international and internal affairs. A revolution within one state was certain to have international repercussions. Metternich's policy was strongly supported by Czar Alexander I of Russia.
3. Nationalists and liberals throughout Europe opposed this policy. They did not want conservative intervention to prevent the emergence of democratic states with a national basis. Foreign governments did not have the right to interfere in the internal affairs of other states.
4. During the period from 1815 to 1848 the conservatives opposed the various liberal and nationalist movements that appeared in Europe.
5. The Treaty of the Holy Alliance was drawn up on September 26, 1815. It emanated from Czar Alexander I. Although Castlereagh and Metternich poked fun at its mysticism and lofty moral principles, the agreement became the ideological basis for the conservative domination of Europe after 1815. The concepts of "Christian charity" and "unalterable good will" merely served to cloak the repressive tendencies of the conservative Northern Courts: Austria, Russia, and Prussia.
6. Although the Czar often invoked the moral principles of this agreement, the Holy Alliance was of little importance in the development of international government by the great powers.
B. Quadruple Alliance
1. This agreement was signed at Paris on November 20, 1815 by Austria, Prussia, Russia, and Great Britain. It reaffirmed the Treaty of Chaumont (March 9, 1814)

which sanctioned "diplomacy by conference" or "congressional government."

2. Thus, Article VI of the Chaumont agreement served as the impetus for international government by the great powers. It was reaffirmed by Article VI of the Quadruple Alliance.

3. The system of international government as laid down by the Quadruple Alliance did last beyond 1823.

4. British adherence to the Quadruple Alliance was based on the concept of preventing any new French disturbance of the 1815 settlement. In particular, she opposed the reappearance of a Bonaparte on the throne of France. Both Castlereagh and Canning pursued this policy. The conservative powers (Russia, Austria, Prussia) took a more international view of their responsibilities. They viewed anti-liberal and anti-nationalistic intervention as a desirable thing regardless of where such action occurred. The inevitable cleavage occurred after the Congress of Verona (1822). After Verona, Great Britain even gave a degree of assistance to liberal and national movements in Portugal, Spain and Greece.

C. Congress diplomacy

1. Aix-la-Chapelle (November 15, 1818)

   a. Since France had shown no signs of aggression and had fulfilled her financial obligations, the allied powers invited the French to join the Quadruple Alliance. It now became the Quintuple Alliance.

   b. Foreign troops were withdrawn from France, and her indemnity reduced.

   c. Czar Alexander's "Holy Alliance" policy of armed intervention wherever absolutism was threatened was blocked by Castlereagh and even Metternich. Castlereagh opposed any intervention of this type, while Metternich desired a more subtle approach to maintain the balance of power.

   d. The five great powers did agree to a general statement which declared that peace could best be maintained by preserving the status quo.

2. Troppau (November, 1820)

   a. This congress was called to consider revolutions in Spain and Italy. The great powers were also concerned by the assassination of the Duc de Berry, nephew of Louis XVIII of France, and the radical Cato Street Conspiracy (1820) in Great Britain. The agitation of such German student societies as the *Tugendbund* and the *Burschenschaften* plus the murder of the Czarist agent Kotzebue also worried the conservative leaders.

b. Metternich was able to secure the approval of his government, Prussia, and Russia for the Troppau Protocol. This document sanctioned intervention against revolutions which endangered peace. Castlereagh dissented because of British public opinion. In his State Paper of May 5, 1820 Castlereagh had opposed intervention in Spain; this he argued was interference in the internal affairs of another state.

3. Laibach (1821)
   a. At this congress, the great powers authorized Austria to restore the despotic Ferdinand I as ruler of the impoverished Kingdom of Two Sicilies. This was done with ease in March 1821.

4. Verona (1822)
   a. Although this last congress was called to deal with the Greek revolution, the question of Spain came up. The revolutionaries had forced Ferdinand VII to accept the liberal 1812 constitution. Czar Alexander was anxious to send his armies into Spain, but the congress authorized a somewhat hesitant France to restore the absolutism that had prevailed before 1820.
   b. Canning, the new British foreign secretary, protested vehemently. Although a French army restored Ferdinand VII in 1823, the concert of Europe would now have to operate without Great Britain.
   c. Under Canning, the British now began to give active assistance to liberal and nationalist movements.
   d. Canning even approached the American minister in London, Richard Rush, with a proposal of joint Anglo-American action to prevent the Spanish reconquest of her Latin American colonies with the assistance of the conservative powers of Europe. The United States preferred to issue a unilateral warning to the Holy Alliance in the form of a presidential message to Congress. This was the Monroe Doctrine (December 2, 1823). It was British seapower and the

British desire to maintain her lucrative trade with Latin America that really prevented an attempt to restore the old position of Spain in the New World.

5. The breakdown of congress diplomacy was also visible after 1823 in Greece, the Danubian Principalities, Spain, Portugal, and Belgium.

6. The Greek revolt (1821–1829)

    a. The influence of the French Revolution, the hopes raised by Catherine the Great's "Greek scheme," and the cultural and economic renaissance in early nineteenth Greece all helped bring on the revolt.

    b. The influence of the secret revolutionary society, the *Hetairia Philiké*, and its leader, Alexander Hypsilanti, was significant.

    c. The Greeks fought alone against the Turkish-Egyptian army and navy until 1827. Russia saw an opportunity to intervene profitably, but she was joined by Great Britain and France.

    d. When the Turks refused to agree to an armistice and continued to land forces in Greece, a combined Russian, French, and British fleet sent most of the Egyptian squadron at Navarino to the bottom (October 20, 1827).

    e. Only Russia declared war on the Turks, while France remained friendly to the Greek cause. Britain did not like the move for fear of Russian expansion. Metternich could do nothing to stop conservative Russia from aiding the Greek nationalists.

    f. Russian successes forced Turkey to sign the Treaty of Adrianople (September 14, 1829). Greece won her independence, but she was restricted in size to the area south of the Gulf of Volo—Gulf of Arta line.

7. Danubian Principalities (Rumania)

    a. Russia had occupied the two principalities of Moldavia and Wallachia during her war with Turkey (1828–1829).

    b. Russia occupied these provinces until 1834, pending payment of an indemnity by Turkey.

    c. The Treaty of Adrianople (1829) added more fuel to the nationalist fires which were threatening to destroy the Metternichian system. The princes (*hospodars*) were now to be elected by the Rumanian nobles. In addition, the *hospodars* could control internal affairs and maintain a militia.

   d. The Organic Statute of 1832 gave both Moldavia and Wallachia the same law, and helped pave the way for a union of the two principalities (as Rumania) in 1859.

8. Spain
   a. Although the European concert had restored Ferdinand VII (1814–1833) in 1823, his death ten years later saw the liberal cause revive. Again, Metternich was unable to stem the tide.
   b. During the Carlist War (1834–1839) Maria Cristina (the regent for Isabella II) led the liberals to victory over the conservative forces of Don Carlos, brother of the late Ferdinand VII.
   c. France, England, Spain, and Portugal even concluded a Quadruple Alliance in support of the constitutionalist parties of the latter two states.
   d. The moderate Constitution of 1837 was won, but bickering among the liberals led to the dictatorship of General Narvaez.

9. Portugal
   a. In 1820 a revolution against the rule of the British soldier, Marshal Beresford, occurred. This was in Oporto.
   b. A liberal constitution was promulgated, the Inquisition suppressed, and feudalism ended. John VI swore allegiance to the new document in 1822.
   c. The restoration of Ferdinand VII in Spain encouraged a revolt by the reactionaries under Dom Miguel in 1823–1824. Another revolt under Dom Miguel was encouraged by Metternich, but a British force helped suppress it (1827–1828).
   d. Dom Miguel soon started a new insurrection (Miguelite Wars, 1828–1834). With the assistance of the Quadruple Alliance of Great Britain, France, Spain, and Portugal, the constitutionalist party was victorious.

10. Belgium
   a. The Belgians had long been restive during the fifteen years of Dutch domination. The overthrow of the

Bourbons in France in 1830 was the signal for a liberal revolution in Brussels (August 25, 1830).

b. Complete independence was declared on October 4, 1830, and the Dutch were driven out. A very liberal constitution was promulgated in February, 1831.

c. To prevent the conservative powers from intervening, Great Britain and France called a conference on Belgium. In December, 1830 the great powers agreed to give Belgium her independence. Russia agreed only because she was occupied with the Polish revolt of 1830–1831. Austria and Prussia followed suit. Belgian neutrality was declared in January, 1831, but the Dutch did not agree to either her independence or neutrality until 1839.

11. Evaluation of the Congress System

a. Despite initial Metternichian successes in Italy and Spain, the solid front of great powers disintegrated after Verona (1822).

b. Both Britain and France, despite deep suspicion of each other, encouraged liberalism and nationalism in Greece, Portugal, Spain, Belgium, and Latin America.

c. The "cardboard" alliance of Great Britain and France against the conservative Northern Courts was almost wrecked by the Mehemet Ali crisis in 1840. The affair of the Spanish marriages in 1846 caused a rupture that was not healed until the Crimean War.

III. France After Napoleon

1. In 1815 France was still a rural country. Even as late as 1846 a census showed 75% of the people lived in rural areas.

2. The revolution had seen the emergence of a large number of small landholders. They were generally conservative, and anxious to hold their plots even after the return of the Bourbons. The peasants were content to salt away their savings, live meagerly, and be let alone.

3. Bourbon France was not the France of 1789. The privileges that the nobility enjoyed under the Old Regime were gone. Even the estates of many nobles (as well as the Church) had been broken up and sold during the revolutionary years.

4. The returning Bourbons were supported by an alliance of clericals and royalists—"the altar and the throne."

5. Louis XVIII (1814–1824)

a. This Bourbon monarch had been permitted to return because of the influence of Czar Alexander I.

b. In June 1814 he granted a *Charte Constitutionnelle* (Constitutional Charter) which provided for hereditary monarchy, an upper house (Chamber of Peers) nominated by the king, and a lower house (Chamber of Deputies) elected by a small fraction of the populace. Only those who were thirty years old and paid a tax of 300 francs annually could vote in contests for the lower house. Candidates for seats in the Chamber of Deputies had to pay a yearly tax of 1000 francs.

c. The Restoration was given a rude shock when Napoleon suddenly returned from Elba for the famous Hundred Days (March–June 1815). After Waterloo the French reactionaries (Ultras) carried out the White Terror against their enemies, particularly in southern France.

d. The first election was held in the middle of the White Terror and yielded an Ultra-dominated parliament, the *Chambre introuvable* (unanticipated chamber). New elections in 1816 produced a moderate majority in the lower house. A moderate ministry under the Duc de Richelieu took office and remained in power until 1818.

e. The trend to the left enabled the Decazes ministry to stay in power from 1819 to 1820, but the assassination of the Duc de Berry in 1820 saw the return of the more conservative Richelieu (1820–1821).

f. After 1820 Louis XVIII yielded more and more to the Ultra policies of his brother, the Count of Artois. Ultra influence was so strong that Richelieu resigned (1821) in favor of the more reactionary Villèle (1821–1828).

g. Several liberal plots against the Bourbon regime were smashed: the "Bazar Français" (1820), the Conspiracy of Saumur (1822), and the disaffection of several non-commissioned officers associated with the *Charbonnerie* (charcoal burners) at La Rochelle (1822).

    h. Louis XVIII died in 1824 and was succeeded by his brother, the reactionary Count of Artois.

6. <u>Charles X (1824–1830)</u>

    a. With the accession of Charles X, the entire government was Ultra.

    b. Charles X wanted to drop the semblance of constitutional government that existed and return to the conditions of absolute monarchy that prevailed prior to 1789.

    c. The first attempt was <u>Villèle's Indemnification Act of 1825.</u> The French nobility was to be compensated by a bond issue of one billion francs for the lands they lost during the revolution. This move alienated the French peasantry.

    d. A severe press law pushed journalists like Thiers and Guizot into the opposition.

    e. The opposition to Charles X built up so quickly that the moderates and independents were able to defeat Villèle in the election of November, 1827.

    f. The weak Martignac cabinet struggled against opposition from the left and the Ultras during 1828 and 1829.

    g. The rightist Polignac ministry (1829–1830) spelled the end of Bourbon rule in France. By 1830 opposition elements began to join hands against the Ultras and their clerical allies of the "Congregation."

    h. On March 18, 1830 the parliamentary opposition made a critical reply to the speech of Charles X that had opened the session of the chambers. This was passed 221–181. <u>"The 221"</u> became a symbol of constitutional opposition to Charles X.

    i. When Charles X attempted an anticonstitutional coup d'état with his <u>Four Ordinances</u> (actually five if a list of Ultra appointments to high office is included) on July 26, 1830, a coalition of moderates deposed him.

    j. A group of 91 deputies led by Thiers and Guizot and supported by the more republican Lafayette called Louis Philippe to the throne (August 7, 1830).

7. <u>The Orleanist (July) Monarchy (1830–1848)</u>

    a. Louis Philippe, the "Citizen King," was the son of Philippe Égalité, Duke of Orleans. Égalité had been executed in 1793. Louis Philippe could claim descent from a younger brother of Louis XIV.

b. This new businessman's government had the support of bankers like Lafitte, diplomats like Talleyrand, and journalists like Thiers and Guizot. Even republicans supported it until its anti-liberal tendencies became apparent.

c. Almost from the outset Louis Philippe was determined to be a strong king. The republican and working-class elements were quickly disillusioned. Only 200,000 Frenchmen could vote because of the requirement that the franchise be limited to citizens who paid taxes of 200 francs. Candidates for the lower house had to pay taxes of 500 francs. It was to be a government run by the bourgeoisie, the bankers and businessmen of France. Even the lower middle class (shopkeepers, professional men, small factory owners) were denied the franchise.

d. High unemployment and low wages plagued the factory workers. High tariffs protected many inefficient industries. In 1836 some 30,000 Parisian workers (out of a total of 250,000) were unemployed. Riots occurred in Paris and Lyons in 1831 and 1834, and many attempts were made on the life of Louis Philippe.

e. Child labor was common, and the incidence of tuberculosis high. A 16 to 18-hour working day was not uncommon in the silk mills. Unions were banned, and it became a crime to criticize the government.

f. Louis Napoleon Bonaparte, the future Napoleon III, made two unsuccessful attempts to overthrow the unpopular regime: at Strasbourg in 1836 and Boulogne in 1840.

g. The regime was rendered still more unpopular by its pacific foreign policy. Most Frenchmen still longed for the glory and power France enjoyed under Napoleon Bonaparte. A Napoleonic legend persisted until its beneficiary, Louis Napoleon Bonaparte, capitalized on it by winning the presidency of the Second Republic in 1848.

h. The "Guizot ministry" from 1840–1848 added still more to the burden of the regime's unpopularity.

Bribes, favors, and corruption cost the government what popular support it had. The lower house was controlled with the help of 149 "place men" (1842), public officials who were allowed to sit as deputies in the lower house. A business depression in 1847 and the rejection of a program of moderate reform in the same year caused the opposition to stage a "banquet campaign."

i. The moderate opposition, led by Barrot, Pagnerre, and Recurt staged some seventy political banquets in 1847 and 1848.

j. When Guizot stopped one Parisian banquet in January, 1848 the opposition sought to bring a test case to the courts by holding a <u>Grand-National banquet in Paris on February 22, 1848.</u>

k. But the radical newspapers of Paris called for a procession to the banquet which was illegal. The moderates had only wished to test the legality of public political meetings, but the situation got out of hand when troops fired on the crowd near Guizot's home (February 23, 1848). All Paris was now aroused, and Louis Philippe abdicated.

l. A moderate provisional government under the poet Lamartine now took control.

IV. Great Britain After 1815

1. <u>The Tories had been in control almost continuously since 1770.</u> After the end of the Napoleonic wars the Tories were faced by a major economic depression.

   a. The markets of Europe were unable to absorb the huge stocks of manufactured goods that had accumulated during the war.

   b. The government no longer required large quantities of military supplies.

   c. The ranks of the unemployed were swelled by the addition of 400,000 demobilized soldiers and sailors.

   d. Prices dropped sharply.

2. <u>Tory remedies</u>

   a. To protect the landowners from an influx of cheap grain from North America, the Tory-dominated Parliament passed the Corn Law of 1815. This kept the price of bread high, and caused considerable suffering.

b. The Tories also abolished the 10 per cent income tax (1816), but added new duties on many articles. This raised prices for the bulk of the population.

c. The factory workers felt that the only hope for improvement was in parliamentary reform. But the excesses of the French Revolution made the Tories suspicious of any liberal reform. Even the Whigs equated democracy with mob rule.

3. Agitation for reform to 1832

a. This actually began in 1769 when Wilkes was elected by a Middlesex constituency, but was denied his seat in Parliament because of royal and ministerial pressure. By 1782, however, Parliament did remove the resolution that denied Wilkes his seat. This helped establish the principle of free election to the House of Commons.

b. After 1771 Commons reluctantly permitted the publication of its speeches.

c. Further reform was delayed by the excesses of the French revolutionaries. Both Tories and Whigs were horrified by this example of liberalism.

d. After 1815 journalists like William Cobbett *(Register)* began to agitate for parliamentary reform. "Orator" Hunt argued that universal suffrage and annual parliaments would save England. A London tailor named Francis Place worked on union organization despite the restrictive Combination Acts of 1799–1800.

e. The Spa Fields meeting (December 2, 1816) near London called attention to the need for reform and the large number of hungry Englishmen. It was dispersed by force.

f. The agitation for change led the Tories to pass the Coercion Acts (1817) which suspended *habeas corpus* and made "seditious" meetings unlawful.

g. The Peterloo Massacre (August 16, 1819) occurred near Manchester when police violently broke up a peaceable demonstration against the Corn Laws. This led to the Six Acts (December, 1819): trials of offenders were speeded up, unauthorized military drills were outlawed, libelous printed matter could be seized, public meetings were banned, a stamp tax was placed on political tracts, and justices of the peace were empowered to search dwellings for arms.

h. A few months later (February, 1820) the famous Cato Street Conspiracy was thwarted. The plotters had hoped to blow up the entire cabinet while they dined, seize the Bank of England, and establish a new government.

i. During the 1820's radicalism seemed to wane. The improvement in business, more generous poor relief, and temporary cowing of the agitators were all contributory factors.

j. Liberal Tories like Robert Peel (1770–1850) introduced legislation to remove 100 offenses from the capital punishment list. The free trade advocate Huskisson won the reduction of duties on wool, silk, iron, wines, sugar, and coffee. The agitation of Francis Place even secured the repeal of the Combination Acts (1824), but a new law of 1825 virtually prohibited the strike. Even the reactionary Wellington was forced to modify the Corn Law of 1815 in order to permit the easier importation of inexpensive foreign grain. In addition, Wellington and Peel pushed the Catholic Emancipation Act (1829) through Parliament to prevent further Irish unrest: this repealed the Test Act of 1673 which had prevented Catholics and nonconformists from holding public office.

k. The accession of William IV to the throne necessitated a general election in which reform of the House of Commons became the leading issue (1830). The Whigs under Grey, Russell, and Lord Durham adopted a platform of reform and won the election of 1830. The new Whig cabinet of Earl Grey was now committed to reform by both its election platform and a new wave of popular agitation.

l. The reformers wished to do away with the pocket boroughs where a single powerful leader could name the member of Parliament. In addition, they wished to drop the rotten boroughs where bribery and pressure could swing the election because of the very small number of eligible voters. In 1830 only a third of the House of Commons was freely elected in the so-called open boroughs.

m. The first reform bill was killed in committee in March, 1831, while the House of Lords defeated a second bill (October, 1831). When the third reform bill also seemed headed for defeat in the Lords, popular agitation and the king's threat to appoint new peers to the upper house caused the House of Lords to capitulate. The Reform Bill of 1832 added some 250,000 voters to the rolls, but the workers and farmers were still without the ballot. The beneficiaries of this legislation were the propertied men of commerce and industry. In addition, many towns and counties received representation in Parliament for the first time, while 111 members from pocket and rotten boroughs were dropped.

4. Reform and agitation (1832–1848)

a. In 1833 a bill carried to abolish slavery in the colonies of Great Britain. This was the successful culmination of a long campaign led by William Wilberforce.

b. The Factory Act of 1833 was also passed despite Tory and laissez-faire Whig opposition. Children under 9 could not be employed, and those under 13 had to have two hours of school per day. Children between 9 and 13 were limited to a 48-hour week.

c. Trade unionism continued to grow under the leadership of John Doherty and Robert Owen. The confusion of practical trade union objectives and utopian socialist dreams caused the Grand National Consolidated Trades Union to be dissolved in 1834. For the moment trade unionism declined.

d. In 1837 the eighteen year old Victoria (1837–1901) came to the throne. She brought a respectability to the monarchy which had been absent for almost a century. In addition, she generally accepted the parliamentary system of government.

e. Chartist agitation for further reform began in 1836 with the Workingmen's Association in London. Under the leadership of Feargus O'Connor the Chartists demanded universal manhood suffrage, election districts of equal population, annual Parliaments,

vote by ballot, and an end to the property qualification for members of Parliament. Chartism gained
strength in the 1840's, but the ludicrous failure of the
petition of five million (actually two million) in 1848
wrecked the movement. The workers now looked to
Liberal politicians in Parliament and more moderate
trade union leadership.

f. The conservative Peel cabinet (1841–1846) sought to
mollify the demand for free trade and the end of the
Corn Law by several moves. Duties were lowered on
the importation of grain in 1842. In addition, import
and export duties on wool were removed. But the
anti-Corn Law and free trade agitation continued
under the leadership of the Manchester School (John
Bright and Richard Cobden). The poor English har-
vest of 1845 and the famine in Ireland were additional factors that forced Peel to help provide cheap
bread. In 1846 Peel split his party and wrecked his
career by pushing through Parliament a bill to virtually abolish the Corn Law (tariff on imported grain).
A policy of free trade was established that lasted to
the Great Depression.

V. The Germanic Confederation After 1815

1. The Germanic Confederation
   a. The Vienna Final Act (1815) had organized this loose
   confederation *(Staatenbund)* to provide the disunited
   states of Germany with a degree of protection against
   the ambitions of France.
   b. If any member of the Germanic Confederation was
   attacked on Germany soil, the other members of the
   Deutscher Bund were obligated to come to her defense. Since Austria won the presidency of the *Bund*
   diet at Frankfurt, Metternich's anti-liberal and anti-
   nationalistic policies could be implemented more
   easily.
   c. Prussia had been the hope of the German liberals
   everywhere, but with the decline of Hardenburg's
   power that state fell under the control of the reactionaries by 1819. Under Frederick William III Prus-

sia seldom challenged Austria's dominant position in
Germany.

d. A few small German states such as Bavaria, Baden,
and Saxe-Weimar did give their people constitutions.

e. Liberal student societies like the *Tugendbund* and
Burschenschaften did win a considerable following.
Metternich was somewhat concerned when the students from the University of Jena organized the Wart-
burg Festival (1817), but he was moved to action
when the reactionary journalist Kotzebue was assassinated by a student. Using his influence on Frederick
William III and the Diet, Metternich secured passage
of the repressive Carlsbad Decrees (1819).

f. Prussia's only serious challenge to Austrian hegemony
in Germany was her organization of the *Zollverein*
(tariff union). The Prussian tariff union was organized in 1818, but by 1844 it included all of Germany
except for Austria, Oldenburg, Mecklenburg, Hanover, and a few former Hanse cities. But beyond this
tariff union the smaller German states would not go.
They distrusted the aggressive and ambitious Prussians, and preferred the less efficient Catholic
Hapsburgs.

g. Yet, German nationalists found it hard to place their
hopes in the multinational and polygot empire of
Austria. How could a German nationalist movement
be led by a state that was about 80 per cent Slavic,
Hungarian, Rumanian, and Italian?

2. Effect of the 1830 revolution in Germany

a. By 1827 the revolutionary movement in Germany
had revived despite the Carlsbad Decrees.

b. The example of the French revolution of 1830 was
duplicated in Saxony, Hesse-Cassel, Hanover, and
Brunswick where the people won constitutions. Prussia and Austria were untouched, however.

c. At the Hambach Festival (1832) some 25,000 people
demanded that Germany be unified as a republic.
Lafayette, the French republican hero of 1830, was
toasted. Metternich countered this demonstration
with six repressive laws that were rammed through
the diet at Frankfurt. In addition, the new king of
Hanover dropped the liberal constitution (1837),

an act which greatly aroused German constitutional sentiment.

d. The new Prussian king, Frederick William IV (1840–1861), often spoke in liberal terms but did nothing to aid the republican or nationalist cause. He stood in awe of both Austria and Metternich until the fateful days of 1848.

VI. The 1848 Revolutions and Their Aftermath

A. Italy

1. In 1848 Italy was still politically disunited. The virus of nationalism had infected the souls of many Italians through such organizations as the *Carbonari* (Charcoal Burners) and Mazzini's *Young Italy*. Revolutionary uprisings in Naples (1820), Piedmont (1821), the Papal States, Modena, and Parma in 1831 had all been successful. Mazzinian revolts in Savoy (1834) and elsewhere created nothing but martyrs, while Garibaldi's Italian Legion in South America was little more effective. Italians who felt humiliated by foreign domination, the lack of constitutional government, and the division of Italy into a dozen political fragments saw new hope in the events of 1848. This feeling of Italian nationalism was known as the *Risorgimento* (Resurgence). The state that was destined to lead this national movement was Sardinia (Piedmont), the only Italian government with a native dynasty (House of Savoy).

2. The Austrian acquisition of Lombardy and Venetia in 1815 had made any Italian revolutionary movement virtually impossible. The Hapsburg occupation of tiny Ferrara in July, 1847 infuriated Italian opinion. Italians realized that Austria was the main stumbling block to unification. The hopes of Italy were centered on the vacillating Charles Albert (1831–1849) of Sardinia. For all of Charles Albert's boasting *(Italia farà da sè*—Italy will do it herself), he was not the forceful leader that was needed.

3. The revolutionary movement first came into the open in Palermo, Sicily in January, 1848. It spread to Naples, and the tyrannical Ferdinand II *(Bomba)* was compelled to grant the Kingdom of the Two Sicilies a constitution.

    a. The Grand Duke of Tuscany followed suit (February, 1848) as did Charles Albert of Sardinia. The Sardinian *Statuto Fundamentale* later became the basis of the Italian constitution. Even Pope Pius IX made some liberal concessions in March, 1848.

4. Milan's "Five glorious days" (March 18–22, 1848)

    a. Under Cattaneo, the heroic Milanese drove Radetsky's forces out of the city. The Austrians fell back to the four fortresses of the "Quadrilateral": Peschiera, Verona, Mantua, and Legnano.

    b. This victory over the "whitecoats" encouraged all Italy. Coupled with the deposition of Metternich at Vienna (March 13, 1848), this ejection of the Austrian army from Lombardy seemed to indicate the end of Hapsburg domination.

5. New aid for the Italian cause.

    a. Daniele Manin now proclaimed a republic in Venice (March 22, 1848).

    b. On the same day Sardinia declared war on Austria.

    c. A papal army was sent north to aid the national cause by Pius IX (April, 1848).

    d. The Sardinian forces even defeated the Austrians at Goito (May 30, 1848).

6. Turning of the tide

    a. By June, 1848 the Austrian government was ready to yield Lombardy and conclude peace, but General Radetsky induced Vienna to continue the struggle.

    b. Radetsky soon routed the Sardinians at Custozza (July 24, 1848), and then drove them out of Lombardy. An armistice was arranged between Austria and Sardinia in August. Milan was again in Hapsburg hands.

    c. In Naples, *Bomba* had rewon control with the aid of Swiss mercenaries (May 15, 1848). He withdrew an army that had been sent north to aid Sardinia, and quickly rewon Sicily (May, 1849).

    d. After the murder of the moderate prime minister Rossi in Rome in November, 1848, the pope abandoned further liberal experiments and fled. In the early months in 1849 both Garibaldi and Mazzini arrived, and a Roman Republic was proclaimed (February, 1849).

    e. Louis Napoleon Bonaparte now sent a French expedition to retake the city for Pius IX and thereby win favor with French Catholics. This was done after a heroic defense by Garibaldi (June 30, 1849).

    f. After a similar siege, the Austrians broke Venetian resistance on August 28, 1849. Austrian troops also smashed liberal resistance in Tuscany.

    g. A lack of leadership, unity, and power doomed the Italian revolution of 1848–1849. Only the later emergence of Camillo Cavour and the assistance of Napoleon III enabled Italy to achieve unification.

B. France

  1. <u>After the abdication of Louis Philippe in 1848 an uneasy alliance of moderate Republicans and Socialists formed a Provisional Government in Paris.</u> The moderate-dominated government was headed by the poet Alphonse Lamartine, but Socialists like Blanc and Albert had to be included to appease the militant Parisian workers who did not want another 1830-type revolution.

    a. The moderates were compelled to recognize that the government would guarantee work for the army of unemployed in the Paris area (February, 1848).

    b. <u>Louis Blanc</u> was permitted to set up headquarters in the Luxembourg Palace. From here he hoped to implement his idea of socialized workshops as spelled out in *The Organization of Labor.*

    c. But the moderates under Pierre Marie substituted <u>national workshops *(ateliers nationaux)*.</u> This was no more than a large scale relief program to appease the unemployed radicals of Paris.

    d. A radical demonstration in Paris in March, 1848 might have overturned the Provisional Government had Louis Blanc not intervened.

  2. <u>The elections to the National Assembly (April 23, 1848)</u>

    a. The moderate Republicans won a smashing victory by taking 500 seats. The radicals failed to capture 100 seats.

    b. The Legitimists (those who wanted a return of the Bourbons) won about 100 seats, while Orleanists were returned in 200 districts.

  3. <u>Revolt of the radicals</u>

    a. The workers feared that the revolution would now

be nullified by the moderate Assembly in the same way that Louis Philippe had prevented liberal reform after 1830.

b. The Parisian mob broke into the Assembly hall on May 15, 1848, but the insurrection collapsed. Now the moderates joined forces with the monarchists in the Assembly and dissolved the national workshops.

c. The Parisian workers staged a tremendous revolt (June 23–26, 1848) known as the "June Days." After some of the bloodiest street fighting in French history, General Cavaignac ("The Butcher") restored order.

4. Cavaignac and the repression

a. Cavaignac won dictatorial powers and proceeded to suppress radical newspapers and secret societies.

5. Meanwhile, the Assembly had completed a Republican constitution (November 4, 1848).

a. It provided for a strong president and a unicameral legislature.

6. In the election of December, 1848 Louis Napoleon Bonaparte easily outdistanced Cavaignac in the presidential ballot. His triumph was generated because he was a symbol of order to the peasants and bourgeoisie. The Napoleonic legend and the hope for additional glorious exploits after two decades of drab Orleanism were additional reasons for his success. He was also able to win considerable support among the workers because of such vague Socialist tracts as the *Extinction of Pauperism.*

7. The Second Republic (1848–1851)

a. The election of a Legislative Assembly on May 13, 1849 saw the Monarchists elect about 450 deputies. The Republicans took only 80 seats, and the Socialists 180.

b. The dominant Monarchists, the Party of Order, were divided into Bourbons and Orleanists. Both of these groups were actively considering an illegal seizure of power as was President Louis Napoleon Bonaparte.

c. Louis Napoleon kept clear of the liberal-monarchist struggles within the Assembly. He posed as a man above party and factional quarrels, a representative of the nation.

d. Louis Napoleon won considerable Catholic support

after sending an expedition to destroy the Roman Republic and restore the authority of Pius IX (April-June, 1849). He further ingratiated himself by supporting greater Church supervision over the primary schools (Falloux Law, March 15, 1850).

e. The president wisely disassociated himself from a law of May, 1850 which took the vote away from all industrial and migratory workers.

f. In addition, Louis Napoleon appealed to the peasants and bourgeoisie as the one person who could maintain order.

g. Louis Napoleon selected a cabinet of men devoted to him. It was dominated by Rouher.

h. The president took pains to carefully cultivate the army by distributing gifts and honors judiciously. His very name was an asset here.

i. When the Assembly turned down his request that the constitution be amended to allow him a second term as president, the "little nephew" decided on a coup d'état (November 29, 1851). The coup was successfully engineered on December 2, 1851, the anniversary of his uncle's victory at Austerlitz (1805). Numerous uprisings in Paris and the provinces were quelled. A plebiscite on December 21, 1851 approved the coup by better than a ten to one margin. France chose authority over liberty.

j. The new constitution of January 14, 1852 gave Louis Napoleon almost dictatorial control. After a whistle-stop tour through the provinces in September, 1852 to win support for the imperial idea, the Second Empire was established by decree on December 2, 1852. Louis Napoleon took the title Napoleon III.

C. Austria

1. In 1848 the Hapsburg empire was still a land where the clergy and nobility led a privileged existence. Legal distinctions still existed between the nobility and the commoners, while the latter still had to provide the hated labor service (robot). The head of this multinational and polyglot empire was a mediocre epileptic, Ferdinand I (1835–1848). He was King of Hungary and Bohemia, and also ruled Galicia, Ruthenia, part of Transylvania, Lombardy-Venetia, Croatia, Moravia, and

Slovakia. <u>Metternich</u> directed his foreign policy with a capable hand, while <u>Count Kolowrat</u> was his finance minister. By 1848 the Austrian empire was showing the effects of a ponderous inefficiency. But the Hapsburg government muddled on, a despotism that was made palatable by inefficiency. In the last analysis, the empire had survived because the army remained loyal, and because it was possible to play one national group off against another.

2. <u>When Louis Philippe fled from Paris in February, 1848, immediate effects were felt in Budapest and Vienna.</u>

   a. In Budapest the Hungarian patriot Louis Kossuth demanded liberal government in a speech before the Diet at Pressburg (March 3, 1848).

   b. <u>Revolution broke out in Vienna and Metternich was obliged to flee on March 13, 1848.</u> Emperor Ferdinand I issued a constitution providing for responsible government (April 25), but even this did not satisfy the Viennese radicals and the imperial family fled.

   c. Student riots, a scurrilous press, and disorder followed. The middle class elements now began to fear the Viennese radicals.

   d. Dissatisfaction with the imperial constitution and an attempt to disband the <u>Academic Legion</u> caused a Committee of Safety to take control of Vienna from May to October, 1848.

3. <u>Meanwhile, revolution had occurred in Lombardy.</u> Here Radetsky had been forced to fall back on the "Quadrilateral" by an aroused force of Milanese and Sardinians (March, 1848).

4. <u>Revolutionary activity also shook Bohemia to the north,</u> particularly the city of Prague. Had the middle class, landed nobility, peasants, and city workers been united, the liberal Bohemian demands would have been fulfilled by Vienna.

   a. There was also a division between the Czechs and the German minority. The latter did not wish to be overwhelmed by the Czechs in a new Bohemian state.

   b. In June, 1848 a Panslav Congress met in Prague under the leadership of <u>Frantisek Palácky</u>. Although it proclaimed a unity of all Slavic peoples, the various groups were widely separated and were often played off against one another by the Hapsburgs. Emperor Ferdinand even used the Slavic Croats to help crush the Hungarian (Magyar) uprising.

c. Serious riots in Prague caused the Austrian military commander, Prince Windischgrätz, to crush the revolutionary movement in Bohemia (June 17, 1848). This was the first step towards Hapsburg recovery, and was followed by Radetsky's victory of the Sardinian-Italian armies at Custozza on July 24, 1848.

d. Thus far the loyalty of the Austrian army had saved the Hapsburg realm from dissolution. But now the Austrians had to cope with the most serious insurrections of all: those in Hungary and in Vienna.

5. The Croats were desirous of overthrowing the hated Hungarian (Magyar) domination. These rough and tumble frontiersmen found an able leader in Baron Joseph Jellachich, the governor *(ban)* of Croatia.

a. On June 5 the Croatian-Slavonic Diet rejected Magyar authority.

b. The Austrians overcame their dislike of the Croatian national movement because the Hungarian situation threatened to break up the realm.

c. Jellachich was authorized to invade Hungary with a Croatian army (September, 1848), but the Magyars repulsed his force. Now the Hungarians moved to help their fellow revolutionists who were besieged in Vienna by Windischgrätz and Jellachich.

d. The Hungarians were unable to break the ring around Vienna, and the city fell to the Hapsburg armies on October 31, 1848. The revolutionary *Reichstag* (Assembly) had fled north to Kremsier where it was dissolved in March, 1849.

6. End of the Hungarian revolution

a. With Prague, Vienna, Milan, and Croatia quiet, the Hapsburg armies were now able to concentrate their strength against the Magyars.

b. Windischgrätz quickly seized Budapest on January 5, 1849 and won another engagement at Kapolna in February, but a Magyar resurgence under General Görgei drove the Hapsburg armies out of Hungary (April, 1849).

c. A Hungarian republic under Kossuth was proclaimed in April. The new Hapsburg emperor, Francis Joseph (1848–1916), appealed to Czar Nicholas I for assistance and received it. Russian troops entered Hungary along with Hapsburg armies and extinguished Magyar resistance by August, 1849 (Világos). Kossuth fled and Hungary was subjected to severe reprisals by General Haynau.

7. Results of the 1848 in the Hapsburg empire
   a. Feudalism was ended as a result of the Austrian Assembly's Act of Emancipation (September 7, 1848) and the March Laws of the Pressburg Diet.
   b. Francis Joseph (1848–1916) replaced the weak Ferdinand I as emperor. The ruthless and reactionary Felix Schwarzenberg (1800–1852) became his leading minister.
   c. The constitutional promises of Ferdinand I were ignored. Bureaucratic control from Vienna and a policy of Germanization (Bach system) now followed.

D. Germany
   1. The ejection of Louis Philippe in France was also the signal for a series of bloodless revolutions in the numerous German states. Here the demand for constitutional government was coupled with a desire for unification. The German princes yielded everywhere to the revolutionary tide in the spring of 1848. These revolutionary movements were centered in the larger cities like Berlin and Frankfurt. They were led by intellectuals like the historian Dahlmann. The populace often looked to the princes for reform which led the Duke of Saxe-Coburg to remark that "everything is being demanded of us, even the establishment of perfect health and the gift of long life." For the moment, the German liberals foolishly placed their hopes in the vacillating Frederick William IV of Prussia, a weak monarch who equated paternal despotism with liberty.
      a. During the turbulent March Days of 1848 in Berlin, Frederick William IV withdrew his troops, summoned an assembly, indicated his willingness to work for a German constitution, and promised to assume the leadership of all Germany.
      b. The Prussian constituent assembly met on May 22, 1848 and continued its radical discussions over the

summer. It was not dissolved until December 5, 1848, but by that time the momentum of revolution was largely spent.

   c. Frederick William IV did grant a constitution in 1850, but it was illiberal. The three-class voting system permitted the few who paid the first one-third of taxes to elect one-third of the lower house (*Landtag*). 17 per cent of the population elected two-thirds of the *Landtag*. The upper house (*Herrenhaus*) was dominated by the nobility. Voting was public. With all these restrictions, the *Landtag* still had to approve taxes and laws, but the monarch selected his own cabinet.

2. The Frankfurt Assembly

   a. This body of 830 met on May 18, 1848 to write a liberal constitution for all Germany. It was dominated by professors, lawyers, officials, and businessmen—a middle class body.

   b. It has been called "the most distinguished constituent body in history," but its lengthy discussions on a German constitution, the Schleswig-Holstein question, and the area of the new Germany gave the reactionary princes a chance to rewin control (1848–1849).

   c. Archduke John was made imperial regent (*Reichsverweser*) by the Frankfurt Assembly. He headed a provisional government that had no army and little authority.

   d. The Danish occupation of Schleswig (March, 1848) took the attention of the Frankfurt Assembly and Germany from its key task of writing a constitution for a liberal and unified German state.

   e. Another factor which slowed up the work at Frankfurt was the *grossdeutsch-kleindeutsch* controversy. The *grossdeutsch* (Big-German) group wanted to include German Austria and Bohemia in the new German empire. The *kleindeutsch* faction wanted non-German Austria excluded, the solution that was finally accepted in October, 1848. Austrian recovery by that time made the *kleindeutsch* victory meaningless, since the Hapsburgs were unwilling to yield any territory to a new German state that would be led by Hohenzollern Prussia.

    f. The Frankfurt Constitution was finally completed on March 27, 1849. The King of Prussia was declared Emperor of Germany by a vote of 290–248, but he refused the crown because it came from a popular assembly (April, 1840). This move killed the liberal movement.

3. Austro-Prussian rivalry (1849–1850)

    a. Prussia now proposed a unification scheme that would join the Hapsburg empire and the German states into a great central European state of 60 million souls. Prussia would lead an inner confederation of the German states, while Austria would merely control what she already had—the Hapsburg domains. Such a plan would permit Prussia to dominate a formerly divided Germany.

    b. A constitution was drawn up (May 26, 1849) and an assembly representing the members met at Erfurt on March 20, 1850.

    c. Now that the Hungarian rebellion had been crushed, the Austrians reacted vigorously. Schwarzenberg, with the support of several German states, countered the Prussian sponsored Erfurt Union by restoring the old Germanic Confederation at Frankfurt (May, 1850).

    d. Later in 1850 Prussia and Austria almost came to war over the question as to who was to help the ruler of tiny Hesse-Cassel fight his parliament. With Russia supporting Austria, Prussia yielded. This was known as the Humiliation of Olmütz (November 29, 1850). Prussia dissolved her Erfurt Union and agreed to the reestablishment of the Germanic Confederation.

4. Why did the revolution fail in Germany?

    a. There was no revolutionary center like Paris to give the nation liberal leadership.

    b. The revolution was largely a middle class movement which failed to win the workers, peasants, and princes.

    c. The revolutionaries failed to consolidate their hold on the governments of the 39 German states in the spring of 1848. While they debated, the reactionaries quietly rewon control.

    d. The concepts of liberalism did not win a large following in Germany. Autocracy and obedience remained the watchwords.

e. The Austro-Prussian struggle for power also precluded the possibility of liberal inroads.

BIBLIOGRAPHY

Artz, Frederick B., *France under the Bourbon Restoration, 1814–1830* (Cambridge: Harvard University Press, 1931).

Artz, Frederick B., *Reaction and revolution, 1814–1832* (New York: Harper, 1934).

Blum, Jerome, *Noble landowners and agriculture in Austria, 1815–1848: a study in the origins of the peasant emancipation of 1848* (Baltimore: Johns Hopkins University Press, 1948).

Bury, J. P. T., *France, 1814–1840: a history* (3rd rev. ed., London: Methuen, 1954).

Cambridge Modern History, Vol. IX, The growth of nationalities (New York: Macmillan, 1934).

Fejtö, Francois, ed., *The opening of an era: 1848. An historical symposium* (London: Wingate, 1948).

Hammond, J. L. and Hammond, B., *The age of the Chartists, 1832–1854. A study of discontent* (London and New York: Longmans, Green, 1930).

Kissinger, Henry A., *A world restored: Metternich, Castlereagh, and the problems of peace, 1812–1822* (Boston: Houghton-Mifflin, 1957).

May, Arthur, *The age of Metternich* (New York: Holt, 1933).

Namier, Sir Lewis B., *1848: the revolution of the intellectuals* (New York: Oxford University Press, 1946).

Nicolson, Harold, *The Congress of Vienna: a study in allied unity, 1812–1822* (New York: Harcourt, Brace, 1946).

Park, Joseph H., *British prime ministers of the nineteenth century* (New York: New York University Press, 1950).

Pemberton, W. B., *Lord Palmerston* (London: Batchworth Press, 1954).

Plamenatz, John, *The revolutionary movement in France, 1815–1871* (London: Longmans, Green, 1952).

Robertson, Priscilla, *Revolutions of 1848: a social history* (Princeton: Princeton University Press, 1952).

Schapiro, J. S., *Liberalism and the challenge of Fascism: social forces in England and France, 1815–1870* (New York: McGraw-Hill, 1949).

Schoyen, A. R., *The Chartist challenge* (New York: Macmillan, 1958).

Simpson, Frederick A., *Louis Napoleon and the recovery of France, 1848–1856* (3rd ed., London and New York: Longmans, Green, 1951).

Taylor, A. J. P., *The course of German history* (New York: Coward McCann, 1946).

Taylor, A. J. P., *The Hapsburg monarchy, 1809–1918* (London: Hamilton, 1948).

Taylor, A. J. P., *The Italian problem in European diplomacy, 1847–1849* (Manchester: Manchester University Press, 1934).

Webster, Charles, *The Congress of Vienna, 1814–1815* (London: Oxford University Press, 1919).

Wolf, J. B., *France, 1815 to the present* (New York: Prentice-Hall, 1940).

Chapter 7

THE INDUSTRIAL REVOLUTION

I. The Nature of the Industrial Revolution

A. The nineteenth century historian Arnold Toynbee (1852–1883) first used the term Industrial Revolution to refer to the vast economic changes in England between 1760 and 1825. In reality, however, there had been a slow development of industry for two centuries prior to 1760. The period described by Toynbee was an era of expanding industrial, commercial, and banking activity, but it was followed (beginning around 1860) by a century of unparalleled economic growth. The term "revolution" is, therefore, somewhat extreme as a description of economic development between 1760 and 1825. It would be more correct to view this period as a speedup in technological development, factory usage, commercial activity, and the introduction of more sophisticated banking and credit institutions.

B. The basic requirements of industrialization
   1. Technological skill may be considered one of the fundamental needs of an industrial state. In this area, England was easily the undisputed leader. The achievements of Kay, Hargreaves, Arkwright, Cort, Newcomen, and Watt are proof of English technological leadership before 1825.
   2. Still another basic requirement was the possession of raw materials. Iron ore, coal, cotton, oil, and wool were among the more important resources.
   3. An adequate labor supply was an indispensable ingredient. The English enclosure movement of the eighteenth century forced many farmers to move to urban areas.

Here they became part of the labor pool needed by an industrial state.

4. A large supply of investment capital was absolutely necessary. In this respect England again led all other European states. The numerous fortunes based on agricultural and commercial enterprise were often available to finance new technological developments. The development of the joint-stock company also enabled many investors to pool their capital in a single enterprise.

5. In addition, industrialization could proceed only if adequate markets existed to absorb the vast quantities of newly-produced goods. The population of England grew to nine million in 1800, and then more than tripled during the ensuing century (32.5 million in 1900). The French population grew more slowly. Her population of 26 million in 1800 rose to 35 million (1845), and reached 39 million by 1906.

C. Developments leading to the Industrial Revolution

1. One of the key factors was the increased use of power-driven machinery.

2. Still another development was the more efficient production of coal, iron, and steel. After the first oil well was drilled in Pennsylvania (1859), that natural resource became a vital substance for expanding world industry.

3. The rapid development of better means of transportation and communication materially aided industrialization. Railroad, canal, steamship, and airplane development plus the invention of the telegraph, telephone, and the wireless all contributed to industrial growth.

4. The expansion of banking and credit institutions was still another aspect of the industrial era.

5. Another key development was the emergence of the factory system. The new factories rendered the domestic (putting-out) system of production obsolete. The modern capitalist brought his men, materials, and machines together under a single roof to insure more efficient production. A division of labor occurred in which each man was given a specialized task.

6. Some large scale industry existed before 1760, however. The Imperial Wool Factory at Linz, Austria employed about 25,000 workers, while John Winchcomb, the most

important English manufacturer of cloth in the sixteenth century, employed about 1,000 workers.

II. The Role of the Machine

A. Mechanical inventions preceded the beginning of the Industrial Revolution, but they could not be compared to the vastly more significant accomplishments after 1760.

B. The most phenomenal development of machinery was in the manufacture of cotton cloth. Despite the opposition of English woolen interests in Parliament, the output of cotton cloth doubled between 1700 and 1750.

  1. John Kay's Flying Shuttle

    a. This semiautomatic device, when adapted to a loom, made it possible to weave cloth much more quickly. It was also possible to weave wider cloth.

  2. James Hargreaves' Spinning Jenny (1767)

    a. Even before the invention of the Flying Shuttle, the spinners could not meet the demands of the weavers. The Flying Shuttle made the need for yarn even more imperative.

    b. Hargreaves' Spinning Jenny made greater yarn production possible, but the threads spun were not strong enough for certain fibers.

  3. Richard Arkwright's Water Frame (1769)

    a. This machine was driven by water power. It produced thread of excellent quality and strength, and thus eliminated the one problem left by the Spinning Jenny.

  4. Samuel Crompton's Mule (1779)

    a. Arkwright had perfected a device which produced thread for calico warps. Now a machine was needed to spin a fiber type of yarn.

    b. Crompton's mule could spin some 400 threads at the same time, and could be run by steam or water power.

  5. Edward Cartwright's Power Loom (1785)

    a. By 1785 the advances in spinning threatened to create an oversupply of yarn. Cartwright's power loom opened the door to the development of a more efficient way of weaving cloth. By 1820 the power loom replaced the antiquated weaving devices of the previous century.

6. Eli Whitney's Cotton Gin (1793)
   a. This machine made a more plentiful supply of American cotton available for the mills of England. The cotton gin removed the seeds from cotton, a process by hand.

C. The steam engine
   1. After its perfection by Newcomen, the steam engine quickly replaced water power in the iron and textile industries.
   2. Thomas Savery (1650–1715)
      a. The concept that steam expansion could be used as a source of power was known in antiquity.
      b. Savery perfected a crude (and dangerous) steam engine in 1698 which was able to pump water out of shallow mines.
   3. Thomas Newcomen (1663–1729)
      a. In 1712 Newcomen devised a better steam engine to pump water out of coal mines. But Newcomen's "Miner's Friend" could not convert straight-line movement into rotary action.
   4. James Watt (1736–1819)
      a. Watt improved the steam engine considerably by devising a way to convert the movement of the piston into circular action. This made the improved steam engine a valuable industrial machine. By 1800, 320 of Watt's steam rotary engines were being used in Great Britain.
   5. The steam engine ended the old dependence on water power. No longer would a factory have to be located along a stream. In addition, the steam engine provided a cheap source of power to drive the large industrial machines already developed. This new device helped speed up the production of goods and resources, and fathered a revolutionary advance in the development of transportation.

III. Coal, Iron, Steel, and Oil Production

A. Industrial expansion after 1760 sharply increased the demand for iron and steel. This, in turn, required a much greater supply of coal, since the old method of smelting iron ore with charcoal had depleted the forests of Great

Britain. Coal, on the other hands, was available in large quantities near Newcastle and in Wales.

1. Abraham Darby the elder (1677–1717) had perfected a method of smelting pig iron with coke around 1712. Since coke could easily be made from English coal, the process stimulated the production of pig iron. Abraham Darby the younger (1704–1776) improved his father's process, and by the middle of the eighteenth the use of coke for iron-smelting was common.

2. In 1784 Henry Cort perfected a way of stirring (puddling) molten iron ore to burn off impurities. Only now could tough wrought iron be produced. In 1786 Cort perfected the rolling mill. Now sheet iron could be manufactured.

3. Nevertheless, an inexpensive, and simple way to produce steel was required. Benjamin Huntsman (1704–1776) was able to produce a high quality steel for cutlery and other products at Sheffield, but the perfection of a large scale process did not come until 1856 when Bessemer unveiled a new way of eliminating the impurities in iron by shooting jets of compressed air into the molten metal.

4. Less than a decade later (1865) Sir William Siemens developed a still better method of producing steel. Improvements on the Siemens process were later made by Pierre Martin. The Siemens-Martin technique was more popularly known as the open hearth process.

   a. The molten metal was poured into a shallow trough. Air and gas were played upon it. This new process produced about 10 per cent more steel than the Bessemer method, and it superseded it by World War I.

5. The introduction of the Bessemer and Siemens-Martin processes decreased the price of steel by 50 per cent between 1856 and 1870.

6. In 1877 the Thomas-Gilchrist process was discovered which enabled steelmakers to use iron ore with a high phosphorus content.

B. Increase in coal production

   1. By 1860 Great Britain led the world in coal production with a total output of 80 million metric tons. The United States was second with 15.2 million metric tons,

Germany third with 12.3, Belgium fourth with 9.6, and France fifth with only 8.1. By 1913 the United States had wrested world leadership from Great Britain with an output of over 617 million metric tons.

C. Increase in steel production
1. In 1865 Great Britain was the leading European producer of steel with an output of 225,000 metric tons. The various German states combined were second with 97,000. France stood third with 41,000, an augury of her imminent political decline. By 1900 Germany led Europe in steel production.

D. The development of the oil industry
1. The first oil well was drilled in Pennsylvania in 1859. United States leadership in oil production was a constant factor until 1914. During that year American oil production totaled 407,554,000 barrels.
2. Russian production near the Caspian was considerable, while Rumanian output was also a factor of importance. The other states of Europe were largely dependent on imports from the United States and the Middle East.

IV. Improvements in Transportation and Communication

A. Transportation
1. Road construction
   a. European roads in 1700 were either nonexistent or so poorly paved that travel was both time-consuming and uncomfortable. This totally inadequate "system" of roads had scarcely been improved since the days of Julius Caesar. It was completely unsuitable for the needs of an industrial world.
   b. The French engineer Pierre Trésaguet (1716–1796) developed a fine system of roads and bridges in his homeland, but two Scots, Thomas Telford (1757–1834) and John McAdam (1756–1836), helped make road construction a science. Telford stressed the importance of drainage, while McAdam constructed his roadbeds with layers of crushed stones of increasingly smaller size. By 1830 most British highways were surfaced with broken stone ("macadamized"). A fast (ten miles per hour) stagecoach and mail service was in operation in Britain by 1784.

2. Canal construction
   a. Both the Dutch and French had long employed canals as a means of cheap transportation. Under the leadership of James Brindley (1716–1803), an era of canal building was inaugurated in Great Britain. From about 1770 to 1830 about 3,000 miles of canal were dug, mostly in and about such industrial centers as Manchester and Birmingham.
   b. Elsewhere in the world the canal boom spread. The Erie Canal (1825) was the best example of the American effort to link the Atlantic seaboard with the trans-Appalachian region.
   c. In 1869 the Suez Canal was completed by De Lesseps. Now the long voyage around Africa could be avoided.
   d. The important Kiel Canal (1895) materially shortened the route from the North Sea to the Baltic, while the Panama Canal (1914) made the lengthy voyage around Cape Horn unnecessary.

3. The steamship
   a. Although Robert Fulton's *Clermont* is often thought of as the vessel that inaugurated an era of steam transportation (1807), James Rumsey (1785) and John Fitch (1790) actually operated steam-powered vessels at an earlier date.
   b. The first steamships crossed the Atlantic in 1838, but they failed to oust the speedy clipper ships for four decades. In 1882 the first steel ship crossed the Atlantic in one week.

4. Railroads
   a. Richard Trevithick (1771–1833) actually developed the first steam-powered locomotive, but it attracted no public attention.
   b. George Stephenson (1781–1848) was able to reduce the weight and improve the efficiency of the locomotive. He helped complete the first railroad in 1825. After 1830 railroad construction proceeded in Great Britain and the United States at a rapid tempo: Britain possessed 20,000 miles of track in 1890, while the United States had already constructed 167,000. The greatest era of railway construction came after 1850.

5. The automobile
   a. Although <u>Daimler and Benz</u> had developed crude gasoline vehicles after 1880, Levassor was probably the first to use the principle of an internal combustion engine. Two decades later (1908) Henry Ford began to produce autos on a mass production basis.
6. The airplane
   a. For centuries man had experimented with various types of flying machines, but not until 1890 was any significant progress made by <u>Otto Lilienthal</u> and <u>Samuel Langley</u>.
   b. In 1903 the <u>Wright brothers</u> made the first successful airplane flight in a motor-driven craft. The English Channel was crossed in 1909 by plane, and Charles Lindbergh flew across the Atlantic in 1927.
B. <u>Communication</u>
   1. The telegraph
      a. Although Wheatstone and Steinheil contributed to the development of the telegraph, <u>Samuel Morse's</u> improvements enabled him to get the first line constructed between Baltimore and Washington (1844). By 1866 the first cable had been laid under the Atlantic.
   2. The telephone
      a. The first telephone was developed by <u>Alexander Graham Bell in 1876</u>. Within a year the Bell Telephone Company was established.
   3. The wireless
      a. The first successful wireless was developed by <u>Guglielmo Marconi in 1895</u>. In 1901 the first signals were successfully sent across the Atlantic.

V. The Expansion of Banking and Credit Facilities

A. <u>The need for capital</u>
   1. The new industries that began to emerge after 1750 required large sums of money for equipment, buildings, sites, raw materials, and manpower.
   2. Most of the new enterprises were small at first because of the shortage of capital.
      a. England, however, had more money available for investment than the other states of Europe because of

the numerous fortunes already amassed in agriculture and commerce.

    b. The establishment of joint-stock companies to accumulate capital from many small investors was encouraged by the principle of limited liability. In 1844 legislation extended this principle to railroad investment. It was applied to other industries at a later date.

    c. Private "merchant bankers" (such as those in London) also lent considerable sums to finance industrial expansion. By 1800 London had replaced Amsterdam as the banking hub of the world.

  3. Capital was much scarcer in eighteenth century France. Prior to 1800 France lacked the stabilizing influence of a central bank. In addition, the huge expenditures of Louis XIV and his successors ruined the credit of France, and helped bring on the financial crisis of 1788–1789.

    a. After the fiasco of John Law's Mississippi Company (1720), joint-stock companies were unpopular in France.

B. The growth of banks

  1. Several great international banking houses emerged during the nineteenth century. Among the more significant were the houses of Baring (London) and Rothschild (Paris, London, Vienna, Frankfurt, Naples). These international banks, though conservative in their policies, enabled citizens of a given country to invest their surplus funds abroad.

  2. Banks also aided industrial expansion by pushing the use of banknotes and checks rather than specie. In Great Britain, however, the Bank of England received the sole right to issue paper currency in 1844. This right was won by the Bank of France four years later because of the desperate plight of the provincial banks.

  3. Central banks became increasingly important during the Industrial Revolution.

    a. This type of bank usually conducted all of the banking operations for a given government.

    b. It often won the exclusive right to issue banknotes which could circulate as legal tender.

    c. The first such bank was probably the Bank of Venice

(1157). More recent central banks were the Bank of Genoa (1407), the Bank of Amsterdam (1609)—succeeded by the Bank of the Netherlands (1814), the Bank of England (1694), and the Bank of France (1800).

d. In Germany the *Reichsbank* (1876) superseded the old Bank of Prussia. This credit institution was permitted to issue banknotes in excess of its specie holdings, but by a fixed amount. A tax of five per cent on notes issued beyond this limit served to check over-issuance, but when more notes were required it was not an insurmountable barrier.

VI. The Spread of Industrialization

A. The beginning of the Industrial Revolution in England around 1750 was an event that had international importance.

1. By the second decade of the nineteenth century the United States had a thriving textile industry in New England. Whitney had invented the cotton gin (1793), McCormick the reaper (1831), Singer the sewing machine (1851), and Morse the telegraph (1846). The Civil War saw the United States shift from an economy based on agriculture to one based on the output of coal, steel, textiles, and other industrial products.

2. After Otto von Bismarck had paved the way for German unification in 1871, that new state began to challenge Great Britain for the industrial supremacy of Europe. By 1910 German steel production was twice that of Great Britain.

3. Despite the efforts of Napoleon III (1852–1870) to develop French industry, France lagged behind. Her steel production in 1910 was about one-quarter that of Germany; French coal output was less than one-sixth the quantity of her neighbor across the Rhine.

4. The Industrial Revolution came to Belgium after 1830, and began to make itself felt in Russia in the 1890's under the aegis of Count Witte.

B. The consequences of industrialization

1. One of the key effects was the rapid growth of population. The population of Europe doubled between 1800

and 1900 (187 million to 401 million), while that of heavily industrialized Great Britain tripled in the same period (9 million to 32.5 million). France again lagged behind: her population was 35 million in 1845 and but 39 million in 1906.

2. Urbanization was still another important feature of the new industrial society. Such English cities as Manchester and Leeds grew rapidly. Urban centers in the Ruhr, Saar, and lower Rhine valleys mushroomed, as did cities in the Rhone and Seine valleys. Berlin, Hamburg, Vienna, and Budapest also grew because of the influx of heavy industries. These new cities were often plagued by inadequate housing, sewage disposal, recreational facilities, streets, water, police and fire forces.

3. The new productive facilities brought mass produced goods to the consumer at relatively low prices. In time, this helped bring about a substantially higher standard of living.

4. As the productive facilities of Europe were able to fully meet the needs of the home market by 1870, a race for overseas markets developed. This, among other reasons, led to the New Imperialism in Africa, Asia, and the Middle East. These underdeveloped areas also offered attractive possibilities to the many entrepreneurs with surplus capital to invest.

5. The Industrial Revolution saw the bourgeoisie oust the old landed nobility from their position of political dominance. It also saw the emergence of a working class in the factory towns: despite the terrible working conditions and factory discipline, they were probably better paid than the agricultural workers of the period. With the development of unions, the lot of these workers improved substantially.

VII. Liberalism

A. The new factory system soon won for itself a host of defenders and opponents. Many "economic liberals" came to the defense of the new industrialists. They argued that government should not interfere with business, for this would upset the natural laws of economics.

1. Adam Smith (1723–1790) argued along this line in his

famous *Wealth of Nations* (1776). He lived in an era which extolled the virtue of observing the immutable laws of nature in all areas of endeavor. Smith argued for a policy of laissez-faire: government should leave business alone, since this was in accord with the dictates of nature.

B. The "classical economists"

1. Thomas Malthus (1766–1834) argued that population was increasing at a much faster rate than the food supply. Only the reduction of the birth rate would help. Famine, disease, and war might be valuable aids in addition to the "moral restraint" needed to reduce the birth rate. It is little wonder that the new owners of industry received his *Essay upon the Principles of Population* (1798) with enthusiasm.

2. David Ricardo (1772–1823): Under the direct influence of Malthus, the wealthy Ricardo proposed his "iron law of wages." Wages cannot rise above the minimum needed for bare subsistence. If wages rise above this level temporarily, workers will have more children. This increase in the labor supply will depress wages to the subsistence level. Ricardo also propounded a law of rent and a theory of value.

C. Jeremy Bentham (1748–1832) and utilitarianism

1. This wealthy eccentric tossed aside all ideas of natural laws, and seized upon the "principle of utility." Utility became the criterion by which all things were measured. Bentham generally favored a policy of laissez-faire by the state unless a few tended to work against the best interests of the general public. In this way Bentham opened an avenue of retreat from the philosophy of laissez-faire.

D. John Stuart Mill (1806–1873)

1. Still another step away from the narrow laws of the "classical" economists was the more humane approach of Mill. Mill rejected the gloomy approaches of both Malthus and Ricardo.

   a. Workers could form cooperatives and unions, and could seek higher wages.

   b. Mill generally opposed state intervention in economic matters, but he felt legislation was the only way to protect children and women who worked in factories.

c. Mill believed that women should enjoy the same privileges as men. He regarded the Reform Act of 1832 in England as insufficient, and urged that the ballot be given to all men.

d. His best known works are the *Autobiography* (1873) and his essay *On Liberty* (1859).

E. The Manchester school

1. Like the "classical economists" this school of English economists argued on behalf of laissez-faire. They urged that restrictions on trade (tariffs, quotas) be kept to a minimum.

2. These pioneers of the free trade movement were led by John Bright and Richard Cobden.

VIII. Socialism and Communism

A. What is socialism?

1. The term was first used in England in 1825. Essentially it involves state ownership of the basic productive facilities: steel, coal, railroads, oil, and textiles. These properties would be owned collectively. Socialists believe that the wealth produced should be distributed more equitably, that distribution in a capitalist economy was unfair. Unlike the communists, socialists would make these changes peaceably and by legal means.

2. The idea of common ownership of property is quite old. It existed in some of the early Christian communities, and was mentioned by Plato in his *Republic*. Thomas More suggested it in his *Utopia* (1516), and the cry was taken up two and a half centuries later by Rousseau, William Godwin (*Enquiry Concerning Political Justice*, 1793), and Babeuf.

3. The great socialist leaders of the nineteenth century came largely from the middle and upper classes. The workers themselves were generally aloof to the ideas of these men prior to 1860.

B. The utopian socialists

1. Claude Henri de Saint-Simon (1760–1825)

a. This French nobleman believed that the men of industry, science, and the arts should be the leaders of society.

b. Although Saint-Simon was deeply concerned with the welfare of his fellow humans, he believed that man should be employed where his ability could be utilized the best. Rewards were to be in proportion to his performance. Saint-Simon had no time for the lazy or idle rich.

c. His plans for a very mild form of socialism appear in *L'Industrie* and *Nouveau Christianisme*. Among his more important disciples was Emperor Napoleon III.

2. Charles Fourier (1772–1837)

   a. This utopian socialist had a basic dislike of the competition, greed, and deceit he saw in the world of commerce. Harmony and cooperation seemed more important, and he resolved to set up ideal communities called "phalanxes."

   b. Each phalanx was to contain about 1620 people and have one square league of ground. The people could live communally, that is, in one large building. In this way their desire for companionship would be met.

   c. Since Fourier believed that humans were guided by the law of "passionate attraction," he tried to take into account the passions that motivated people: sex, companionship, food, etc. The desire for companionship was met by living in one large building. To satisfy the human need for sex, Fourier decided to abolish marriage. In the popular mind this tended to discredit utopian socialism, since it soon became identified with free love.

   d. Fourier insisted that all members of the phalanx work. Work was made as pleasant as possible, and unpleasant jobs carried greater rewards. People could go to work to the strains of music, and could obtain sparkling wine and pastry when they so desired. Dirty and unattractive work would be done by hordes of children who would kill vermin, repair roads, work in slaughterhouses, and attend animals.

   e. Fourierist communities were started in New Jersey, Wisconsin, and Massachusetts in the 1840's, but they failed. Nevertheless, Fourier's ideas received a great deal of attention in France and Russia. Even in the United States Emerson, Greeley, Lowell, Hawthorne, and Albert Brisbane were attracted.

3. Robert Owen (1771–1858)
   a. This English industrialist was the father of English socialism. After amassing a fortune, Owen and some partners developed a model industrial community at New Lanark, Scotland. Despite the success of New Lanark, Owen's partners complained because the many services he provided cut profits.
   b. Owen now turned to small rural communities of a cooperative nature. His experiment at New Harmony, Indiana failed (1826–1828), however.
   c. Despite this failure, Owen took up the fight for remedial factory legislation in Parliament. His socialistic ideas inspired a later generation of leaders in Great Britain.

C. Christian socialism
   1. Among the more important leaders were Charles Kingsley (1819–1875) and Frederick Maurice (1805–1872).
   2. These men hoped that working men and the church could together combat the evils of industrial society. The failure of Chartism in 1848 saw the movement spread in England.
   3. In addition to the publication of many periodicals, associations of workers were promoted. The producer cooperatives they sponsored failed, however.
   4. The traditions of English Christian socialism were carried on by the Fabian Society later in the nineteenth century. In the main, these traditions centered around an attack on materialism, and the belief that Christian love was preferable to competition and exploitation.

D. Communism
   1. The appearance of Karl Marx (1818–1883) and Friedrich Engels (1820–1895) added a new element to the peaceful and evolutionary types of socialism that had been proposed prior to 1848. This new ingredient was the prediction that social betterment could only occur through a violent revolution of the working class.
   2. The dogmatic Marx saw in history a rhythm, a pattern which would explain the future.
   a. The existing history of mankind was a series of class

struggles between exploiters and exploited. In ancient Rome this struggle involved the patricians and plebeians; in the Middle Ages it existed between the nobility and the serfs. Marx believed that a class struggle was now taking place in the modern industrial world, the world of capitalism. This combat was between the owners of industry (bourgeoisie) and the propertyless workers (proletariat).

b. Marx believed that all changes in history were due to economic causes. In pushing this concept of economic determinism, he argued that all institutions and human endeavor had an economic basis. Marx' view of history could, therefore, be regarded as materialist.

c. Marx indicated that in the ensuing struggle between the proletariat and bourgeoisie, the former would win. He regarded the ultimate victory of communism as historically inevitable.

d. Marx stated that the victory of the working class would lead to the temporary dictatorship of the proletariat. After a period of time, a classless society would emerge in which all would labor according to their abilities and be compensated in accordance with their needs. The means of production would be controlled by the state.

3. These Marxian concepts were dogmatically formulated in the *Communist Manifesto* (1848).

a. Among the many sources which Marx tapped was the philosophy of Hegel. He appropriated the Hegelian dialectic of thesis, antithesis, and synthesis for his explanation of the class struggle during different stages of history.

b. Surprisingly enough, even Adam Smith influenced Marxian philosophy. Smith's labor theory of value suggested that the worth of an item was equivalent to the labor expended to produce it.

c. David Ricardo's "iron law of wages" helped convince Marx that a worker could never rise above a subsistence income in a capitalist economy.

4. In *Das Kapital* (1867) Marx formulated his concept of surplus value.

a. This theory is based on the tenet that the value of an article is in direct proportion to the labor needed to make it. Thus, according to Marx, the worker alone creates the total value of a given item.

b. Marx went on to say that the worker received only a portion of the price for which the article was sold. The rest was surplus value, the amount taken by the entrepreneur as profit. In this way the bourgeoisie was exploiting the proletariat, while the worker was unable to purchase many of the things he produced.

5. Organized Marxian socialism after 1848

a. In 1864 Marx helped found the First International Workingmen's Association. Marx desired international cooperation among the various worker's parties in order to achieve the goals of socialism.

b. The Geneva conference (1866) produced sentiment for an eight-hour day, while the 1867 session urged that communication and transport industries be nationalized.

c. When Bakunin and his anarchists joined the 1869 meeting grave dissension followed. The anarchists were expelled in 1872.

d. Although the First International may have had as many as 5 million members in its loosely run organization, it had little authority and accomplished nothing. It was abandoned in 1876.

e. In 1889 the Second International was organized. This international combination of Marxian revolutionary parties, gradualist reformers, and trade unionists managed to stay together until 1914.

f. In its many congresses from Brussels (1891) to Basle in 1912 the Second International remained a collection of national parties. It was split by several key questions: (1) Should socialists accept cabinet posts alongside members of nonsocialist parties? (2) What policy should socialists follow if their country became involved in war? Despite the objection of Jean Jaurès, many socialists cooperated politically with nonsocialists. The second question was never resolved, although an inocuous general statement was issued at the 1907 Stuttgart congress.

IX. Other Responses to Industrialization

A. <u>Anarchism</u>
  1. Anarchists believed that all forms of government were oppressive. They were not satisfied with the Marxian promise that the state would eventually disappear. To achieve this end at once they resorted to the assassination of many public figures, a policy that achieved nil.
  2. Perhaps the best known anarchist was <u>Mikhail Bakunin (1814–1876)</u>. He urged that all existing institutions be abolished, and each man be allowed to act without restraint. All forms of authority had to be abolished at once.
  3. <u>Pierre Joseph Proudhon (1809–1865)</u>
      a. In his book *What is Property?* (1840) Proudhon stated that private property was "theft." In addition, he wished to put an end to all government.
      b. No form of authority over man was the ideal he pursued.
      c. Proudhon was particularly incensed over the charging of interest. He disliked the accumulation of wealth and property unless it was gained by work. His ideal was the formation of a People's Bank where all could secure credit. In this way, the workers could raise their incomes and eventually join the bourgeoisie.
      d. This new society would be based on associations of producers which would somewhat resemble the producer cooperatives of today. Political control would be vested in a loose union of these associations.

B. <u>Syndicalism</u>
  1. Although syndicalism had no single recognized leader, its foremost spokesman was <u>Georges Sorel (1847–1922).</u>
  2. In the *Reflections on Violence* (1908) Sorel urged a campaign of violence on the workers: sabotage and strikes backed by force were emphasized.
  3. Sorel believed that a violent general strike of all workers was the ultimate revolutionary weapon.

BIBLIOGRAPHY

Ashton, T. S., *The Industrial Revolution, 1760–1830* (New York: Oxford University Press, 1948).

Berlin, I., *Karl Marx: his life and environment* (2nd ed., New York: Oxford University Press, 1948).

Bowden, W., *Industrial society in England towards the end of the eighteenth century* (New York: Macmillan, 1925).

Bowden, W., Karpovich, M. and Usher, A. P., *An economic history of Europe since 1750* (New York: American, 1937).

Carr-Saunders, Alexander, *World populations past growth and present trends* (New York: Oxford University Press, 1937).

Clapham, J., *An economic history of modern Britain,* 3 vols. (2nd ed., Cambridge: Cambridge University Press, 1930–1938).

Clapham, J., *The economic development of France and Germany, 1815–1914* (Cambridge: Cambridge University Press, 1936).

Dietz, Frederick, *The Industrial Revolution* (New York: Holt, 1927).

Dunham, A. L., *The Industrial Revolution in France, 1815–1848* (New York: Exposition Press, 1955).

Heaton, H., *Economic history of Europe* (Rev. ed., New York: Harper, 1948).

Knowles, Lillian C., *Economic development in the nineteenth century* (London: Routledge, 1932).

Mantoux, P., *The Industrial Revolution in the 18th century* (Rev. ed., New York: Harcourt, Brace, 1929).

Manuel, Frank E., *The new world of Henri Saint-Simon* (Cambridge: Harvard University Press, 1956).

Podmore, F., *Robert Owen, a biography* (New York: Appleton, 1924).

Redford, Arthur, *The economic history of England, 1760–1830* (New York: Longmans, 1931).

Schwarzchild, L., *The Red Prussian: the life and legend of Karl Marx* (New York: Scribner's, 1947).

Sée, Henri E., *Economic and social conditions in France during the eighteenth century* (New York: Knopf, 1927).

Toynbee, Arnold, *The Industrial Revolution* (Boston: Beacon Press, 1957).

Chapter 8

SCIENCE, THOUGHT, AND ART IN THE NINETEENTH CENTURY

I. The Romantic Era

A. <u>Romanticism</u>
   1. The Romantic movement had its roots in the latter part of the eighteenth century, but it reached the zenith of acceptance between 1800 and 1850. In the musical world it remained a powerful force during the entire nineteenth century.
   2. <u>Romanticism was a revolutionary reaction against the classicism of the preceding century.</u> Classicism had been inspired by the culture of Greece and Rome: this could be seen in the buildings, sculpture, ideas, and art of eighteenth century. In addition, the men of the Enlightenment had placed great faith in reason as an instrument of human improvement.
   3. <u>The romantics believed that the classicists had neglected the emotional and the sentimental.</u> Too much emphasis had been placed on cold reason. In addition, the romantics rebelled against the simplicity and starkness of classical culture. They looked for beauty in nature, and often found a stimulus in the medieval past. Many romantics found a source of inspiration in the liberal revolutions of the nineteenth century, while others sought solace in a utopian future. In essence, romanticism was a rebellion against authority and rules.

B. <u>Science</u>
   1. <u>Louis J. Daguerre (1789–1851)</u>
      a. In 1839 this Frenchman managed to produce the first photograph in the space of a thirty-minute period. His "daguerreotype" was made by exposing sensitive

chemical plates to sunlight. Within a few years, however, Fox Talbot perfected an instantaneous method
of photography.

2. Michael Faraday (1791–1867)
   a. This British scientist made several significant innova-
      tions in the area of applied science. His study of the
      element carbon was useful to the coal industry, while
      his research on chlorine was of value to the bleaching
      industry. More important was his work in electroly-
      sis. Around 1830 it led to the perfection of the elec-
      troplating process. Faraday had learned how to in-
      duce chemical action by using electrical current.
      Soon thereafter Faraday discovered that electric cur-
      rent could be produced by moving a conductor in an
      electrical field. This basic principle was the founda-
      tion for the development of the first dynamo.

3. John Dalton (1766–1844)
   a. Although the concept that matter was made up of
      tiny particles (or atoms) was one that had been de-
      veloped in antiquity by Leucippus and Democritus,
      Dalton was the first to clearly define the theory. This
      Quaker schoolmaster was able to demonstrate that
      the atoms of one element were distinguishable from
      those of another element because they had different
      relative weights.

4. Charles Lyell (1797–1875)
   a. In his three volume *Principles of Geology* Lyell took
      up the old Hutton thesis that the appearance of the
      earth had been changed over the centuries by such
      natural phenomena as volcanoes, earthquakes, rain,
      frost, and the action of rivers. This challenged the
      Biblical view that the earth had remained unchanged
      since the time of creation.

5. Theodor Schwann (1810–1882)
   a. This anatomy professor formulated the important
      "cell theory" in 1839. Professor Schwann developed
      the concept that all living organisms grow in small
      units called "cells." This concept was modified
      within a decade by physiologists who found that the
      cell could be further subdivided into smaller parts.

6. Jean Baptiste de Lamarck (1744–1829)
   a. This French nobleman shook the entire scientific

world with his *Natural History of Invertebrate Animals*. Lamarck set forth several general laws of evolution, some of which are open to serious question. Lamarck believed that evolution proceeded from simpler to more complicated forms, that a new organ could be added if the need was continually felt. He believed that organs developed in a direct ratio of their use. Considerable debate was generated by Lamarck's belief that new organs acquired by a body were transmitted to the next generation.

7. Johannes Müller (1801–1858)
   a. Professor Müller won early fame for his teaching at the University of Berlin as well as his *Handbook* on human physiology. In his law of specific energies he showed that a definite sensation results when a sensory nerve is stimulated.

8. Claude Bernard (1813–1878)
   a. This great physiologist at the Sorbonne was responsible for the discovery of the vaso-motor system. He did considerable work on the problem of digestive processes, particularly on internal secretions and glands.

9. Christian Thomsen (1788–1865)
   a. This Danish investigator laid the foundation for the study of the prehistoric era. He suggested the idea that early men may have lived in different stages: stone, bronze, and iron.

C. Philosophy
   1. Georg W. F. Hegel (1770–1831)
      a. Hegel taught at the universities of Jena, Heidelberg and Berlin. It was during his sojourn at Berlin (1818–1831) that he won an esteemed position in the intellectual world.
      b. Hegel believed that a given idea (thesis) held sway only until it was effectively challenged by a new proposition (antithesis). From the clash emerged a third concept (synthesis) which was somewhat closer to the truth than the initial two ideas. This new idea would cause the dialectic to start afresh until a new triad was completed. The dialectical process formulated by Hegel was to continue indefinitely.
      c. Hegel argued that there were three general stages

of human development: the "oriental" (only the ruler is free), the "classical" (only the nobility have freedom), and "German" where ordinary man is liberated "as man." He regarded the Germans of the nineteenth century as a people chosen to lead the world. His ideas in this direction helped to inspire a generation of nationalists who sought German unification.

d. Unfortunately, this concept of German superiority plus his deification of the state left a legacy that was fully exploited by the Nazi regime after 1933. It might also be noted that Hegel paid little heed to individual rights. He believed that each person was obliged to serve the state and obey the laws.

e. Aside from his contribution to political conservatism, Hegel helped provide the philosophical basis for Marxism through his dialectic.

2. Auguste Comte (1798–1857)

a. This French social reformer was associated with Saint-Simon from 1818 to 1824. Comte believed that society had a powerful effect on the individual, and that his main objective must therefore be the reorganization of society.

b. He believed that societies had laws, and coined the term "sociology" to denote such concepts.

c. His Law of the Three Stages stated that society had gone through a theological, metaphysical, and positivist stage. During the theological stage man looked to the supernatural for explanations. In the second stage metaphysical ideas sufficed, while in the third stage (the positive) only scientific explanations would do. Positivism was the only way to achieve harmony among nations and individuals.

D. Literature

1. Poetry

a. Romantic poetry in England reached the peak of its development under a succession of brilliant versifiers. One of the best known was William Wordsworth (1770–1850) whose forthright passion for freedom and pantheism can be seen in "The Prelude" and "Tintern Abbey." Samuel Taylor Coleridge (1772–1834) received acclaim for his "Ancient Mariner" and

"Kubla Khan," while Lord Byron (1788–1824) won plaudits for "Childe Harold's Pilgrimage" and his battle for Greek independence. Even more rebellious in his contempt for traditional ideas and conformity was Percy Bysshe Shelley (1792–1822). His hopes for equality and freedom were passionately expressed in "Prometheus Unbound." Still another important poem by Shelley was his "Adonais," a contribution written to express his deep sorrow over the death of his friend and fellow poet Keats. John Keats (1795–1821) made a lasting mark on the world of letters because of the imagery and beauty of the "Eve of St. Agnes" and "Endymion." The "Ode on a Grecian Urn" is still another example of Keats' acceptance of beauty as a standard in itself. Alfred Tennyson (1809–1892) won acclaim for such poems as "Locksley Hall" and "Morte d' Arthur" in which he questioned the materialism of the industrial society and suggested a new and more mystical faith. *In Memoriam* (1850) indicated his steadfast devotion to the idea of immortality. Robert Browning (1812–1889) excelled in his use of the dramatic monologue, particularly in "Fra Lippo Lippi" and "Andrea del Sarto." His greatest work was *The Ring and the Book*. Matthew Arnold (1822–1888) best exemplified the romantic pessimism of nineteenth century poetry in his "Dover Beach" and "Isolation: To Marguerite."

b. One of the outstanding figures of romantic poetry in France was the brilliant but pessimistic Charles Baudelaire (1821–1867). His only poetic contribution was *Les Fleurs du Mal*. Victor Hugo (1802–1885) was probably the greatest French poet of his time. His imagery and color can be seen in such great lyric poems as "Les Orientales," "Les Voix Interieures," and "Les Contemplations."

c. German romantic poetry produced the great Heinrich Heine (1797–1856) and Johann Wolfgang von Goethe (1749–1832). Heine was best known for his liberalism and revolutionary ideals, although he was capable of the bitterest satire. His *Buch der Lieder* brought him initial fame, as did his later *Neue Gedichte*. Schumann and Schubert set many of his *lieder* to music. Goethe made his greatest poetic contribution in *Faust,* a verse drama on a pact between a man of letters and the devil. This man of diverse intellectual attainments made Weimar the temporary literary hub of Germany.

d. Adam Mickiewicz (1798–1855) was the greatest Polish poet of the romantic era. His *Sir Thaddeus* and *The Ancestors* called on all Poles to enlist in the national cause, and Mickiewicz himself participated in several revolts against the Russians.

e. Alexander Pushkin (1799–1837) was the leading Russian poet of the period. Under the influence of Byron, a torrent of poetry which raised hopes for liberty came from Pushkin's pen: *The Gypsies, Poltava,* and *The Bronze Horseman.* His greatest work was *Eugen Onegin,* a masterpiece that depicted the life of the Russian gentry and also pleaded for freedom.

f. Edgar Allan Poe (1809–1849) was one of the great men of American letters during the first half of the nineteenth century. In addition to his short stories and newspaper work, Poe's rhythmic and melancholic poetry marked him as a literary great. His best known poems were "Israfel," "The Raven," "The Bells," "Ulalume," and "Annabel Lee." Nathaniel Hawthorne (1804–1864) and Herman Melville (1819–1891) were better known for their bizarre novels and short stories, while William Cullen Bryant (1794–1878) produced such beautiful nature poetry as "To the Fringed Gentian" and "The Death of the Flowers." Walt Whitman (1819–1892) won fame for his free-verse poetry, particularly *Leaves of Grass, Drum Taps,* and "When Lilacs Last in the Dooryard Bloom'd."

2. Drama

a. French playwrights such as Victor Hugo dominated the stage of early half of the nineteenth century. His romantic *Hernani* caused a storm among the classicist critics. Eugene Scribe (1791–1861) depicted the life of the new bourgeoisie and mirrored liberal thought in various comedies. He also wrote librettos for Verdi, Meyerbeer, and Auber. The dominant figure among German playwrights was the Austrian dramatist <u>Franz Grillparzer (1791–1872)</u>. Among his better known plays were *Die Ahnfrau* and the romantic *Der Traum: ein Leben*.

3. Romantic novelists

    a. <u>Sir Walter Scott (1771–1832)</u> chose to extol the colorful and exciting past of medieval England in *Ivanhoe* and *Kenilworth*. His *Waverly Novels* also helped to create a great interest in the folk traditions, chronicles, and tales of the Middle Ages. <u>Charles Dickens (1812–1870)</u>, on the other hand, preferred to depict the wretched condition of the poorer people of nineteenth century England. His portrait of the newly-industrialized England plus his demands for change in education and the courts helped provide ammunition for the forces of liberalism. Dickens is best known for such novels as *Oliver Twist, A Tale of Two Cities,* and *Bleak House*.

    b. In France <u>Victor Hugo</u> seemed to share Sir Walter Scott's enthusiasm for the medieval past in his great novel, *Notre Dame de Paris*. Hugo's *Les Miserables* dealt with the more contemporary problems of ordinary citizens. <u>Alexandre Dumas (1802–1870)</u> also harked back to the Middle Ages in *Le Tour de Nesle,* but won much wider acclaim for *The Three Musketeers* and *The Count of Monte Cristo*. <u>Honoré de Balzac (1799–1850)</u> won fame for his ability to portray the individual. His *Human Comedy* poked fun at the foibles of the French middle class, but he is equally well-known for *Pére Goriot* and *Eugénie Grandet*.

    c. <u>Alessandro Manzoni (1785–1873)</u>, under the influence of Scott, turned to the medieval world of sixteenth century Milan for the theme of *I Promessi Sposi (The Betrothed)*. The theme ostensibly dealt with Spanish oppression in medieval Italy, but was designed to rouse Italy against the heavy hand of Austrian domination in the nineteenth century.

    d. <u>Nikolai Gogol (1809–1852)</u> was not only a great novelist, but a fine playwright and writer of short stories. He won fame with romantic Cossack tales such as *Mirgorod* (particularly the part called "Taras Bulba"). His later novels were the more realistic *The Overcoat* (on the poorer folk of St. Petersburg) and *Dead Souls,* a tale of peasant misery in Russia. It might be noted that his later trend toward realism foreshadowed a turning point for Russian literature as a whole.

e. Washington Irving (1783–1859) made himself the outstanding figure of American letters by publishing "Rip Van Winkle" and "The Legend of Sleepy Hollow." His interest in the American West led to *A Tour of the Prairies* and *Astoria*. James Fenimore Cooper (1789–1851) won initial fame for a novel on the American Revolution, *The Spy*. Cooper's novels of the sea and the American frontier proved to be his most popular. Among these was *The Last of the Mohicans*. Henry Thoreau (1817–1862), one of the great transcendentalists, sought a life of individual independence and depicted his existence in *Walden*. His essay on "Civil Disobedience" also attracted considerable attention.

E. Art

1. The romantic tradition in art differed sharply with the classicist concepts of orderliness and exact draftsmanship. The revolutionary heroes of Jacques David (1748–1825) yielded to an emphasis on color, emotion, and imagination. There emerged several great romantic artists on both sides of the English Channel: Turner, Constable, Delacroix, and Corot.

2. The nature painting of Turner and Constable

    a. John Constable (1776–1837) was one of the most popular painters of his time. His portrayal of the English countryside won him fame, particularly "Dedham Vale" and "Salisbury Cathedral."

    b. J. M. W. Turner (1775–1851) also achieved considerable fame as a landscape painter. His work in water color was outstanding. Turner's use of beautiful color and light can be seen in his paintings of Venice, medieval Scotland, ancient Carthage, sunsets, rivers, and sea scenes. Among his more famous paintings are "Calais Pier," "The Fighting Téméraire," and "Approach to Venice."

3. Ferdinand Delacroix (1798–1863)

    a. Under the influence of Constable, Delacroix became the leader of the romantic school in France. With the exhibition of one of the earliest paintings, "Dante and Vergil," Delacroix soon showed his ability to use vivid color and depict individual passions and sentiments. His subjects were more often drawn from history than nature. "The Entry of the Crusaders into Constantinople" and "The Massacre of Scio" are two representative works of this type.

4. The Barbizon (Fontainebleau) school

a. This school of French painters took its name from the village of Barbizon which was located near the forest of Fontainebleau. The painters of this school emphasized a rather direct portrayal of nature, and probably paved the way for the later impressionistic and realistic schools.

b. Among the more important painters of this school are Theodore Rousseau (1812–1867), J. B. C. Corot (1796–1875), and Jean F. Millet (1814–1875). Millet also painted several scenes of peasants at work, a fact that caused him to be associated with Courbet and Daumier as another social realist.

5. Honoré Daumier (1808–1879)

a. Daumier excelled as a cartoonist, lithographer, and painter. His 4,000 cartoons (in lithographic form) found their way into such journals as *Caricature* and *Charivari*. Daumier was imprisoned for a political cartoon ("Gargantua") in 1832. He found time to complete some 200 fine canvasses, among them "The Republic" and "Don Quixote."

F. Architecture

1. Romantic architecture did not exhibit the same spirit of change and innovation to be found in both literature and music. Classical forms retained their vogue in the architectural world of the nineteenth century. These concessions to the architecture of ancient Greece and Rome can be seen in the public structures of the United States and the buildings of Second Empire France. The new public structures that housed the romantic spirit of nineteenth century nationalism were, therefore, buildings of a more orderly and disciplined classical era.

2. By 1830 the classical dominance was briefly challenged by a "Gothic revival" in Great Britain and France. As in the literature of Hugo and Scott, architects sought inspiration in the pointed arches and pinnacles of the

medieval past. Sir Charles Barry's work in rebuilding the palace at Westminster was one of the best examples of the "Gothic revival" in England. In France a major achievement of the Gothic school was the restoration of the Notre Dame cathedral in Paris by Viollet-le-Duc.

3. In Italy a "primitive classical" school harked back to the architectural styles of the Renaissance. The revival of this "Italian style" soon spread into Germany, England, and Austria.

G. Music

1. The sentimental and melancholy music of the romantic era was a distinctive change from the precision and regularity of the classical era. Ludwig von Beethoven (1770–1827) best represented this change from classicism to romanticism. His emotional and dynamic music shocked many critics of his time, but he succeeded in breaking away from the musical formalism of the eighteenth century by employing a larger orchestra and new harmonies. Like many other romantic composers, Beethoven was influenced by the nationalistic movements of his time. His *Fifth Symphony* (1809) was a tribute to emerging German national movement.

2. The music of this era thus took on a national tone. This was particularly true of the music of Richard Wagner (1813–1883) as exemplified by his *Ring Cycle.* Like the writers of this period, Wagner derived his material from the folk tales and literature of medieval Germany. The leading figure in the world of Italian opera was Giuseppe Verdi (1813–1901). Like Wagner, he was a devoted nationalist. His *Requiem* in honor of Manzoni typifies this trend, although he is better known for such great operas as *Il Trovatore, La Traviata,* and *Aïda.*

3. Another trend in the romantic music of the nineteenth was composition of many beautiful *lieder* (songs) by Franz Schubert (1797–1828), Robert Schumann (1810–1856) and Johannes Brahms (1833–1897). This solo song had a piano accompaniment of equal importance. Many *lieder* were inspired by such contemporary poets as Heine.

4. The more popular light opera of Auber, Meyerbeer, and Offenbach won the plaudits of the emerging middle classes. Light themes, scenic beauty, and witty situations

characterized these productions, although *Masaniello* by Auber helped precipitate the Belgian revolution of 1830.

5. The romantics did important work in reviving or re-interpreting many of the forgotten works of the past. Felix Mendelssohn's (1809–1847) performance of the *St. Matthew Passion* in 1829 started a great Bach revival in Germany.

6. Some of the great virtuosos of the era were also outstanding composers. Particularly important in this dual capacity were Frédéric Chopin (1810–1849), Franz Liszt (1811–1886) and Niccolo Paganini (1782–1840).

II. The Age of Realism

A. During the first half of the nineteenth century the romantics had held public attention with their emphasis on feeling, emotion, and instinct. Despite the vogue of romanticism, classicism persisted in the arts. After 1850, however, men began to look away from the ancient models and rationalism of the classicists. They also questioned the emotional basis of romanticism with its emphasis on medieval models. The new industrial society looked for a new explanation of man and his surroundings. This it found in realism, the identification of truth with that which could be readily observed in the contemporary world.

B. Science
 1. Charles Darwin (1809–1882)
   a. Three major influences helped point Darwin in the direction of a new theory of biological evolution. Darwin was greatly influenced by a five year voyage to the South Seas and the South American littoral. His observation of many living creatures led him to consider the possibility that differences in environment might cause variations in a given species. Lyell's *Principles of Geology* also had a profound influence on Darwin. Darwin was very impressed by Lyell's thesis that changes in the earth's crust might be due to the action of natural processes (floods, earthquakes, volcanoes). Was there, then, a possibility that nature held the secret of biological evolution? Darwin was also interested in Malthus *Essay on Population*, a tract which claimed that human population is related to a

struggle for existence. Did Malthus' concept offer a basic explanation for biological evolution which could also explain the variation of species?

b. These thoughts were best expressed in *Origin of Species* (1859) and the *Descent of Man* (1871). In these volumes Darwin stressed the idea that the existing species were not fixed eternally by some divine force. They were, Darwin argued, different because of the influence of their environment over the centuries.

c. Darwin believed in the concept of "natural selection." He argued that the fittest of each species survived because these particular speciments deviated from the normal in such a way as to give them a special advantage in the battle for survival. Such differences occurred in each succeeding generation until an entirely new species evolved.

d. Outside the field of science, Darwinism found its champions also. The rising business moguls saw in Darwinism a justification for keen competition, while nationalists won solace for their tough diplomacy.

2. Gregor Mendel (1822–1884)

a. This Augustinian monk did considerable research in hybridization. His results modified Darwin's concept of "natural selection."

b. Mendel's experiments led him to conclude that separate characteristics are inherited independently of each other. Mendel also learned that within each reproductive cell some factors were dominant while others were recessive.

3. Dmitri Mendeleev (1834–1907)

a. This great Russian chemist first formulated the "periodic law." Mendeleev classified the known elements in the order of their atomic weights. From the gaps in his table he predicted the discovery of elements not as yet found.

4. Joseph Lister (1827–1912)

a. While professor of surgery at Glasgow, Lister began to experiment with the idea that carbolic acid might help end many of the infections which accompanied operations. His work in bacteriology and the introduction of carbolized catgut were significant contributions to aseptic surgery.

5. Louis Pasteur (1822–1895)
   a. Pasteur's work with bacteria demolished the old theory of spontaneous generation. His work with wine and vinegar led to the process we now call pasteurization.

6. Sigmund Freud (1856–1939)
   a. The great contribution of this Austrian psychiatrist was his pioneering work in the field of psychoanalysis. In work with Josef Breuer considerable study was devoted to the use of hypnosis in the treatment of hysteria.
   b. Freud noted that many problems of his mentally ill patients were traceable to serious difficulties very early in life. Treatment consisted of helping the patient recall and then discuss these traumatic problems while under hypnosis. In effect, this would be a catharsis.
   c. Freud traced many of the problems of the mentally ill to early difficulties in life that had a sexual basis. He also dropped hypnosis and replaced it with the free association of ideas technique. This, he hoped, would help the patient consciously recognize many things in his unconscious.
   d. Freud's emphasis on infant sexuality and the Oedipus complex caused a break with Jung and Adler.

C. Philosophy
   1. The second half of the nineteenth century was an era which extolled materialism and science. Fewer men concerned themselves about the world of the spirit. The new world of applied science demanded an emphasis on the factual and the pragmatic. It promised a new era of prosperity and comfort on earth. Few advocates of spiritual universe could be heard above the throng of pragmatists, positivists, and scientists.

   2. Friedrich W. Nietzsche (1844–1900)
      a. Nietzsche vaulted in prominence with the publication of *Thus Spake Zarathustra*. In this philosophic poem the traditional morality of the Judaic-Christian past was rejected as the code of the weak. Nietzsche preferred the irrational philosophy of the *Übermensch*

(superman) in which only the strong would survive. This philosophy of force undoubtedly had Darwinian overtones, and had a strong influence on the German racists as well as Hitler and Mussolini.

3. Arthur Schopenhauer (1788–1860)
   a. Another advocate of pessimistic realism was Schopenhauer. He won fame for his tome entitled *The World as Will and Idea*. Schopenhauer, also a good Darwinian, saw the world as a battleground of wills. As the actions of an individual failed to meet the demands of his will, the only escape appeared to be in a Buddhist renunciation of this world, a world of unsatisfied desire.

4. Henri Bergson (1859–1941)
   a. Bergson believed that human activity was dominated by a vital spirit *(élan vital)*. Although this was a break with the rationalism of the eighteenth century, Bergson was not far removed from Schopenhauer's belief in the dominance of the will over reason. His philosophy must be viewed as still another manifestation of irrationalism.

5. The pragmatism of William James (1842–1910) and John Dewey (1859–1952)
   a. Both Dewey and James rejected the possibility that absolute truths might exist. The truth was what was applicable to a given situation. The true test of anything was how it worked out in a practical situation. This utilitarian philosophy was called pragmatism, although Dewey's particular contribution has often been termed instrumentalism.

D. Literature
   1. Realism and naturalism
      a. The accent on realism which characterized the last half of the nineteenth century had stressed the observable, the practical, and the material. The new realistic literature emphasized the psychological approach to the individual, and the study of social and family problems. What was the proper relationship of the individual to his traditional background and the accepted ethics and mores of society? Should women be placed on an equal footing with men? How could the condition of the worker be improved?

All these questions were treated in the realistic literature after 1850.

b. Emanating from the realistic literature of this era was a new trend that might be termed naturalism. As exemplified by Zola, this school felt that realism was insufficiently realistic. To reflect the contemporary scene was not quite enough: one had to do this, of course, but it had to be supplemented by an explanation of how things came to be and what they might be in the future.

2. Poetry
   a. Charles Péguy (1873–1914) was both a distinguished poet and writer. His religiosity caused him to infuse a spiritual meaning in his poetry and prose. Best known of his poems is *Le Mystère de la charité de Jeanne d'Arc*, an exposition on a personal symbol of greatness.
   b. Stéphane Mallarmé (1842–1898) was the founder of the French symbolist school. His obscure poetry suggested sound and color, and presented the haunting ideas of another world. Later in life he abandoned punctuation. His *Après-midi d'un faune* won him fame and inspired the composer Debussy.
   c. Paul Verlaine (1844–1896) was probably the greatest "decadent" of the *fin de siècle* French school. His later conversion to Catholicism injected a religious tone into his mystical and symbolist poetry. Verlaine is known for his *Sagesse, Romances sans paroles, Jadis et Naguère,* and *Parallèlement*.
   d. English poetry of this era was represented by Algernon Swinburne (1837–1909). Swinburne could be considered the English counterpart of the "decadent" French symbolists. His *Poems and Ballads* marked a sharp departure from the usual Victorian poetry because of their impressionism, pessimism, and sensuality. In his *Songs before Sunrise* Swinburne showed the same stripe of intellectual revolt exhibited earlier by Byron: this time the attack went forth against Christianity (like Nietzsche) and traditional morality.

3. Drama
   a. The Norwegian realist Henrik Ibsen (1828–1906) won acclaim for a series of social dramas in which he pro-

claimed his personal set of values. Ibsen was particularly interested in the individual's conflict with society. Among his better known plays were *Brand, Peer Gynt, A Doll's House, Ghosts,* and *An Enemy of the People.*

b. <u>August Strindberg (1849–1912)</u>, a Swedish playwright, originally won fame for a naturalistic novel entitled *The Red Room.* His seventy dramas reflect mysticism and naturalism as well as his three very unhappy marriages. Among his better known plays are *The Father, Julie,* and *After the Fire.*

c. <u>Anton Chekhov (1860–1904)</u> won fame for his excellent short stories as well as his plays. His pessimistic realism showed the stagnation of Russian life as well as its dullness and frustration. His better known plays were *Ivanov, The Sea Gull, Uncle Vanya,* and *The Cherry Orchard.*

d. <u>George Bernard Shaw (1856–1950)</u> won fame as a novelist, music critic, socialist, and dramatic critic before turning to the stage. Under the influence of Ibsen, Shaw's realism took in such diverse subjects as prostitution *(Mrs. Warren's Profession),* pacifism *(Heartbreak House),* the Salvation Army *(Major Barbara),* and dramatic critics *(Fanny's First Play).* Shaw's *Devil's Disciple* used the American Revolution as its theme, while *Caesar and Cleopatra* turned to a phase of ancient history for its background. Among his other well-known plays were *Arms and the Man, Pygmalion,* and *Saint Joan.*

4. The novel

a. <u>Gustave Flaubert (1821–1880)</u> won fame as a realistic novelist for his great *Madame Bovary.* Despite the moral uproar that this novel of marital infidelity caused, Flaubert's fame grew. His later novels included *Salammbô* and *The Temptation of St. Anthony.* Alphonse Daudet (1840–1897) also specialized in realistic tales of love-affairs, but often lapsed into romantic stories such as *Tartarin of Tarascon.* Guy de Maupassant (1850–1893) was the master of the short story before he lost his sanity. His 300 short stories and novels are excellent examples of psychological realism. Among his better short stories are

"Boule de Suif" and "L'Héritage." Émile Zola (1840–1902) was both a journalist and a novelist. His republican inclinations even caused him to play a considerable role in the Dreyfus case. Zola's passion for the naturalistic novel compelled him to depict life exactly as it was. Scientific accuracy and precise description made his novels complete but burdensome with detail. Zola's series of twenty novels (*Les Rougon-Macquart*) show the decline of a family because of drink, illness, and degeneracy. *Nana, Germinal,* and *L'Assommoir* are the best known individual novels in this series. The last of the important French novelists of this era was Anatole France (1844–1924). His scepticism and cleverness was coupled with frontal assaults on religion and politics. This nineteenth century Voltaire was best known for such novels as *The Crime of Sylvestre Bonnard, Thaïs, The Gods Thirst, Penguin Island,* and *The Revolt of the Angels.*

b. Among the great Russian novelists of the nineteenth century was Ivan Turgenev (1818–1883). His best novels were written in the decade after 1850 and included *Rudin* and *On the Eve.* In *Fathers and Sons* (1862), Turgenev's greatest work, the growing sentiment for revolution was portrayed. In his *Sportsman's Sketches* he dealt the dying institution of serfdom a serious blow. Fedor Dostoievsky (1821–1881) made his reputation as a writer of short stories and novels. He was also something of a journalist and a socialist revolutionary. Troubled with family difficulties, a prison sentence in Siberia, epilepsy, and an addiction to gambling, Dostoievsky nevertheless wrote a long list of fine novels in which his understanding of poverty, evil, and other human problems was evident. Leo Tolstoi (1828–1910) was a Russian noble who spent his life as a writer-philosopher. His *War and Peace* was a powerful advocacy of pacifism. Mysticism crept into his later and more realistic novels, particularly *The Kreutzer Sonata.* Maxim Gorky (1868–1936) won fame as a social realist through his novels, short stories, and plays. He dealt with such problems as slums, tramps, and the middle class in his literary works. His better novels include *Foma Gordeyev, Mother,* and *The Confession.*

c. <u>George Meredith (1828–1909)</u> was one of the more important English realists of this period. His clipped style of writing prevented recognition until *Diana of the Crossways* was published. Such psychological novels as the *Ordeal of Richard Feverel* also won acclaim. Thomas Hardy (1840–1928) preferred to write about the problems of village life in Wessex. Among the better known novels of this period were *The Return of the Native, The Mayor of Casterbridge,* and *Tess of the D'Urbervilles.* When some of these novels were denounced as indecent, Hardy temporarily turned to poetry.

d. <u>H. G. Wells (1866–1946)</u> was one of the first novelists to deal with topics that we now call science fiction. These included *The Time Machine, The Island of Dr. Moreau,* and *The Invisible Man.* His witty and realistic novels on the current scene were used to convey his social ideas. Among the best of these were *Kipps, Tono Bungay, The History of Mr. Polly,* and *Joan and Peter.* His later novels included the prophetic *World Brain* and *Mind at the End of Its Tether.*

e. <u>Rudyard Kipling (1865–1936)</u> was more of a romantic than a realist in his novels, short stories, and poetry. His interpretation of India and the "enlightening" role of British rule can be seen in such poems as "Gunga Din" and "The White Man's Burden." Some of his better known novels of the jungle and the sea included *The Jungle Book, Kim,* and *Captains Courageous.*

f. <u>Thomas Mann (1875–1955)</u> was the greatest German novelist of the twentieth century. He won fame for his great novel *(Buddenbrooks)* on the rise and fall of an important German merchant clan. Mann's preoccupation with problems of the mind can be seen in such later novels as *Tonio Kröger* and *Death in Venice. The Magic Mountain* involved Mann in the complexities of Freudian psychology before he began his Joseph tetralogy in 1926. His later novels included a tale of Indian antiquity *(The Transposed Heads)* and a twentieth century version of the Faust legend (*Dr. Faustus*).

g. <u>William Dean Howells (1837–1920)</u> emerged as one of the great American writers of realistic fiction with *The Rise of Silas Lapham*. He reflected the American scene in *A Modern Instance* and *Indian Summer,* but showed a trace of utopian socialism in *A Traveler from Altruria*. <u>Mark Twain (1835–1910)</u> combined wit and satire in his five novels of boyhood surroundings in Missouri. The best of these novels were *Tom Sawyer* and *Huckleberry Finn*. He also had considerable success with two historical novels: *The Prince and the Pauper* and *A Connecticut Yankee in King Arthur's Court*. Misfortune in later life caused him to pen the pessimistic *The Man That Corrupted Hadleyburg*. <u>Jack London (1876–1916)</u> won fame as a writer of adventure stories of the Klondike and elsewhere. The best known are *Call of the Wild, The Sea-Wolf, White Fang,* and *Martin Eden*. Some of his novels on current social problems (*The People of the Abyss*) also attracted favorable attention. <u>Upton Sinclair (1878–   )</u> devoted the bulk of his novels to the industrial and social problems of his time. Beginning with a critique of the Chicago stockyards (*The Jungle*) in 1906, Sinclair published *King Coal* and *Oil!* within the next two decades. *Boston* was an analysis of the Sacco-Vanzetti trial.

E. <u>Art</u>
   1. <u>Impressionism</u>
      a. This late nineteenth movement in art (and music) was largely centered in France. It was somewhat related to the realistic trend in literature whereby the writer tried to record things with scientific accuracy. The impressionists of Paris sought to depict the initial impression a scene made on them. They attempted to free themselves from subjective influences, and became quite concerned with the effect of light and color. They broke with the traditional reliance on form and opened the way to a new emphasis on motion. The classical emphasis on clarity was largely dropped, and the way was paved for Post-Impressionism.

    b. The leading figure of the Impressionist school was <u>Edouard Manet (1832–1883)</u>. His "Olympia" and "The Music Lesson" are well-known. <u>Edgar Degas (1834–1917)</u> excelled a depicting motion in paintings of ballet dancers, workmen, and jockeys. Pierre <u>Auguste Renoir (1841–1919)</u> did fine work in landscapes, portraits, opera scenes, and pictures of the Seine. His use of light and color to catch a momentary scene was complemented by a greater than usual dependence on solidity. <u>Claude Monet (1840–1926)</u> also used light and color in a suggestive manner to depict cathedrals, cliffs, and Parisian scenes. His "Seine River at Argenteuil" is a good example of the use of brilliant and solid color to achieve a sense of space and depth.

2. <u>Post-Impressionism</u>

    a. This late nineteenth century school was dissatisfied with objective and improvised nature of Impressionistic painting. <u>Paul Cézanne (1839–1906)</u> used brilliant color and greater solidity than the Impressionists in his pictures of card-games, landscapes, and still lifes. Cézanne was able to embody a great deal of personal feeling in these canvasses, and thus pave the way for the later Expressionists.

    b. <u>Paul Gaugin (1848–1903)</u> broke not only with the Impressionist school, but with artistic traditionalism in general. His mastery of color, symbolism, and subjective approach made him a key Post-Impressionist figure.

    c. <u>Vincent Van Gogh (1853–1890)</u> was a great Dutch figure of the Post-Impressionist school. He worked with Gauguin at Arles, France for a period of time. Despite periods of madness, he turned out a large number of extraordinary still lifes, landscapes, and portraits. Vivid color, emotion, and a Japanese influence touched much of his work. Some of his best canvasses were "Sunflowers," "Bedroom at Arles," and "The Starry Night."

3. <u>Expressionism</u>

    a. Van Gogh is often cited as the painter who paved the way for this school. The Expressionists emphasized a subjective approach to art, one in which the accurate representation of nature was subordinated to an emotional and intuitive approach. Even distortion was acceptable to the Expressionists. The Expressionists were sometimes called *les fauves* ("the wild beasts").

b. Henri Matisse (1869–1954) was one of the leading proponents of Fauvism. His sojourns in Morocco inspired many still lifes and interiors. His use of vivid color, sensitive line, and rhythmic form can be seen in "Goldfish and Sculpture," "Girl in Green," "Three Sisters," and "Interior with Violin Case." Another advocate of Fauvism was the talented Georges Rouault (1871–1958). His canvasses of judges, clowns, and the suffering of Jesus show a deep sympathy for human misery and a hatred of injustice.

4. Cubism
   a. This school originated in France around 1910. Among its early devotees were Pablo Picasso, Juan Gris, and Georges Braque. The Cubists attempted to portray what they saw as a three-dimensional geometrical design. Cubism was one of the earliest ventures into abstract art. After World War I futurism, lyricism, and surrealism all came into vogue.

F. Architecture
   1. The Age of Realism continued to exhibit interest in the "Gothic revival" but to a considerably lesser degree after 1870. Some churches and colleges in the United States and Great Britain used the style. It was also incorporated into the Hungarian parliament building in Budapest.
   2. A decorative classicist style was more prevalent, however. Although these classic structures contained newer materials such as concrete, they often showed some Japanese, Gothic, or even Egyptian influences. The Church of the Sacred Heart in the Montmartre section of Paris showed a revival of Byzantine architectural lines.
   3. The late nineteenth and early twentieth centuries saw the development of a new school of architecture. This school of functionalism cut its ties from the romantic, Gothic, and classical past and adapted itself to the new materialistic machine age. The functionalists insisted that the appearance of a building must be related to its

actual use. They also believed that a structure must fit into the environment so that a coordinated whole emerged after the completion of a new edifice.

  a. One of the early European functionalists was Otto Wagner (1841–1918). Wagner designed the Vienna railway station.

  b. The functionalist tradition was continued in Europe by Walter Gropius who established the Bauhaus school at Weimar (later Dessau) in 1919. Ludwig Miës van der Rohe was another leading figure of this school.

G. Music

  1. Despite the emphasis on realism in the latter half of the nineteenth century, romanticism (with a touch of nationalism) continued to prevail.

  a. Perhaps the most outstanding figure of German romanticism was Johannes Brahms (1833–1897). In addition to his four great symphonies, Brahms composed superb chamber music, and the revered Piano Concerto in B Flat plus the Violin Concerto in D. His *Schicksalslied* (Song of Destiny) and many *lieder* (songs) also won wide acclaim.

  2. Charles Gounod (1818–1893) led the way among the French composers of opera. *Faust, Mireille,* and *Romeo and Juliet* are his outstanding operatic works. Georges Bizet (1838–1875) made his greatest contribution to the repertory of opera with the beautifully orchestrated and emotional *Carmen.* Charles Camille Saint-Saens (1835–1921) won plaudits for the beautiful opera *Samson et Dalila.* His Third Symphony and *Danse Macabre* also received critical acclaim. Jules Massenet (1842–1912) added 20 operas to the existing repertory. Among the better works were *Manon* and *Le Jongleur de Notre Dame.*

  3. Anton Dvorák (1841–1904) helped to establish a Czech national school of music. He won fame for his Slavonic Dances. While his operas did not receive acclaim outside his native land, the *New World Symphony* and his *Stabat Mater* brought fame.

  4. Edvard Grieg (1843–1907) used his melodic ability to popularize the folk music of his native Norway. His

beautiful Piano Concerto in A Minor was hailed as was his incidental music for Ibsen's *Peer Gynt*.

5. Nineteenth century Russia produced several outstanding composers. Peter Tschaikovsky (1840–1893) excelled in the melodious Slavic themes. His opera *Eugen Onegin* was based on a folk tale by Pushkin. Tschaikovsky's six symphonies and such ballets as *Swan Lake* and *The Sleeping Beauty* won him world fame. Modeste Moussorgsky (1839–1881) was much more of a nationalistic composer. His great opera *Boris Godunov* was based on a Pushkin play. The unfinished opera *Khovanshchina* and his piano suite *Pictures at an Exhibition* also won acclaim. Nicholas Rimsky-Korsakov (1844–1908) was best known for such operas as *The Snow Maiden, Sadko,* and *Le Coq D'Or*. His *Scheherazade* was most often performed as ballet music.

6. Claude Debussy (1862–1918) was one of the great innovators of this age. Debussy was one of the chief exponents of impressionism in music. He began to toy with unusual technical innovations: new scales and dissonances which could create a special mood. This could be seen in the prelude *"L'Après-midi d'un faune"* ("Afternoon of a Faun"). Another rebel against the prevailing romanticism of his time was Richard Strauss (1864–1949). Turning from romantic *lieder,* he produced the operas *Hero's Life* and *Elektra* plus the great tone poems *Don Juan, Death and Transfiguration* and *Der Rosenkavalier*. Igor Stravinsky (1882–   ) tossed aside melody and startled the musical world by the dissonances of his ballet *Le Sacre du Printemps* (1913). His use of polytonality and dissonant harmonies continued to bewilder the musical world long after 1913. His ballets *The Fire Bird* and *Petrouchka* won fame as did the *Histoire du Soldat* (which was to be read, danced, and played). Arnold Schönberg (1874–1952) also turned from the romantic tradition of Brahms to the use of atonality, the lack of a fixed key. One of the earliest evidences of atonality in Schönberg's work can be seen in the *Kammersymphonie* (1906) and the *Second String Quartet* a year later. In 1914 he developed his famous twelve-tone system which was later used for the first time in *Serenade* (1924).

7. In Italy <u>Giacomo Puccini (1858–1924)</u> replaced Verdi as the leading musical figure. His great operas included *Manon Lescaut, La Bohème, Tosca,* and *Madame Butterfly.* The last exhibited a contemporary emphasis on things Japanese. Puccini's *Girl of the Golden West* turned to America for its inspiration. Melody, romanticism, and a tremendous theatrical sense characterized the operas of Puccini.

BIBLIOGRAPHY

Barzun, Jacques, *Romanticism and the modern ego* (Boston: Little, Brown, 1945).

Brandes, G., *Main currents in nineteenth century literature,* 6 vols. (New York: Boni and Liveright, 1923).

Brinton, Crane, *Nietzsche* (Cambridge, Mass.: Harvard University Press, 1941).

Craven, T., *Modern Art* (New York: Simon and Schuster, 1934).

Faure, E., *History of art,* 5 vols. (New York: Harper, 1921–1930).

Gray, C., *History of music* (New York: Oxford University Press, 1947).

Hoffding, H., *A history of modern philosophy,* 2 vols. (New York: Macmillan, 1900).

Lang, P. H., *Music in western civilization* (New York: Norton, 1941).

Merz, J. T., *A history of European thought in the nineteenth century,* 4 vols. (New York: Scribner, 1896–1914).

Pledge, Humphrey T., *Science since 1500* (New York: Philosophical Library, 1947).

Raynal, M., *The nineteenth century: Goya to Gauguin* (New York: Skira, 1951).

Sears, Paul B., *Charles Darwin* (New York: Scribner, 1950).

Shryock, R. H., *The development of modern medicine* (New York: Knopf, 1947).

Singer, Charles, *A history of biology* (New York: Schuman, 1950).

Wittels, Fritz, *Freud and his times* (New York: Grosset, 1958).

Chapter 9

THE UNIFICATION AND DEVELOPMENT OF GERMANY AND ITALY

I. German Unification

A. <u>After the Congress of Vienna had finished its deliberations in 1815, Germany still did not exist.</u> Instead, a patchwork of 39 states was left, but only two were of any importance: Prussia and Austria. Although Austria was given the presidency of the new Germanic Confederation (*Deutscher Bund*), her multi-national character made her the implacable foe of all national movements—even that in Germany. In fact, Metternich found it difficult to convince Germans that Austria was their natural leader while the largely German state of Prussia existed. Prussia had become even more German after the Vienna settlement by acquiring the valuable Rhine valley and Westphalia, and yielding part of her Polish lands to Russia. This gave Prussia a clear advantage over the polyglot Hapsburg empire, an advantage which became more telling in the fiercely nationalistic nineteenth century. Austria, nevertheless, was the dominant power in Germany from 1815 to 1858. The emergence of Prussia as an equal during the "New Era" after 1858 brought on the final struggle for supremacy in Germany.

B. <u>Factors favoring unification</u>
   1. The great surge of national consciousness during the period 1806–1815 was an important factor. Germans as a whole bitterly resented the French invasion under Napoleon. They were angered by the collective inability of the German states to oust the French prior to the War of Liberation in 1813. Many intellectuals and bourgeois elements were won over to the concept of a united Germany; a few even desired a liberal Germany.

2. Of more lasting influence were the ideas of various German intellectuals. Fichte's *Reden an die deutsche Nation (Addresses to the German Nation)* in 1807–1808 were a clarion call to those Germans who desired nationhood. The Grimm brothers did extensive research to show that German was the fountain head of all language *(Ursprache)*. The historians Ranke and Treitschke also fired up German national feeling by extolling the great past of the German people. Arndt's poetry and Körner's music added still more to the spirit of nationalism.

3. The formation of the Germanic Confederation, weak as it was, still gave impetus to the German national movement. Despite the Austro-Prussian rivalry and particularism of the lesser states, the *Bund* was clearinghouse for ideas and debate. It served to deter French ambitions beyond the Rhine and became a waystation on the road to complete unification.

4. Another powerful factor that helped pave the way for later unity was the evolution of the Prussian-dominated *Zollverein* (Tariff Union) between 1818 and 1844. Despite the fact that each state had a veto in the *Zollverein* legislature, and notwithstanding the fact that Austria attempted to wreck the organization in 1852, the idea that economic cooperation was possible in Germany served as a stimulus to the unification movement.

5. After 1840, the Schleswig-Holstein problem with Denmark served to ignite German nationalism.

6. The growth of an educated middle class also contributed to the desire for German unification. This powerful group regarded the political divisions within Germany as a source of weakness. They looked with favor on the *Zollverein,* and were encouraged by Friedrich List's advocacy of the national state as the most efficient economic unit.

C. Factors hindering unification

1. The most important reason was the Austro-Prussian struggle for the domination of Germany. Only the great Prussian victory at Königgrätz (Sadowa) in 1866 drove Austria out of Germany.

2. Fear of Prussian ambition pushed many of the German secondary states into Austria's camp. Some of the smaller states even harbored the idea of the "third Germany."

3. Particularism was still another impediment. This was the desire of the lesser German states to preserve their independence and territorial integrity despite the economic and political pressure for a unified Germany. These divisive tendencies were deeply wedded to a tradition emanating from the medieval past.

4. The Lutheran tradition of Prussia, in contrast to the Catholic background of Austria and the south German states, was still another point of division.

5. French pressure for a divided (and weak) Germany also formed a serious obstacle until the Franco-Prussian War.

6. The *grossdeutsch-kleindeutsch* controversy was another roadblock for German nationalists. A *grossdeutsch* solution would have included Austria and her non-German territories in the new German state; the *kleindeutsch* solution would have excluded Austria entirely, except for Austria's German section *(Ostmark)*. This question plagued the Frankfurt Parliament until 1849 when it decided to offer the crown of the proposed German Empire to Frederick William IV of Prussia.

D. Austrian domination of Germany, 1815–1858

1. During the "Metternich era" from 1815 to the revolutionary year of 1848, Austria clearly dominated the German scene. Yet, during this era her financial position worsened, her bureaucracy became more inefficient, and her army deteriorated. Prussia, on the other hand, was gaining strength because of her efficient and dedicated civil service and army. In addition, Prussia was well on her way toward industrialization by 1848, while tradition-bound Austria lagged behind. Although Austria was still somewhat stronger in 1848, Prussia had thrust herself on the stage of German affairs as an astute competitor.

2. The ouster of Metternich in March, 1848 brought down the old and traditional Hapsburg state. The March Days in Berlin also seemed to herald a more liberal era. Meanwhile, the liberal nationalists of the various German states met at Frankfurt in May, 1848. Here they organized a weak central government for Germany and completed a constitution by March, 1849. At this point the movement for a unified Germany received a crippling blow. The Assembly, by a narrow margin, accepted

the *kleindeutsch* viewpoint and offered the crown of a proposed German empire to the vacillating Frederick William IV of Prussia. Despite his earlier acceptance of liberal and national ideas, Frederick refused the crown: he still felt that Austria should retain a hazy leadership in Germany, and also believed that such an offer would be meaningful only if it came from the princes. Following Frederick's refusal Austria, Prussia, and Saxony withdrew their deputies from Frankfurt. The Frankfurt Assembly was at an end, and hopes for a liberal and united Germany were gone. Germany might still be unified, but the process would be completed by either an autocratic Prussia or a conservative Austria.

3. Frederick William IV now moved to achieve German unification on Prussian terms. A plan was drawn up for a great central European state with a population of 60 million people. An inner confederation, under Prussia, would include most of Germany; the Austrian state would remain intact, but also be part of this new bloc. Austria would not be a member of the inner confederation.

   a. Many of the small German states joined the Prussian Union out of fear. Its assembly met at Erfurt in October, 1849, and the Prussian-dominated group soon came to be known as the Erfurt Union.

   b. Due to the vacillation of Frederick William IV, the Erfurt Union grew weaker during 1850. In the meantime, Austria (with Russian aid) had put an end to the Hungarian uprising. Under Schwarzenberg, the Austrians now initiated a stronger German policy. They reopened the old Germanic Confederation in May, 1850 and at Olmütz humiliated Prussia by forcing her to abandon the Erfurt Union and recognize the restored *Deutscher Bund* at Frankfurt.

   c. Until the premature death of Schwarzenberg in 1852, Austria continued to dominate German affairs. Even until 1858 Prussia seemed willing to accept a secondary role in Germany despite the anti-Austrian gestures of Bismarck in Frankfurt. Within Prussia, the landed nobility regained their old position, while life was made hard for the liberals, the 1850 constitution notwithstanding.

4. The "New Era" in Prussia
   a. Late in 1858 Frederick William IV was adjudged insane, and Prince William became regent. William became king in 1861 upon the death of his brother.
   b. The new Prince Regent ended many of the restrictive measures in Prussia. Again, German liberals and nationalists began to look to Berlin for leadership.
   c. The successes of the Italian nationalists in 1859 and 1860 gave the German national movement great impetus. An example of this new feeling was the *Nationalverein* (National Association) of Rudolf von Bennigsen. This active organization dedicated itself to a liberal and united Germany.
   d. The Hapsburg defeat in the Austro-Sardinian War of 1859 also had an influence on the new Prince Regent of Prussia. He saw that even in defeat Austria was unwilling to share the leadership of Germany in exchange for Prussian help along the Rhine. William also noted that the inefficient mobilization of Prussia's armies in 1859 made an overhaul of her armed forces necessary. To bring about the desired changes, Albrecht von Roon was made Minister of War. General Helmuth von Moltke became head of the General Staff.
   e. The threat of Napoleon III temporarily brought Austria and Prussia together at Teplitz (July, 1860), but the struggle for primacy in German affairs saw the old tug-of-war resumed in 1861.
E. The emergence of Otto von Bismarck
   1. The battle over army reform
      a. In 1860 the Prince Regent proposed a comprehensive plan of army reform to the liberal Prussian Parliament *(Landtag):* the army was to be increased from 200,000 to 371,000 men, and the length of military service was to be increased from two to three years. The cost was 9.5 million thalers.
      b. The liberal-dominated lower house grudgingly went along with the proposals in 1860, but determined to fight the king and his reactionary-military clique. In the 1861 elections the liberals won an overwhelming majority in the Prussian lower chamber, and on the basis of this victory, demanded an itemized budget

and a reduction of military service to two years. The real issue was autocracy versus responsible government.

c. William dissolved the lower house in 1862, but new elections returned an even larger liberal majority. William now faced a choice: abdicate, or drop the idea of army reform. The latter course meant parliamentary government. In this crisis, William was induced to send for Otto von Bismarck and offer him the position of Minister-President. Bismarck accepted the challenging position, and remained in office until 1890.

2. Otto von Bismarck

   a. This conservative Junker had represented Prussia at Frankfurt (Germanic Confederation) from 1851 to 1859. In this post he had fought a running battle with the Austrians, and had decided that Prussia could unify Germany only by defeating the Hapsburg armies.

   b. From 1859 to 1861 Bismarck had represented his country at St. Petersburg. Here he won the personal friendship of Tsar Alexander II which proved to be of great value in 1866 and 1870.

   c. In 1862 Bismarck was sent to Paris as the Prussian ambassador. He learned much about the desires and character of Napoleon III before being recalled to Berlin by William I.

   d. Upon his return to Berlin, Bismarck took office with the understanding that William I would not abdicate. When the lower house rejected the budget, Bismarck sent them away and ruled without a budget. Prussian liberalism had been dealt another severe blow.

   e. When the Polish revolt broke out in January, 1863, Russia was hard pressed by the rebels and the diplomatic pressure of Austria, France, and Great Britain. Bismarck wisely supported the Tsar against the rebels, and won his gratitude. This proved almost indispensable in 1866 and 1870.

   f. In August, 1863 Austria tried to rally liberal opinion in Germany against Bismarck's Prussia. Franz Joseph called for a congress of princes, but Bismarck wrecked Austria's scheme by refusing to let his sovereign attend. A German conference without Prussia was worthless, and the Hapsburg effort failed.

F. The Schleswig-Holstein question

1. The new Danish king, Christian IX, came to the throne in November, 1863. He signed a new constitution which incorporated the duchy of Schleswig into Denmark. Holstein's status was left unchanged: it remained a member of the Germanic Confederation, and was tied to Denmark only by a personal union with the Danish crown.

2. Holstein was almost entirely German, while Schleswig was also German except for its northern section. German public opinion was greatly aroused and desired a solution that would give the two duchies to Duke Frederick of Augustenburg. This settlement would permit the duchies to dissolve their ties with Denmark and enter the Germanic Confederation. Bismarck, on the other hand, wanted to incorporate the duchies. He, thus, sought and won Austrian backing for a policy of maintaining the old status quo for the duchies, i.e., personal union with Denmark, but not incorporation. This meant abrogation of the new Danish constitution, and Bismarck correctly calculated that the Danes would fight first. War with Denmark would give Prussia a chance for territorial gain even if the hated Austrians were their allies.

3. Austro-Prussian forces quickly defeated the Danish armies in the early months of 1864. After a futile conference in London (April–June, 1864), war resumed and the Danes were again defeated.
   a. By the Treaty of Vienna (October, 1864), the Danes yielded Schleswig, Holstein, and Lauenburg to Austria and Prussia.
   b. For the moment, Bismarck agreed to joint rule, but he was determined to win the duchies ultimately.

4. Austria and Prussia now seemed to be moving in the direction of war over Schleswig-Holstein.
   a. Vienna continued to support the claims of the Duke of Augustenburg until the summer of 1865.
   b. A new Austrian ministry came to power in July, 1865 and agreed to the Treaty of Gastein (August 14, 1865).

5. The Treaty of Gastein (August 14, 1865)
   a. Prussia was permitted to purchase Lauenburg.

        b. Austria was given control over Holstein, but Prussia obtained Schleswig.

        c. Prussia gained the use of the port of Kiel in Holstein plus military roads through that duchy.

        d. Austrian-held Holstein was thus completely surrounded by Prussian territory. Bismarck now looked for some additional support before precipitating war with the Hapsburgs.

    6. The Biarritz—Paris talks (October–November, 1865)

        a. Napoleon III and the French were disturbed by Gastein, because they sensed it might mean a reconciliation between Austria and Prussia.

        b. To placate Napoleon III and try to learn what France would do in the event of an Austro-Prussian war, Bismarck visited France in the fall of 1865.

        c. In these discussions with Napoleon III and other French leaders, Bismarck dangled the possibility of gains in Belgium and along the Rhine before their eyes. In exchange, he apparently won French neutrality in the event of a war with Austria. Napoleon III also placed no obstacle in the way of a Prusso-Italian agreement.

G. The Austro-Prussian War of 1866

    1. Soon after returning from France, Bismarck signed a commercial agreement with Italy. In April, 1866 a formal alliance was concluded. Napoleon III gave it his blessing, since he believed Austria to be the stronger of the two German powers.

    2. Bismarck now proposed to goad Austria into war by a proposal for a united Germany (under Prussia) that would exclude the Hapsburg domains.

    3. Both Austria and Prussia mobilized, and when Austria proposed that the Germanic Confederation settle the Schleswig-Holstein question, Bismarck sent his forces into Holstein. War was inevitable (June, 1866). When it came most of the secondary states of Germany sided with Austria.

    4. At the last moment Austria did something that should have been done many months earlier: she agreed to give Venetia to France (for retrocession to Italy) whether she won or lost the coming war. In return, France would stay neutral, and might erect a neutral buffer state in the

Rhine Valley (June, 1866). But the offer was late.

5. The ensuing war was brief. Austria was crushed at Königgrätz (Sadowa) on July 3, 1866. Despite the Austrian victories in Italy, the war had been settled in Bohemia.

6. It was now obvious that Prussia had emerged as the leading power in Germany. Napoleon III failed to act along the Rhine while Prussia was occupied, a mistake he soon regretted. After Prussia and Austria had concluded a preliminary peace treaty at Nikolsburg (July 26, 1866), French requests for compensation (1814 frontiers, Belgium, or Luxemburg) were suggested in Berlin. Since his hands were now free, Bismarck gently put the French demands off until a personal illness saved him further embarrassment (September–December, 1866).

7. Even in 1866 Bismarck saw that war with France was inevitable. His definitive treaty with Austria (Treaty of Prague, August 23, 1866) was notably lenient. Austria lost no territory except Venetia, and paid only a moderate indemnity. French demands for territorial compensation also caused Bismarck to be lenient with the south German states of Baden, Württemberg, Bavaria, and Hesse-Darmstadt: they concluded a military alliance with Prussia which would be operative in the event of a French attack. Bismarck also planned for the future by obtaining a copy of French territorial demands in 1866, the famous Benedetti Memorandum. This he used to win over British public opinion in 1870.

8. The 1866 conflict with Austria won only 1300 square miles of territory for Prussia. The south German states and Saxony were permitted to retain their sovereignty, but a new Prussian-dominated North German Confederation was to be organized. This new confederation was formally established in April, 1867.

H. The French reaction to Sadowa

1. Both the French leadership and French public bitterly resented the diminished position of France in Europe. France had also been disgraced by the disastrous Mexican expedition, and had been taxed by commitments in Algeria, Indo-China, and Rome.

2. To help restore her prestige and win a strategic border post, Napoleon III pressured Bismarck to agree to the

cession of Luxemburg over the winter of 1866–1867. The Dutch king, owner of Luxemburg, refused to sell the Prussian-garrisoned area without Bismarck's approval. Bismarck arranged for the news of the negotiations to leak out. With German public opinion now aroused, Bismarck could not yield.

3. The British sponsored a conference in London which ended the Prussian occupation of Luxemburg. However, France was again humiliated, since she obtained nothing to counterbalance the large Prussian gains in Germany.

4. Napoleon now spent the next three years in an attempt to win an alliance with Austria and Italy. The new Dual Monarchy of Austria-Hungary (after 1867) was a stumbling block, because the Hungarian element was unwilling to fight for Austrian domination of Germany. In addition, the Austrians were unwilling to join such a Triple Alliance until Italian participation was assured. Italy refused to join until France guaranteed her Rome, an act Napoleon III could not do without alienating Catholic opinion in France. Despite lengthy negotiations, the alliance never materialized.

5. French attempts to rearm (Niel Law) were also insignificant when compared to the great war machine Prussia had assembled.

6. In 1870 a frustrated France stood alone. It was at this moment that the Hohenzollern Candidature issue arose.

I. The Franco-Prussian War, 1870–1871

1. In 1868 the debauched Isabella II was driven from the throne of Spain by a revolutionary junta under Serrano and Prim.

2. For almost two years the Spanish sought a successor.

3. In July, 1870 the French learned that the vacant Spanish throne had been offered to Prince Leopold of Hohenzollern-Sigmaringen, the Catholic branch of the royal house of Prussia. To France a Hohenzollern south of the Pyrenees (as well as east of the Rhine) meant encirclement. Instead of a sixteenth century Hapsburg ring Napoleon III faced a nineteenth century Prussian noose. Whether Bismarck deliberately planned this to provoke a weaker France into a declaration of war is not known, but it seems likely.

4. France implied that war would result if Prince Leopold's candidacy was not withdrawn. To Bismarck's dismay, Leopold's father had him withdraw. But now the frustrated French issued a demand to King William that this plan never be revived (<u>Ems: July 13, 1870).</u> William courteously informed Benedetti, the French ambassador, that Prince Leopold had withdrawn and that the matter was at an end. William then sent the famous Ems dispatch to Bismarck informing him of the French request. In turn, Bismarck issued a changed version of King William's Ems telegram, one that was calculated to arouse the French. It did, and France declared war on a stronger Prussia (July 19, 1870).

5. Severe French defeats at Sedan (where Napoleon III was captured) and Metz wrecked the regular army. A republic was set up in Paris and resistance continued on a sporadic basis. In January, 1871 the new German Empire was proclaimed in the Hall of Mirrors at Versailles. In subsequent months the pressure of public opinion and the Prussian victory over France compelled the south German states to enter the new German Empire.

6. <u>The Treaty of Frankfurt (May 10, 1871)</u> gave the new Germany Alsace-Lorraine plus a supposedly crippling indemnity of 5 billion francs.

II. The German Empire, 1871–1914

A. <u>Government of the new Second *Reich*</u>
1. <u>A federal system was set up by Bismarck</u> which allowed the states to retain certain powers. Some of the concessions were made to assuage the old particularism.
2. <u>The supreme executive authority was vested in the new Kaiser (and King of Prussia), William I.</u> The chancellor, Bismarck, was responsible only to the Kaiser, not the elected legislature. The "cabinet" was merely a group of administrators who were responsible solely to the chancellor. In addition, the Kaiser was commander-in-chief of the armed forces.
3. <u>In the upper house or Federal Council *(Bundesrat)* of the new legislature, Prussia had a veto.</u> The members of the *Bundesrat* represented the states, not the people.
4. The lower house or Imperial Diet *(Reichstag)* was

elected by all men over 25, but the lower chamber of the powerful state of Prussia remained conservative because of Three-Class system of voting. The *Reichstag* was weak for several reasons: it could be dissolved by the Kaiser with the consent of the *Bundesrat,* it had only a limited power over the purse because many of the revenue laws were permanent, and it could consider only those bills presented to it by the chancellor and *Bundesrat.* In short, the *Reichstag* could not make governments, policies, or ministers. At best, its numerous parties could only modify the wishes of the Kaiser and chancellor.

B. In this government the state of Prussia emerged as the leading political entity. Prussia had swallowed the whole of Germany after 1871.

C. Otto von Bismarck stood out as the leading political figure of the Second *Reich.* He used the various political parties of the *Reichstag,* but was beholden to none of them. During the period 1870–1878 he depended on the relatively progressive National Liberals because the more conservative parties did not appreciate the need for minimal concessions. Bismarck was willing to make a few gestures in behalf of liberalism if it would help him knit the particularist states of Germany into a powerful and unified whole.

D. *The Kulturkampf*

1. This struggle between the new Germany and the Catholic church was a continuation of the old struggle between king and priest.

2. In 1870 the Doctrine of Papal Infallibility was declared an article of faith. This plus the appearance of the Center Party, the political voice of the church, seriously worried Bismarck. The new Center *(Zentrum)* worried Bismarck further by its demand that the German states be given a large measure of autonomy. With the capture of 63 seats in 1871, the Center party was the third largest political entity.

3. A few Germans, the "Old Catholics" like Döllinger, refused to accept the Doctrine of Papal Infallibility. Despite a request from the Vatican, Bismarck refused to dismiss the "Old Catholics" from their church positions. In 1872 a law was passed expelling the Jesuits from Germany.

4. These measures were followed by the drastic May (Falk)

Laws (1873–1875): a civil ceremony was made compulsory for all marriages, most monastic orders were dissolved, members of religious orders were not permitted to teach in the schools, and the government was given the power to block church appointments.

5. Feeling in Germany now turned against Bismarck, even among Protestants. The Center party won 92 seats in the *Reichstag* in 1877 and momentarily became the largest party. Bismarck made some conciliatory gestures to the new Pope, Leo XIII, in 1878. After 1880 the harsh "May Laws" were gradually withdrawn.

E. Bismarck and the Socialists

1. In 1848 socialism had no real base in Germany, but as industrialization proceeded to take hold in the next three decades the number of workers grew rapidly. After 1848 the writings of Karl Marx and the socialists began to influence the new working class as well as the German intellectuals.

2. Ferdinand Lassalle (1825–1864) was the founder of the first socialist political organization in Germany, the Universal German Workmen's Association. After Lassalle's death, the leadership shifted to such Marxian Socialists as Wilhelm Liebknecht and August Bebel. Only at the Gotha Congress (1875) did the Lassalean and Marxian factions join forces and support a moderate program. In 1890 the name Social Democratic Party was adopted.

3. Bismarck detested the socialist platform of democracy, antimilitarism, and social reform. He did not move against the socialists before 1878 because he was deeply involved in the *Kulturkampf*.

4. The drastic anti-socialist law of October, 1878 practically drove the socialists underground. In the *Reichstag*, however, they had a haven and increased their representation to 35 seats in 1890 and 110 seats in 1912. Despite Bismarck's attacks until 1890, the Social Democrats grew to be the largest party in Germany prior to World War I. But it should be noted that the gradualist philosophy of Eduard Bernstein had toned down the more strident demands of earlier socialism. The new goal was social reform through the evolutionary possibilities offered by parliamentary democracy.

F. The Germany of William II

1. In 1888 the aged William I died. Although Bismarck had respected the dead emperor, he was almost always able to dominate him and thus run Germany. Now the situation had changed: for three months the dying Frederick III (1831–1888) ascended the throne, only to be succeeded by the impetuous and erratic William II (1888–1918). Within two years several serious rifts occurred between Bismarck and the young emperor: the emperor's desire to end the war against the socialists, the emperor's hope for closer ties with Great Britain and Austria-Hungary rather than Russia, and the Kaiser's wish to set aside Bismarck's prerogative to be present when the emperor met with a minister.

2. The basic question was whether William II or Bismarck would rule Germany. Bismarck resigned on March 18, 1890 and the emperor selected the capable General Georg Leo von Caprivi (1890–1894) as the new chancellor. He soon won the enmity of the Center Party over school legislation as well as the dislike of the conservative agrarian interests for negotiating commercial treaties that cut the price of food. Caprivi was succeeded by the compliant Prince Hohenlohe-Schillingsfürst (1894–1900) during whose tenure the Kiel Canal was opened (1895) and a new civil code enacted (1900). Count Bernhard von Bülow (1900–1909) was preoccupied with colonial and foreign questions, and was succeeded by the unimaginative bureaucrat Dr. Theobald von Bethmann-Hollweg (1909–1917).

3. The Germany of William II, like that of Bismarck, was dominated by a conservative agrarian-military-industrial coalition. This anti-parliamentary alliance along with the government bureaucracy effectively blocked the development of responsible, parliamentary government. They also offered vigorous opposition to the socialists and the national minorities (Polish, Danish, and French) within Germany.

4. By 1913 the Junker-dominated German army was increased to the then-unprecedented size of 870,000. Even the Socialists voted to finance this program, although they voted against the military measures for which the funds were intended.

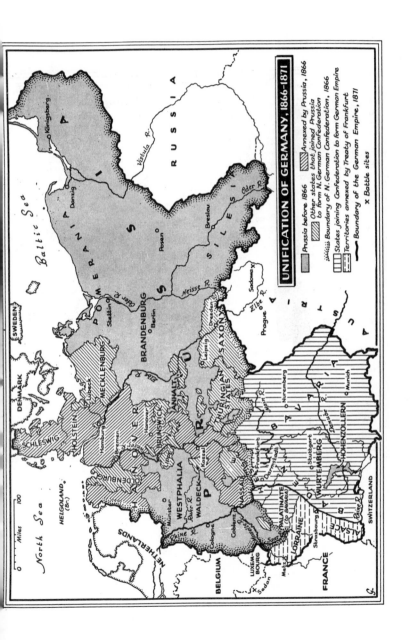

UNIFICATION OF GERMANY, 1866-1871

- Prussia before 1866
- Annexed by Prussia, 1866
- Other states that joined Prussia to form N. German Confederation
- Boundary of N. German Confederation, 1866
- States joining Confederation to form German Empire
- Territories annexed by Treaty of Frankfurt
- Boundary of the German Empire, 1871
- x Battle sites

North Sea

Baltic Sea

SWEDEN

DENMARK

SCHLESWIG

HELGOLAND (Br.)

NETHERLANDS

BELGIUM

LUXEM-BOURG

FRANCE

SWITZERLAND

RUSSIA

AUSTRIA

POMERANIA

SILESIA

BRANDENBURG

MECKLENBURG

HANOVER

WESTPHALIA

WALDECK

OLDENBURG

HOLSTEIN

BRUNSWICK

ANHALT

SAXONY

THURINGIAN STATES

NASSAU

BAVARIA

WÜRTEMBERG

HOHENZOLLERN

BADEN

ALSACE

LORRAINE

Königsberg

Danzig

Posen

Breslau

Stettin

Berlin

Leipzig

Dresden

Lübeck

Hamburg

Kassel

Münster

Cologne

Coblenz

Frankfort

Darmstadt

Strasbourg

Metz

Sedan

Nuremberg

Stuttgart

Munich

Prague

Sadowa x

Vistula R.

Oder R.

Neisse R.

Elbe R.

Oder R.

Elbe

Weser R.

Rhine R.

Ruhr R.

Main R.

Saar R.

Danube R.

Rhine R.

0 Miles 100

UNIFICATION OF ITALY
1859-1870

▮ Kingdom of Sardinia before 1859

To Kingdom of Sardinia:
▥ 1859   ▨ 1860

To Kingdom of Italy:
▧ 1866   ▩ 1870

▨ Italia Irredenta
X Battle site

SWITZERLAND   AUSTRIA

FRANCE

SAVOY
Magenta   LOMBARDY   VENETIA
Novara X   Milan   Trieste
Turin   Solferino   Verona
PIEDMONT   Mantua   Venice
TO FRANCE   Genoa   PARMA
1860   MODENA
ROMAGNA
NICE
Nice   THE RIVIERA   Leghorn   Florence   THE MARCHES
TUSCANY   Adriatic   DALMATIA
CORSICA   UMBRIA   PAPAL
(French)   Rome   STATES   Sea
SARDINIA   Naples   APULIA   ALBANIA
Bari
SARDINIA   Taranto
Tyrrhenian   KINGDOM OF THE TWO SICILIES
Sea   CALABRIA
Palermo   Straits of Messina
Mediterranean   SICILY
AFRICA   Sea
Tunis
MALTA   0   Miles   200
(Br.)

G. German economic development
   1. The new Germany had a population of 41 million after the conclusion of the Treaty of Frankfurt in 1871. This made Germany the second most populous state in Europe (Russia: 87 million), but in industrial development she soon surpassed even Great Britain in many fields. This industrial growth coupled with the efficient army of the Second *Reich* made Germany the strongest power in Europe by 1914.
   2. By the 1860's Germany was crisscrossed by six great rail lines of great commercial and military value. By 1914 virtually all of the railroads of Germany were owned by the state governments.
   3. Germany also excelled in the production of steel and coal. By 1910 German steel production was over 13 million metric tons, almost twice that of Great Britain and four times that of France. By 1913 German coal production reached 190 million metric tons; over 87 million metric tons of lignite were also mined.
   4. The German chemical and electrical industries also developed significantly after 1871. Her dye and pharmaceutical industries won special acclaim.

III. Italian Unification

A. The initial push for Italian unification came from the creation of a puppet Kingdom of Italy by Napoleon I. This act lessened the particularist tendencies of the past centuries, and coupled with the nationalistic influence from revolutionary France, caused a powerful movement for Italian unification to develop among the intellectuals and bourgeoisie. Italy was still a geographical expression in 1815, but the nationalistic hopes of many patriots had been aroused. This desire for Italian unity was gradually translated into successful action during the next half century, the era of the *Risorgimento* (resurgence).

B. The Austrian acquisition of Lombardy-Venetia by the 1815 Vienna Final Act made Metternich particularly careful to restore as much as possible of the old particularist Italy. The "new" states of Italy were Sardinia (Piedmont), Modena, Parma, Lucca, Tuscany, the Papal States, and the Kingdom of the Two Sicilies. Tiny San Marino and

Monaco played little part in the coming *Risorgimento.*
From their vantage point in Lombardy-Venetia, the Hapsburg armies gave effective support to the reactionary band
of princes who returned to Italy after the downfall of Napoleon I.

C. The *Risorgimento* differed from its German equivalent in
at least two important ways: the nationalist movement had
a powerful democratic counterpart, and Italy had but one
state strong enough to lead—Sardinia. But prior to the
emergence of Cavour in 1850 even Sardinia lacked the industrial and commercial devolopment that her mission required. Cavour reduced the tariffs, improved the Sardinian
army, completed an armaments industry, and vastly expanded Piedmont's railroad and canal network.

D. Public opinion in both Great Britain and France remained
sympathetic to the Italian cause. In the case of Great
Britain, commercial hopes played a part. French sympa-
thies were not translated into assistance prior to 1848, since
many French statesmen viewed a united Italy or Germany
as additional dangers to French security. Only with the
election of Louis Napoleon as President of the Second
French Republic (1848) did the attitude of the French government begin to change.

E. One of the first signs of an active Italian nationalist movement was the emergence of a secret revolutionary organization known as the *Carbonari* (Charcoal-Burners). This
organization spread north from the Two Sicilies, and was
responsible for a series of unsuccessful revolutions after
1820. Mazzini's Young Italy took on the burden of revolutionary activity after 1831.

F. Still another impetus for the Italian national cause came
from important literary sources. Allessandro Manzoni's *I
promessi sposi (The Betrothed)* was a powerful nationalistic
spur. The romantic tales of Italian medieval heroes by
Guerrazzi and Grossi awakened patriotic hopes: perhaps
the new Italy could rival their exploits over the French and
Arabs. Some even felt the new Italy could be the beginning
of another Roman Empire. The patriotic poetry of Leo-
pardi and some of the great arias from Verdi's operas also
served to stimulate the *Risorgimento.* And finally, Gioberti's
The Moral and Civil Primacy of the Italians (1843), grandi-
ose as it was, breathed an element of self-confidence into

those Italians who were chagrined by criticism of Italy's weak political position. These men of letters did much to break down the provincialism that had divided Italy since the downfall of Rome. The people of Sicily, Tuscany, and Piedmont may not have considered themselves Italians by 1848 (if by 1861), but the idea of unification had been implanted.

G. The revolutionary failures, 1820–1849

　1. Encouraged by the success of the Spanish revolutionaries in 1820, the *Carbonari* in the army of Two Sicilies under General Pepe revolted against the despotic Ferdinand I (1751–1825). The frightened Bourbon king quickly granted a constitution similar to that introduced by the British in Sicily in 1812.

　2. The conservative Concert of Europe was concerned. Led by Metternich, the Troppau protocol (1820) was issued as a warning against revolution that might endanger the existing political structure. The Congress of Laibach (1821) authorized Austria to forcibly restore Ferdinand I to his former position, a mandate that was executed with ease.

　3. A *Carbonari* uprising in Piedmont forced Victor Emmanuel I (1802–1821) to abdicate (1821). He was succeeded by Charles Felix (1821–1831), but the constitutional party was defeated at Novara by the Austrians and Piedmontese royalists.

　4. In 1831 a series of revolts broke out in Modena, Parma, and the Papal States. They had been inspired by the July Revolution in France which had ejected the Bourbon monarch Charles X. Failure was again the rule in Italy, however, as Austrian troops helped defeat the insurrectionists.

　5. In 1831 Mazzini founded a new revolutionary society— *Young Italy*. A general revolution was planned for 1832, but the plans became known to Piedmontese authorities and the uprising was checked. Another Mazzinian revolt in Savoy was a ludicrous failure (1834).

　6. The election of the liberal Pope Pius IX in 1846 gave Italian nationalists renewed hope. He relaxed the tight censorship and permitted Rome to have a municipal council. Unfortunately, the revolutionary events of

1848–1849 cooled his enthusiasm for liberalism, and made him an implacable foe of unification.

7. In 1848 a Sicilian revolution forced Ferdinand II (*Bomba:* 1830–1859) to issue a liberal constitution. Grand Duke Leopold of Tuscany followed suit (February, 1848). The great French revolution that ejected Louis Philippe soon followed, and gave the Italian revolutionary movement greater impetus.

8. The vacillating <u>Charles Albert (1831–1849)</u> of Sardinia now gave his people a constitution that was the basis of the later Italian constitution (March, 1848). Pope Pius IX granted the Papal States a constitution a few days later.

9. In Austrian-held Lombardy, the courageous Milanese drove the Austrians out of their city. Radetsky fled eastward to the safety of the Quadrilateral forts (March, 1848).

10. The temporary successes continued as Manin established his Venetian Republic and Piedmont declared war on Austria (March, 1848). Italian contingents from all over the peninsula joined the Sardinian army, but a great Austrian victory at <u>Custozza (July 24, 1848)</u> crushed Italian hopes.

   a. In the meantime the revolt in the Two Sicilies collapsed.

   b. Revolutionaries set up a Roman Republic (February 9, 1849).

   c. The pressure of the revolutionaries forced Charles Albert to renew the war against Austria. Sardinia was again beaten, this time at <u>Novara (March 23, 1849)</u>.

   d. <u>Charles Albert abdicated in favor of his more resolute son, Victor Emmanuel II (1849–1878).</u>

11. The French landed near Rome, crushed Garibaldi, and smashed the Roman Republic (July, 1849). French troops stayed in Rome until 1866, and returned from 1867 to 1870.

12. The last revolutionary stronghold in Venice surrendered in August, 1849 after a heroic defense.

13. <u>The futility of the Italian revolutions of 1848–1849 revealed the weakness of the unification drive.</u>

   a. Italy lacked the military strength to drive out the

Austrians, a prerequisite for unification. Italy could not do it alone as Charles Albert had suggested.

b. The nationalist movement needed a shrewd political leader, not a romantic like Mazzini nor a blunt soldier like Garibaldi. The emergence of Camillo Cavour as Minister of Agriculture and Commerce of Piedmont in 1850 gave the Italian liberal-nationalists the man they needed.

H. Count Camillo Benso di Cavour

1. Cavour was a moderate liberal who distrusted visionary revolutionists like Mazzini. His concessions to democracy came more from the need to appease liberal public opinion rather than personal conviction. His admiration of the British parliamentary system assured Piedmont of gradual reform in the direction of democracy.

2. Cavour exhibited his ability and progressive ideas by introducing scientific farming on his father's lands. In 1842 he founded the Agrarian Society to promote this idea throughout Piedmont. Cavour also played a significant role in promoting railroad construction and the establishment of banking institutions. He believed all these changes were needed to transform Piedmont from a political and economic backwater to the leader of the national crusade.

3. Cavour founded a whist club in Turin as a cloak for political discussions. When the censorship was relaxed in 1847, he helped found *Il Risorgimento,* a newspaper devoted to the cause of Italian independence. Despite the fact that republicans regarded him with suspicion (they believed him to be an aristocrat at heart), Cavour was in the forefront of those who won a constitution for Piedmont in 1848. He became increasingly prominent after Piedmont was humbled by Austria in 1848–1849.

4. Cavour worked behind the scenes to curb the power of the Church of Piedmont (1850). Later that year he became Minister of Agriculture and Commerce (1850–1851).

5. In November, 1852 Cavour was named Prime Minister. He held this post for the next seven years.

a. Once in office Cavour was determined to strengthen Piedmont economically and militarily. Tariffs were lowered to increase foreign trade, railroad construction was pushed (in 1859 Piedmont had half the Italian trackage), irrigation projects were expedited (Cavour Canal begun in 1857), and an armaments industry was founded.

b. Considerable French and English capital was invested in Piedmont. In this way, those two governments had a financial as well as a political interest in Italian unification.

c. Cavour rejected the Mazzinian approach to unification. He felt that spontaneous popular revolts had been disproven as a technique by events since 1820. Cavour also showed little interest in Mazzini's desire for a republic. On the other hand, the more moderate Gioberti approach never won the sympathy of Cavour: he could not accept an Italian confederation under the presidency of the reactionary Pius IX. Cavour probably would have settled for a compact north Italian state under Piedmontese leadership so long as it was a constitutional monarchy. But the great opportunities of 1860 permitted him to go much further.

IV. The Road to Unification, 1852–1870

A. The Crimean War, 1854–1856

  1. France, Great Britain, and Turkey had been engaged in the bloody and painstaking assault on Sevastopol for a year. Fresh troops were sorely needed by 1855.

  2. Cavour saw an opportunity to win the gratitude of Napoleon III and the British. At the same time it would give him a chance to bring the "Italian question" before all Europe at the peace conference.

  3. Sardinia entered the war in January, 1855 and gained prestige by its part in the victory at Chernaia (August, 1855).

  4. At the Paris peace conference Cavour greatly impressed the statesmen of Europe by his moderation and ability. At the same time he clearly outlined the problems of Italy before an international forum.

B. The Austro-Sardinian War, 1859

  1. For two years Napoleon III's interest in Italy waned. Then in January, 1858 an Italian patriot, Felice Orsini,

attempted to assassinate the French emperor on a Parisian street.

2. This episode apparently spurred Napoleon III to secretly met with Cavour at Plombrières (July 20, 1858). Despite Catholic opinion in France and the influence of Empress Eugénie and Walewski (foreign minister), Napoleon agreed to join Piedmont in a war against Austria if Cavour could provoke Austria into a declaration of war or otherwise justify it in the eyes of the world. Napoleon also agreed to an Italian confederation under the presidency of the pope: Piedmont would head the powerful Upper Italian Kingdom to be composed of Piedmont, Lombardy-Venetia, Modena, Parma, and a part of the Papal States (Papal Legations). A Kingdom of Central Italy, a small papal domain around Rome, and a southern Kingdom of Naples were also planned. France was to receive Nice and Savoy for her services, and the daughter of Victor Emmanuel II was to marry the debauched Prince Jerome Bonaparte, cousin of Napoleon III.

3. Cavour had yielded little in agreeing to permit Pius IX to be president of the proposed confederation. The Upper Italian Kingdom obviously would dominate the new confederation.

4. Napoleon III somewhat strengthened his position by signing a treaty of benevolent neutrality with Russia in March, 1859. Prussia stood aloof, and the new Derby government in Great Britain was somewhat suspicious.

5. Nevertheless, Sardinian armaments, propaganda, and French support brought an Austrian declaration of war in April, 1859. British attempts to settle the question by a European congress failed.

6. The French and Piedmontese armies drove the Austrians from Lombardy by their victories at Magenta and Solferino (June, 1859). Before the allies could move into Venetia, Prussian mobilization along the Rhine, battle losses, and clerical opinion in France forced Napoleon III to make an armistice at Villafranca (July, 1859) without consulting Cavour.

7. Cavour resigned in anger, but the Villafranca arrangements were generally preserved in the final Treaty of Zürich (November, 1859): Piedmont won Lombardy,

but Venetia remained in Austrian hands. The small Italian states of Parma, Tuscany, Modena, and Romagna were not compelled to take back their pro-Austrian rulers who had been ousted by revolutions during the course of the recent war.

C. The growth of Piedmont in 1860

1. Because of strong Catholic sentiment in France, Napoleon III publicly opposed Sardinian annexation of the central Italian states that had ousted their rulers in 1859. Privately, both he and Victor Emmanuel II encouraged them to join Piedmont.

2. In August and September of 1859 assemblies in these states publicly refused to allow the former rulers to return, and asked for union with Piedmont.

3. In January, 1860 Cavour again became Prime Minister. To settle the problem of the central Italian states, Cavour worked out a secret arrangement with Napoleon III: Piedmont could annex the central Italian principalities if plebiscites were first held. In return, France would get Nice and Savoy, areas she would have acquired after the Austro-Sardinian War had Piedmont won Venetia (not merely Lombardy). Napoleon III wished to reward France for her losses and somewhat trim the size of the growing Piedmontese kingdom.

4. In March, 1860 the plebiscites were held, and as expected, the populace voted for union with Sardinia. Piedmont, in turn, ceded Nice and Savoy to France by the Treaty of Turin (March 24, 1860). This cession (and revision of the Vienna settlement) so frightened Prussia along the Rhine that she moved closer to Austria for the next year.

5. The loss of his native Nice to France incensed the blunt Garibaldi. In addition, an abortive revolt in Sicily aroused this gallant soldier (April, 1860). Under the watchful and not altogether approving eye of Cavour, Garibaldi fitted out his Red Shirts in Genoa and sailed for Sicily (May, 1860). He evaded both the Piedmontese and Neapolitan fleets and landed at Marsala, in western Sicily.

6. By the end of July, 1860 Garibaldi's army had conquered all of Sicily. In the process it had grown considerably. The skeptical Cavour now tried to forestall

Garibaldi by inspiring a more conservative revolution in Naples, but Garibaldi seized that city (September, 1860) and prepared to march north and take Rome from the pope.

7. Cavour realized that such a move would compel the friendly French forces in Rome to fire on Garibaldi. The French help that was still required to complete the unification of Italy might be lost. Even Austria might intervene to help Pius IX.

8. A revolt in the Papal States (September, 1860) gave Cavour an excuse to send his army into Umbria and the Marches. Except for Rome and the area immediately nearby, Piedmont seized all of the Papal States on the pretext of maintaining order. The Piedmontese army quickly marched into the Two Sicilies, joined forces with Garibaldi, and under the threat of civil war, stopped Garibaldi's march on Rome and forced him to yield Naples and Sicily to Piedmont. The acquisition of the Marches, Umbria, and the Kingdom of the Two Sicilies completed Italian unification except for Venetia and Rome.

D. On March 17, 1861 the Kingdom of Italy was proclaimed. The 1848 Piedmontese constitution was its fundamental law. Soon thereafter, on June 6, 1861, the great Camillo Cavour died. The archietect of unity had passed away before the completion of the edifice.

1. Cavour's successor was the great Tuscan patriot, Baron Ricasoli (1861–1862).

2. Under Ricasoli, the agitation for annexation of Rome continued.

3. Ricasoli was succeeded by Rattazzi who went back to Cavour's policy regarding Garibaldi and the Roman question: keep the old soldier on the verge of insurrection to justify the Italian government's more moderate methods of achieving the same goal.

E. In June, 1862 Garibaldi went to Sicily with the knowledge of the government. Using the cry "Rome or death," Garibaldi left Catania, Sicily with 3,000 men and landed in Calabria.

1. Here a government force dispersed Garibaldi's surprised troops who thought that the cabinet had approved of

their march on Rome by not breaking up the expedition
in Catania.

2. The <u>Aspromonte skirmish</u> caused the downfall of
Rattazzi.

3. After a short interlude under the deranged Farini,
<u>Marco Minghetti</u> became Premier.

F. <u>The September Convention (September 15, 1864)</u>

1. The Italian desire for Rome did not end with the Aspro-
monte affair. Despite papal occupation, Rome still was
desired as the capital of a united Italy. How to accomplish this with the presence of a French army of occupation was a difficult problem.

2. Minghetti believed that if the French could be induced
to leave, Rome might eventually fall into Italian hands.
Napoleon III, however, had to have assurances that the
new Italy would forget her Roman ambitions. Only this
could placate French Catholic opinion in the face of a
withdrawal from Rome.

3. In the September Convention, France agreed to withdraw her troops within two years if the Italian government agreed to move her capital from Turin to Florence.
Minghetti agreed, but only to get the French out of Italy
by 1866.

4. Minghetti (from Bologna) also had the satisfaction to
see the capital moved out of Piedmont. The move to
Florence delighted the provincially-minded Italians of
southern and central Italy.

G. <u>The acquisition of Venetia in 1866</u>

1. Bismarck's conversations with Napoleon III at Biarritz
and Paris in the fall of 1865 convinced the Prussian
statesman that the French would not stand in the way of
a Prusso-Italian alliance.

2. Napoleon III could thus help Italy secure Venetia and
clear his conscience for his shabby treatment of Cavour
in 1859.

3. Under the new Premier, <u>General La Marmora,</u> Italy ne-
gotiated with both Prussia and Austria well into 1866.
<u>On May 12, 1866 the alliance with Prussia was signed.</u>
Although Austria soon realized her error and offered
Italy Venetia to stay out of the coming German war, the
Italians believed a military victory was needed to cement
the unity of their particularist state.

4. Italy suffered military defeats on land (Custozza) and at sea (Lissa). Only the great Prussian victory at Königgrätz and the mediation of Napoleon III won Venetia for Italy.

H. The winning of Rome in 1870

1. The acquisition of Venetia after military defeat left Italian patriots with a sense of disillusionment. The Italian armed forces proved themselves deficient in training, leadership, equipment, and spirit except for the few Garibaldians who did well in the Trentino. The new Italy was being forged, but the mass of Italians regarded it as just another master. Poverty, not Austria, remained the chief enemy. High taxes and inflation, mainly at the expense of the peasantry, caused additional disillusionment with the state. The middle and upper class Italians scarcely realized that a serious social problem existed.

2. Disillusionment and poverty notwithstanding, the Roman question was still unsolved. By the terms of the 1864 September Convention, the last French troops left Rome in December, 1866.

3. The government again encouraged a move on Rome by Garibaldi: Rattazzi hoped for a revolution within Rome that would give him an excuse to intervene. But he did not act as Garibaldi moved on Rome.

4. The French quickly returned (October, 1867) and helped papal troops rout Garibaldi with their new *chassepot* rifles (Mentana, November 3, 1867).

5. This event embittered Franco-Italian relations for the next three years. It prevented the formation of a Franco-Austrian-Italian alliance against Prussia, and left France isolated in 1870.

6. When the Franco-Prussian War broke out, French troops were withdrawn from Rome. An Italian army under General Cadorna quickly occupied Rome (September 20, 1870). Rome was now made the capital.

7. In an effort to placate Pius IX and world Catholic opinion, the Law of Papal Guarantees was passed (May 13, 1871). It guaranteed to the pope complete freedom to exercise his spiritual functions. Representatives of foreign states to the Vatican were granted full diplomatic rights. The pope was to have an annual income of 3,-

250,000 lire, an amount he enjoyed from his former lands. Pius IX rejected the offer. He and all subsequent popes until Pius XI regarded themselves as prisoners. Only the Lateran Treaties of 1929 eased the situation.

V. The Development of Italy, 1870–1914

A. End of enlightened conservatism
  1. During the relatively quiet period from 1869 to 1876 the capable and enlightened statesmen of the Right continued to hold power: Giovanni Lanza (1869–1873) and Marco Minghetti (1873–1876) were typical of the devoted and skilled men who had led Italy to unification and beyond.
B. The first ministry of the Left came to power in 1876 under Agostino Depretis.
  1. Like his more conservative predecessors he worked with all moderate elements to the right and left of the center. Only clerical extremists and Mazzinian leftists were avoided. This system of moderate political alliances (*trasformismo*) gave Depretis control of parliament for the bulk of the period to his death in 1887.
  2. The policy of *trasformismo* tended to blur or postpone serious issues between the left and right. Nevertheless, it remained a political pattern until the advent of Mussolini.
  3. Depretis also won considerable parliamentary support by alliances with local political bosses. The use of government pressure and the promise of government contracts also were employed by Depretis and his subordinates.
  4. In 1878 King Victor Emmanuel II died, and was succeeded by the more dignified Humberto I (1878–1900). In the same year Leo XIII (1878–1903) became pope, but efforts to settle the Roman question were to no avail.
  5. The electorate was increased from 600,000 to some 2 million in 1881 by reducing the voting age to 21 and by halving the tax-paying requirement.
  6. Poor administration of the compulsory elementary school education act (children six to nine) made that reform valueless.

C. The first ministry of Francesco Crispi, 1887–1891
   1. After the death of Depretis, the republican and anti-clerical Crispi became Premier. He pushed through laws abolishing compulsory religious instruction in the elementary schools, and almost caused Pope Leo XIII to leave the Vatican by erecting a statue of the heretic-scientist Giordano Bruno near the Holy See.
   2. His imperialistic tendencies soon won for Italy a protectorate over Ethiopia (Treaty of Ucciali, 1889). During Crispi's second ministry 1895–1896) war with Ethiopia resulted from conflicting interpretations of this agreement. Italy suffered a disastrous defeat at Adowa (March, 1896), and abandoned her Ethiopian hopes until 1935. She retained Eritrea along the coast of the Red Sea.
   3. The Sicilian conservative Di Rudini succeeded Crispi as Premier in 1891–1892. This aristocrat with a red beard and a monocle continued the old policy of transformism: he appointed many moderate deputies of the Left to his cabinet—even Nicotera who had served in a Leftist ministry under Depretis. This move by Di Rudini symbolized the lack of clear-cut party division in Italy. Di Rudini was content to balance the budget and play down the jingoism of his predecessor.
   4. The more moderate Giolitti was selected for his first ministry (1892–1893). Like his predecessors, both Rightist and Leftist, he successfully used government pressure to win 380 out of a possible 508 seats. The corrupt political atmosphere helped. But his majority was elected on no single issue; they were also easily pushed apart, since they belonged to no one party.
      a. Giolitti was overthrown within a year when scandals involving the *Banca Romana* were made public.
D. The second Crispi ministry, 1893–1896
   1. The fears of socialism and peasant revolts in Sicily forced the middle and upper classes to accept the strong but Leftist government of Crispi.
   2. The ideas of Garibaldi, Mazzini, plus the anarchism of Bakunin all aided the development of socialism. The Marxist writing of Antonio Labriola and Pisacane also were a key element.
      a. The peasants of the poverty-stricken south were the

most vulnerable, although Milan became the center of Marxism.

b. When the revolt against unbearable social conditions occurred, it came in Sicily. The socialists merely associated themselves with it (1893).

c. Groups of workers *(fasci)* occupied the communal lands in Sicily which had been taken from them. These untutored peasants knew nothing of Marxist doctrine, but Crispi used this as a scare for a severe and unwarranted repression.

3. Despite the repression and financial scandal that surrounded Crispi, his Minister of Finance, Sidney Sonnino, succeeded in balancing the budget in 1896. This was a great feat in view of the expenditures for the Ethiopian fiasco.

4. The humiliating defeat at Adowa forced Crispi to resign. He was too closely associated with the desire for grandeur through an east African empire to escape the responsibility for defeat. His political repression and failure to cope with the social unrest in southern Italy and Sicily also helped force his retirement at the age of 80.

E. The second Rudini ministry, 1896–1898

1. Rudini wisely pardoned the leaders of the Sicilian *fasci,* and tried to initiate some reforms on his home island.

a. Rudini still had to cope with the same basic social problem Italy had faced since her birth: the widespread hunger and joblessness.

b. City workers joined the peasantry on the Marxist left in larger numbers. New industry had attracted millions from the countryside (Turin grew from 250,000 to 500,000 from 1871 to 1921), but during periods of unemployment these workers were fertile material for socialist agitators.

c. Even Pope Leo XIII urged social betterment for the poorer classes in the encyclical *Rerum novarum.* But the great gulf between wealth and poverty was not so easily bridged.

d. Bread riots throughout Italy forced Rudini to resign in 1898.

F. The government of General Luigi Pelloux, 1898–1900

1. The crisis seemed to call for a strong hand, but Pelloux

became a tool for those who wished to strengthen the executive over the legislature.

    a. In June, 1899 Pelloux astounded the country by declaring that he would rule by royal decree alone.

    b. The Left continued to resist against his arbitrary rule. Even the liberals joined them in a successful defense of the constitution.

    c. The new coalition gained in the elections of 1900 and Pelloux chose to resign. The unpopular king, Humberto, was assassinated and was succeeded by the more liberal Victor Emmanuel III.

G. The Giolitti era, 1901–1914

    1. In 1903 Giolitti again became Premier. He was to hold the office five times. Even when he was out of power during this era, his liberal influence could be felt.

    2. Giolitti excelled in his knowledge of finance and in the area of administration. He was not a flamboyant speaker, but was a good judge of men.

    3. Giolitti was an ardent advocate of parliamentary government. He was determined to avoid the repressive practices of Pelloux and Crispi, but was not averse to dealing with local party losses or using the transformist technique in parliament.

    4. Giolitti was one of the first liberal leaders to understand the reasons for the growth of socialism in Italy.

        a. He did not blame, for example, the Sicilian uprising of 1893 on radical doctrine, but rather on the poverty of the area and the government's unwillingness or inability to improve the situation. Even in the industrialized and relatively wealthy city of Milan the socialists made considerable electoral gains after 1900.

        b. Giolitti believed that social reforms would rewin the urban proletariat and the impoverished farmers. He also adopted the new policy of not making the police the instrument of the employers. In this way, the poorer elements of Italian society began to regard the state less and less as an enemy.

        c. The safety valve that perhaps prevented a social revolution in southern Italy and Sicily was mass emigration to the United States, Brazil, and Argentina. By 1914 almost six million Italians had left their homeland. Thirty-five million remained.

d. But even under Giolitti there was more talk than action to improve rural conditions. Twenty-two years (1905–1927) were required to complete an aqueduct to carry water from the Apennines to arid Apulia.

e. The general election of 1913 showed an increase in socialist strength from 41 to 78 seats in the lower chamber. Also important was the larger number of Catholic deputies: 14 to 35.

f. Despite the numerous strikes (which Giolitti handled with moderation), Giolitti still felt that liberal concessions would win the discontented. In June, 1912 the vote was given to almost everyone.

5. <u>Giolitti was not the usual table-thumping Irredentist who felt he had a mission to make Italy great.</u>

a. Fortunately, the tariff war with France had been ended in November, 1898. In exchange for a free hand in Morocco, France gave Italy to understand that she would not oppose her acquisition of Tripoli (1900).

b. Despite the rapprochement with France, the Triple Alliance with Germany and Austria-Hungary was renewed in 1902, 1907, and 1912. But Italy continued to flirt with both the French and the Triple Entente. Unfortunately, Giolitti never gave foreign affairs the same meticulous attention he devoted to domestic problems.

c. Nationalistic pressure at home and approval of the great powers abroad induced Italy to seize Tripoli (1911–1912). As in Eritrea, she had merely annexed a sandy waste. Tripoli was not another Tunisia.

6. <u>The leftist gains in the 1913 elections showed that the liberalism of Giolitti had already passed its peak.</u>

a. Despite Giolitti's enlightened views (as against accomplishments), the socialist groups captured about one-quarter of the seats. The constitutional liberals still had a large majority, but their numbers were reduced from 370 to 318.

b. Giolitti, however, had to soften his anticlericalism to hold many Catholic deputies in his new coalition. It was obvious that the liberals were merely holding on:

the extremists on the left and right were gaining strength.

7. <u>By 1914 Giolitti's star began to wane.</u>
   a. The 1913 elections had been so corrupt, even by Italian standards, that Giolitti's popularity virtually disappeared.
   b. Many left of center deputies left the Giolitti coalition.
   c. Giolitti resigned in 1914. He hoped this would be another temporary withdrawal, but except for a brief ministry in 1920–1921, Giolitti's political career was over.
   d. The corruption and anarchism of Giolitti's Italy were the products of an unhealthy social, economic, and political environment. Theft, nepotism, bribery, brigandage, and violence were all part of the contemporary scene. Giolitti did not invent them, but he made good political use of the existing situation.

H. <u>The Italian economy after 1870</u>
   1. The bulk of Italian industry was concentrated in the north. Milan, Genoa, and Turin paced the peninsula as the great centers of commerce and industry.
   2. After 1900, Italy again enjoyed a period of prosperity.
      a. The tariff war with France had been ended in 1898 by the conclusion of a commercial treaty.
      b. Emigration abroad eased the problem of a mushrooming population.
      c. The cooperative movement and greater use of electricity were also important factors.
      d. Wages rose considerably, since labor disputes were settled without government intervention on behalf of employers.
      e. The Italian treasury enjoyed a surplus during the period 1899–1910. In addition, foreign trade grew tremendously between 1890 and 1910. The port of Genoa was the third most important Mediterranean stopping point.
      f. Despite the economic upswing, per capita income in Italy was half that in France and only one-third the British level.
   3. Italy had little coal, but the generation of hydroelectric power was encouraged until the pressure of World War I.

    a. Even as late as 1914 Italy had to import 12 million tons of coal annually.

    b. The import of this coal plus the increase in the amount of electricity generated gave many new industries a chance to prosper.

    c. The high cost of imported raw materials doomed these new industries. Many collapsed in the 1919 recession.

4. Land reclamation remained a serious problem for the Italian government. The area around Rome contained the Pontine marshes. To the north of Rome was the large marshland of Maremma. Still another great swamp was located near Ferrara.

    a. But despite brave statements, the mosquito-infested swamps were not drained to provide sorely needed land.

5. Still another serious problem was the indiscriminate use of forest resources in the Apennines and Sardinia.

    a. The result was the loss of valuable timber lands. A good deal of rural unemployment followed. Flooding and the loss of vital topsoil were additional problems.

BIBLIOGRAPHY

Albrecht-Carrié, Rene, *Italy from Napoleon to Mussolini* (New York: Columbia University Press, 1950).

Binkley, R. C., *Realism and nationalism, 1852–1871* (New York: Harper, 1935).

Bruun, Geoffrey, *Revolution and reaction, 1848–1852* (Princeton: D. Van Nostrand, 1958).

Case, Lynn M., *Franco-Italian relations; the Roman question and the Convention of September* (Philadelphia: University of Pennsylvania Press, 1932).

Clark, Chester W., *Franz Joseph and Bismarck: the diplomacy of Austria before the war of 1866* (Cambridge, Mass.: Harvard University Press, 1934).

Craig, Gordon A., *The politics of the Prussian army, 1640–1945* (New York: Oxford University Press, 1955).

Croce, B., *A history of Italy, 1871–1915* (Oxford: Clarendon Press, 1929).

Dawson, William H., *The German Empire, 1867–1914.* 2 vols. (New York: Macmillan, 1919).

Eyck, Erich, *Bismarck and the German Empire* (London: Allen and Unwin, 1950).

Hales, E. E. Y., *Pio Nono: a study in European politics and religion in the nineteenth century* (New York: Kenedy, 1954).

Hayes, Carlton J. H., *A generation of materialism 1871–1900* (New York: Harper, 1941).

Henderson, W. O., *The state and the industrial revolution in Prussia, 1740–1870* (Liverpool: Liverpool University Press, 1958).

Hentze, Margot, *Pre-fascist Italy: the rise and fall of the parliamentary regime* (London: Allen and Unwin, 1939).

Kohn, Hans, *The idea of nationalism: a study in its origins and background* (New York: Macmillan, 1944).

Lord, Robert H., *The origins of the war of 1870. New documents from the German archives* (Cambridge, Mass.: Harvard University Press, 1924).

Mosse, W. E., *The European powers and the German question, 1848–1871* (London: Cambridge University Press, 1958).

Oncken, Hermann, *Napoleon III and the Rhine: the origin of the war of 1870–71* (New York: Knopf, 1928).

Passant, E. J., *A short history of Germany, 1815–1945* (London: Cambridge University Press, 1960).

Pinson, Koppel S., *Modern Germany* (New York: Macmillan, 1954).

Robertson, C. G., *Bismarck* (New York: Barnes and Noble, 1947).

Salamone, A. W., *Italian democracy in the making, 1900–1914* (Philadelphia: University of Pennsylvania Press, 1945).

Smith, D. Mack, *Italy* (Ann Arbor: University of Michigan Press, 1959).

Sprigge, C. J. S., *The development of modern Italy* (New Haven: Yale University Press, 1944).

Steefel, Lawrence D., *The Schleswig-Holstein question* (Cambridge, Mass.: Harvard University Press, 1932).

Taylor, A. J. P., *Bismarck: the man and the statesman* (New York: Knopf, 1955).

———, *The course of German history* (New York: Coward-McCann, 1946).

Whyte, A. J., *The evolution of modern Italy* (Oxford: Blackwell, 1944).

Chapter 10

GREAT BRITAIN AND FRANCE: MIDCENTURY TO WORLD WAR

I. The Legacy of 1848 in Great Britain

A. <u>Although Chartism seemingly came to an ignonimous end with the failure of Feargus O'Connor in 1848, most of its requests were won ultimately.</u> Among these were universal suffrage, annual parliaments, and voting by ballot rather than openly. Another lasting achievement of Chartism was its sponsorship of the cooperative movement. From its beginning in 1844 under the two dozen Rochdale Pioneers, the movement has continued to grow.

B. After the business recession of 1847 and the peak of Chartist agitation in 1848, British economic recovery was rapid. Railway construction paved the way for the boom times that followed. The Great Exhibition of 1851 in Hyde Park was a public tribute to the great new industrial age.

   1. With the rise in employment came better wages.

   2. The trade union movement also gained strength and became a permanent feature of the British scene. By 1876 most legal restrictions against unions were removed. After 1900 unions and workers entered British politics through the Labor Party.

C. <u>The Irish problem</u>

   1. The problem of longstanding Anglo-Irish bitterness had been aggravated after 1840.

     a. The population of Ireland had risen from 2.5 million in 1760 to 8 million in 1840. The result was overpopulation.

     b. Landlord rapacity, frequent famines, and overdependence on the potato crop were additional problems.

  c. Famine and disease between 1845 and 1849 were particularly devastating. The potato blight plus large case exports of food by the landowners brought many Irishmen to the edge of starvation.

  d. Some 780,000 people left Ireland in the decade 1841–1850. An additional 914,000 emigrated between 1851 and 1860, and 655,000 more from 1881–1890.

  e. Even the repeal of the Corn Laws by Peel in 1846 failed to help, since the potato crop failed that year.

  f. The Irish also resented the high rents they paid to absentee British landlords, and felt that they were the real owners of the soil.

  g. Money paid to support the established (Anglican) church caused considerable bitterness.

  h. Still another grievance was the fact that Irishmen had no say in making the laws of their own land. An independent Irish parliament had been abolished after a 1798 rebellion, and an <u>Act of Union (1800)</u> required Irish M.P.'s to sit in the British parliament in London.

 2. After the death of the moderate <u>Daniel O'Connell</u> in 1847, leadership of the Irish national movement passed into the more radical hands of William Smith O'Brien and his Young Ireland Party.

  a. An attempted revolt at Tipperary (July, 1848) failed, but the ardor of the national movement was not dampened.

II. British Political Evolution, 1846–1867

A. <u>Effect of Corn Law repeal</u>

 1. Peel's repeal of the Corn Laws in 1846 not only enabled the British worker to buy cheaper bread, but it wrought a political revolution.

 2. Both the old Tory and Whig parties had been divided into conservative, liberal, and radical factions. After 1846 the gulf between the conservative Tories and the more liberal Peelites became immense. For a few years Disraeli led the conservative and protectionist-minded Tory wing, but even he abandoned high tariffs in 1852.

 3. The Whigs were also divided. The more conservative Whigs were led by <u>Lord John Russell</u>, while the liberal

Manchester-oriented Whigs followed <u>John Bright</u> and <u>Richard Cobden.</u>

a. From such divergent groups little cooperation resulted. The result was little important legislation during this period.

b. Nevertheless, the new Liberal and Conservative parties emerged. The political instability which yielded eight ministries between 1846 and 1868 could not prevent this political evolution.

c. Generally, Whig-Liberal coalitions dominated the scene. A typical coalition was the Whig-Peelite alliance under Lord Aberdeen from 1852–1855.

B. <u>Poor management of Crimean War affairs led to the downfall of the Aberdeen ministry. He was succeeded by the unpredictable and audacious Palmerston (1855–1858).</u>

1. Palmerston was ejected when he tried to pass a measure to increase the penalty for conspiracy to murder. This resulted from French protests regarding Orsini's attempt to kill Napoleon III. The French believed the Orsini plot originated in England.

C. <u>The second Derby ministry, 1858–1859</u>

1. The Conservative Derby had been Prime Minister briefly in 1852.

2. His ministry ended all property requirements for members of Parliament, and removed legal disabilities on Jews.

3. The Derby ministry removed all political authority over Indian affairs from the British East India Company. This was a direct result of the Sepoy Mutiny of 1857.

D. <u>The second Palmerston ministry, 1859–1865</u>

1. One of the greatest achievements of Palmerston was the free trade agreement with France known as the Cobden-Chevalier Treaty of 1860. Tariffs were lowered on British coal, iron, tools, and textiles, and British levies were lowered on French wines, silks, hats, and dresses.

2. Great Britain came close to war with the United States in 1861 when a Federal vessel seized two Confederate commissioners from the British steamer *Trent*. The release of Mason and Slidell averted war.

3. The Palmerston ministry of 1859–1865 was also significant for its part in the consolidation of British politics along Liberal and Conservative party lines. The former

Peelites and Whigs were joining forces under Gladstone; Palmerston was probably "the last of the Whigs." At the same time the conservative factions in the old Whig and Tory parties were beginning to coalesce under Benjamin Disraeli.

4. The death of Palmerston (October, 1865) paved the way for the coming Liberal-Conservative battle between Gladstone and Disraeli.

E. The Reform Bill of 1867

1. Lord John Russell now became prime minister for the second time (1865–1866). He had proposed measures to broaden the electorate in 1851, 1852, and 1853, but had failed each time. The defection of a group of Liberals under Robert Lowe (Adullamites) defeated Russell's fourth reform bill.

2. Russell was succeeded by Lord Derby who now formed his third ministry (1866–1868). Disraeli successfully prevailed on both Lord Derby and Queen Victoria to support the nationwide demand for electoral reform.

3. By this bold stroke Disraeli hoped to catch the reform-minded Liberals by surprise and make it known to all classes that the Conservative Party was also the champion of the people. He was about to begin a program of "Tory democracy."

4. After considerable amendment in a liberal direction, the reform bill became law (August 15, 1867). Small house-owners and artisans (the bulk of the English workers) now won the right to vote in the boroughs and counties. The electorate had been doubled and the boroughs with less than 10,000 people could no longer send two members to the Commons. The mushrooming cities such as Manchester, Leeds, Liverpool, and Birmingham gained seats. In all, the towns and cities won 19 new places, while the counties added some 25.

5. When Lord Derby retired in February, 1868 Disraeli succeeded him as prime minister. His ministry was short lived, however. When Gladstone again pressed the question of a solution to the agitation in Ireland, the divided Liberals joined forces and defeated the Conservatives. In the ensuing general election, the newly enfranchised householders turned on Disraeli and helped

produce a major election victory for the Liberals and Gladstone.

III. Gladstone and Disraeli, 1868–1894

A. The Great Ministry of Gladstone, 1868–1874

1. The devout Gladstone was a former Peelite who gradually moved into the ranks of the new Liberal Party. He was particularly able in matters of finance, and possessed a strong humanitarian streak that hampered him in the great imperialistic scramble after 1871. Gladstone was also determined to improve conditions in Ireland.

2. Despite the opposition of the Conservatives, the Anglican (Episcopalian) clergy, and the House of Lords, Gladstone made the Disestablishment Act of 1869 law. No longer would Irish Catholics be obliged to support a church of which they were not members. The law took effect in 1871. Gladstone now tried to remedy the serious problem of land tenure in Ireland. British landlords in Ireland made few improvements for their Irish tenants, and often evicted them without compensation for improvements they had made. The Irish Land Act of 1870 gave the tenant compensation for improvements should he be evicted. Government loans were to be made to those who wished to buy their land. Unfortunately, the act accomplished very little. Rents could still be raised indiscriminately, and tenants were still evicted arbitrarily. The Irish question was still unsolved as an 1870 rebellion in County Mayo indicated.

3. Education Bill of 1870
   a. This bill helped improve the backward British school system. Board schools under the control of locally elected officials were established. They were supported by government funds, local taxes, and fees by parents. The question of compulsory attendance was to be settled locally. This was made a requirement for all in 1880. Church schools that met government standards would receive government grants, but no funds from local taxes,

4. Civil service reform (1870)
   a. From this time on, except for the Foreign Office, all

civil servants were to be hired on the basis of competitive examinations.

5. The Army Regulation Bill (1871)
   a. Under the leadership of Edward Cardwell, the secretary of war, the old system of purchased commissions was ended.

6. Ballot Act of 1872
   a. Secret voting replaced oral and public voting.

7. Judicature Act of 1873
   a. The existing courts were reorganized and divided into two new divisions: the high court of justice, and the court of appeal. Appeals could be made to the House of Lords from the latter court.

8. End of the Great Ministry
   a. Gladstone's many reforms had alienated various special interest groups. The Education Bill of 1870 had offended the extremists (nonconformists and high churchmen). The end of purchased commissions alienated the wealthy, while Gladstone's pacifist foreign policy disturbed the numerous jingoes of all classes. Other irritating items were the tax on matches and premature temperance legislation.
   b. In the general election of 1874 the Conservatives were victorious and Benjamin Disraeli became prime minister.

B. The Second Disraeli Ministry, 1874–1880
   1. Even the conservative Disraeli continued the parade of reforms begun by his antagonist Gladstone.
      a. The Public Health Act of 1875 is still the basis of British sanitary law.
      b. The Artisans Dwelling Act of 1875 was an important government attempt to improve the housing of the poor. Authorities in the larger cities were permitted to demolish buildings unsafe for habitation.
      c. The Factory and Workshops Act of 1878 regulated working conditions and hours.
   2. Foreign policy
      a. Even before coming to office Disraeli had promised a more adventurous foreign policy. The British public had watched Gladstone permit the Russians to remilitarize the Black Sea (1871). In addition, Russian moves near Afghanistan caused concern.

b. Disraeli caught the public's imagination by his masterly, if illegal, purchase of 177,000 shares (44 per cent) of Suez Canal stock from the bankrupt khedive of Egypt. With the approval of only the cabinet (parliament was not sitting), Disraeli borrowed £4 million from the Rothschilds and purchased the shares before the French could take advantage of the situation. This gave the British control of almost half the stock, and prevented French control of a waterway whose traffic was eighty per cent British.

c. To tie India more securely to Britain and also please Queen Victoria, Disraeli pushed the Royal Titles Bill through parliament. The law gave Victoria the title Empress of India.

d. The Near East crisis of 1875–1876 now absorbed much of Disraeli's energy. The original revolt in Bosnia-Herzegovina against Turkish misgovernment quickly spread to Montenegro, Serbia, and Bulgaria. Austria, Russia, and Prussia pressed the Turks to treat their Christian populace decently, and Disraeli reluctantly followed suit. He did not wish to weaken Turkey and allow Russian penetration to the Mediterranean. The Turks knew this but the British public and Gladstone badgered Disraeli to do something in the face of the Bulgarian Massacres. Russia declared war on Turkey in 1877, and after reaching the vicinity of Constantinople, forced the harsh Treaty of San Stefano on Turkey. Disraeli objected vigorously and war appeared imminent, until it was agreed to meet at the so-called Congress of Berlin under the "honest" eye of Otto von Bismarck. Russian demands were scaled down, Bulgaria was divided into two autonomous parts, Austria won the right to administer Bosnia and Herzegovina, and Disraeli came home with the triumphal annexation of Cyprus. This was the high point of Disraeli's popularity.

e. The Afghan War of 1878–1879 and the war against the Zulus in the Transvaal brought the powerful moral wrath of Gladstone down upon the government. This coupled by the severe decline in agriculture (due to American production) hurt Disraeli.

3. The campaign of 1880

    a. Gladstone barnstormed the country attacking Disraeli's imperialistic policies. Disraeli preferred to use Commons, partly because of personal inclination and partly due to illness.

    b. The election results signaled a great Liberal victory. Disraeli resigned and was succeeded as prime minister by Gladstone.

    c. Disraeli died in 1881. Salisbury succeeded him as head of the Conservative Party.

C. The Second Gladstone Ministry, 1880–1885

  1. The Irish question

    a. Under the leadership of Charles Parnell the Home Rule party sought a separate legislature for Ireland in the 1870's.

    b. In addition to the usual coercive measures, Gladstone attempted to improve the lot of the Irish by his Land Act of 1881. Fair rentals were to be set by an impartial judge, but nothing was said about the rents already in arrears. Those who rented won greater security, and could be compensated for improvements they made if the land was sold. Neither the landlords nor the farmers were pleased.

    c. Parnell was imprisoned for urging his followers to intimidate those who took advantage of the Land Act of 1881. He was released in 1882 when he agreed to end the "boycott."

    d. Parnell repudiated all connection with the Phoenix Park murders (Dublin) of Lord Cavendish and Thomas Burke (1882). Trial by jury was suspended and the police were given power to search and arrest on mere suspicion. The Irish nationalists continued their campaign of terrorism despite these measures.

  2. Foreign problems

    a. Although Gladstone had based his 1880 platform on an anti-imperialistic stand, circumstances compelled him to send troops into Egypt in 1882. The Egyptian nationalists under Ahmed Arabi were defeated at Tel el-Kebir.

    b. The prestige of the Gladstone government fell when it failed to rescue General Gordon at Khartoum (January 26, 1885)

    c. The cabinet was also hurt by the crisis that followed

the Russian attempt to penetrate Afghanistan. The government's attempt to settle the crisis by negotiation succeeded, but was portrayed by the Conservatives as a sign of weakness (1885–1886).

3. Representation of the People Act of 1884
   a. This law gave the ballot to agricultural workers, a group that had been passed over in 1867. Some two million new voters were added to the rolls.
   b. Almost all males could now vote except for domestics, bachelors living with their families, and those with no fixed home.

4. Redistribution of Seats Act of 1885
   a. This act was a significant step in the direction of apportioning parliamentary seats in proportion to population.
   b. Boroughs with less than 15,000 people were merged with counties. Two-member districts having less than 50,000 inhabitants lost one seat. With a few exceptions, single-member constituencies became the rule except in the larger cities and boroughs.

5. Resignation of Gladstone (June 9, 1885)
   a. The loss of prestige in foreign affairs plus disunity in the ranks of the Liberals so weakened Gladstone that he was forced to resign.
   b. Disunity among the Liberals continued to plague the party from 1880 to 1905.
   c. The Conservative leader, Lord Salisbury, took office briefly (June, 1885–January, 1886).

D. The Third Gladstone Ministry, February–July, 1886
   1. Split in the Liberal Party
      a. In the election of December, 1885 the Liberals won 335 seats, the Conservatives 249, and the Home Rule (Irish Nationalist) Party of Parnell 86. Parnell's faction held the balance of power, and he supported Gladstone when the latter promised to fight for a home rule bill.
      b. This bill split the Liberals. Many feared for the Protestant minority in Ireland, while others believed the Irish might be disloyal in time of war. These men, led by Joseph Chamberlain, Lord Hartington, and John Bright, were called Liberal Unionists because they favored the continued union of Ireland

and England. Most of them left the Liberal ranks, and that party lost power for 20 years except for a single interval.

c. Gladstone had done to Liberals in 1886 what Peel had accomplished in 1846.

d. The First Home Rule Bill (1886) was rejected 343–313.

E. The Second Salisbury Ministry, 1886–1892

  1. Election of 1886

    a. This election, based on the issue of home rule, was a defeat for the Liberals. Salisbury formed a cabinet and made his nephew Arthur Balfour chief secretary for Ireland.

    b. A Crimes Act (1887) was passed to help repress Irish violence. In addition, Balfour continued Salisbury's policy (Ashbourne Act of 1885) of granting government loans so that Irish tenants could purchase their land.

    c. Meanwhile, indiscretions in Parnell's private life caused Gladstone to drop him. It also led to a split in Irish nationalist ranks until the emergence of John Redmond in 1899.

F. The Fourth Gladstone Ministry, 1892–1894

  1. Election of 1892

    a. Using the home rule issue plus a series of planks on domestic legislation, Gladstone and his Irish allies won a majority of the parliamentary seats.

  2. A second home rule bill passed Commons, but was rejected by Lords, 419–41.

    a. Gladstone was persuaded by his colleagues not to go to the country. Meanwhile, a peaceful era began in Ireland, and home rule was forgotten for 20 years.

    b. The ailing and elderly Gladstone resigned in 1894. He was succeeded by the imperialist Liberal, Lord Rosebery.

    c. Rosebery could get little legislation through with a divided Liberal party. He resigned after a minor defeat in June, 1895.

  3. In the meantime an avowedly socialist party had formed in 1893. It was the Independent Labor Party.

    a. Its roots lay in the Fabian Society of Sidney and George Bernard Shaw plus H. M. Hyndman's Social

Democratic Federation.
b. The emerging socialists were generally of the gradualist variety: they fought for representative government, universal suffrage, and state action to improve the condition of the workers.
c. Two socialists won election to parliament in 1892. One was James Keir Hardie, one of the founders of the Labor Party.

IV. A Decade of Conservative Rule, 1895–1905

A. The Third Salisbury Ministry, 1895–1902
1. The new Conservative government included Salisbury himself as foreign secretary and Balfour as head of the exchequer. Liberal Unionists like Joseph Chamberlain were included. Chamberlain had ample room for his imperial notions as colonial secretary.
2. The new government was forced to devote most of its energies to foreign policy.
   a. Almost at once a dispute arose over the border between British Guiana and Venezuela. President Cleveland rushed to Venezuela's assistance by invoking the Monroe Doctrine. War appeared certain in 1895 until the boundary question was settled by arbitration.
   b. Anglo-American relations seemed to improve from the low point of 1895. During the Spanish-American War only Great Britain was friendly to the United States. The Hay-Pauncefote Treaty of 1901 even gave British sanction to a solely American canal across Panama.
   c. When British diplomacy failed to halt foreign incursions into China after the Sino-Japanese War of 1894–1895, Britain took Kowloon and Weihaiwei.
   d. In 1902 Great Britain concluded an alliance with Japan. This defensive pact might help contain Russian moves in the direction of Manchuria and Korea.
   e. Still another problem was the Fashoda crisis of 1898–1899. The occupation of Fashoda on the Nile by Marchand brought Kitchener to the scene. After a period of tension, France yielded the area because of the Dreyfus problem and her lack of military prepa-

ration. Anglo-French relations soon began to improve under the influence of the French foreign minister, Théophile Delcassé.

f. Perhaps the most trying foreign problem was the Boer War of 1899–1902. The Boers had left Cape Colony early in the nineteenth century to settle in the Transvaal and Orange Free State. The discovery of gold in the Witwatersrand brought a huge influx of non-Boers into the area. Under the leadership of Cecil Rhodes and Lord Carnarvon, a clash was inevitable as the Kruger-led Boers attempted to restrict the "outlanders" by heavy taxation and denial of the franchise. In the war that followed, superior British and imperial forces subdued the brave Boers after a three year resistance. The generous Treaty of Vereeniging ended the war.

3. In 1901 the beloved Queen Victoria died. During her sixty-four year reign she gradually yielded more and more power to the cabinet. By 1901 Great Britain had become one of the world's greatest industrial powers. Her population reached 37 million, and her empire was the greatest ever assembled.

a. Victoria was succeeded by the gay Edward VII (1901–1910)

B. The Balfour Ministry, 1902–1905

1. In 1902 Lord Salisbury retired and was succeeded by the able Arthur Balfour.

2. Although the Conservatives generally made few reform proposals, the Education Act of 1902 was a significant piece of legislation. This act amended the 1870 law to give new local and borough councils control of secular education in all schools. These councils would replace the local school boards, and would be under the minister of education. Private schools could continue to give religious instruction.

3. Meanwhile, the Balfour government ran into several serious political storms: the house of lords in the 1901 Taff Vale decision had made unions financially liable for the acts of their members. This allowed employers to sue for damage suffered in labor disputes. The decision cost the Conservatives considerable support among the workers.

4. The Liberals also attacked Balfour for the poor treatment accorded imported Hindu and Chinese laborers in South Africa.

5. Balfour suffered the loss of Joseph Chamberlain who resigned in September, 1903 over the issue of an imperial preferential tariff.

    a. Chamberlain urged that tariff preference be given to the dominions and colonies that accorded similar treatment to Great Britain. This would strengthen imperial ties, give British industry the markets of the empire, and assure Great Britain of an adequate food supply.

    b. The Conservatives were divided, and the Liberals rose to the attack on a free trade platform.

6. Balfour resigned and the Liberal Sir Henry Campbell-Bannerman became prime minister in December, 1905.

    a. Herbert Asquith headed the exchequer, Sir Edward Grey took over the foreign office, and Richard Haldane became head of the war office.

    b. In the election of 1906 the Liberals won a clear majority in parliament with 379 seats. The Conservatives won but 132, the Irish Nationalists 83, and the rising Labor Party 51.

    c. A short-lived Liberal-Labor alliance based on social reforms resulted. In the long run the laissez-faire Liberals and the socialists were destined to split.

V. The Era of Liberal Power, 1905–1914

A. The stated policy of Campbell-Bannerman was a program of social reform. The Conservatives viewed such a policy with alarm, but were reassured by their control of the house of lords.

1. The house of lords rejected a measure approved in the lower house (Liberal Education Bill of 1906) to place private schools under the minister of education.

2. The Trades Disputes Bill of 1906 did pass, however. It nullified the Taff Vale decision.

3. The Provision of Meals Act of 1906 allowed school authorities to feed children who came to school hungry. Money could be obtained later from parents if they could pay.

4. The Workmen's Compensation Bill of 1906 liberalized the legislation of 1880 and 1897. Under the new law, most workers earning less than £250 a year were entitled to compensation from their employers for occupational illness or industrial accidents.

5. The Medical Inspection Act of 1907 made it possible for all school children to obtain a checkup by a physician.

6. Despite vigorous Conservative opposition, the Old Age Pensions Bill of 1908 became law. It passed the house of lords, but a showdown on the veto power of that body was imminent.

B. The Ministry of Herbert Asquith, 1908–1916

   1. In April, 1908 Campbell-Bannerman resigned because of poor health. He was succeeded by Herbert Asquith.

   2. In 1909 the Liberals passed three important pieces of social legislation.

      a. The Labor Exchanges Act of 1909 provided 350 offices in 11 districts where the unemployed could get information on vacancies.

      b. The Trade Boards Act of 1909 established trade boards consisting of an equal number of employers and employees in industries which had exceptionally low wages.

      c. The House and Town Planning Act of 1909 was a bold attempt to improve the substandard housing that many were compelled to occupy. Landlords were made responsible for the condition of their houses. Back to back houses were forbidden, cities were given permission to demolish condemned structures, and government aid was to be supplied for the construction of new housing.

C. Limiting the power of the house of lords

   1. The Lloyd George budget of 1909

      a. Lloyd George, chancellor of the exchequer, and the Liberals in general were determined to make the wealthy classes pay for the new social legislation and the naval expansion program made necessary by German efforts under Tirpitz.

      b. The budget passed commons, but was rejected by the house of lords (November, 1909). The lords did not appreciate the Liberal attempt to redistribute the national income via a "People's Budget" despite the fact that it was against all custom for the upper chamber to interfere in financial matters.

2. Asquith denounced the action of the house of lords as unconstitutional, and called for a general election in 1910 on this issue.

   a. The Liberals also backed home rule for Ireland.

   b. The election of January, 1910 diminished Liberal voting strength, but with the support of the Irish Nationalists and the Laborites they still had a majority.

   c. With this coalition in hand, the budget passed commons and the lords yielded.

3. The victorious coalition now turned to the task of limiting the power of the house of lords.

   a. The death of Edward VII brought his son George V (1910–1936) to the throne. The new monarch did what he could to work out a settlement.

   b. Asquith introduced a bill in the autumn of 1910 to allow the house of lords to delay a money bill only one month. All other bills passed by three consecutive sessions of commons would automatically become law if two years elapsed between introduction of the bill and final passage. In addition, the life of a parliament was to be limited to five years instead of the usual seven.

   c. The house of lords rejected the parliament bill, and a new election was held in December, 1910. Both the Liberals and Conservatives won 272 seats. The Irish Nationalists and Labor Party again held the balance of power. They continued to support Asquith.

   d. The Parliament Bill was again passed by the house of commons in February, 1911. The house of lords attached so many weakening amendments that Asquith won the king over to the idea of appointing enough Liberal peers to the upper chamber to insure passage of the bill. The legislation now squeaked through the house of lords 131–114 as many Conservatives absented themselves.

4. The house of commons now voted a salary of £400 a year for its members. This aided several Labor members who lacked financial resources, but who were unable to accept union funds because of the Osborne judgment of 1909 by the house of lords.

5. The National Insurance Act of 1911 was also made law.
   a. Wage earners between 16 and 65 (2¼ million) in industries subject to business fluctuation were required to purchase insurance designed to give them a maximum of 15 weeks of benefits.
   b. Sick benefits were provided for almost 15 million workers earning less than £160 a year.

D. Labor unrest
   1. Despite the substantial benefits won by the workers through the mass of Liberal legislation since 1906, they were seriously hurt by the substantial rise in prices between 1900 and 1910.
      a. The workers did not understand the problem of foreign tariffs, the role of vast British investments abroad, and the formidable economic competition of Germany and the United States.
      b. The workers now turned to trade unions and strikes rather than the Liberal and Labor parties.
   2. An epidemic of serious strikes occurred in 1911–1912. The most serious were among the transport workers and miners.
      a. The key problem remained: stationary wages and rapidly rising prices.

E. Revival of the Irish problem, 1912–1922
   1. The economic situation in Ireland had improved substantially since Gladstone introduced his home rule measure in 1886. Many Irishmen took advantage of Conservative legislation and purchased their farms. Emigration also declined. In addition, Asquith had promised to reintroduce a home rule bill in exchange for Irish Nationalist support on the Parliament Bill of 1911.
   2. In 1912 the bill was introduced with the support of John Redmond, leader of the Irish Nationalists.
      a. The people of the Protestant counties of Ulster under Sir Edward Carson protested vigorously. They did not wish to be dominated by the Catholic and agricultural south. The Conservatives supported their position.
      b. In January, 1913 the house of commons passed this third home rule measure. Despite the opposition of the house of lords, it would now become law in two

years if three successive sessions of the lower house passed the legislation.

c. The bill passed again in May, 1914.

d. In the meantime, war loomed between the Ulsterites and the Irish Nationalists. Only the occurrence of World War I prevented a civil conflict.

e. After the war a new home rule bill became law in December, 1920. Northern and southern Ireland each won a parliament of their own, and each kept their representation in the British Parliament. A Council for Ireland was to handle common problems.

f. Despite the continued revolutionary activities of the Sinn Fein, the Irish Free State was recognized as a dominion in 1922.

VI. France at Midcentury

A. The historian David Thomson has suggested that the 1815–1848 was the era "which the locusts ate" in France. France had failed to work out a compromise between the traditions of the Old Regime *(ancien régime)* and the ideas of the new revolutionary tradition since 1789. The efforts of Louis XVIII were wrecked by his autocratic successor, Charles X (1824–1830). Even under Louis Philippe (1830–1848) a division of authority existed between the monarch and the legislature. The idea of ministerial responsibility had not taken hold.

B. As of 1848 the French had failed to see a correlation between government and democracy. Government was regarded as an object of suspicion, while democracy as embodied in the revolutionary tradition, was held to be desirable. In this sense democracy was the expression of what Rousseau called the "general will."

C. The revolutionary tradition had gradually become alienated from the compromise path of constitutional monarchy. Such a course had not been fruitful enough under the Restoration (1815–1830) or during the July Monarchy (1830–1848). Now Louis Napoleon Bonaparte, president of the Second Republic (1848–1852), was asserting the validity of popular sovereignty. Such lip service proved to be a sham once Louis Napoleon had used Bonapartism to restore the empire. Plebiscites without democracy discredited

Bonapartism as a democratic force during the Second Empire (1852–1870). Louis Napoleon's rather close relationship with Roman Catholicism also precluded the possibility that the church would ever be accepted as party of the revolutionary tradition after 1870.

D. The French liberals gradually drifted to the right during the first half of the nineteenth century. These liberals did not see the need for cooperation with the voteless masses; they did not see the value of ministerial responsibility so long as they were to be the ministers. Guizot was typical of the early nineteenth century liberal who lost the confidence of the French people. The liberals of 1830 had become the conservatives of 1848.

  1. The leaders of the 1848 revolution—men like Lamartine and Marie—were suspicious of the new socialism of Louis Blanc, although French radicalism helped fill the void left by the end of the Old Regime. French liberalism had failed to expand democratic institutions. Such changes as occurred in 1830 and 1848 came through revolution. The British example of liberal reform from above (1832) was not appreciated.

  2. By 1851 a more conservative revolutionary appeared in the person of Louis Napoleon Bonaparte. For the moment Bonapartism became the driving force of the revolutionary tradition.

E. Louis Napoleon Bonaparte (1808–1873)

  1. Louis Napoleon was the son of Hortense de Beauharnais (daughter of Empress Josephine) and King Louis of Holland (brother of Napoleon I).

  2. As a youth his mother instilled in him the fact that he carried the hopes of all Bonapartists. Only he could erase the shame of the 1815 treaties, and restore France to her former grandeur.

  3. The death of the Duke of Reichstadt in 1832 elevated Louis Napoleon to the leadership of the Bonapartist cause. His *Rêveries politiques* (1832) soon made him better known in France. The long casualty lists provided by his uncle were forgotten. They were replaced by a Napoleonic legend, a *mystique* which gloried in the achievements of the Bonapartist past and attacked the pacifism and lack-lustre of the Orleanist regime. The Bourbons had threatened a return to the autocratic

past, and the Orleanists had failed to establish a liberal present. Bonapartism, said Louis Napoleon, would restore French greatness. Whether such greatness included democracy was another matter. For the moment it was enough to use plebiscites to cover up the deficiency.

4. In 1836 (Strasbourg) and again in 1840 (Boulogne) Louis Napoleon made two vain attempts to overthrow Louis Philippe with army support.
   a. Louis Napoleon was imprisoned at Ham until 1846 where he wrote the semi-socialistic *Extinction of Pauperism*. The utopian socialist influence can be seen by his hope that the poor could be settled in profitable agricultural colonies. Although the ideas were never put into operation, they served to win valuable support for Louis Napoleon in 1848. He was trying to be all things to all men.

5. In the economic sphere Louis Napoleon could be classed as an exponent of free trade. In this respect, his stay in England (after the escape from Ham in 1846) undoubtedly played a part.
   a. Louis Napoleon admired the free trade platform of Peel. He later fought the protectionist industrialists of France, and signed the Cobden-Chevalier agreement of 1860.

6. Louis Napoleon was also solicitous of the interests of French Catholicism.
   a. He dispatched troops to Rome in 1849, and helped restore Pius IX. The Falloux Law of 1850 gave the Church greater control over primary schools.

7. As a Bonaparte he paid particular attention to the army. While his name alone won support after his election as president in 1848, he strengthened his position by the distribution of honors, medals, and good food. Troops were encouraged to shout *"Vive l'empereur"* as he passed.

8. Louis Napoleon also made a determined effort to win middle class support by posing as the defender of the *status quo.* Only he could bring France, if not Europe, peace and prosperity. And these, he promised, could be won without disturbing the existing social order.

9. But despite his promise of peace, he often noted the need to revise the 1815 treaties to the advantage of

France. This he stated in the famous *Les idées napo-léoniennes* (1839). In addition, Louis Napoleon showed a genuine interest in the national aspirations of the Germans, Italians, Hungarians, Poles, and Rumanians.

F. Establishment of the Second Empire

1. Louis Napoleon's overwhelming victory in the presidential election of December, 1848 was probably the result of many of the aforementioned factors.

2. There, nevertheless, ensued a deadlock between the new president and the monarchist assembly. Both the Legitimists and Orleanists were temporarily united as the Party of Order, but they each hoped to place their candidate on the throne by a *coup d'état.*

   a. When the assembly refused to revise Article 45 of the constitution and permit Louis Napoleon to run for a second term, he and his followers seized power during the night of December 1–2, 1851.

3. December 2 was chosen, since it was the anniversary of his uncle's victory at Austerlitz in 1805. The president's half brother, Morny, and his devoted follower, Persigny, played key parts in the seizure of power.

4. Meagre opposition in Paris (December 4, 1851) and 13 departments was crushed by the Algerian veterans of Saint-Arnaud and Magnan. Over 25,000 from all classes were imprisoned. By December 15, 1851 all resistance had been crushed.

5. Plebiscite of December 21, 1851

   a. Under the direction of Morny, this "prepared" election gave Louis Napoleon permission to revise the constitution. The vote was 7,500,000 to 640,000.

   b. The French were weary of the parliamentary bickering of the Second Republic. Many desired a strong hand to fend off the menace of radicalism. The size of the affirmative vote may have been due in part to its oral nature.

   c. It should be noted that the vote in Paris was fairly close: Yes: 133,000 to No: 80,000. This may have reflected the repression of Magnan on December 4.

6. The new constitution of January 14, 1852

   a. The new constitution gave Louis Napoleon great authority. He alone commanded the armed forces. He could make peace or war, and initiate laws plus decrees to carry them out.

b. The president could choose a Council of State. This body could work out legislation in secret.

c. The Senate, also chosen by the president, could pass on the constitutionality of the laws. They could also amend the constitution with a *senatus consultum* if the president also agreed.

d. The Legislative Assembly *(Corps législatif)* could accept or reject legislation. It had no authority to initiate laws or amend them.

e. The authoritarian nature of the new constitution could be seen from the statement it contained on the president's authority: he governed "by means of" the Council of State, the Senate, and the Legislative Assembly.

7. Beginning of the authoritarian regime

a. It was estimated that the new regime exiled over 10,000 souls to Algeria. Over 25,000 were arrested.

b. Freedom of the press was ended. Each paper posted a large bond as a guarantee of its good behavior. Many papers became government organs, but a few like the *Siècle* managed to survive.

c. All political meetings and clubs were abolished.

d. Orleanist properties were confiscated.

e. All prefects were Bonapartist appointees.

f. Elections to the *Corps législatif* were rigged.

g. Louis Napoleon was in complete control of the entire government and the armed forces.

8. The provincial tour of September, 1852

a. This tour, arranged by the Minister of the Interior, Persigny, was designed to prepare the French public for the announcement that the empire had been established.

b. Handpicked prefects arranged for cheers and cries of "*Vive l'empereur.*"

9. Proclaiming the empire

a. The Senate passed an amendment to the constitution *(senatus consultum)* that created the empire. It was confirmed by a plebiscite.

b. On December 2, 1852, the forty-seventh anniversary

of his uncle's victory at Austerlitz, the Second Empire was proclaimed.

10. Establishing a dynasty
   a. On January 30, 1853 the new emperor, Napoleon III, married Eugénie de Montijo, Countess of Téba. Eugénie became the head of the clerical faction at court. Both Napoleon III and the new empress aided church schools and missions with funds and friendship, while the liberal Catholicism of Montalembert was kept at arm's length.
   b. On March 16, 1856 the Prince Imperial was born. A successor to the throne now seemed to assure the Bonapartist dynasty the continuity it lacked.

11. Foreign recognition of the Second Empire
   a. To reassure the worried Great Powers, Louis Napoleon had stated in his Bordeaux speech of September 27, 1852 that "the empire means peace."
   b. They still had memories of Ulm and Austerlitz, and were worried by the new emperor's stated intention of changing the Vienna treaties. In addition, the powers assembled at Vienna had decided that a Bonaparte should never again sit on the throne of France. Napoleon's choice of the numeral III was a challenge to the conservative courts.
   c. Led by Czar Nicholas II's grudging recognition, Austria and Prussia also opened relations with the new government. British recognition came more willingly.

G. The economic policy of Napoleon III
   1. Good Saint-Simonian that he was, the new emperor did much to industrialize France, improve her commercial position, and aid the poorer classes. His Bordeaux talk of September 27, 1852 gave the country a glimpse of his intentions regarding railway, harbor, and canal construction. As J. M. Thompson indicated, he made economic prosperity a consolation prize for the loss of liberty.
   2. Until the advent of the Second Empire banking had been under the control of conservative families like the Rothschilds. The new dynasty wanted more banking facilities, institutions that would make credit more readily available for the projects desired by the regime.
   3. The Péreire brothers founded the *Crédit mobilier* in

1852. It made loans to the government, but also financed the feverish industrial expansion. Unlike the family-controlled banks, its shares were sold to the public. Industrial growth was also pushed by the *Crédit foncier,* the *Comptoir d'Escompte,* and the more ancient *Banque de France.* Even the conservative Rothschilds invested heavily in railroads and ironworks; they also formed a company to exploit the resources of Algeria, an area of special interest to Napoleon III.

4. Napoleon III took a personal interest in expanding French railway construction. During his two decades in power, trackage increased five fold.

5. The new regime also completed the telegraph system, subsidized key steamship lines, and had the city of Paris rebuilt into the magnificient tourist center of today.

   a. Baron Eugène-George Haussmann was largely responsible for the reconstruction of Paris. New boulevards, stores, banks, additions to the Louvre, plus a new opera house made Paris a prime tourist attraction. Its population grew from 1 million in 1851 to 1.8 million in 1870.

6. Napoleon also made substantial efforts to modernize French industry.

   a. The Cobden-Chevalier Treaty of 1860 was a blow to the backward and protectionist-minded French industrialists. They now had to compete with the more efficient heavy industry of Great Britain.

   b. Once the protectionist-shackles had been broken, Napoleon offered French businessmen loans to modernize and thus meet the problem of foreign competition. Particular concern was shown for the coal and iron establishments. The continuing coal shortage may have been partly responsible for Napoleon III's great interest in Belgium, Luxemburg, the Saar, and the Rhineland.

7. The government-backed industrial expansion helped create a boom from 1852 until the panic year of 1857. The worst effects of this depression were over by 1859. Another business crisis occurred in 1866, but it too was weathered by the growing French economy. Not even the financial drains of the Crimean, Austro-Sardinian, and Mexican ventures seriously hurt France. She was

able to publicly cover the war loan of 1870 and quickly pay the huge indemnity resulting from defeat in the Franco-Prussian War.

8. Napoleon III and the workers
   a. Napoleon III generally sided with the captains of industry by breaking up strikes and keeping wages low.
   b. However, Napoleon III, in true Saint-Simonian fashion, redressed the balance in favor of the worker by initiating old age pensions, accident insurance, free lawyers, and free burial. Abolition of the identity card *(livret)*, compulsory state insurance, and the equality of the employer and employee before the law were further benefits.
   c. The French demand for trade unions became great after a group of French workers visited the London Exhibition of 1862 and made contact with their British counterparts.
   d. In 1864 unions were legalized. Strikes could also occur, but their value was impaired by the provision in this law which stated that the government could intervene if violence occurred or if serious attacks were made on the "liberty to work."

H. Political evolution of the Second Empire
   1. The authoritarian empire, 1852–1860
      a. During this era the press was kept under tight control. Each paper had to deposit 50,000 francs as a guarantee of good behavior. The minister of the interior could suspend editors at any time.
      b. Napoleon III completely dominated the government. He appointed the entire Council of State and the Senate. His prefects managed to return a lower house *(Corps législatif)* that was almost entirely Bonapartist before 1863.
      c. Louis Napoleon, mindful of Louis Philippe's weak foreign policy, became involved in the Crimean War (1854–1856). He hoped to restore the prestige of France, humble an ancient adversary of his uncle (Russia), rearrange the Vienna treaties, break up the "alliance" of the Northern Courts, and increase his stature in Europe. He succeeded in doing all these things, and probably reached the peak of his power

at the Congress of Paris (1856) which ended the Crimean War.

d. From 1856 to 1859 he vacillated between retaining the Crimean alliance with Great Britain and making a new arrangement with Russia. The English became more and more suspicious of his territorial aims in Europe, while the Russians would come to no understanding with him unless he agreed to abrogate the Black Sea demilitarization clause of the Congress of Paris agreement.

e. In the meantime, Napoleon III and Cavour had become embroiled in the unpopular Austro-Sardinian War of 1859. It cost Napoleon III considerable battle casualties, money, and Catholic support in France. His acquisition of Nice and Savoy in 1860 worried all of Europe, and the territorial losses of Pope Pius IX in that year further angered French Catholics. Napoleon III had also alienated French industrialists by the anti-protectionist Cobden-Chevalier agreement of 1860.

2. The liberal reform of 1860

a. A combination of pressures thus induced Napoleon III to make a small political concession. On November 24, 1860 a decree was issued to permit the legislature to debate the speech from the throne. The work of the legislature could also be reported in the press. Although this was a minor political opening, it did enable the few opposition members to criticize government policy.

3. The election of 1863

a. Despite government pressure and influence, the opposition won two of the eight million votes cast. This new Third Party took 32 seats, but the government still retained 250. It was the size of the opposition vote that alarmed the regime.

4. The effect of Sadowa (1866)

a. The great Prussian triumph over Austria in July, 1866 seriously hurt the position and prestige of Napoleon III. His failure to intervene along the Rhine while Prussia was busy in Bohemia cost France the only opportunity she had to obtain compensation. Prussia's enlarged power as the North German Con-

federation alarmed the French and hurt Napoleon III's popularity within France.
  b. Napoleon III even failed to win tiny Luxemburg in 1867.
5. The liberal concessions of 1867
  a. The regime hoped to recoup some of its support by a substantial concession at home. Ministers could henceforth be interpellated by the legislature. Some restrictions on public meetings were lifted, and the press was made answerable to the courts and not the government-appointed prefects.
6. The election of May, 1869
  a. Prior to the election Leon Gambetta, a leader of the republican opposition, came forward with the liberal Belleville Program: freedom of assembly, liberty for the press, separation of church and state, free, secular, and compulsory elementary education, election of all public officials, and the abolition of all standing armies. This program was not realized in 1869, but it foreshadowed the republican program during the Third Republic.
  b. Although the government won the bulk of the legislative seats, the total vote of the opposition rose from 2 to 3.5 million. The vote for government candidates dropped from 6 to 4.5 million.
7. Reforms of July 12, 1869
  a. The *Corps législatif* was now given the power to initiate and amend laws. It could also vote the budget item by item, and discuss what it wished.
  b. The Senate was given the right to interpellate the government. This body was now permitted to amend or veto laws passed by the *Corps législatif.*
  c. Ministers could now also be deputies, but were appointed by and still responsible to Napoleon III.
8. The "Constitution of 1870"
  a. On April 20, 1870 a *senatus consultum* was passed which codified the constitutional changes since 1860.
  b. Ministers were still to be appointed by the emperor, but were now "responsible" to the legislature. France had now achieved constitutional monarchy.
  c. A plebiscite was held on May 8, 1870 on the question of the liberal changes of the previous decade. The

rural vote resulted in a substantial show of support for Napoleon III: 7,359,000 to 1,572,000. There were 1,894,000 abstentions. The larger cities such as Paris, Bordeaux, Marseilles, and Lyons voted against the government.

9. The Franco-Prussian War of 1870–1871

   a. Since the Prussian victory at Sadowa, France had been worried by the political complexion of Europe. Prussia through the new North German Confederation was clearly the leading power in Europe.

   b. French resentment was further embittered by her failure to win compensation in Belgium, Luxemburg, or along the Rhine. She also failed to cement an Austro-Italian-French alliance against Bismarck. To make matters worse, France failed to rearm sufficiently, while her military forces were led by men of lesser ability.

   c. The inevitable war came after Bismarck pushed the candidacy of Leopold, a Hohenzollern prince, for the vacant Spanish throne. French protests caused Leopold to withdraw his candidacy, but when a demand was made that the attempt never be made again, war resulted.

   d. The North German Confederation, supported by the four Catholic states of south Germany, quickly overwhelmed the French. Napoleon III himself was taken prisoner at Sedan with an entire army (September 2, 1870).

   e. Soon after the debacle at Sedan, a mob invaded the hall of the Legislative Assembly in Paris. They obliged the members of the lower chamber to proceed to the Hôtel de Ville where Gambetta and Favre led in the proclamation of a republic. Gambetta became the driving force behind the new Government of National Defense. By September 19, 1870 the Germans had surrounded Paris, but Gambetta escaped by balloon. While General Trochu was content to stay surrounded in Paris and while General Bazaine surrendered Metz and 175,000 men, Gambetta organized a desperate volunteer resistance. Paris finally surrendered on January 28, 1871, and Bismarck agreed to an armistice which would allow the election of a new

National Assembly. He proposed to deal only with this body, since it would be the most recent expression of the national thinking.

f. Elections were held on February 8, 1871 and the National Assembly met in Bordeaux five days later. Of the 650 deputies, only 200 were republicans; the majority were monarchists of Legitimist, Orleanist, or Bonapartist persuasion. It was a "republic without republicans." Thiers was made Chief of the Executive Power.

g. Thiers and Favre now completed the unpleasant task of signing a peace treaty with Bismarck. The Treaty of Frankfurt was completed on May 10, 1871 and provided for the cession of Alsace-Lorraine, an indemnity of five billion francs, and an army of occupation until the indemnity was paid.

I. The Third Republic, 1870–1914

1. From the proclamation of the Third Republic in September, 1870 until its dissolution in 1940 France enjoyed its longest period of political continuity.

2. The Paris Commune, March–May, 1871

a. Trouble was brewing in Paris as early as October 31, 1870 when socialists and other radicals made an attempt to seize control. It was unsuccessful, but the resentment over General Trochu (President of the Government of National Defense) and his incompetent defense of Paris remained.

b. The Parisians were also alarmed by the monarchist composition of the National Assembly elected on February 8, 1871. Republican Paris also resented the assembly's decision to meet at Versailles, a site associated with the Bourbon past.

c. The Germans had failed to disarm the National Guard in Paris. Thiers sent troops into Paris to seize their cannon, but the soldiers fraternized with the Parisians and permitted the mob to execute Generals Lecomte and Thomas.

d. The rebels declared Paris an independent commune and elected a municipal council that included followers of Blanqui, Proudhon, Jacobins of the 1793 type, moderate republicans, and some socialists. No definite program could emerge except a demand for decentralized government throughout France that was based on powerful municipalities.

e. Troops loyal to the Versailles government took the offensive in April, 1871 and crushed the desperate resistance of the Communards during the bloody week of May 21–28, 1871. About 38,000 Communards were arrested, and many were given prison terms, sentences of death, or were shipped to New Caledonia.

f. The harshness of the monarchist-middle class National Assembly was due to their fear of the radicalism represented by the Paris Commune. Law and order was their passion; socialism and anarchy was their nemesis.

3. The republic of Adolphe Thiers, 1871–1873

    a. The National Assembly contained about 200 Legitimists who supported the Bourbon pretender, the Count of Chambord. It also seated 200 Orleanist sympathizers who wished to see the Count of Paris made king. In addition 30 Bonapartists were elected. The new legislature contained about 200 republicans, but they succeeded in enlarging their numbers considerably in the next decade under the leadership of Leon Gambetta.

    b. The Bordeaux Pact between Thiers and the National Assembly (March 10, 1871) saw Thiers promise not to give any one political faction an undue advantage over the others.

    c. The Rivet Law of August 31, 1871 gave Thiers the title President of the Republic. Thiers now became an advocate of a conservative republic because it was "the government which divides us least." The Rivet Law also proclaimed the sovereignty of the National Assembly. The new president and the ministry were responsible to the legislature. This was an important step in the consolidation of the Third Republic, but the monarchists pushed it through with the idea in mind that since they controlled the legislature this seemingly republican institution could be used to eject Thiers at the right moment.

    d. Meanwhile, by-elections in 1871–1872 saw the republicans under Gambetta gain 23 seats.

    e. Through two government loans during 1871–1872

Thiers raised the funds needed to pay the German indemnity. The last German soldier left France in September, 1873.

    f. The monarchists then defeated the Thiers government as not being sufficiently conservative (360–344). This was on May 24, 1873.

4. The presidency of Marshal Marie MacMahon, 1873–1879

    a. MacMahon was an avowed monarchist whose chief purpose was to pave the way for a restoration.

    b. Within a few months (August, 1873) the Count of Chambord and the Count of Paris agreed to a plan of restoration. The childless Chambord would be restored first, and would be succeeded by the younger Count of Paris. The plan came to nothing a few months later when Chambord insisted on the white Bourbon flag instead of the tricolor.

    c. The stunned monarchists attempted to hold on by passing the Septennate Law (November 20, 1873). This would give President MacMahon a seven year term, and enable the monarchists to find a royal candidate. Nevertheless, the Bourbons and Orleanists failed to join forces despite several additional attempts.

    d. The growth of republican sentiment was thus fostered by the sorry picture of monarchist squabbles. In addition, threats of a new Bonapartist coup between 1872–1874 also strengthened the republican cause. The standing threat of monarchism was an important reason for the steady growth of republican sentiment.

    e. The new president, MacMahon, was a political neophyte. Unlike Thiers, he seldom ventured into politics. The few exceptions to this rule ended in failure. MacMahon thus set the pattern for the presidency until 1940: dignity without participation. The *Loi des Trente* of March, 1873 further reduced the importance of the president. From this time he could only communicate with the legislature through his ministers. The real head of government would be the "Vice President of the Council of Ministers."

    f. The ministries of the Duc de Broglie indicated the beginning of a new phase of the Third Republic. A monarchical restoration no longer seemed likely, and Broglie accordingly placed greater emphases on conservative government. Broglie placed conservative appointees in many administrative prefects. A law was even passed giving the government the right to appoint mayors. Even when Broglie was driven from office in 1874, he was replaced by the conservative General Cissey. By 1875 the French government was in the hands of conservative administrators or generals.

g. The tide now began to turn in the direction of republicanism. In July, 1874 Gambetta pushed a law through the legislature which permitted all males to vote at age 21.

h. The Wallon amendment (January 30, 1875): This key amendment was the crucial test for the so-called "Constitution of 1875" (Law on the Organization of the Public Powers, etc.). The amendment stated that the "president of the republic" would now be elected by the Senate and Chamber of Deputies sitting together as a National Assembly. The word "republic" was the key; acceptance of the amendment implied acceptance of the Third Republic. The dissension among the monarchists and numerous republican victories in by-elections helped push the amendment through 353 to 352.

i. The new president had a seven year term and was eligible for reelection. His powers were quite large on paper, but only a strong president like Poincaré ever exercised the full authority of the office. All presidential acts required the counter-signature of the proper minister. The new Senate was to have 300 members, 225 chosen by a system of indirect election for nine years and 75 to be chosen by the National Assembly for life. Except for financial legislation, the Senate shared the right to initiate laws equally with the new 618 member Chamber of Deputies. The lower house was to be elected for four year terms by universal manhood suffrage. It could be dissolved by the president if he had the approval of the Senate.

j. The most amazing feature of the "Constitution of 1875" was the fact that it was passed by a monarchist legislature during the tenure of a right-wing government.

k. The newly elected legislature met for the first time in 1876. The Chamber of Deputies was overwhelmingly Republican, but the Senate had a monarchist majority.

l. Coup de Seize Mai (May 16, 1877): This was the first major test of the new republic. President MacMahon dismissed Premier Jules Simon because the latter did not sufficiently oppose the anticlericalism of the republicans. The key issue involved was control of the ministry. Was the ministry to be responsible to the Chamber of Deputies or the president? MacMahon asked the Orleanist Duc de Broglie to form a new ministry, but it was given a vote of no confidence by the republican Chamber of Deputies. MacMahon dissolved the lower house and called for new elections, but despite some losses, the republicans still won. By December, 1877 MacMahon admitted defeat when he appointed Jules Dufaure to be Premier. No president again tampered with the responsibility of the ministry to the Chamber of Deputies.

m. Parliamentary sovereignty became a permanent feature of the Third Republic. The president and the Senate lost much of their importance after 1877. The unfortunate concomitant of a powerful Chamber of Deputies was political instability. The prevalence of many small parties made coalition government a necessity. These coalitions often broke up when one or two parties dropped out because of differences with the government on a single issue. From 1874 to 1915, for example, France had 52 cabinets. Their average life was about nine months. Some continuity was preserved by the survival of certain individuals from one government to another. The government bureaucracy was more important in this respect, however.

n. In 1879 the republicans gained 58 seats and won control of the Senate. McMahon decided to resign (January 30, 1879) and was replaced by Jules Grévy, a republican.

5. The presidency of Jules Grévy, 1879–1887

a. The republicans now enjoyed control over the Chamber of Deputies, the Senate, and the presidency. Despite the fact that they were conservative republicans, they soon took up the cudgels of anticlericalism.

b. In 1880 all unauthorized religious associations were given three months to regularize their position. Within two years 300 congregations were dissolved, but the Trappists and Carthusians were not disturbed. The Jesuit order was broken up by decree.

c. In 1882 a primary education law was passed to undermine the position of the church schools. A primary school for each commune that provided only secular education was the objective of this law.

d. The republicans reversed the Broglie policy of government-appointed mayors. From 1882 mayors were to be elected by municipal councils.

e. In 1884 a Trade Union Act was passed which gave unions legal recognition. This law aided the revival of the labor movement which now began to take a Marxian turn under the leadership of Jules Guesde (1845–1922).

f. The republicans also pushed through a law ending the life membership for 75 senators. All senators were now to be elected (1884).

g. In 1885 the Ferry cabinet (1883–1885) fell over a minor defeat in Indo-China. The republicans still retained 372 seats (spread over various factions, but the forces of the right increased their numbers to 202.

h. In 1887 the son-in-law of President Grévy was caught using his influence to secure membership in the Legion of Honor for those who paid well. Daniel Wilson's indiscretion forced Grévy to resign although he had done nothing dishonest. The Wilson scandal shook the entire Third Republic, and gave the monarchist-military-clerical clique of the right renewed hope.

i. Marie Francois Sadi-Carnot succeeded Grévy as president (1887–1894).

6. The Boulanger affair, 1886–1889

a. Through the intercession of Georges Clemenceau, General Georges Boulanger was made minister of war in the Freycinet cabinet (1886–1887). Boulanger had won popular acclaim by his dashing appearance on horseback. He was popular in the army for improving the food and living conditions of the soldiers. Boulanger won further popularity when he demanded the return of the spy Schnaebelé (1887) who had been seized by the Germans. His demands helped breathe spirit into the concept of *revanche* (revenge) against Bismarck's Germany.

b. Boulanger became so popular, that he was sent to an unimportant command in Clermont-Ferrand in 1887. But the advent of the Wilson scandal shook the republican government. Boulanger, meanwhile, maintained good relations with the more radical republicans and Orleanists.

c. When the worried government retired him in 1888, Boulanger was easily elected to the Chamber of Deputies. He advocated revision of the constitution and dissolution of the lower house. To enforce his demands, he resigned his seat (July, 1888), but was simultaneously reelected in three different constituencies in the following month.

d. When Boulanger was again elected in Paris in January, 1889 many believed he was about to seize power. But he failed to act. The worried republican cabinet now made it known it was going to have him tried for treason, and Boulanger fled to Belgium. Two years later he took his life.

e. The republicans had weathered another storm. The elections of 1889 were a great triumph for them and the Third Republic. The forces of the reactionary right were to have another opportunity, however.

7. The *Ralliement*
   a. The failure of Boulanger was such a blow to the Church that Pope Leo XIII attempted to reconcile French clericals to the existence of the Third Republic.

   b. This policy of reconciliation was called the *Ralliement* or rally movement.

   c. Despite opposition by both clericals and monarchists on one hand and republicans on the other, the *ralliement* introduced a brief era of good church-state relations. Its high point was the Méline ministry of 1896–1898.

     d. The Dreyfus affair ended the era of good feeling.
8. The Panama scandal
     a. Under the leadership of Ferdinand de Lesseps, a company (*Compagnie du canal interocéanique*) had been founded to build a canal across Panama. French investors of all classes purchased 1.5 billion francs worth of stock. Poor management and corruption caused the collapse of the company in 1889, but no action was taken against it until November, 1892.
     b. The investigation that was finally begun revealed that many deputies, cabinet members, and newspapermen had accepted gifts for their support of the project. A prominent Jewish banker who had been associated with the venture, Baron Jacques Reinach, committed suicide. His connection with the scandal helped fan the flames of antisemitism.
     c. The Panama scandal visibly weakened the Third Republic, but the greatest threat was now to come.
9. The Dreyfus affair, 1894–1906
     a. On November 1, 1894 Drumont's antisemitic paper, the *Libre parole,* revealed that Captain Alfred Dreyfus had been arrested for giving secret information to a foreign power. Dreyfus was the first Jew to be appointed to the French general staff.
     b. Dreyfus was arrested because his handwriting seemed to resemble that found on the *bordereau* (memorandum) found in the wastebasket of the German military attaché in Paris. Graphologists could not agree as to whether Dreyfus' handwriting resembled that on the *bordereau,* but he was still convicted and sent to Devil's Island (December, 1894).
     c. In 1896 the new head of the French intelligence service, Colonel Georges Picquart, found proof that the handwriting on the *bordereau* was that of Major Esterhazy, not Dreyfus. Picquart also noted that the Germans were still getting information although Dreyfus was in prison. The worried army transferred Picquart to an obscure post in Tunisia.
     d. For the army it was no longer a question of whether Dreyfus was innocent or guilty. Its honor was at stake, and Dreyfus had to remain "guilty." The monarchist-clerical officer corps, deeply tainted with anti-

semitism, also hated the Third Republic. In a short time the issue would be joined between the defenders of the Third Republic and Dreyfus on one side, and the enemies of the republic and Dreyfus on the other.

e. When Dreyfus' brother independently discovered that the *bordereau* was written by Esterhazy, the latter was brought to trial. A military court still acquitted him to save the honor of the army (January, 1898).

f. Émile Zola, the great French novelist, now published his famous *J'accuse* letter in which he publicly named the officers associated with the dishonest condemnation of Dreyfus (January 13, 1898). Seven months later it was learned that a key document used against Dreyfus had been forged by Colonel Henry, the new head of French intelligence.

g. In the meantime, the country was split. Republicans were now joined by the socialists in defending Dreyfus. His defense, as all knew, was synonymous with the defense of the Third Republic. The leading Dreyfusards were Anatole France and Charles Péguy. The antisemitic officer corps plus many monarchists and clericals bolstered the anti-Dreyfusard ranks. Battles in the streets and in the press resulted.

h. When President Felix Faure, an opponent of retrial for Dreyfus, died in February, 1899 he was succeeded by Émile Loubet (1899–1906).

i. In June, 1899 the *cour de cassation,* the highest French appeal court, ordered a new military trial for Dreyfus. Despite the evidence, Dreyfus was again found guilty "with extenuating circumstances." He was given a ten year sentence, but President Loubet pardoned him. In 1906 Dreyfus was fully cleared and decorated with the Legion of Honor.

j. The Dreyfus affair resulted in a crushing defeat for the monarchist-clerical enemies of the republic. A republican-socialist coalition formed behind the moderate René Waldeck-Rousseau (1899–1902).

10. The ministry of Waldeck-Rousseau, 1899–1902

a. The new coalition, victors in the Dreyfus affair, was now determined to carry out one of the key republican demands: separation of church and state. The anti-Dreyfusard stand taken by most clericals played a major role in pushing the republicans along this course.

b. The Associations Law of 1901 was passed after the victory of the republican and left of center parties. The Concordat of 1801 between Napoleon I and the papacy had legalized the position of only the secular clergy. Convents, monastic orders, and religious congregations had to obtain state authorization to exist as did any other association. Many of these groups were allowed to exist during the nineteenth century because the government, as under the Second Empire, looked the other way. But they did not exist legally, and could be regulated whenever the state desired to do so. The law of 1880, for example, had forced the dissolution of 300 congregations. It was under Émile Combes, the anticlerical Minister of Public Instruction, that the 1901 law was vigorously enforced. Some 3,000 congregations were closed, and then refused authorization to reopen. Most of the orders fled to Belgium, Great Britain, or the United States.

c. Waldeck-Rousseau was unsympathetic with such extreme anticlerical measures, and resigned in favor of Combes (June, 1902).

11. The ministry of Émile Combes, 1902–1905

a. In July, 1904 this anticlerical ministry pushed through legislation that forbade teaching by religious congregations. In addition, all congregations were to be dissolved within 10 years.

b. Meanwhile, Pope Leo XIII had died in 1903 and was succeeded by the less conciliatory Pius X (1903–1914). Since the seizure of Rome by Italy in 1870, the papacy had urged the heads of all foreign governments to avoid that city. However, France and Italy had become more friendly since 1902. In 1904 President Loubet of France visited Italy, an act which embittered relations between France and the papacy.

c. Combes now introduced a bill which would completely separate church and state, legislation that would eradicate the Concordat of 1801. Although Combes fell from power in January, 1905, Aristide Briand pushed through a somewhat different bill.

Under the new law the state would not pay the salaries of the clergy and would not have the right to appoint them. Church property would be taken over by voluntary religious associations who would pay the salaries of the clergy. If such associations were not formed, then the local communities became the owners of church property.

d. This complete separation of church and state was accomplished. The end of Gallicanism could also be seen in this law. Now the pope was the supreme head of the French church. By 1918 anticlericalism had become a less important issue in French politics.

e. The ultimate victory of the state can be seen in the attendance figures of the primary schools. In 1886 state primary schools enrolled 3,598,000 as against 1,919,000 in church primary institutions. By 1925 the state schools had 3,061,000 to but 767,000 for similar church schools.

12. By 1905 the question of monarchy or democracy had been temporarily resolved. The Third Republic had survived, but the cement that held its supporters together was hostility against the clericals, the monarchists, and the army. So much effort was spent resisting these reactionary elements that little attention was paid to the socio-economic questions of twentieth century society. The republicans had lost much support among the growing working class in the 1890's by simply ignoring the reforms that were soon won in Great Britain. When Clemenceau attempted to pass his 17 point reform program in 1906, the legislation was blocked. The conservative peasantry and lower bourgeoisie plus republican-socialist differences were largely responsible. The disillusioned workers preferred to place their reliance on trade unions after 1906, but the power of these groups frightened their logical allies, the republicans. A large number of serious, and sometimes violent, strikes occurred between 1906 and 1911. In addition, the forces of the left used much of their energy in a pacifist crusade. Within the army the authoritarian and antirepublican tradition remained strong, while on the right the semi-Fascist *Action Française* remained a standing threat.

BIBLIOGRAPHY

Arnaud, René, *The Second Republic and Napoleon III* (New York: Putnam, 1937).

Aubry, Octave, *The Second Empire* (Philadelphia: Lippincott, 1940).

Binkley, Robert C., *Realism and nationalism* (New York: Harper, 1935).

Brogan, D. W., *France under the Third Republic* (New York: Harper, 1940).

Bruun, Geoffrey, *Clemenceau* (Cambridge, Mass.: Harvard University Press, 1943).

Bury, J. P. T., *France, 1814–1940, a history* (London: Methuen, 1949).

Campbell, P., *French electoral systems and elections, 1789–1957* (New York: Praeger, 1958).

Case, Lynn M., *French opinion on war and diplomacy during the Second Empire* (Philadelphia: University of Pennsylvania Press, 1954).

Chapman, G., *The Dreyfus case* (New York: Viking, 1957).

Chapman J. M. and Brian, *The life and times of Baron Haussmann* (New York: Macmillan, 1958).

Christie, O. F., *The transition to democracy, 1867–1914* (London: George Routledge, 1934).

Cole, G. D. H. and Postgate, R., *The British people, 1746–1946* (New York, 1946).

Ensor, R. C. K., *England, 1870–1914* (London: Oxford University Press, 1936).

Hale, R., *Democratic France: the Third Republic from Sedan to Vichy* (New York: Coward-McCann, 1941).

Magnus, P., *Gladstone* (New York: Dutton, 1954).

Marriott, J. A. R., *Modern England, 1885–1932* (London: Methuen, 1934).

Maurois, André, *A history of France* (New York: Grove Press, 1960).

Monypenny, W. F., and Buckle, G. E., *The life of Benjamin Disraeli,* 6 vols. (New York: Macmillan, 1910–1920).

Morley, John, *The life of William Ewart Gladstone,* 3 vols. (New York: Macmillan, 1903).

O'Connor, James, *History of Ireland, 1798–1824,* 2 vols. (Garden City: Doran, 1926).

Pearson, H., *Dizzy: the life and personality of Benjamin Disraeli* (New York: Harper, 1951).

Thomson, David, *Democracy in France. The third and fourth republics* (3rd ed., London: Oxford University Press, 1958).

Wolf, J. B., *France, 1815 to the present* (New York: Prentice-Hall, 1940).

Chapter 11

EASTERN EUROPE DURING THE NINETEENTH CENTURY

I. The Emergence of Russia After 1815

A. Alexander I (1801–1825)
1. Russia had emerged from the Napoleonic wars with great prestige because of her key role in the defeat of France. Liberals had been encouraged when Alexander I had made Finland an autonomous grand duchy (1809). Six years later Poland was given a separate administration and a relatively liberal constitution. The hopes of liberals in Poland were dashed by 1820 by the czar's failure to call for a meeting of the diet.
2. At home Alexander's talk of reform gradually disappeared. The experience of the Hundred Days and the influence of Metternich pushed Alexander in the direction of reaction. This can be seen in the selection of Alexis Arakcheev who introduced a system of "military settlements" throughout the country. In 1821 a secret police organization was established.
3. Even the one solid reform that Alexander pushed to a conclusion fared badly. His emancipation of the serfs in the Baltic area was a serious failure, since they were freed without land and had no means of support.
4. During the latter years of Alexander's reign groups of army officers formed several revolutionary secret societies. The first such group was organized (1817) by Pavel Pestel in St. Petersburg. This Union of Salvation, later called the Union of Welfare, wished to curb the autocratic powers of the czar, end the military colonies, and abolish serfdom. Pestel was transferred to Kiev where he organized the more active Southern Society. Nothing

would have come of these efforts had there not been some confusion over the succession to the throne when Alexander I died in the Crimea (December, 1825).

B. The Decembrist uprising
  1. In 1822 the successor to the throne, Grand Duke Constantine, renounced his heritage. Tsar Alexander I accepted it, and decreed in August, 1823 that his brother Nicholas should be next in line. This simple arrangement might have avoided the Decembrist revolt had it been made public. But the document was kept secret, and all were stunned when Constantine did not immediately take control in December, 1825. Nicholas at first hesitated to declare himself tsar despite another renunciation by Constantine.
  2. On December 13, 1825 the Northern Society, successor to the Union of Salvation, assembled 3000 troops in St. Petersburg. After negotiations failed, Nicholas broke up the demonstration with artillery fire. The revolt of the Southern Society under Pestel and Muraviev-Apostol was also crushed.
     a. The Decembrist revolt made Nicholas I wary of innovation and reform. He placed no reliance on the younger nobility, but preferred a supine bureaucracy.
     b. The Decembrist uprising was not without result, however. Certain reforms were initiated by Nicholas. More important was the inspiration it offered to later revolutionaries like Alexander Herzen. In turn, the agitation of Herzen became the foundation for the more radical Menshevik and Bolshevik groups who emerged toward the end of the nineteenth century. A liberal revolutionary tradition had been established.
C. Nicholas I (1825–1855)
  1. From his education and marriage to the daughter of the Prussian king Nicholas inherited a devotion to autocracy that was unequalled in Europe. He despised constitutional government, and believed it to be one of the prime causes of western decline.
  2. Nicholas I paid scrupulous attention to the workings of his government. He took a painstaking interest in the army, and had Michael Speransky draw up a legal code.
  3. The Third Department under Benckendorff was the

hated secret police. This organization handled the censorship and watched all who might be a threat to the regime. Nicholas viewed the right to dissent as a sign of weakness and an invitation to anarchy.

4. Education was also tailor-made to serve the state. Under Count Sergei Uvarov, the minister of education, the school system was to help perpetuate the status quo. Peasant children were not permitted to go beyond the primary school, but children of the nobles and bureaucracy could go on to secondary schools and universities. By 1850 only 3000 students enrolled in the five Russian universities.

5. The serf problem became quite serious after 1825. While the number of serfs increased by one million between 1816 and 1835, they could no longer be profitably absorbed in agriculture. Both the nobility and the serfs sensed that this situation could not continue much longer, but Nicholas refused to tamper with the existing order.

6. Under the leadership of Count Kankrin, tax collections improved and rigid economies were observed. Russian paper money even had a metal basis prior to the Crimean War. As a result, her credit was good.

7. The Poles, as well as other national minorities, did not fare well under Nicholas I. The constitution promised by Alexander I was often a dead letter. In 1830 a revolution broke out in Poland. A republic was proclaimed. Nicholas I sent Field Marshal Ivan Paskevich to Poland, and after seven months of bitter fighting, the Poles were subdued. Disagreement within Polish ranks, their exaggerated demands for portions of Russia, and the lack of active support from the West doomed the revolt. After 1831 a policy of Russification was pursued, but it did not eradicate Polish national feeling.

8. Nicholas I and the 1848 revolutions
   a. The success of the revolutionaries in France (February, 1848) concerned Nicholas I. He worried about the events in Germany and Austria even more, since they were close at hand. Using revolution as a pretext, he seized the Danubian Principalities (later Rumania), but Anglo-French pressure compelled him to withdraw. Nicholas, nevertheless, sent his troops into

Hungary in 1849 and smashed the forces of Kossuth. Revolution in Hungary was a danger to his regime because of its proximity to Russia.

9. The Slavophil-Westerner cleavage

   a. The founder of Russian Slavophilism was probably Ivan Kireevski (1806–1856).

   b. Kireevski believed that religious differences made Russia and Europe fundamentally different. Russia, he argued was a land of faith unlike the Protestant and Catholic states of western Europe. Kireevski belittled the institution of private property as practiced in the West, and upheld the collectivist tradition of the Russian village commune *(mir)*. And finally, since Moscow was the Third Rome, Russia obviously had been chosen to dispense the blessings of civilization to the West.

   c. The Slavophils also belittled western individualism, rationalism, and abhorrence of violent methods. This signified weakness and decay.

   d. Ivan Aksakov (1823–1886), another important Slavophil, felt that the Russian Orthodox church was the only true form of Christianity. He believed that Russia had a holy mission to free those in the West from Catholicism and Protestantism.

   e. Those who wished to accept the cultural and parliamentary tradition to Europe were called Westerners. These men were led by Alexander Herzen (1812–1870), Vissarion Belinsky (1811–1848), and Peter Chaadayev (1794–1856). The Westerners accepted rationalism, and rejected the Orthodox faith for agnosticism in many cases. They believed that Russia had much to learn from the West, and denied that Russia had a unique development, particularly one which yielded her any great advantages. Like the Slavophils, however, they idolized the *mir* and the Russian peasant. In addition, neither group saw any merit in the middle class society of Europe.

10. Panslavism

    a. This movement emerged from the more religious Slavophil ideas. Panslavism was a political movement. It suggested that the superior Byzantine-Russian civilization would triumph over the decadent

Germano-Latin civilization of the West—but by war.

b. In his book *Russia and Europe,* Nikolai Danilevsky (1822–1885) argued that Slavic Russia was the heir to the dying civilization of the West. Justice guided the Slavs, while material gain was the driving force of the westerners. It was Russia's destiny to expand into central Europe until she controlled all of the territory east of a line from Stettin on the Baltic to the Adriatic Sea on the south. Only then would all the Slavs (plus many Germans and Magyars) be united under the aegis of Russia. Danilevsky, like the later Marxists, was certain that history was on Russia's side. In the 1870's Panslavism played a brief role as an instrument of Russian foreign policy.

11. Death of Nicholas I (1855)

a. Throughout his reign Nicholas had played the role of Europe's great reactionary, the policeman of Russia, and the watchdog of the continent. Liberalism was his enemy, change his *bête noire.* To the end he upheld the formula of "orthodoxy, autocracy, and nationalism."

b. In 1854 he became engaged in the Crimean War with Great Britain, France, and Turkey. As the allies were pressing the siege of Sevastopol in March, 1855 Nicholas I died. His successor, the more liberal Alexander II, soon made peace because of the loss of Sevastopol and the threatening position of Austria.

D. Alexander II (1855–1881)

1. Defeat in the Crimean War was made definitive by the 1856 Congress of Paris. Although Russia lost no territory, the defeat caused a reevaluation of her internal problems. The new czar realized that the serf problem, this above all others, now had to be settled by emancipation. When Alexander II announced the 1856 peace settlement to his people, he coupled it with a promise of reform within Russia.

2. Although Alexander II's training reflected stringent militarism and considerable discipline, his tutor Moerder also instilled a strong humanitarian spirit in the young man. It was this spirit and a strong personal determination that enabled Alexander to emancipate the serfs in 1861.

3. Emancipation of the serfs (February 19, 1861)
   a. The intellectual climate of mid-nineteenth century Russia was an important factor in the emancipation question. Alexander Herzen and his journal *Kolokol* ("The Bell") was a powerful influence. The poet Nekrasov attacked conditions in his country in his famous ode "Who Lives Happily in Russia." Turgenev's novel *Sportsman's Sketches* tore the veil from the sordid features of rural life, while Alexander Pushkin openly assaulted the autocracy in his *To Chaadayev*.
   b. Serf discontent could be seen in numerous rebellions. In addition, the serf assumption that the land worked was really their property served as an additional pressure on Alexander II.
   c. The surplus of serfs in many parts of Russia plus the low productivity of serf labor were two economic factors that helped the cause of emancipation.
   d. Alexander began to attack the emancipation problem in 1856, but it was not until February 19, 1861 that a final act resulted. During the years of discussion the serfs were never consulted. In addition, there was never any question as to who owned the land. The property rights of the landlord were unquestioned.
   e. The emancipation act finally signed by the "Tsar-Liberator" transformed the serfs from mere property to people who had certain rights: they could marry without permission, enter business, etc. The landlords could still punish them until *volost* (a group of village communes) courts were established.
   f. Though the peasants gained legal freedom in 1861, they received less land than the amount needed. The government reimbursed the landlords, while the peasants repaid the government over a 49 year period. The "redemption payments" were often high, and in later years frequent defaults forced the government to write off these debts.
   g. Since the peasants were tied to a village commune (*mir*), it was this organization that actually received the land. The *mir* then redistributed the land to individual farmers. Periodic redistributions occurred every 10 or 12 years. The members of each *mir* were

jointly responsible for "redemption payments." Since the peasants could not live on the small allotments of land given to them, many had to rent or purchase more land from landlords or work for wages. High rentals and low wages caused a deep bitterness between the peasants and landlords.

h. In the meantime, it should not be forgotten that the power of the aristocracy had been broken by emancipation. This power had rested on the land and the serfs. Now it declined rapidly.

4. The Zemstvo law (February 13, 1864)

a. Russia was divided into 360 districts. Each was empowered to establish a *zemstvo* or district assembly. The members of this assembly were elected by a three-class system of voting: peasants, private landowners, and townspeople.

b. Although no one class was to predominate, the aristocracy was usually able to name almost half the members to each *zemstvo*. After 1890 the aristocracy increased their control. Yet, it should be noted that the three groups worked well together. In addition, the newly-freed peasants were seldom in a position to govern wisely. They needed training and time, and many received it in the *zemstvo*.

c. The *zemstvo* had responsibility over hospitals, schools, bridges, roads, and charity. They were to aid agricultural development, and determine local taxes. In 1889, during the reactionary reign of Alexander III, the powers of the various *zemstvos* were curtailed by the appointment of a land captain *(nachalnik)* in each district.

5. The judicial reform of 1864

a. The ignorance of many judges and their willingness to accept bribes was one of the worst features of the Russian courts. In addition, there was a confusingly large number of different courts. The rules of evidence were notoriously unfair: credibility was based on rank and education.

b. The great hopes of the reformers were only achieved for those above the peasant class. Peasants remained under the old *volost* courts and law. In the new courts, those above peasant rank could enjoy equality before the law. Trial by jury was the general rule except in treason cases and press matters. Judges were more independent than before, but only the minister of justice could promote them.

6. Educational reforms
   a. With the appointment of a new minister of education, A. V. Golovnin, the control of universities was given to the faculties.
   b. In December, 1864 the Gymnasium and Real School were established. The former prepared students for the university, while the latter trained students for technical institutes. The Elementary School Code of June, 1864 authorized the *zemstvos* and city governments to maintain such institutions.
   c. Much of this progress was soon undone when Count Dmitri Tolstoy became minister of education in 1866.

7. Army reform
   a. Under the brilliant and enlightened war minister, Dmitri Miliutin, much was done to improve the Russian army after the Crimean disaster.
   b. The Military Service Law of 1874 required that all young men of 20 serve six years in the regular army. This was to be followed by a 14 year period in the reserves.

8. Assessment of the reform era
   a. Many peasants were dissatisfied with the land reform that accompanied emancipation. Tax payments plus serious crop failures in 1867 and 1870–1873 contributed to the numerous peasant rebellions. In addition, they were unable to live on the land alloted them by the *mir*.
   b. The gentry generally remained conservative and opposed to reform. More important was the fact that the old imperial bureaucracy often carried out the reforms without relish, if they carried them out at all.
   c. The intelligentsia were also dissatisfied, and were quick to make their demands known. Many had been won over to socialism. Others demanded political freedom and immediate social and economic reform. Some spoke against the monarchy, the church, and even the family. To combat the writers and editors emanating from this group, the government moved

to suppress all unfavorable criticism. Sympathy among the educated classes for the Polish rebellion of 1863 plus an attempt to assassinate Alexander II in 1866 caused such repression that many liberals broke with the government.

9. The beginning of a revolutionary movement
   a. Alexander Herzen (1812–1870) was one of the most influential revolutionary leaders. Through a journal that was regularly smuggled into Russia, "The Bell," Herzen advocated a socialistic state based on the *mir*. It was he who first advocated that the intelligentsia should go to the people *(narod)* in order to both help and arouse them.
   b. The go-to-the-people movement was called *narod-nichestvo* or populism. Those who participated were called *narodniki*. Peasant distrust and indifference plus police suppression and spies doomed this intellectually-inspired effort of the 1870's to failure.
   c. Nevertheless, many of the *narodniki*, now turned to a new organization whose methods involved terrorism and assassination. This was a secret society called *Land and Liberty (Zemlya i volya)*. Political murder and socialism became the tenets of this group. The heroine Vera Zasulich (1849–1919) was its most famous leader. In 1879 the society split into two groups: the *Narodnaya volya* (People's freedom) used terror to win support for its program of socialism, while the *Cherny peredel* (Total redistribution of the land) emphasized the peasant's need for more land which would be won by peaceful methods.
   d. On March 13, 1881 the *Narodnaya volya* succeeded in assassinating Alexander II. This untimely act ended further reform that was being contemplated by Count Mikhail Loris-Melikov, the new interior minister.

E. Alexander III (1881–1894)
   1. The new tsar was determined to rid Russia of all revolutionary activity. He firmly believed that the concessions granted by his father, limited as they were, had opened the door to revolutionary activity. It was this subversion that had culminated in the assassination of his father, and he was determined to make no further concessions. His policy for the next 13 years was firm

support of autocracy and the Russian Orthodox Church. These were the twin pillars upon which his Russia rested. So stringent were the efforts of Alexander III and his advisers in the direction of authoritarianism, that the revolutionary movement seemed to come to a halt. This, however, proved to be but a temporary setback.

   a. The manifesto of May 11, 1881 made it clear to all that the credo of the new tsar was autocracy.
   b. The moderate ministers, including Loris-Melikov, resigned.
   c. From this time on the two great influences on the tsar were thoroughly reactionary: Constantine Pobedonostsev (Procurator of the Holy Synod from 1880–1905) and the Slavophil Ivan Aksakov. Aksakov's Panslavism had an important effect on the tsar, but it was the "philosopher of reaction" Pobedonostsev who influenced many of the policies of Alexander III and his successor.

2. Constantine Pobedonostsev (1827–1907)
   a. Pobedonostsev believed that Russian Orthodoxy, Russian nationalism, and autocracy had to be firmly established as the bulwarks of the monarchy.
   b. He firmly opposed the introduction of the usual civil liberties of the West, and rejected parliamentary government and an independent judiciary. A free press was unthinkable, and academic freedom was beyond discussion.
   c. Pobedonostsev's ideas also contributed to the weakening of the *zemstvos.*
   d. His policy of Russification caused terrible depredations against the Jews. These violent attacks, or *pogroms,* were often sanctioned or encouraged. Jews had to live in western or southwestern Russia, and only in towns. They were effectively kept out of the professions by a quota system after 1887. Jews were forbidden to acquire agricultural property.

3. The plight of the peasant
   a. Although the amount of land owned by the peasants increased steadily after 1861, it was only 13 per cent in 1887 and 24 per cent in 1905. But these benefits were not distributed evenly. In addition, many of

the poorer peasants did not use their lands fully or effectively.

b. It is estimated that the peasants paid 95 per cent of all taxes on agriculture. Over half their income was eaten up by taxes. The great poverty of the peasantry had not been solved by emancipation. So great was the burden that unpaid taxes became commonplace.

c. These heavy taxes forced the government to reduce "redemption payments" in 1882 and abolish the poll tax of Peter the Great in 1883.

d. The peasants lacked capital to buy more land, and were unable to afford migration to the east. The establishment of a Peasant Land Bank in 1881 did not help.

e. When drought came to Russia in 1891 a serious famine occurred. Only the efforts of the zemstvos prevented a catastrophe.

f. And so the peasant problem continued to be the great economic cancer.

4. Industrialization

a. One of the early figures associated with the growth of industry in Russia was M. K. Reitern, minister of finance from 1862 to 1878.

b. Reitern was responsible for the organization of Russia's first private lending institution in 1860, the Imperial Bank. His free trade formula from 1868 to 1877 was switched to a protectionist policy. The peak of protectionism was reached in 1891. Many credit protectionist tariffs as the reason for the enormous development of Russian industry after 1890.

c. Reitern pushed railroad construction, since he believed it would help increase productivity. The period 1870–1875 and 1891–1901 were periods of impressive growth in railway trackage. By 1901 Russia had over 37,000 miles of track, much of it built with French capital. Nevertheless, the Russian government owned 75 per cent of the trackage as late as 1900, a fact that made nationalization under the Communists comparatively easy.

d. In the 1890's, a period of enormous industrial growth, the leadership of Count Sergei Witte was instrumental. Much of the growth was achieved at the expense of the peasantry, since large amounts of wheat were exported and high tariffs were levied on imported manufactured articles. Witte, the minister of finance after 1893, was able to show treasury surpluses and place the ruble on a gold basis. This attracted foreign investment capital for Russian industry, particularly French and Belgian money. The debt of the Russian government quadrupled between 1894 and 1914. France alone held 80 per cent, but half of Russia's imports in 1913 came from Germany.

  e. In pig iron production Russia produced only 1.3 million tons in 1894. A spectacular jump to 5.1 million tons was achieved by 1913. Coal production, another good industrial indicator, rose to 40 million tons by 1913 from a mere 5 million tons in 1890. There is little doubt that Russia was well on its way to industrialization prior to the 1917 revolution.

F. Nicholas II (1894–1917)
  1. The weak Nicholas II came to the throne with the idea of preserving autocracy in Russia. His resolve to preserve the old regime was strengthened by his strong-willed wife, Alexandra Federovna, and by the omnipresent Constantine Pobedonostsev. The son of the royal couple and heir to the throne also presented serious problems. Little Alexius was a hemophiliac, a fact that produced a profound feeling of guilt in the tsarina, since she knew that it was hereditary and transmitted only through the female. This guilt made her more determined than ever to see Alexius survive and preserve the autocracy. Her determination on this point plus a baffling superstition soon placed the royal family and the Russian government at the mercy of charlatans like Gregory Rasputin.
  2. Advisers of Nicholas II
    a. Pobedonostsev continued to exert a tremendous influence on the pliable tsar. It was he who urged Nicholas to rebuke the *zemstvos* for their demands in the direction of representative government.
    b. Count Witte continued to be an influential adviser even in matters beyond industrialization.
    c. Vyacheslav Plehve (1846–1904), as minister of the interior, followed a policy of antisemitism as well

as Russification in Finland and Poland. He was
assassinated in 1904.

3. The development of political opposition
   a. The failure of the idealistic *narodniki* and the revo-
      lutionary *Narodnaya volya* in the 1870's did not com-
      pletely extinguish the desire for change.
   b. Beginning in 1894 under the leadership of Dmitri
      Shipov the *zemstvo* reformers began to agitate for
      change. They even published a paper in Stuttgart,
      Germany called "Liberation." All hoped to win po-
      litical freedom for the individual through an associ-
      ation called the Union of Liberation.
   c. The largest revolutionary party to develop at the turn
      of the century was the Social Revolutionary Party.
      They were also known as the Essars (S.R.). After
      their organization in 1901 they pushed for a socializa-
      tion of agriculture as the best means of improving the
      lot of the peasant. Their interest in the city worker
      was secondary. Among their more important leaders
      were Victor Chernov and M. Gotz.
   d. Marxism made up the third important revolutionary
      force. Beginning with small study groups in St. Peters-
      burg, Kazan, and Vilna, it soon attracted revolution-
      aries like Nikolai Lenin and Julius Martov. Under
      the leadership of Lenin they soon came to place
      greater interest in the industrial workers (proletariat),
      since the peasants were regarded as essentially capi-
      talist in their orientation. The various Marxist
      groups met at Minsk in February, 1898 and organized
      the Russian Social Democratic Workers' Party. The
      new party organization was disabled by many arrests,
      and by Lenin's attacks. Lenin would not agree that
      the main task was better wages and stronger unions.
      After Lenin's exile was over in 1900 he became one
      of the editors of *Iskra* ("The Spark") and urged noth-
      ing less than a revolutionary overturn of capitalist so-
      ciety. In July, 1903 a second congress of the party met
      in Brussels and then continued its sessions in London.
      At these meetings Lenin fought for a small, disci-
      plined party of revolutionaries who would lead the
      workers in an effort to overthrow capitalistic soci-
      eties. Lenin would admit only active revolutionaries

to the party organization. Julius Martov took the opposite view. He felt that anyone who accepted the party's platform should be welcomed, even if the recruit was not active. Martov's view won, but when the moderate representatives of the Jewish *Bund* withdrew, Lenin's group was in the majority. This majority group came to be called Bolsheviks, while the new minority under Martov and G. Plekhanov were soon known as Mensheviks.

4. The crisis of 1904–1905

    a. Despite the warnings of Witte that Russian pressure in Korea and Manchuria would soon lead to war with Japan, Witte was dismissed. The Russians treated Japanese efforts to negotiate with such disdain, that the latter began hostilities on February 8, 1904.

    b. The Russo-Japanese War of 1904–1905 saw the corrupt government and inefficient armies sustain a series of defeats. The hated Plehve was assassinated in July, 1904, and was replaced by a more moderate minister of the interior.

    c. A *zemstvo* congress was even permitted to meet in St. Petersburg in November, 1904. In "eleven theses" the congress demanded the convocation of a representative legislature and a guarantee of civil liberties.

    d. Bloody Sunday: January 22, 1905. A peaceful procession of workers led by Father George Gapon walked toward the Winter Palace of the tsar. They hoped that the "little father" would somehow improve social and economic conditions. All faith had been lost in the ministers, but not the tsar. The peaceful procession was broken up by gunfire.

    e. Nicholas II now made a tardy and inadequate concession. In August, 1905 a manifesto was issued creating an imperial Duma. This proved to be a sham, since the proposed body could discuss problems, but not legislate. Meanwhile, the war with Japan continued to go badly, and a beaten Russia signed the Treaty of Portsmouth. Russia lost southern Sakhalin, all treaty rights in Manchuria, and recognized the independence of Korea with special emphasis on the predominant position of Japan in that country. A mutiny on the warship Potemkin followed by an effective general strike (October, 1905) forced Nicholas II to make substantial, if insincere, concessions.

f. Manifesto of October 31, 1905. The tsar agreed to call for the election of a Duma with full legislative power. A wide variety of civil rights were conceded. For a moment, the beginnings of liberty seemed to be at hand. The more radical elements now launched less effective second and third general strikes followed by a bloody insurrection in the streets of Moscow (December 22, 1905–January 1, 1906). Moderates felt that the city socialists had gone too far. The government, once again sure of the army, prepared to whittle down its promises of October 30. Witte even arranged for a large foreign loan early in 1906 so that the government would not be dependent on the Duma for funds.

5. The first Duma (May, 1906)

a. Before the Duma had met all signs of revolution had been extinguished. All who were suspect by the police were jailed. A few days before the Duma met, several laws were proclaimed: the tsar was referred to as an autocrat, and he kept complete control over the executive, foreign affairs, and the armed forces. He could veto new laws, and appoint half the members of the upper house (Imperial Council). In addition, the tsar could rule by decree when the Duma was not in session. These laws left the lovers of liberty very little.

b. The leftist parties boycotted the elections with the result that the largest party was the Constitutional Democrats or Cadets with 184 seats. Under Paul Miliukov they hoped to make the Duma a house of commons. In turn, socio-economic reforms would follow. There were no other well-organized parties. Over 100 deputies refused to join any party, another 105 were to the left of the Cadets, 17 were S-R's, 2 were Social Democrats, 38 were moderate rightists, and 7 were extreme rightists. A tug of war developed on the issue of more land for the peasants. In addition, the Duma failed to dislodge the ministers after a vote of censure. After 73 days the Duma was prorogued.

c. Peter Stolypin now emerged as the leading minister

of Nicholas II. It was he who had engineered the dismissal of the First Duma. His platform was "first order, then reform!" Over 600 persons were executed, but Stolypin also threw the corrupt out of their government positions. In addition, he pushed through land reform laws in 1906 and 1907 that permitted the individual peasant to petition the *mir* for withdrawal of his land in one piece. In the period 1906–1914 half of the 12 million farm families in European Russia petitioned to receive their shares. Stolypin's plan for a vigorous peasantry as an antidote to revolution had some success. More would have been achieved had the petitions been translated into deeds of ownership for the peasantry. Stolypin, nevertheless, emerged as an autocratic reformer of the Bismarckian variety.

6. The second Duma (March, 1907)

   a. The second Duma was far more to the left than its predecessor. Those Cadets who had signed the Viborg Appeal (advocated resistance to the government for dissolving the first Duma) were barred. In addition, the leftists now participated. Some 216 elected were to the left of the Cadets, the Cadets had 99, while 52 were to the right of the Constitutional Democrats. A bitter fight between revolutionaries and reactionaries doomed the second Duma to dissolution within three months.

7. The third Duma, 1907–1912

   a. Stolypin now changed the election laws to insure the return of a conservative third Duma. Almost half of the new members were landowners. The Essars were wiped out, the Cadets lost half their seats, while the social Democrats dropped two-thirds of their representation. An enlightened rightist group, the Octobrists, dominated. This Duma and its successor were never able to control ministerial appointments, although their pressure caused a number of resignations. Stolypin continued to dominate Russian affairs until his assassination in 1911. A noteworthy achievement of the third Duma was the doubling of funds expended on education. The percentage of children receiving an elementary education also dou-

bled between 1907 and 1912. The literacy rate rose
to 43 per cent by 1914.

8. The fourth Duma, 1912–1916
   a. This Duma had a conservative composition similar
      to that of its predecessor.
   b. After the assassination of Stolypin in 1911, decadence
      and corruption in the government became rampant.
      The debauched Gregory Rasputin soon gained more
      and more influence because he was able to "relieve"
      the Tsarevich, Alexius, from several attacks of hemo-
      philia. Soon no minister could hold office without the
      approval of the corrupt "monk" Rasputin.
   c. The outbreak of war in 1914 temporarily united all
      of Russia behind the tsar. But a serious defeat at
      Tannenburg (1914) soon hurt morale. The Austro-
      German offensive of 1915 cost Russia enormous cas-
      ualties plus Poland and Lithuania. Poor administra-
      tion, inadequate military leadership, and corruption
      ruined the heroic efforts of the soldiers.
   d. The baleful influence of Rasputin was increased by
      unscrupulous and neurotic intriguers like A. D. Pro-
      topopov, the interior minister. The Duma leaders
      such as Miliukov bluntly called for constitutional
      government. Even as this occurred Rasputin was
      murdered in December, 1916. This did not help, for
      Boris Stürmer, a criminal, became prime minister.
      With such leadership it is no wonder that Russian
      casualties from 1914 to 1917 have been estimated at
      nine million. Strikes reached epidemic proportions
      by February, 1917 and were not quelled by the inter-
      ior minister Protopopov.
   e. When the revolution occurred in March, 1917 the
      apathetic tsar was taken by surprise. The government
      simply vanished from St. Petersburg.

II. The Ottoman Empire, 1815–1914

A. Turkish decline
   1. The Ottoman Empire had probably reached its peak
      during the reign of Suleiman the Magnificient (1520–
      1566). At that time an element of later weakness was in-
      troduced when Francis I of France allied himself with

the sultan. The French did this to check the growing power of the Hapsburgs, but as a gesture of goodwill the Turks permitted Frenchmen residing in their empire to enjoy the capitulations (1535). Austria and England soon won these privileges: their citizens paid no taxes to Turkey, were not subject to Turkish law, and were to be tried in the consular court of their respective country. By the nineteenth century the abuse of these capitulations by foreign residents was a symptom of Turkish decadence.

2. The ideological influence of the French Revolution stirred up the Christian subjects of the sultan. A great wave of liberalism and nationalism permeated Serbia, Montenegro, Greece, Rumania, and Bulgaria in the nineteenth century. Even among the Moslem subjects of the Ottoman Empire the demand for constitutional reform became strong.

3. Russia's desire to press south and occupy Constantinople was still another pressure on the declining empire. From 1672 to 1914 twelve wars occurred between Russia and Turkey. By 1789 Catherine the Great had occupied the Crimea and the entire northern shore of the Black Sea. She had reached the Dniester to the west. Only now did Great Britain and France come to the aid of the dying Ottoman Empire. Their main role in the nineteenth century was to help the Turks fend off Russia, and reduce Russian gains whenever possible. In turn, Russia posed as the Christian friend of the Bulgars, Serbs, and Armenians, a policy that brought on violent Turkish attacks against these minorities. The Russians also used the Panslavic ideological magnet to encourage the Serbs. After 1840 Tsar Nicholas I even discussed the dissolution of the Ottoman Empire with the British, but the Crimean War shattered this dream.

4. Still another problem for the declining Turkish Empire were the Janissaries (Yeni Ceris) or the "new army." This system began in the fourteenth century. The sons of Christians in the conquered provinces of southeastern Europe were enrolled in the army of the sultan. They were given an excellent education and military training before becoming the personal guard of the sultan. After 1582 the Janissaries became a menace to each sultan. At

that time foreigners entered the service and the quality of the former membership was weakened. It was not until the reign of Mahmud II (1808–1839), in June of 1826, that the Janissaries were thoroughly crushed.

5. Turkish decline can be traced from their naval defeat at Lepanto (1571) and their failure to push the Hapsburgs out of Vienna in 1683. But a succession of weak sultans after 1683 left power in the hands of Grand Viziers, the Janissaries, or the religious leaders of the Ulema.

B. Mahmud II (1808–1839)

1. The dethronement of the reform-minded Selim III (1789–1808) by the Janissaries and the Ulema caused the new sultan to move cautiously.

   a. Only in 1826, when popular opinion was on his side, did he smash the Janissaries.

   b. Prussian military instructors were brought in and a military academy established. In addition, a medical school was founded.

   c. Primary school education was now required, and literature was distributed on the problem of infectious disease.

   d. A postal service was established. Mahmud II also laid the foundations of a national police force.

   e. The sultan enforced the use of the fez instead of the distinctive headdress that divided his subjects.

2. Foreign affairs

   a. Turkish internal security was already undermined to a considerable degree by Clause 7 of the Treaty of Kutchuk Kainardji (1774). This clause gave Russia the right to protect Orthodox Christians in any part of the Ottoman Empire. Russia thus had a pretext to intervene whenever it was useful to do so. The Treaty of Bucharest (1812) gave Russia not only Bessarabia, but the right to protect Christians in the Danubian Principalities (the future Rumania).

   b. A second Serbian revolt forced the Turks to recognize Milosh Obrenovich as Prince of Serbia (1817). The Serbs had won little territory, however.

   c. The Greek war of independence, 1821–1830: The revolt which began in 1821 had been inspired by the "Greek Scheme" of Catherine the Great, Russian encouragement through Count Capo d'Istria, the ideas of the French Revolution, and the work of the revolutionary society *Hetairia Philiké*. Alexander Hypsilanti led the uprising. The war dragged on until 1824 when the sultan appealed to a powerful vassal for aid: Mehemet Ali of Egypt. Mehemet Ali sent aid through his son, Ibrahim. The Greeks were in a hopeless position until a great wave of sympathy (Philhellenism) in western Europe saved them. Concerted Russian, French, and English support for the Greek cause resulted in the defeat of the Egyptian fleet of Ibrahim at Navarino (October, 1827). Russia, hopeful that Turkish dissolution was at hand, declared war (April, 1828). Her troops captured Varna, and then plunged south to Adrianople, just 30 miles from the Dardanelles. In the Caucasus, the Turks lost Kars and Erzerum, and Turkey seemed about to collapse. Only disease and fear of Anglo-French intervention forced the Russians to halt short of Constantinople.

d. Treaty of Adrianople (September 14, 1829): Russia gave up her enormous Balkan gains, but saw her frontier moved from the northern to the southern mouth of the Danube where it emptied into the Black Sea. Russia was allowed to occupy the coveted Danubian Principalities until the Turks paid an indemnity. The Turks also accepted the London Protocol of March, 1829 establishing a Greek state. The autonomy of Serbia was affirmed.

e. The London Conference of November 30, 1829 granted Greece complete independence. A second London Protocol (February 3, 1830) restricted the territorial size of Greece. In 1832, the Greek frontier was moved north to the Volo-Arta line, and a Bavarian prince named Otto was placed on the throne.

f. Treaty of Unkiar Skelessi (July 8, 1833): When Mehemet Ali of Egypt demanded that Mahmud II give him Syria as payment for his assistance against the Greeks, an internal revolt occurred. Ibrahim seized Syria, and invaded Anatolia itself. It appeared that the Ottoman dynasty was over, until Tsar Nicholas I offered Russian "aid." Mahmud reluctantly accepted this support, and Russian troops quickly moved to Bosporous (February, 1833). The alarmed British and French forced the sultan to give Mehemet Ali Syria and Adana, and thus make Russian troops around Constantinople unnecessary for the sultan's defense. Palmerston and Guizot had a combined fleet sent to the Dardanelles (June, 1833). The Russians agreed to leave, but only after the Treaty of Unkiar Skelessi had been concluded in July, 1833: an eight year defensive alliance was arranged, and the Straits were to be closed to all foreign warships except Russian. There is some doubt that this interpretation of Unkiar Skelessi was correct: the Russians seemed more interested in establishing their right to intervene in a declining Turkey, rather than win the exclusive right to use the Straits. Nevertheless, Britain and France believed Unkiar-Skelessi gave Russian war vessels the exclusive privilege of entering or leaving the Black Sea.

  g. The Münchengrätz Agreement of 1833, signed by Austria, Russia, and Prussia, guaranteed the preservation of the *status quo* in the Ottoman Empire. This was a tripartite endorsement of Russian gains at Unkiar Skelessi.

C. Abdul Mejid (1839–1861)
  1. Under the influence of the statesman-ambassador, Reshid Pasha, the young sultan Abdul Mejid (1839–1861) inaugurated a program of reform known as *Tanzimat* ("Regulation"). The *Tanzimat* reforms were contained in the Imperial Decree of Gülhane of November, 1839.
    a. In part, these reforms were to improve the lot of Christians in Turkey so that Russian excuses for intervention would be removed. Turkish involvement in foreign problems took the attention of her leaders from the *Tanzimat* program. The Ottoman government's main interest was to unite all religious groups in undivided loyalty to the state. Christians and Jews were no longer to be second class citizens in the courts.
    b. The *Tanzimat* reforms included a modern commercial code, a criminal law based on the Napoleonic Code of 1804, a system of fixed taxation to be collected by governors on a regular salary, and freedom

from arbitrary government.

c. Little was done in the field of education. Those who visited western Europe, however, began to bring back new ideas. These new influences were soon to generate the Young Turk movment of Namik Kemal.

2. The Near Eastern crisis of 1839–1840

  a. In July, 1839 Mehemet Ali and his son Ibrahim moved against the new boy-sultan, Abdul Mejid. The sultan would have yielded to the superior Egyptian forces had the British and French not come to his assistance. These powers feared that Russia would invoke the 1833 Treaty of Unkiar Skelessi to seize the Straits under the pretext of defending them against the Egyptians. An Anglo-French fleet was dispatched, but Russia indicated that she preferred collective action by the five great powers.

  b. Once Russian aggression was removed as a political possibility, Palmerston demanded that Mehemet Ali be dealt with severely. Thiers, the French foreign minister, disagreed and gave Mehemet Ali his support. Great Britain now joined Austria, Russia, and Prussia (Treaty of London, July 15, 1840) and compelled France to withdraw her support of Mehemet Ali. Thiers resigned in October, 1840 and Mehemet Ali gave up claims to Syria in exchange for the hereditary rule of Egypt (Convention of Alexandria, November 27, 1840).

  c. Meanwhile, Anglo-Austrian cooperation in the Near East worried Russia so profoundly that she agreed to a new multilateral treaty for the Straits.

3. Straits Convention of July 13, 1841

  a. This convention replaced the unilateral guarantee of the Straits given to Turkey by Russia in 1833 at Unkiar Skelessi. The western powers suspected that only Russian warships could use the Straits by the Unkiar Skelessi agreement.

  b. Whether this was true or not, the new 1841 convention was a guarantee by all of the great powers that no foreign warships would use the Straits.

  c. The agreement apparently cost Russia nothing, but did end Anglo-Austrian cooperation in the Near East.

4. The Anglo-Russian "gentlemen's agreement" of 1844

a. In 1844 Nicholas I visited Queen Victoria. He and Nesselrode, the Russian foreign minister, had conversations with Lord Aberdeen, the British foreign secretary. Both Nesselrode and the tsar came away with the impression that if Turkey collapsed Russia and Great Britain would consult each other as to what action was to be taken.

b. A serious crisis in Anglo-Russian relations occurred in 1849. The Russians had occupied the Danubian Principalities in 1848 to preserve order. They did not leave until 1851.

c. More serious was the help Nicholas I sent into Hungary in 1849 to quell the uprising of Louis Kossuth and his followers. The 90,000 Russian troops saved the Hapsburg cause in Hungary, but the revolutionary leaders fled to Turkey. When Nicholas I joined Austria in a demand that the Turks return the revolutionaries, the British and French sent a fleet to the Straits (November, 1849). War was averted, but Nicholas continued to believe that Great Britain would cooperate with Russia should Turkey collapse.

5. The Crimean War, 1854–1856

a. Among the basic causes of this unwanted conflict was the British desire to thwart further Russian expansion southward into Turkey, Iran, Afghanistan, and India. The Russians regarded such expansion as legitimate, and resented British efforts despite the 1844 "gentlemen's agreement." Britain was also anxious to preserve Turkish independence because of the dominant commercial position she enjoyed in the Ottoman Empire. The British were large buyers of Turkish grain, a fact that gave them greater than a passing interest in the existence of the Ottoman Empire. In addition, the British supported the Turks to protect their trade routes to India from Russian and French incursions. The Russophobia of Lord Palmerston and the distrust it inspired among Russian leaders played a significant role in the deterioration of the Near Eastern situation. Franco-Russian disharmony was another key factor in bringing on the Crimean War. Nicholas I treated the new French emperor, Napoleon III, as a parvenu. Napoleon's personal pique plus his desire

to win control of the Palestinian Holy Places for
Roman Catholic monks brought a collision with Russia. Nicholas I, the defender of the Greek Orthodox
position in the Holy Places, was bitter over the turn
of events by December, 1852.

b. Nicholas I now approached the British ambassador
in St. Petersburg, Lord Seymour, regarding the 1844
Anglo-Russian understanding on Turkey. For the
moment the British seemed receptive (January–February, 1853).

c. The tsar now sent the <u>Menshikov mission</u> to Constantinople (February–May, 1852) to demand concessions
on the control of the Holy Places plus the right to
protect Christians in Turkey. The new British ambassador at Constantinople, Lord Stratford de Red-
cliffe, induced the Turks to reject most of these demands (May, 1853).

d. In June, 1853 an Anglo-French fleet arrived at Besika
Bay to support the Turkish position. Russia countered by occupying the Danubian Principalities.
Further negotiations were fruitless despite Austrian
efforts.

e. <u>Turkey alone declared war on Russia (October, 1853)</u>
but suffered a serious naval reverse at Sinope next
month. In January, 1854 an Anglo-French fleet entered the Black Sea to protect the Turkish coast.

f. In February, 1854 Great Britain and France sent an
ultimatum to Nicholas I to evacuate the Danubian
Principalities. When no reply was received, they declared war on Russia (March, 1854).

g. <u>Austria and Prussia now made an alliance.</u> They
agreed to oppose Russian annexation of the Danubian Principalities (Rumania), and warned the tsar not
to go beyond the Balkan Mountains in any offensive
against Turkey (April, 1854).

h. <u>In June, 1854 Turkey agreed to let Austria occupy
the Danubian Principalities.</u> Russia withdrew in
August, 1854. The tsar's fury against Austria was un-
bounded: Russia had saved Hungary for the Hapsburgs in 1849, but five years later Austria showed her
ingratitude by forcing Russia out of the strong position she held in the Danubian Principalities.

    i. Russian evacuation of the Danubian Principalities shifted the campaign from the Balkans to the Crimea. For two years the Allies inched along. Sevastopol fell in September, 1855.

    j. An Austrian ultimatum in December, 1855 forced Russia to agree to peace talks.

    k. Congress of Paris (February–March, 1856): Napoleon's hope to use the peace conference to revise the 1815 treaties failed. The conferees agreed to respect the integrity of Turkish soil. Russia yielded a small part of Bessarabia and the mouths of the Danube. In addition, Russia gave up the privilege of protecting Christians within the Ottoman Empire. Russia was forced to agree to the neutralization of the Black Sea.

  6. The establishment of a Rumanian state

    a. In 1857 Austria evacuated the Danubian Principalities of Moldavia and Wallachia.

    b. Within a year Napoleon III was able to get the great powers to agree to the creation of the United Principalities of Moldavia and Wallachia. Two separate administrations were set up by the powers.

    c. However, both the Moldavians and the Wallachians elected the same man as their prince: Colonel Alexander Cuza. For practical purposes a united Rumania had been formed by this action in 1859.

    d. In 1862 the Turkish sultan agreed to the union of the two principalities as Rumania.

D. Abdul Aziz (1861–1876)

  1. The association with Great Britain and France during the Crimean War aided the spread of western ideas.

  2. The desire for reform was not satisfied by change from above, for what the sultan gave he could withdraw.

  3. Literary revival accompanied the tide of reform. The dramatist and political writer, Namik Kemal, translated Rousseau and Montesquieu. He also headed the new Young Turk (Society of New Ottomans) movement.

  4. The Young Turk movement began in June, 1865. It's key plank was the establishment of a constitutional monarchy. The Young Turks also sought to improve the condition of Christians in the Ottoman Empire.

  5. The Young Turks were disbanded in 1872, but its membership continued to work for constitutional government.

    a. By 1876 the sultan, Abdul Aziz, was deposed. The despotic and extravagant sultan had offended the reformers, the Ulema, the army, and the people.

    b. The reform leader who led the revolt was Midhat Pasha. The reform-minded Murad V became sultan, but insanity ended his reign after three months.

6. The Cretan revolt, 1866–1868

    a. The Turks crushed the rebellion and temporarily halted the movement for the union of Crete and Greece.

7. In 1869 the Suez Canal was opened to international commerce. Benjamin Disraeli purchased 177,000 shares of its stock in 1875 and made certain that Great Britain would be the largest stockholder. The British occupied Egypt in 1882.

8. Russia repudiates the Black Sea clauses of the Treaty of Paris (October 31, 1871):

    a. Russia took advantage of the Franco-Prussian War to unilaterally abrogate the hated Black Sea clauses of the 1856 Treaty of Paris. She was now free to fortify the northern shore of the Black Sea, and maintain naval vessels on that body of water.

    b. An international conference at London confirmed what Russia had already done. At the same time the conferees aligned themselves against unilateral changes in international treaties.

E. Abdul Hamid II (1876–1909)

1. The new sultan owed his position to the liberal leader, Midhat Pasha. Midhat was made Grand Vizier, and in December, 1876 promulgated a new constitution.

2. Abdul Hamid quickly dropped Midhat Pasha in February, 1877 and prorogued the newly elected Turkish parliament the following year.

3. The Russo-Turkish War of 1877–1878

    a. In 1875 an insurrection occurred in the Turkish provinces of Bosnia and Herzegovina. A Bulgarian uprising soon followed.

    b. In 1876 the independent states of Serbia and Montenegro declared war on Turkey. Russia had encouraged their hope of annexing Turkish territory inhabited by their fellow Slavs.

    c. At this juncture the Austrians and Russians signed

the Reichstadt Agreement of July, 1876. This secret document would guarantee the *status quo ante bellum* should Serbia lose, but would yield Russia the province of Bessarabia and give Austria-Hungary most of Bosnia and Herzegovina.

d. The Serbs were crushed in September, 1876 at Alexinatz and appealed to the great powers for intervention. Russia forced the sultan to grant Serbia an armistice and then won an Austrian promise to stay neutral in the event of a Russo-Turkish conflict (January, 1877).

e. Russia declared war on Turkey in April, 1877. After the capture of the strong fortress of Plevna in December, 1877 the Russians swept to the outskirts of Constantinople before an armistice was concluded (January, 1878). Austria now proposed a European peace conference, and the aroused British sent their fleet to Constantinople.

f. The Russians forced the humiliating treaty of San Stefano on the Turks in March, 1878, but Great Britain vigorously objected to the erection of the strong Bulgaria envisioned in the agreement. A secret Anglo-Russian understanding to reduce the size of Bulgaria and divide it into two sections was worked out by the new British foreign secretary, Lord Salisbury, and the Russian ambassador to Great Britain, Count Peter Shuvalov (May, 1878).

g. The British now came to a secret agreement with Turkey in June, 1878. They agreed to defend Turkey against any attacks in Asia Minor in return for Cyprus.

h. A secret Anglo-Austrian agreement reconciled the Hapsburgs to a divided Bulgaria.

4. The Congress of Berlin (June–July, 1878)

a. Otto von Bismarck acted as host to the conferees. His self-styled role was that of an "honest-broker." The congress generally endorsed the agreements reached secretly by the powers just before the meeting.

b. A Bulgarian state of small size was created north of the Balkan Mountains. South of the Balkans, the state of Eastern Roumelia was established as a semiautonomous principality. Macedonia was left to Turkey.

   c. Austria-Hungary was allowed to occupy Bosnia and Herzegovina plus the Sanjak (district) of Novi Bazar, a strip of territory that separated Montenegro and Serbia.

   d. Russia won southern Bessarabia from Rumania, the area she lost in 1856. As compensation, Rumania was given Dobrudja.

   e. Formal independence was accorded to Serbia, Rumania, and Montenegro. Serbia and Montenegro were given small territorial additions at Turkish expense.

   f. In Asia Minor, Russia received Batum, Kars, and Ardahan.

   g. The Turks promised to make reforms to better the conditions of their Christian subjects in Macedonia and Armenia.

   h. Not only were the Russians furious with the relatively small gains won at Berlin, but the aspirations of Greece, Serbia, and Bulgaria were largely unfulfilled. The weak Ottoman regime was permitted to retain a small fragment of European territory.

   i. Serbia felt her Slavic Russian friend had deserted her at Berlin, and made a secret agreement with Austria-Hungary to attract support from the Hapsburgs (1881). For the same reason, Rumania allied herself with Austria-Hungary and Germany in 1883.

5. Insurrection in Eastern Roumelia (1885)

   a. In September, 1885 a revolution occurred in Eastern Roumelia. Prince Alexander of Bulgaria quickly proclaimed the union of his country and Eastern Roumelia. Since the tsar disapproved, Great Britain and Austria took a favorable attitude. Turkey did nothing.

   b. At this juncture the Serbs saw their hopes for aggrandizement dwindle. They declared war on Bulgaria (November, 1885), but were routed. Only Austrian intervention saved them.

   c. The Greeks now sought territory from Turkey, but the powers restrained them (January, 1886).

   d. In February, 1886 the Turks accepted the "personal

union" of Bulgarian and Eastern Roumelia under
Prince Alexander. Russia soon agreed to the compromise plan.

e. Bulgaria and Serbia made peace by the Treaty of
Bucharest (March, 1885).

f. In the meantime, Austro-Russian rivalry in the Balkans had reached a point of no return. Even Bismarck was unable to get his friends to delimit the
Balkans into two distinct spheres of influence.

g. In the <u>Reinsurance Treaty</u> that Bismarck arranged
with Russia in 1887, Bismarck tried to appease Russia by promising her diplomatic support in Bulgaria
and friendly neutrality should she move on the
Straits.

h. The abdication of Prince Alexander of Bulgaria in
1886 was the result of Russian pressure. Only the
election of Prince Ferdinand of Saxe-Coburg by the
Bulgarian Assembly in 1887 temporarily quieted the
Balkan situation.

i. By 1896 Bulgaria and Russia achieved a reconciliation. The powers recognized Prince Ferdinand as
ruler of Bulgaria. In 1908 Ferdinand proclaimed
himself Tsar of Bulgaria, and declared Bulgaria an
independent state.

6. Revival of the Young Turk movement

a. In the 1890's the Young Turk movement revived
after an interval of two decades. Most of the Young
Turks were exiles in Great Britain, France, and
Switzerland. Some were to be found in Cairo and
Naples, as well as among many of the young army
officers in Turkey itself.

b. The Young Turks blamed the decline of Turkish
power and her financial woes on the despotic Sultan
Abdul Hamid II.

c. A Committee of Union and Progress was formed, but
coordinated revolutionary activity proved impossible
in the face of spies, repression, and factionalism.

d. A Macedonian revolt in 1902–1903 saw Russia and
Austria compel Turkey to accept the Mürzsteg reform
program. Foreign inspectors were attached to the
gendarmerie and some judicial reforms were made.

e. In December, 1907 the various Young Turk groups

met at Paris to coordinate their work and establish a link with discontented army officers like Enver Bey and Mustafa Kemal. Even Masonic lodges in Salonika and other cities were among the revolutionary elements.

f. The Anglo-Russian rapprochement of 1907 caused the Young Turks serious concern. So long as these powers had remained unfriendly Turkey had managed to survive. Fear of Germany and Austria-Hungary drove them together. In June, 1908 the Russians agreed to a more extensive British plan for reform in Macedonia. The Young Turks felt that this was a prelude to the loss of Macedonia, and under Niazi Bey, revolted against the sultan in July, 1908. Troops sent to end the rebellion went over to the side of the Young Turks, and Abdul Hamid II agreed to democratic reforms.

g. The first parliament met in December, 1908. Almost at once a schism developed between the representatives of the various subject nationalities (Liberal Union) and the Turkish nationalists (Committee of Union and Progress). The Turkish group was unwilling to compromise regarding demands of the various Christian minorities; it was supported by Germany. The Liberal Union won British support, and the British soon won the reputation of backing dissident minorities who were blocking Turkish national hopes. Autocratic Germany appeared to be the real friend of the resurgent Young Turks.

h. Abdul Hamid II attempted to restore the autocracy in April, 1909 because of the split between the Young Turks and the national minority groups. The Young Turks quickly seized Constantinople and deposed the sultan.

7. Mohammed V (1909–1915)
  a. The new sultan was the weak and colorless Mohammed V.
  b. With a chance to effect great changes, the Young Turks failed to break the power of *Ulema* (a committee of religious leaders) and achieve equality before the law for Christians and Moslems. The hated capitulations remained.

c. In 1909–1910 the Young Turks did establish the principle of universal military service and universal suffrage. But Turkey remained an empire, and refused to work out a law for all subjects or grant Christian provinces like Macedonia autonomy. Given a long era of peace, the Young Turks might have worked out the nationality problem and the evolution of democratic institutions. War, however, was their portion for the eleven years after 1911.

d. Turkish democracy was short-lived. In 1913 the pro-German Enver Bey led a Young Turk *coup d'état*. All opposition was suppressed by a Young Turk triumvirate of Enver Bey, Talaat, and Jemal.

e. The influence of Enver Bey was instrumental in pushing Turkey into World War I on the side of Germany in November, 1914.

8. The Tripolitan War, 1911–1912
   a. Having won assurances of goodwill from the great powers, the Italians seized Tripoli in October, 1911. Within a year most of the Libyan coast and the Dodecanese Islands were occupied.
   b. The Turks were compelled to agree to the seizure by the definitive Treaty of Lausanne (October 18, 1912).

9. The First Balkan War, 1912–1913
   a. In March, 1912 Bulgaria and Serbia allied themselves. The alliance had been encouraged by Russia who regarded it as a protection against Austria. The pact envisaged gains for both participants following a successful war against Turkey.
   b. In May, 1912 an alliance was made between Greece and Bulgaria. The stage was now set for an anti-Turkish crusade.
   c. In August, 1912 the Bulgarians demanded that Turkey make reforms to improve the condition of the populace in Macedonia. The great powers selected Austria and Russia as their agents. These states were to seek reforms in Macedonia, and thus avoid a Balkan conflagration.
   d. The Balkan states were not anxious to wait for reforms. Turkey was already reeling from the defeat in the Tripolitan War at the hands of Italy. Opportunity was now at hand.

    e. Led by tiny Montenegro, the Balkan states of Bulgaria, Greece, and Serbia declared war on the dying Ottoman Empire. The Turks were dealt a series of defeats: the Bulgarians approached Constantinople and the Serbs and Montenegrins reached the Adriatic. A serious crisis ensued in November–December, 1912 when Austria and Italy launched vigorous objections to a Serbian state on the Adriatic.

    f. Pressures by the great powers after the opening of the London peace conference in December, 1912 brought about an armistice in April, 1913. The Serbians and Montenegrins reluctantly abandoned their gains in Albania.

    g. The Treaty of London (May 30, 1913): this treaty ended the First Balkan War, but only Bulgaria had achieved the territorial gains she desired. Serbia was displeased with her small share of Macedonia and the loss of northern Albania. Greece and Montenegro were also frustrated. Albania was created as an independent state.

10. The Second Balkan War, 1913

    a. Soon after a Serbian-Greek alliance had been concluded in June, 1913, Bulgaria attacked without warning. Turkey and Rumania now entered the war against a surrounded Bulgaria.

    b. Bulgarian defeat was rapid. Peace came with the Treaty of Bucharest on August 10, 1913.

    c. Rumania acquired northern Dobrudja. The Greeks and Serbs made gains in Macedonia at Bulgarian expense with Serbia nearly doubling her territory. Turkey recovered Adrianople.

    d. The Balkan wars of 1912–1913 greatly increased the tensions in Europe. The Sarajevo incident of 1914 that sparked the beginning of the First World War was made all the more dangerous by the existing level of frustration and tension in the Balkans.

III. Austria, 1849–1914

A. Austria in 1849

    1. The multinational Austrian Empire had managed to survive the series of revolts that ranged from Prague to

Budapest in 1848–1849. The loyalty of the army and the divisions among the revolutionaries enabled the Hapsburg regime to weather the crisis everywhere except in Hungary. Only the intervention of Russia saved the Magyar realm for Austria.

2. Austrian prestige had also been restored in Germany after Prussian hopes for its Erfurt Union had been smashed at Olmütz (November, 1850). Under the leadership of Felix Schwarzenberg Austria again assumed the presidency of the Germanic Confederation (1851) and the leadership of Germany.

3. The liberal Kremsier constitution of March, 1849 was a compromise attempt to satisfy the various nationalities within the empire. Local government and local control of schools was proposed, but under the overall control of the Hapsburg monarchy. This constitution said nothing about the serious Hungarian problem.

4. The Kremsier assembly was dissolved in March, 1849. Schwarzenberg, Stadion, and Alexander Bach plus conservative Magyar leaders now joined hands to sidestep the liberalism of 1848 and the feebleness of pre-1848. Count Francis Stadion hastily drafted a new constitution which superceded the Kremsier document. The entire empire, despite its polyglot nature, was treated as a unified and centralized state.

   a. A single imperial parliament was established. It was elected by universal suffrage.

   b. A responsible government under a prime minister was another feature of the Stadion constitution.

   c. Hungary was divided into provinces. Like the other provinces, they were administrative divisions. Thus, the Austrian empire was treated as if it had a single nationality and similar traditions throughout. In reality it was a conglomeration of nationalities whose aspirations, culture, and stage of development differed widely.

5. The new Stadion constitution was promulgated in March, 1849, but it was not to come into effect until "the provisional emergency" was over. Thus the cabinet of Schwarzenberg was responsible only to Emperor Franz Joseph (1848–1916), not the paper parliament of the

Stadion constitution. A decade of absolutism was to follow.

6. In August, 1849 the Hungarian army was finally crushed at Világos. As a result of their insurrection, the Magyars lost their constitution. Croatia, loyal to the Hapsburgs throughout 1848–1849, also lost her Diet and local self-government. For the next ten years Austria remained a centralized absolutism.

B. The Bach system, 1849–1860

1. Alexander Bach had succeeded Count Stadion as Minister of the Interior in the summer of 1849. He inaugurated a vigorous policy of Germanization during the ensuing decade.

a. A single law code was formulated for the entire empire.

b. A single administration run by German officials was established for the whole country. These officials were not German nationalists, but it was hoped by men like Bruck that Austria could dominate the revived Germanic Confederation and Prussian *Zollverein*.

c. Even the tariff barrier between Austria and Hungary was divided into five administrative areas run by German officials, while southern Hungary, Croatia, and Transylvania became separate provinces.

d. The inoperative Stadion Constitution of March, 1849 was formally ended by the Sylvester Patent of December 31, 1851. Franz Joseph now became an absolute monarch. Felix Schwarzenberg's death in April, 1852 removed the only prime minister to serve under Franz Joseph. When Bach was suggested as his successor, Franz Joseph's advisers objected on the grounds that absolutism was incompatible with the presence of a prime minister.

2. By 1852 even Bach gave up all hope that the new absolutism could be changed, that a liberal constitution was possible. He became a supporter of absolutism in order to preserve the centralized administrative machine that had been created.

3. In 1855 a concordat was made with the Roman Catholic Church by which that institution was given considerable control over education. It was hoped that a union of the

altar and the throne would help to counter the new forces of revolution and nationalism.

4. The discontent of all national groups within the Hapsburg Empire continued during the 1850's. The memories of 1848 could not be eradicated by the bureaucratic Bach system.

5. One of the greatest problems of the Austrian government was the precarious state of its finances. Unbalanced budgets were common because of the cost of bureaucracy and the need to maintain the army on a war footing during the Crimean War (1854–1856). The financial panic of 1857 cost the Hapsburg government the support of the Vienna business community, but Bach hung on grimly.

C. The October Diploma (October 20, 1860)

1. The defeat of the Hapsburgs in the Austro-Sardinian War of 1859 shook the government violently. To appease public opinion, Bach was dropped as Minister of the Interior in July, 1859.

2. After a delay of almost a year, Franz Joseph issued the famous October Diploma of October 20, 1860.

a. Provincial diets, controlled by the nobility, were established. These *Landtage* were given the right to legislate on many matters. A centralized legislature called the *Reichsrat* met occasionally to work on legislation the provincial diets were not permitted to handle.

b. Nothing was done for the proud and angry Magyars.

c. Franz Joseph hoped that his gesture to the nobility would stifle liberalism.

d. The October Diploma had been but a conservative pose for Franz Joseph as he went to Warsaw to meet Tsar Alexander II and the prince regent of Prussia. His hopes of resurrecting Metternich's Holy Alliance failed, for Prussia had aspirations in Germany and Russia hoped to overturn the Black Sea clauses of 1856 Treaty of Paris.

D. The February Patent of 1861

1. In December, 1860 the somewhat more liberal Anton von Schmerling became Minister of State.

a. He, too, believed that the Bach system should continue.

     b. Schmerling would not consider a new constitution for Hungary because of the 1848–1849 revolution.

     c. Schmerling wished to return to the unitary and centralized state system of Bach, not the federal system of the October Diploma.

  2. The February Patent, originally designed to interpret the October Diploma, was really designed to destroy the earlier document and return to a centralized state.

     a. A bicameral *Reichsrat* was established to handle most matters.

     b. The provincial diets became units of administration rather than state legislatures.

     c. The diets acted as electoral bodies to select members for the *Reichsrat*. They were packed to insure the election of propertied Germans. The poor and the non-German were largely unrepresented.

     d. It was believed that the German majority would gratefully help maintain the centralized empire against Hungarian pressure for change. This same group would also aid the Hapsburg cause in Germany.

     e. When the Hungarian Diet, under the leadership of Francis Deák, asserted it was the successor of the 1848 legislature (and demanded the 1848 laws) it was dissolved.

E. The *Ausgleich* (Compromise) of 1867

  1. From 1861 to 1865 the Magyars continued to insist that Hungary should have some separate status and the 1848 constitution. Schmerling refused to yield.

  2. The struggle with Prussia for the leadership of Germany forced the hand of Franz Joseph. By 1865 war seemed inevitable, and should it occur, Magyar assistance would be indispensable. Schmerling was, therefore, dismissed in July, 1865.

  3. Negotiations for the enlargement of Magyar prerogatives proceeded into 1866. The stunning Austrian defeat at Sadowa in July, 1866 merely speeded up the process. The Hapsburgs had been ejected from Germany. If they wished to increase their power in the Balkans, a *rapprochement* with the Magyars was necessary.

  4. Under the leadership of Francis Deák and Julius Andrássy, the Hungarians won a series of important concessions known as the *Ausgleich* of October, 1867.

a. Hungary won a separate legislature on a par with the Austrian *Reichsrat*. A responsible ministry was also promised.

b. The two states were joined in a personal union through Franz Joseph. He was emperor of Austria, but king of Hungary. The Magyars insisted that the new state be called the Austro-Hungarian monarchy, not the Austro-Hungarian empire.

c. Hungary thus won control of her internal affairs. There was, however, a common ministry for foreign affairs, finance, and war. The imperial chancellor was also given the foreign affairs portfolio.

d. Sixty members were elected by the Austrian *Reichsrat* and the Hungarian Diet to settle other problems of mutual concern. These delegations had to communicate with each other in writing three times on an issue before they could meet. If such a meeting occurred, the delegations could vote, but not debate. This restriction was designed to prevent the formation of a central legislature.

e. Just as the Magyars dominated the other peoples of the new Hungary, the Germans emerged as the leaders of the seventeen Austrian provinces. Austria was run under the February Patent of 1861.

f. Franz Joseph still retained much of his power, but now he ruled through two responsible ministries—one in Vienna, the other in Budapest.

g. The new state was thus a dual monarchy. The Slavic demand for a federal state in which all nationalities had autonomy was junked in favor of a dual monarchy run by Magyars and Germans.

h. By 1890 the population of the polyglot Austro-Hungarian monarchy was about 40 million. Only 10.5 million were German, while 7.5 million were Hungarian. The remaining 22 million (55 per cent) were Czechs, Slovaks, Poles, Croats, Serbs, Ruthenians, Slovenes, Rumanians, Italians, and Gipsies.

F. The Dual Monarchy, 1867–1914

1. In Austria a ministry of German Liberals under Count Auersperg (1867–1870) took office, while Count Julius Andrássy headed the first Hungarian ministry (1867–1871).

2. The Hungarians agreed to a common army, and yielded a point by agreeing to German as the language of command (May, 1868).
3. In September, 1868 the Austrians made a concession by permitting the reunion of Croatia and Hungary.
4. The Concordat of 1855 was suspended abruptly in 1870 as a reaction to the new dogma of papal infallibility.
5. Meanwhile, the Bohemian Diet demanded for the Czechs a position in Austria similar to that won in Hungary by the Magyars.
   a. This killed the Hohenwart government in 1871.
6. Second Auersperg ministry, 1871–1878
   a. This second ministry of German Liberals in Austria was hurt severely by the panic of 1873 and financial speculations by several Liberal ministers. The German Liberals soon broke up into quarrelsome factions.
7. The Kálámán Tisza ministry in Hungary, 1875–1890
   a. The Tisza government made an intensive effort to Magyarize the Slavic minorities in Hungary. School and language restrictions had some success to about 1900, but a new surge of national feeling prior to World War I undid much of the Magyarization.
8. The Taaffe ministry in Austria, 1879–1893
   a. Count Eduard Taaffe handled the nationality question differently in Austria.
   b. The defection of the German Liberals forced Taaffe to form a coalition of Poles, Czechs, and German Conservatives. He made various concessions on language rights to keep the coalition afloat.
9. The Badeni language ordinances, 1897
   a. Count Casimir Badeni, who headed a ministry from 1895–1897, attempted to conciliate the nationalities in Austria by placing German and the local language in a given district on a par.
   b. Violent German resistance forced Badeni to resign. The monarchy was faced by a grave crisis and widespread disorders.
   c. Even the later ministry of Ernst von Körber (1900–1904) failed to solve the language crisis. He was forced to rule by decree.
10. Breakdown of parliamentary government, 1907–1914

a. Although universal suffrage was introduced for parliamentary elections in 1907, the nationality question was never solved.

b. Meanwhile, in Hungary there developed a strong demand to make Magyar the language of command in the army. The demand was dropped in 1906 when Franz Joseph threatened to push universal suffrage in Hungary. Such a law would have given the more numerous Slavs control of the Hungarian parliament, so the Magyars withdrew their language demand for the army.

c. From 1907 to 1914 the ministries in Austria lacked parliamentary majorities. They often ruled by decree. In Hungary Count Stephen Tisza, son of Káláman Tisza, was the dominant figure after 1905. He formed the last Magyar ministry within the Dual Monarchy (1913–1917).

BIBLIOGRAPHY

Charques, R., *The twilight of imperial Russia* (New York: Oxford University Press, 1959).

Jászi, O., *The dissolution of the Habsburg monarchy* (Chicago: University of Chicago Press, 1929).

Kann, R. A., *The Habsburg empire* (New York: Praeger, 1957).

Lewis, Geoffrey, *Turkey* (New York: Praeger, 1955).

Marriott, J. A. R., *The eastern question* (New York: Oxford University Press, 1940).

May, A. J., *The Habsburg monarchy, 1867–1914* (Cambridge, Mass.: Harvard University Press, 1951).

Mazour, A., *Rise and fall of the Romanovs* (Princeton: D. Van Nostrand, 1960).

———, *The first Russian revolution, 1825; the Decembrist movement, its origins, development, and significance* (Berkeley: University of California Press, 1937).

Miller, William, *The Ottoman Empire and its successors, 1801–1927* (New York: Macmillan, 1936).

Pares, Bernard, *The fall of the Russian monarchy. A study of the evidence* (New York: Knopf, 1939).

Price, M. P., *A history of Turkey* (London: Allen and Unwin, 1956).

Ramsaur, Ernest, *The Young Turks* (Princeton: Princeton University Press, 1957).

Robinson, G. T., *Rural Russia under the Old Regime* (New York: Macmillan, 1949).

Seton-Watson, Hugh, *The decline of imperial Russia, 1855–1914* (London: Methuen, 1952).

Sumner, B. H., *Tsardom and imperialism in the Far East and the Middle East, 1880–1914* (New York: Oxford University Press, 1942).

Taylor, A. J. P., *The Habsburg monarchy, 1809–1918* (London: Hamish Hamilton, 1948).

Walsh, Warren B., *Russia and the Soviet Union* (Ann Arbor: University of Michigan Press, 1958).

Chapter 12

INTERNATIONAL RIVALRY AND WORLD WAR, 1871–1919

I. The New Imperialism

A. The first great age of empire-building had begun with the extensive Portuguese explorations in Africa after 1450. Tiny Portugal was joined in the race for empire by Spain, Holland, France, and Great Britain. For the next three centuries imperial and trade wars realigned the holdings of the great powers to the advantage of Great Britain.

B. By the end of the Seven Years' War in 1763 France had lost most of her overseas holdings in Canada and India to the British. Spain continued to dominate Latin America, but with a feeble hand. Within the next 60 years she was forced to relinquish the bulk of her possessions in the western hemisphere. Portugal managed to maintain her hold over Angola and Mozambique, while the Dutch entrenched themselves in the East Indies (Indonesia). Greatest of all the colonial domains was the British empire. Despite the loss of its American colonies, the empire embraced much of Canada, India, and Australia by 1788. The British later won Ceylon and Cape Colony at the Congress of Vienna (1815), and announced their sovereignty over New Zealand in 1840.

C. In general, the period from 1783 to 1871 marked a sharp decline in imperial activity. The military and administrative cost of maintaining colonies proved to be large. In addition, the British loss of her American colonies made many states wonder whether overseas holdings could be held long enough to make them pay. Domestic problems in Europe also occupied the powers prior to 1871: French revolutions in 1830 and 1848, British internal reform after

1832, the 1848 revolutions, the Crimean War of 1854–1856, and the troublesome questions of German and Italian unification.

D. Causes of the new imperialism
   1. Imperial prestige
      a. In all of the great states tremendous pride was taken in every territorial acquisition. This feeling could be found in all social and economic classes. Latecomers to the imperial race like Germany and Italy were under even greater pressure from colonial societies: they had to make a showing before all the desirable areas had been claimed. Publicists like Sir John Seeley, Leroy-Beaulieu, and Karl Peters also played a key role in increasing the enthusiasm for colonial expansion.
   2. Economic reasons
      a. The great increase in the productivity of European industry by 1880 placed pressure on each of the powers to find new markets for their excess capacity. The need for raw materials was also a consideration.
      b. In addition, the mature industrial states of Europe had large amounts of surplus capital to invest. The backward areas of Africa and Asia appeared to offer excellent possibilities.
      c. The new cycle of protectionism that began in the 1870's also helped to intensify the race for colonies. Great Britain was already thinking about the idea of an "imperial federation" in which preferential tariff rates would be given.
   3. Surplus population
      a. Many imperialists argued that the backward areas of the world were needed to absorb the growing population of Europe.
   4. Moral reasons
      a. Many regarded the acquisition of colonies as a way to give the backward peoples of Africa and Asia a spiritual and material uplift. As Kipling put it, this task was the "white man's burden."
      b. Missionary activity was often an entering wedge for imperialism. Devoted men like David Livingstone worked against the evil effects of the Arab slave trade, but in doing so opened up east Africa to colonial

enterprise. Missionary groups like the French *Société des missions africaines* under Cardinal Lavigerie often pressured their governments for a more energetic colonial policy.

5. Military factors
   a. The occupation of a given area was undertaken in many cases because of the strategic value of the region. The British occupation of Egypt in 1882 was undertaken to protect the route to India, while her acquisition of the Chinese port of Wei-hai-wei in 1898 was a move to counter the Russian acquisition of Port Arthur.

II. Imperialism in Africa

A. In 1871 little was known of the great interior of Africa: France had begun the occupation of Algeria in 1830, but the rest of north Africa remained under Ottoman control—at least in name. The British were established in the Cape Colony by 1815, but the Boers moved north into the Orange Free State and the Transvaal during the Great Trek (1835–1837). The British had acquired Sierra Leone, Gambia, and the Gold Coast in west Africa by 1821, and forty years later entered Nigeria via the port of Lagos. French activity in west Africa was centered around Senegal, the Ivory Coast (1842), Guinea (1849), and Dahomey (1863). Spain occupied tiny Fernando Po in 1843, and later won the worthless Rio de Oro and Spanish Guinea (1885), while the Portuguese continued to hold their ancient bases in Angola and Mozambique.

B. Interest in the unknown interior of Africa was sparked by a series of brilliant explorations.
   1. As early as 1795–1796 Mungo Park had explored the west African areas of Gambia and the Niger river valley.
   2. In 1812–1814 the Swiss explorer J. L. Burckhardt moved up the Nile and crossed over to the Red Sea.
   3. A three man expedition crossed the Sahara from Tripoli to Lake Chad in 1822–1825.
   4. During the years 1840–1843 C. T. Beke mapped most of Ethiopia.
   5. Speke discovered Lake Victoria in 1858, and Baker found Lake Albert six years later.

6. David Livingstone's extensive travels uncovered the full course of the Zambesi River as well as the region around Lakes Tanganyika and Nyasa. The imagination of the world was touched when Henry M. Stanley finally located Livingstone on Lake Tanganyika in 1871.

7. Stanley later completed a thorough investigation of the Congo basin (1878). DeBrazza was also active in this area.

C. The race for Africa

   1. Under the leadership of Disraeli, Great Britain acquired 44 per cent of the Suez Canal shares in 1875. When a native nationalist movement threatened Britain's position, even the pacific Gladstone occupied Egypt in 1882.

   2. After the British defeat at Majuba Hill by the Boers in 1881 war was inevitable. The British victory in the Boer War (1899–1902) ended the independence of the Boer republics of Transvaal and the Orange Free State, but the Dutch were able to dominate the new Union of South Africa after 1910.

   3. Berlin Conference of 1885
      a. Called by Germany and France, this conclave set the ground rules for the further division of Africa. Effective occupation was made the key criterion.
      b. Freedom of navigation on the Niger and Congo rivers was guaranteed.
      c. The slave trade was to be abolished.

   4. Soon after the conference King Leopold of Belgium announced his personal sovereignty over the Congo. His old International Association took the name Independent State of the Congo.
      a. Exploitation of the copper mines and other resources became the chief aim of the unscrupulous regime.
      b. Belgium finally annexed the Congo in 1908.

   5. French ambitions in Africa were fired by the able Jules Ferry.
      a. The French occupied Tunis in 1881 to the chagrin of Italy.
      b. The Exploration of DeBrazza gave the French an excuse to occupy French Equatorial Africa, the area north of the Congo River. From here they pushed into the interior and reached Lake Chad.

c. Thus, Senegal, the Ivory Coast, and Guinea were joined into a great French west African bloc.

d. France also acquired Djibouti on the Red Sea in 1888. Their interest in the Sudan and Abyssinia soon caused a clash with the British at Fashoda in 1898. The British prevailed in the Sudan, and French hopes for a belt of territory across Africa from east to west were dashed.

6. British hopes for a Cape to Cairo railway

   a. Although the British were able to consolidate their position in the west African territory of Nigeria by 1894, their hopes for a Cape to Cairo railroad never materialized.

   b. The Anglo-German Treaty of 1890 gave the British Uganda and Kenya, but forced the British to yield Tanganyika to Germany. This ended the British dream of a Cape to Cairo railroad despite the British acquisition of Bechuanaland and the Rhodesias.

7. German acquisitions

   a. Prior to the acquisition of German East Africa in 1890, the Kaiser's government had proclaimed Southwest Africa a protectorate (1884). This angered the British. They assumed that everyone realized Britain intended to occupy the area between Angola and Bechuanaland.

   b. Germany acquired two valuable west African areas when Gustav Nachtigal proclaimed protectorates over Togoland and the Cameroons in 1884.

   c. Germany had thus acquired a considerable African domain despite the fact that she was a tardy contender for empire.

8. Italian territorial gains

   a. The Italian struggle for unification was completed by 1870. This plus the poverty of the new state gave the other European states a decided advantage.

   b. Italian hopes were centered on Tunisia until the French, with Bismarck's encouragement, seized the prize in 1881.

   c. An Italian attempt to seize Ethiopia in 1895–1896 ended in disaster. As early as 1885 the Italians had established themselves at Massawa on the Red Sea.

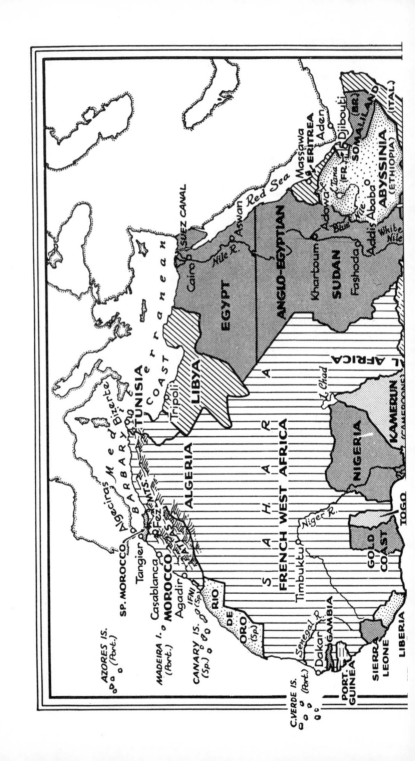

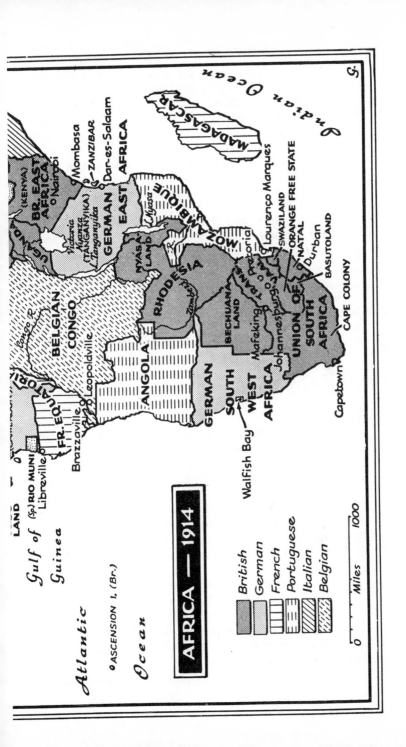

AFRICA — 1914

British
German
French
Portuguese
Italian
Belgian

0   Miles   1000

Atlantic

Ocean

Gulf of
Guinea

ASCENSION I. (Br.)

LAND

(Sp.)RIO MUNI

Libreville

FR. EQUA-
TORIAL

Brazzaville

Congo R.

BELGIAN
CONGO

Leopoldville

ANGOLA

GERMAN
SOUTH
WEST
AFRICA

Walfish Bay

BECHUANA-
LAND

Mafeking

RHODESIA

Zambezi R.

TRANS-
VAAL

Johannesburg

Pretoria

Capetown

UNION OF
SOUTH
AFRICA

CAPE COLONY

BASUTOLAND

NATAL

Durban

ORANGE FREE STATE

SWAZILAND

Lourenço Marques

MOZAMBIQUE

NYASA
LAND

Nyasa L.

GERMAN
EAST
AFRICA

TANGANYIKA)

Tanganyika

L.

Ruanda

Victoria

UGANDA

(KENYA)

BR. EAST
AFRICA

Nairobi

Mombasa

ZANZIBAR

Dar-es-Salaam

MADAGASCAR

Indian Ocean

G.

Five years later this area along the Red Sea was organized as the colony of Eritrea.

d. In 1889 the Sultan of Zanzibar granted Italy possession of a large part of the Somali coast northeast of Kenya. This area became known as Italian Somaliland.

e. When Italy attempted to occupy Ethiopia in 1895, Menelek resisted successfully. His forces crushed the Italians at Adowa in 1896, and Italian hopes had to wait forty years.

f. In 1911 Italy and Turkey became involved in war over Tripoli. Italian successes won Libya, and gave her compensation for French gains in Morocco.

III. Imperialism in Asia

A. (See Chapter 3 for sections on imperialism in India, China, and Japan).

IV. Imperialism in Oceania

A. Following the British entry into Australia (originally a penal colony) in 1788, the Union Jack was placed over New Zealand in 1840.

1. The British continued to expand in this area by annexing Fiji in 1874 and the southeastern portion of New Guinea ten years later.

2. In 1887 Great Britain and France agreed to joint rule over the New Hebrides. Next year the British placed a protectorate over the Cook Islands. This was also accomplished in the Gilbert and Ellice Islands in 1892.

3. A dispute over the Samoan islands involving Great Britain, Germany, and the United States was resolved in 1899.

a. Great Britain obtained several of the Solomon Islands. The United States acquired Tutuila, while Germany received the other Samoan isles.

4. In 1900 the British expanded their Pacific holdings by placing a protectorate over the Friendly Islands.

B. French activity in the Pacific

1. Exploration by men like Freycinet, Duperry, and the

great Dumont D'Urville preceded French annexations in Oceania.

2. In 1842 France annexed the Marquesas and threw a protectorate over the Society Islands and Tahiti. Two years later they placed the Tuamotu Islands under their protection.

3. The important island of New Caledonia was won in 1853, while the Loyalty Islands were secured in 1864.

C. German expansion in Oceania

1. After entering the colonial race in Southwest Africa in 1884, the Germans annexed the Marshall and Solomon Islands.

2. In 1899 Germany secured most of the Samoan chain after an agreement with the United States and Great Britain.

3. Germany had already appropriated northeastern New Guinea and the nearby Bismarck Archipelago.

4. In 1899 the Germans purchased the Marianna and Palau Islands from Spain.

V. Evaluation of the New Imperialism

A. Despite the fact that many were exploited in areas like the Congo or China, imperialism often brought a better educational system, improved health facilities, a transportation network, and the benefits of law. Missionary activity was responsible for much of the educational and spiritual changes.

B. Generally speaking, colonies proved to be a vast financial burden. Individuals and corporations often prospered, but the cost of military and naval establishments outweighed any revenues that governments might obtain. In addition, the colonies never proved to be the great market imperialists hoped they would be because the backward peoples lacked purchasing power. The mother countries did benefit from new sources of raw materials, but they never achieved the ideal of self-sufficiency.

C. The argument that colonies would absorb the surplus population of Europe was proved to be untrue by the very small numbers of Europeans who emigrated to Africa and Asia.

D. Great Britain was the most successful imperialist power in

terms of size, population, and commerce. Almost half her
empire was acquired after 1874.

E. The great imperialistic era from 1871 to 1914 has been followed by a cycle of anti-imperialism after World War I.

VI. The Rival Alliance Systems Prior to 1914

A. The diplomatic situation in 1871
   1. The German victory in the Franco-Prussian War made
      Bismarck's *Reich* the strongest power in Europe.
   2. France never forgave the new Germany for the loss of
      Alsace-Lorraine. She hoped for *revanche* (revenge), but
      needed an ally. Thus, Bismarck was confronted with
      the need to keep France isolated—particularly from
      Russia.
   3. Great Britain absorbed her energies in overseas expan-
      sion. She repeatedly clashed with Russia in Turkey, Per-
      sia, Afghanistan, and Tibet until the *rapprochment* of
      1907. The British generally stayed aloof from conti-
      nental politics before 1904, but soon came to view the
      industrial and naval challenge of Wilhelmine Germany
      with concern.
   4. Russia and Austria-Hungary both viewed each other
      with deep suspicion because of their mutual interest in
      the Balkans and the declining Ottoman Empire. Only
      the skill of Bismarck was able to keep them apart until
      1890.
   5. The new but weak state of Italy aspired to play the role
      of a great power without the resources required for such
      a role. She eventually sought succor from Bismarck's
      Triple Alliance, but sided with France during World
      War I.
B. The Three Emperors' League (1873)
   1. This agreement among the three conservative powers
      was based on the principle of monarchial solidarity
      against revolution. It was the result of a series of meet-
      ings of William I, Franz Joseph, Alexander II of Russia,
      and their foreign ministers. Bismarck, however, was the
      driving wheel.
   2. Bismarck wished the support of Russia and Austria-
      Hungary should a new war occur with France. Austria-
      Hungary saw all hope for revenge against Bismarck van-

ish with the French defeat in 1870–1871. She now hoped to improve relations with the new European colossus. Czar Alexander II, suspicious of Austria-Hungary because of Balkan conflicts, did not want Franz Joseph to move so close to Germany unless he, too, could participate.

3. The agreements
   a. Russia and Austria-Hungary agreed to maintain the *status quo* in the Balkans.
   b. Russia and Germany agreed to assist each other with 200,000 men should either be attacked.
   c. Russia and Austria-Hungary, through the Schönbrunn Convention, agreed to consult each other on cooperative measures should either one be attacked.

4. War scare of 1875
   a. The first test of the loose Three Emperors' League revealed its weakness.
   b. When an inspired article threatening preventive war against France appeared in the Berlin *Post,* both Russia and Great Britain protested vigorously. Neither power wanted France seriously weakened for fear of altering the balance of power still more in Germany's favor.

C. Austro-German alliance of 1879
   1. A revolt against Turkish rule in Bosnia and Herzegovina in 1875 led Serbia and Montenegro to declare war on the Ottoman Empire. Their defeat coupled with the Bulgarian massacres gave Russia an excuse to declare war in 1877. When Russian victories pointed toward her dominance in the Balkans, the great powers secured a revision of her position at the Congress of Berlin (1878). The Russians left the conclave thoroughly dissatisfied and particularly angry with Bismarck.
   2. To protect himself, Bismarck sought a close alliance with Austria-Hungary while the pro-German Count Julius Andrássy was still foreign minister.
      a. The agreement was for five years, but was renewed at regular intervals.
      b. If either party was attacked by Russia, the other would come to its aid.
      c. If either party was attacked by a power other than Russia, the other would stay neutral. It was obvious

that Franz Joseph did not wish to bail Bismarck out of a French conflict. The only point of mutual interest was the eventuality of a war with Russia.

D. The second Three Emperors' League (1881)

1. This secret agreement was desired by the worried Russians, for they did not like the prospect of a strong Austro-Hungarian policy in the Balkans supported by Bismarck. Bismarck insisted that Vienna be included in the new agreement.

2. If one of the signatories became involved in war with a fourth power except for Turkey, the other two were to remain neutral.

3. No changes in the territory of the Ottoman Empire were to be made unless all three powers agreed. If one power had to engage in war against Turkey, it should consult its allies regarding final peace terms.

4. Turkey was to keep the Straits closed. This was designed to keep Great Britain out of the Black Sea and thus protect Russia's southern frontier. The three powers agreed to warn Turkey on this point should she open the Straits.

5. Austria-Hungary was given permission to annex Bosnia-Herzegovina when she felt the time was right.

6. The signatories agreed not to oppose the eventual union of Eastern Roumelia and Bulgaria.

E. The Triple Alliance (1882)

1. This alliance was desired by Italy after the French seizure of Tunisia in 1881. Italy felt isolated diplomatically and worried about French intervention to restore Rome to the pope. Austria-Hungary believed this alliance might calm further Italian claims for her territory (irredentism). Bismarck looked upon the new combination with favor because of the militant Panslavism of Russia and the possibility of a Franco-Russian alliance.

2. Provisions of the alliance

a. If France attacked Italy without cause, Austria-Hungary and Germany would come to her assistance.

b. If France attacked Germany, Italy promised to assist Bismarck.

c. If one or possibly two of the signatories became involved in war with two or more major powers, those in the alliance who were not attacked were obligated to come to the aid of their allies.

    d. If one signatory felt forced to declare war on a great power, the two allies of the contracting state agreed to stay neutral.

3. The Triple Alliance was renewed at five year intervals, but each time Italy demanded additional concessions. In 1887, for example, Italy won the promise of German assistance should war result over problems in North Africa. Austria-Hungary and Italy agreed to maintain the *status quo* in the Near East, but if one should add to its territory, the other state would be permitted to make an equivalent annexation.

F. The Reinsurance Treaty (June 18, 1887)

1. The year 1887 presented Bismarck with a serious diplomatic dilemma. For sixteen years he had kept France isolated, but a threat to this favorable state of affairs now presented itself.

2. Because of serious Balkan problems with Austria-Hungary, Russia refused to renew the 1881 Alliance of the Three Emperors *(Dreikaiserbund)*.

3. Bismarck hoped that a Russo-German agreement would prevent a Franco-Russian combination. He proposed to offer Russia concessions in the Near East that she could never obtain because of Austrian and English opposition.

4. Provisions of the treaty

    a. Germany and Russia promised each other to be neutral in the event one became involved in war. This provision would be void in the event of a German attack on France or a Russian attack on Austria-Hungary.

    b. Germany recognized Bulgaria as a Russian sphere of influence. Both powers agreed to try to maintain the *status quo* in the Balkans.

    c. Germany again agreed to the idea of the closure of the Straits, and secretly promised to aid Russian efforts to win the entrance to the Black Sea.

5. In 1888 Bismarck published the 1879 Austro-German agreement. It was a clear warning to Russian nationalists despite the earlier Reinsurance Treaty.

G. In 1890 the youthful Wilhelm II dismissed Bismarck as chancellor.

　1. The new emperor believed that Germany had to ally herself with Great Britain and Austria-Hungary.

　2. Russian ties, such as the Reinsurance Treaty, were permitted to lapse in 1890.

　3. Russia was now a diplomatic free agent as was France.

H. The Franco-Russian convention of 1894

　1. Repeated Russian efforts to interest Wilhelm II in a new tie failed during 1890–1891. In addition, Great Britain seemed to be moving closer to the Triple Alliance.

　2. The way for a Franco-Russian agreement had been paved by French loans, the Triple Alliance, the lapsing of the Reinsurance Treaty, and indications of Anglo-German friendship.

　3. Provisions of the military convention

　　a. The agreement was classified as a military convention in order to avoid a discussion before the French lower house, a body that constitutionally had the power to review all treaties. The convention was to be operative so long as the Triple Alliance existed.

　　b. If France were attacked by Germany or by Italy supported by Germany, Russia would come to the aid of France.

　　c. If Russia were attacked by Germany or by Austria-Hungary supported by Germany, France would come to the aid of Russia.

I. Great Britain abandons "splendid isolation"

　1. During this era Joseph Chamberlain took the lead in promoting an Anglo-German alliance. The program never won popular support. In addition, the beginning of a vast German naval program under Alfred von Tirpitz in 1898 tended to worsen relations. German insistence that Great Britain join the Triple Alliance and not merely sign a German pact spelled the end of Anglo-German negotiations (1898–1901).

　2. Great Britain now felt so acutely alone, that she abandoned her traditional policy of "splendid isolation." In 1902 she concluded the five year Anglo-Japanese alliance: if either party became involved in war with a third power, its ally agreed to remain neutral. Should one of

the contracting powers be confronted by two adversaries, the other would be obligated to come to its assistance. It was understood that neither party was to enter into any agreement with Russia unless its ally was notified.

J. The *Entente Cordiale* of 1904

    1. The breakdown of Anglo-German talks in 1901 now made a reconciliation between London and Paris possible. In 1903 King Edward VII visited Paris and helped inaugurate a period of improved relations. The return visit of President Loubet began a series of conversations that eventually led to an understanding.

    2. The *Entente Cordiale* was finally completed in April, 1904. It represented a settlement of pressing colonial problems, and paved the way for a military understanding in Europe.

        a. France agreed to recognize the British position in Egypt in return for her support of French interests in Morocco.

        b. France gave up all rights in Newfoundland, but it could still fish in the area. France was compensated for this with small cessions near Gambia and the Niger valley of West Africa.

        c. French and British spheres of influence were clearly delimited in Siam. Additional disputes in the New Hebrides and Madagascar were settled amicably.

    3. In 1906 Anglo-French military conversations began.

        a. The naval and military dispositions agreed upon created what was, in effect, an alliance. Britain had assumed a "moral obligation" to aid France in the event of a German attack.

K. The Anglo-Russian entente of 1907

    1. With French encouragement, this new tie had been discussed since the end of the Russo-Japanese War in 1905. Completion of such an agreement would create, in practice, a rival coalition aimed at the Triple Alliance. This new grouping came to be known as the Triple Entente.

    2. The *rapprochement* of these ancient rivals occurred (as in the *Entente Cordiale*) after several serious colonial problems had been temporarily resolved.

    3. Persia

        a. This was the area of sharpest tension. It was divided into three spheres of influence: a Russian sphere in the north, a neutral sphere in central Persia, and a British sphere in the south.

b. Russia agreed that Afghanistan was not within her sphere of influence, but Great Britain agreed not to interfere in her internal affairs.

c. Great Britain and Russia both agreed to recognize Chinese sovereignty over Tibet.

d. Separate notes saw Russia recognize the Persian Gulf as a British sphere, while Great Britain indicated she would favor a change at the Straits favorable to the Russians.

VII. Crises Prior to World War I

A. The competing Triple Alliance and Triple Entente made for considerable tension in Europe prior to 1914. During the decade prior to World War I a series of crises occurred.

B. The first Moroccan crisis (1905)

1. The settlement of Anglo-French colonial differences in 1904 worried the Germans. After waiting almost a year, they decided to test the strength of the *Entente Cordiale*. Morocco was to be the issue.

2. As a protest to Anglo-French agreements on Morocco without their being consulted, Kaiser Wilhelm II landed at Tangier on March 31, 1905 and declared the sultan to be an independent ruler. In addition, the Germans insisted that the former Anglo-French agreement on Morocco be set aside.

3. The Germans lacked determination to carry out this policy of testing the Anglo-French entente: the Kaiser did not like this policy of bluff. When Delcassé was forced from the French foreign office during this crisis the Germans seemed to have won a great victory. The Germans now insisted on an international conference which met at Algeciras in 1906.

4. When the conference met, Anglo-French opposition stiffened and picked up support from Russia, Italy, and the United States. The final settlement was thus very favorable to France: the police force was to be French and Spanish, but entirely French on the Algerian-Moroccan frontier. France had a leading voice in the new state bank.

C. The Bosnian crisis of 1908–1909
  1. In September, 1908 a conference took place at Buchlau between the Russian foreign minister, Alexander Izvolsky, and the Austrian foreign minister, Count Alois Aehrenthal. The rise of the Young Turk party at Constantinople seemed to indicate an imminent revival of Turkey, a prospect that was unpalatable to both Izvolsky and Aehrenthal. Both men, therefore, came to the following agreement: Austria would be permitted to annex Bosnia-Herzegovina, while Russia could open the Straits for her warships. No precise date for the execution of this agreement was established, and this led to trouble.
  2. In October, 1908 Austria-Hungary unilaterally announced the annexation of Bosnia-Herzegovina. The Russians were caught by surprise, while the other European states registered profound disapproval of the move.
    a. In particular, the Serbs were furious. They had long regarded Bosnia-Herzegovina as an area for their expansion. They now prepared for war with the support of Russia. Vienna also made preparations.
    b. By the spring of 1909 German support of Austria-Hungary and Anglo-French promises to Russia brought the Triple Alliance and the Triple Entente to the brink of war.
    c. When Germany demanded that Russia yield or face war, Izvolsky backed down. Nevertheless, Russia and Serbia were determined not to face such a humiliation again.
D. The second Moroccan crissis (1911)
  1. In the spring of 1911 France sent troops to the Moroccan city of Fez to protect foreign residents from a native uprising. The German reaction was one of opposition. Alfred von Kiderlen-Wächter, the German foreign minister, insisted that France make a proposal to end the Moroccan tension.
  2. In July, 1911 Germany sent the gunboat *Panther* to Agadir. This was meant to frighten the French into making concessions; the Germans finally hit upon cession of the entire French Congo as compensation. Meanwhile, the British feared that what Germany really wanted was a naval base on the coast of Morocco. Lloyd

DIPLOMATIC ALIGNMENTS BEFORE

0   Miles   500

NORWAY

SWEDEN

DENMARK

1907

1894

1887
1890

BERLIN

Vistula R.

RUSSIA

St. Petersburg

Dnieper R.

Dniester R.

1879-82

Vienna

AUSTRIA-HUNGARY

RUMANIA

Black Sea

1882

1882

WITZ.

Danube R.

SERBIA

TRIPLE
ALLIANCE

BULGARIA

Rome

MONT.

ALBANIA

OTTOMAN
EMP.

SARDINIA

GREECE

1914

SICILY

CRETE

Mediterranean Sea

George's Mansion House speech (July 21, 1911) made it clear that Great Britain wanted to be consulted before any final decisions were made in Morocco.

3. The threat of war seemed imminent, but Franco-German talks continued until agreement was reached in November, 1911.

4. Germany gave France a free hand in Morocco in return for a portion of the French Congo. War was again averted, but the level of bitterness had risen appreciably.

E. The Balkan Wars, 1912–1913

1. (For a full account see Chapter 11).

2. In October, 1912 Serbia, Bulgaria, Greece and Montenegro declared war on the declining Turkish Empire. They quickly defeated the Ottoman forces, but soon began an acrimonious quarrel over the spoils. Russia backed Serbian demands for access to the Adriatic, but Austria fought such a move. To prevent war, an international conference created a free Albania and compensated Serbia elsewhere.

3. A second Balkan conflict began in May, 1913. Bulgaria was the chief victim of a combined assault by Serbia, Montenegro, Greece, Rumania, and Turkey.

4. During both Balkan wars a major conflict was avoided only through the efforts of Great Britain and Germany. The British were able to restrain Russia, while Berlin held back the bellicose Austrians.

F. Sarajevo (1914)

1. By 1914 Europe was divided into two hostile armed camps: The Triple Alliance and the Triple Entente. Continuous crises since 1905 had sharpened the ill-feeling that already existed.

2. In addition, there was less willingness to compromise by 1914. Both sides seemed ready for a recourse to violence. Extremism had taken hold.

3. Assassination of Archduke Franz Ferdinand (June 28, 1914)

a. The murder of Archduke Frank Ferdinand and his consort in Sarajevo by the Serbian Gavrilo Princip aroused the bellicose Austro-Hungarian government. There was evidence to indicate that Princip belonged to the anti-Austrian terrorist group known as the Black Hand Society. It was this group that planned the assassination. To make matters worse, the Serbian government knew of the plot and did nothing to prevent it.

b. On July 5, 1914 Germany promised Austria-Hungary her full support. Berlin felt a settlement favorable to Vienna could be won without war.

c. Austria-Hungary wanted to thoroughly humiliate Serbia, and on July 23, 1914 sent Belgrade a list of demands that would have ended the independence of Serbia. Vienna meant to wipe out the Serbian menace, and with a "blank check" from Berlin, refused to ease its demands. Austrian intransigence was strengthened by the fact that the military were in the saddle in Berlin and Vienna.

d. News of a partial Russian mobilization on July 29, 1914 made war inevitable despite the efforts of Lord Grey. Within a week the continent of Europe had entered into the costliest war the world had ever seen up to 1914.

VIII. World War I, 1914–1918

A. Causes
  1. The establishment of the Triple Alliance and the Triple Entente divided Europe into two hostile camps. The members of each coalition felt it was a necessity to support their allies in all crises. As a result, when one or two great powers became embroiled in a crisis—all were.
  2. Militarism
     a. The existence of large standing armies and navies obviously contributed to the miasma of fear and suspicion before 1914.
     b. In addition, the military leaders and their General Staffs had become extremely powerful by 1914. During a crisis their judgments often superceded those of civilian authorities.
     c. The prevalence of fear also contributed to a tremendous arms and naval race. Each state feverishly attempted to keep pace with its rivals.
     d. The General Staffs often worked out secret plans to be used in case of war. These plans were usually based on the element of surprise, and when a crisis

occurred, the military generally advocated action so that their preconceived plans would have the best chance of success.

3. Nationalism
   a. In particular, the French desire for *revanche* because of the loss of Alsace-Lorraine was the most glaring example.
   b. Panslavism and Pan-Germanism also contributed to the vortex of hatred emanating from national desires.
   c. Nationalistic aspirations in the Balkans were a very serious source of trouble to Austria-Hungary and Turkey. Serbian hopes for enlargement at Austrian expense were an additional problem.

4. Economic imperialism
   a. By 1880 most of the countries of Europe, particularly western Europe, had become fully industrialized. Their productivity was so great that national markets were saturated with goods. Tariff wars often resulted. In turn, these frictions seriously disturbed the general political climate.
   b. Many European states sought new markets overseas. Clashes in Africa and Asia further sharpened old European differences. The Kruger Telegram, for example, seriously disturbed Anglo-German relations.
   c. The need for raw materials such as oil and copper increased tensions among the European states.
   d. The desire for a population outlet also led to sharp colonial differences despite the fact that few Europeans ever left their homelands.
   e. Many European states sought colonies in order to provide profitable outlets for surplus investment capital. Concern about these investments, as in Morocco, often led to crises among the great powers.

5. The newspapers
   a. Inflammatory articles in the various presses frequently aroused bitter feelings and suspicion.
   b. These articles often made compromise settlements of an issue impossible, for compromise in the eyes of a jingoistic press was viewed as weakness.
   c. Feuds often developed between the papers of two countries. These feuds embittered the general population and made peaceful relations extremely diffi-

cult. The Austro-Serbian press feud was a good illustration of this problem.

B. The war in Europe
   1. The western front
      a. German strategy was based on the 1905 Schlieffen plan as modified by the head of the General Staff, General Helmuth von Moltke. The plan called for a strong force in the west to wheel through Belgium, encircle Paris, and destroy the French war effort before material assistance could arrive from Great Britain. Moltke transferred some of his strength to Lorraine, and during the advance on Paris, sent six corps to the Russian front. These moves probably saved Paris.
      b. The Germans were stopped at the Battle of the Marne (September, 1914) and Paris was saved. They did occupy Luxemburg and most of Belgium for the remainder of the war.
      c. By the end of 1914 the battle lines were fairly fixed. Not until 1918 was there any appreciable change. The German assault on Verdun in 1916 was halted, while the Anglo-French attack on the Somme that year had only minor success.
      d. In 1918 the Germans launched a major offensive to crush the British and French before American aid could arrive. The Germans moved close to Paris, but strong Franco-American resistance under Foch and Pershing turned the tide. A powerful Allied offensive forced Germany to seek peace. An armistice was concluded in November, 1918.
   2. The eastern front
      a. On the Galician front in 1914, the Rusians recovered from an initial defeat and forced the Austrians to abandon eastern Galicia and Bukovina.
      b. The Serbians held their own, but lost Belgrade in December, 1914. They soon recaptured their capital.
      c. After some Russian successes in East Prussia, Hindenburg and Ludendorff crushed the Russian forces at Tannenburg (August, 1914) and the Masurian Lakes (September, 1914). German forces were then sent south to assist the Austrians in Galicia.
      d. The Russian capture of the fortress of Przemsyl in

March, 1915 forced the Austro-German forces in Galicia to move. A new offensive thoroughly crushed and demoralized the Russians in Galicia, and quickly rewon the entire area. The Germans also took Warsaw (August, 1915) and advanced northward into Vilna and Courland. By the fall of 1915 the Russians had lost one million troops and all of Poland, Lithuania, and Courland.

e. The Russian Brusilov offensive of 1916 was designed to take some pressure off of the Italians in the Trentino. While the Russians took Lutsk and Czernowitz and 500,000 prisoners from the Austrians, the arrival of German help ended the offensive.

f. Meanwhile, in the Balkans Austro-German forces with Bulgarian help occupied most of Serbia in 1915. Austro-German forces eliminated Rumania from the war before the end of 1916; Italy held on precariously until peace came.

g. During 1917 the Russian army collapsed. The Bolsheviks seized power in November, 1917 and concluded an armistice. In March, 1918 Lenin took Russia out of the war via the humiliating Treaty of Brest-Litovsk. Russia yielded Poland, the Ukraine, Finland, the Baltic provinces, and much of the Caucasus.

C. The war in the Near East

1. Turkish entry into the war in November, 1914 saw fighting break out in the Caucasus, in northern Persia, and in the Sinai desert near Suez. Nothing of consequence resulted, however.

2. In 1915 a plan to attack the Dardanelles, seize Constantinople, and thus relieve the pressure on Russia was put into action. Winston Churchill and Lloyd George were two of its chief exponents.

3. The Gallipoli campaign was a failure, and British forces were withdrawn in January, 1916.

4. The campaign in Mesopotamia and Palestine
   a. The initial British thrust won Basra, but after an advance northward some 10,000 British troops were forced to surrender after the seige of Kut-el-Amara.
   b. A second Turkish attack on the Suez was blocked in July, 1916.
   c. In the meantime, Anglo-French negotiations with the

Arabians under Hussein, Grand Sherif of Mecca, led to a revolt against Turkish authority. To support the Arabian revolt, the British cautiously crossed the Sinai peninsula and entered Palestine (1916–1917). General Allenby took Jerusalem, while other British forces seized Baghdad.

d. Most of Syria was occupied by the end of October, 1918 and the Turkish war effort broken. Turkey concluded an armistice with the Allies on October 30, 1918.

D. The war at sea

1. Despite the announced desire of the German and British fleets for a decisive engagement, Von Tirpitz did not venture out of port during 1914. The British were able to send their expeditionary force to France without incident.

2. The Germans emphasized submarine attacks and raids on the English coast by Admiral Hipper. Two small engagements at Heligoland (August, 1914) and Dogger Bank (January, 1915) were indecisive.

3. Eight cruisers of the German overseas fleet did considerable damage to Allied naval and merchant vessels until they were hunted down (1914–1915).

a. In the Battle of the Falkland Islands on December 8, 1914 the British destroyed four of Admiral Von Spee's five ships. The *Dresden* escaped, but was hunted down in March, 1915.

b. The German cruisers *Emden* and *Königsberg* did considerable damage before their destruction in 1915.

4. In February, 1915 Germany announced a submarine blockade of Great Britain. London replied by ordering the confiscation of all things bound for Germany.

a. The sinking of the *Lusitania* with the loss of 139 American lives brought Washington and Berlin to the verge of war. The ship had been carrying munitions.

b. The torpedoing of the *Sussex* in March, 1916 caused a second bitter German-American exchange. For the moment, the Germans gave up unrestricted submarine warfare.

5. Battle of Jutland (May 31–June 1, 1916)

a. When Admirals Hipper and Scheer ventured off the

Norwegian coast, the British quickly engaged them and tried to cut off their line of retreat.

   b. Both sides lost six ships, but German gunnery was superior. British naval superiority forced the Germans to flee, and the German fleet never again ventured into the North Sea.

6. The submarine offensive of 1917

   a. In 1916 the Germans had exacted a fearful toll of Allied shipping. Some 300,000 tons a month were being sunk by the end of 1916.

   b. During 1917 the German submarine fleet was increased to 134. The British countered this by using convoys plus more destroyers and anti-submarine vessels.

   c. Although the Germans sent 8 million tons of Allied shipping to the bottom by October, 1917, they had lost many of their underseas craft. In addition, the Allied construction rate in 1918 exceeded losses. Clearly, the U-boat campaign had failed.

IX. The Peace Settlements

A. The Treaty of Versailles (June 28, 1919)

1. Twenty-seven of the victorious powers sent delegates to Paris to negotiate. The Germans were unrepresented, but had agreed to make peace on the basis of Wilson's Fourteen Points. As negotiations proceeded, the Fourteen Points were often ignored.

2. Woodrow Wilson's idealism seemed to win the approval of all. His willingness to compromise on various things was based on faith in the coming League of Nations.

3. Lloyd George of Great Britain was inclined to a moderate peace treaty, but was bound by wartime promises to make the Germans pay for the conflict.

4. Clemenceau of France candidly advocated a harsh treaty to prevent another German attack on his country.

5. Orlando, prime minister of Italy, and his foreign minister, Sidney Sonnino, vigorously championed their country's territorial claims against Austria and the new Yugoslav state.

6. Russia was not represented, since she was in the throes

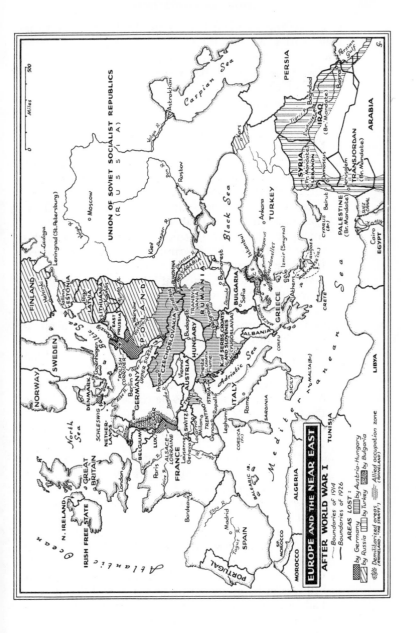

EUROPE AND THE NEAR EAST
AFTER WORLD WAR I

.... Boundaries of 1914
—— Boundaries of 1926

AREAS LOST:

by Germany [illustration] by Austria-Hungary
by Russia [illustration] by Turkey [illustration] by Bulgaria
[illustration] Demilitarized areas [illustration] Allied occupation zone
(RHINELAND, THE STRAITS) (RHINELAND)

Miles 0 500

of a civil war between Lenin's Bolshevik forces and the conservative White armies.

7. The basic decisions were made by the Big Four.
8. Provisions of the Versailles Treaty
   a. An international body for the preservation of peace known as the League of Nations was established.
   b. Germany ceded Alsace-Lorraine to France.
   c. Germany gave Belgium Eupen, Malmedy, and Moresnet.
   d. The Saar was placed under international control for 15 years. A plebiscite would then be held to settle its future. France could obtain the coal output of its mines for 15 years as compensation for the war damage to similar French facilities.
   e. Northern and central Schleswig were to have plebiscites which would determine whether they joined Denmark or remained with Germany.
   f. Germany was to cede most of West Prussia and Posen to the new Polish state. Plebiscites were to be held in parts of East Prussia to determine whether German or Polish control was to be exercised. Such a plebiscite was also to be held in Upper Silesia.
   g. The port of Memel was to be given to the Allied powers.
   h. The Germans yielded all colonial possessions to the Allies. These areas were to be run as mandates under the League of Nations.
   i. Germany was forced to accept the sole responsibility for the war (Article 231).
   j. The German army was limited to 100,000 men. Its navy was to possess but six vessels. No submarines or aircraft were permitted.
   k. The Allies were allowed to occupy the Rhineland for a minimum of 15 years. An area 30 miles wide on the right bank of the Rhine was to be demilitarized.
   l. The Kiel Canal was to be opened to all ships as were all German rivers.
   m. Germany was to pay for all civilian war damage. A bill was to be presented in 1921, but 5 billion dollars had to be paid in the interval. Germany had to give the Allies most of her merchant fleet and one-fourth of her fishing vessels. In addition, she was required

to build 200,000 tons of merchant shipping for the Allies for five years. Germany also had to deliver large quantities of coal to the Allies, and pay áll occupation costs.

n. The United States failed to ratify this harsh treaty because of Wilson's failure to compromise somewhat with the Senate.

B. The Treaty of St. Germain (September 10, 1919)

1. This agreement confirmed the dissolution of the Austro-Hungarian monarchy.

   a. The new state of Austria was forced to recognize the independence of Poland, Hungary, Czechoslavakia, and Yugoslavia.

   b. In turn, these new states were required to protect minorities under their jurisdiction.

   c. Austria also gave up the Trentino, southern Tyrol, Trieste, Istria, and eastern Galicia.

   d. Austria was saddled with an onerous reparation bill. Her army was limited to 30,000 men.

   e. The union of Austria and Germany (*Anschluss*) was forbidden.

C. The Treaty of Trianon (June 4, 1920)

1. This agreement was signed with the new monarchist regime of Hungary headed by Admiral Nicholas Horthy. It followed the suppression of the Bolshevik government of Bela Kun, and the withdrawal of the rapacious Rumanian army.

   a. Trianon cost Hungary 75 per cent of its former territory.

   b. Slovakia was given to the new Czech state, Austria received western Hungary, Yugoslavia obtained Slavonia, Croatia, and part of the Banat, while Rumania gained the remainder of the Banat, Transylvania, and some of eastern Hungary.

D. The Treaty of Neuilly (November 27, 1919)

1. This treaty with Bulgaria cost that state their Aegean toehold plus a reparations bill of $445 million. Her army was limited to 20,000 men.

2. Bulgaria had to recognize Yugoslavia.

E. The settlements with Turkey

1. Allied plans for the partition of Turkey were not carried out in 1919 because of Wilson's opposition and the

bad publicity caused by the Bolshevik publication of the Allied secret treaties.

2. Greek and Italian troops landed in Anatolia, and an international force occupied Constantinople. The weak government of the sultan signed away most of the Ottoman Empire in the Treaty of Sèvres (August 20, 1920).

   a. The Turkish nationalist party under Mustapha Kemal would not accept the Treaty of Sèvres.

   b. They built up a good army and organized a government at Ankara.

3. Mustapha Kemal obtained Italian withdrawal by yielding economic concessions (March, 1921). During the same month he came to an agreement with the Soviet Union: Turkey retained Kars and Ardahah, but returned the port of Batum.

4. Meanwhile, the deep penetration of Anatolia by the Greeks was halted. The Greeks were thrown back and finally crushed with the capture of Smyrna (September, 1922).

5. Treaty of Lausanne (July 24, 1923)

   a. This definitive treaty between the Allies and Turkey saw the Turks yield most of the non-Turkish areas formerly ruled by the Ottoman sultans (Syria, Palestine, Arabia, Iraq).

   b. Turkey held part of eastern Thrace and Constantinople, but yielded most of the Aegean islands to Greece.

   c. Great Britain retained Cyprus, and Italy held the Dodecanese Islands.

   d. The Straits were demilitarized. All ships could pass in time of peace and during war if Turkey was neutral. Neutral ships could pass if Turkey was at war.

   e. The capitulations were ended.

   f. A separate Greek-Turkish agreement provided for a sweeping population exchange.

BIBLIOGRAPHY

Albertini, L., *The origins of the war of 1914*. 3 vols. (New York: Oxford University Press, 1952–1954).

Anderson, E. N., *The first Moroccan crisis, 1904–1906* (Chicago: University of Chicago, 1930).

Birdsall, P., *Versailles twenty years after* (New York: Reynal and Hitchcock, 1941).

Bruun, G., *Clemenceau* (Cambridge, Mass.: Harvard University Press, 1943).

Earle, E. M., *Turkey, the great powers, and the Baghdad railway* (New York: Macmillan, 1923).

Fay, S. B., *The origins of the world war* (New York: Macmillan, 1928).

Hayes, C. J. H., *A generation of materialism* (New York: Harper, 1941).

Hoskins, H. L., *European imperialism in Africa* (New York: Holt, 1930).

Langer, W. L., *European alliances and alignments* (2nd ed., New York: Knopf, 1950).

————, *The diplomacy of imperialism* (2nd ed., New York: Knopf, 1951).

Moon, Parker T., *Imperialism and world politics* (New York: Macmillan, 1947).

Nicolson, H., *Peacemaking, 1919* (Boston: Houghton Mifflin, 1933).

Schmitt, B. E., *Triple Alliance and Triple Entente* (New York: Holt, 1934).

Sontag, R. J., *European diplomatic history, 1871–1932* (New York: Appleton-Century, 1933).

Temperley, H. W. V., *A history of the peace conference of Paris*. 6 vols. (New York: Oxford University Press, 1920–1924).

Thomson, M., *David Lloyd George* (London: Hutchinson, 1948)

Townshend, M. E. and Peake, C. H., *European colonial expansion since 1871* (Philadelphia: Lippincott, 1941).

Winkler, H. R., *The League of Nations movement in Great Britain, 1914–1919* (New Brunswick: Rutgers University Press, 1952).

Chapter 13

EUROPE BETWEEN THE TWO WORLD WARS

I. The Russian Revolution.

A. The Russian revolution occurred as a result of the combination of the <u>legacy of unsolved problems</u> and intolerable conditions of the nineteenth century joined with the <u>ineffectiveness of the tsarist government</u> in meeting the challenge of World War I.

1. World War I was the most total war up to that time, but in Russia nationalist minorities and political parties who desired fundamental changes were less than eager to support the autocracy.

   a. The middle class in Russia, however, were very loyal and wanted to win the war.

   b. Commercial and industrial leaders were shocked by the government's glaring mismanagement of the war effort: two million Russian casualties in seventeen months, inadequate transport, severe shortages of weapons and ammunition.

   c. The government refused to cooperate with any efforts originating outside its own bureaucracy. Attempts of the middle class to aid the war effort were fruitless.

2. <u>The imperial court only made matters worse.</u> The tsar had good intentions, but he was an ineffective ruler.

   a. The tsar, <u>Nicholas II</u>, was dominated to a considerable degree by the <u>Tsarina Alexandra.</u>

   b. Alexandra, in turn, was under the unfortunate influence of the "mad monk," <u>Rasputin.</u>

   c. Rasputin earned Alexandra's support by presumably preventing the crown prince, who suffered from hemophilia, from bleeding to death.

    d. Rasputin was barely literate, but the tsar apparently accepted his advice on conducting the war. It was almost impossible for anyone to interview the tsar without the permission of Rasputin, who also established a bureau where he sold government jobs.

    e. By December, 1916, when Russian war casualties had reached the staggering total of six million, the statistics were increased by one when a group of aristocrats murdered Rasputin.

3. In the autumn of 1916, the issues of liberalism and constitutionalism, which had been so important in the Revolution of 1905, arose again.

    a. The Duma (parliament) had been prorogued since the beginning of the war. After much agitation that it be summoned again, the tsar ordered the Duma to meet in November, 1916.

    b. The Duma of 1916 was composed of very conservative members, but it was extremely indignant about the manner in which the war was being conducted.

    c. The tsar was deeply concerned by the Duma's protests and possibly fearful of revolution. He dissolved the Duma.

    d. The dissolution of the Duma produced a critical shift in public opinion. If the tsar could not conduct the war effectively and would not accept advice or aid from his own subjects, then the government would have to be changed, even if it was necessary to use violence.

4. During World War I food shortages occurred in all belligerent countries. The Russian government was too inefficient to ration food and control food prices effectively.

    a. On March 8, 1917, food riots broke out among the workers of Petrograd (St. Petersburg, the capital of Russia, was renamed in 1914 to get rid of the German suffix. The Communists later changed the name to Leningrad and moved the capital back to Moscow).

    b. Revolutionary agitators soon had the mobs shouting "Down with the tsar."

    c. Troops summoned to quell the rioters refused to fire on the rebels. The army, which had remained loyal during the Revolution of 1905, deserted the tsar.

B. In only a few days, rival authorities emerged, each trying to direct the course of events.

1. On March 12, 1917, delegates from the Petrograd army garrison, labor leaders, and some of the more radical members of the Duma met and formed the Soviet of Workers' and Soldiers' Deputies. (The term, "soviet," means "committee" or "council.")

2. A majority of the members of the Duma, however, elected a Temporary Committee (also known as an Executive Committee) to govern Petrograd until the situation clarified.

3. Meanwhile, Tsar Nicholas II was at the front trying to inspire the troops. When he heard of the Petrograd uprisings, he tried to return to the capital city.

   a. His train was halted by revolutionary troops.
   b. Both the Temporary Committee and the tsar's generals advised him to abdicate because they could not depend on the loyalty of the army.
   c. The Temporary Committee suggested that Prince Lvov should be head of a provisional government. Nicholas II agreed and abdicated in favor of his brother, Grand Duke Michael.
   d. Grand Duke Michael refused the crown, however, and his refusal and Nicholas' abdication were announced the same day.
   e. On March 17, 1917, Russia became a republic.

C. The new Provisional Government had assumed power on March 16, and was soon involved with the Petrograd Soviet as each group tried to control the development of the revolution.

1. Led by Prince Lvov and dominated by liberals who desired a constitutional government, the Provisional Government proclaimed a three-point program.

   a. Elections would be arranged to establish a Constituent Assembly to write a constitution for Russia.
   b. The war against Germany would be continued.
   c. A land reform program favorable to the peasants would be created.

2. The Petrograd Soviet, spurred on by the continued food shortages and need for immediate relief, demanded more radical measures.

a. The Petrograd Soviet was urged on by revolutionary agitators.

b. Among the most extreme agitators were the Bolsheviks, many of whom returned from exile or prison to support the revolution.

c. Stalin arrived in Petrograd from Siberia in March; the German army helped Lenin get from Switzerland to Petrograd, hoping his revolutionary ideas would further damage the Russian war effort. Lenin reached Petrograd in April; and in July, Leon Trotsky arrived from America.

d. Lenin was the outstanding leader among the radicals. His concern in 1917 was to get power, and he was willing to adapt his Marxian theories to the political needs of the moment.

e. The program supported by Lenin and the Bolsheviks was aimed at getting immediate support from the workers and troops in Petrograd.

f. Lenin demanded immediate peace with the Central Powers (Germany, Austria-Hungary, and Turkey); bread for the workers; the control of factories and mines by committees of workers; redistribution of land for the peasants; and, most important of all, the recognition of the soviets, rather than the Provisional Government, as the supreme power in Russia.

D. During the summer of 1917 the Bolsheviks continued their efforts to gain complete control of the Petrograd soviet while the Provisional Government struggled to carry out its policies.

1. The Provisional Government ordered a military offensive against the Austro-Hungarian army on July 1. The Germans reinforced the Austrians, however, and the Russians were badly defeated.

2. Diplomatic failures and division within the Provisional Government further undermined its popularity.

3. The Petrograd soviet and the Bolsheviks then attempted to seize control of Petrograd by armed force, but the uprising was poorly planned and was dispersed.

   a. Evidence of the dealings between German agents and the Bolshevik leaders was made public.

   b. Trotsky was arrested, and Lenin fled to Finland.

4. Continued division within the Provisional Government

led to the assumption of leadership by <u>Kerensky</u>, a Social Revolutionary.

5. In September, Kerensky found the Provisional Government threatened anew, this time from the extreme right.

   a. General Kornilov, the new commander-in-chief of the army, attempted to use the army to seize Petrograd, planning to crush the soviet and take control of the Provisional Government.

   b. To meet Kornilov's threat, Kerensky relaxed the measures against the Bolsheviks. The soviet, the Bolsheviks, and the Provisional Government united and broke up Kornilov's advance. Kornilov was arrested.

6. Kerensky had been forced to rely on the Bolsheviks to stop Kornilov, whose attempt to seize power had discredited the conservatives.

   a. To regain public support, Kerensky assembled a parliament on September 27 and another October 20 which represented all the factions.

   b. The Bolsheviks, however, knowing they could not control these assemblies, boycotted both meetings.

   c. The Bolsheviks continued to concentrate their efforts to get complete control of the Petrograd soviet, together with the military forces it represented.

   d. On October 23 the Bolshevik Central Committee approved the plan for an armed uprising against the Provisional Government.

E. <u>During the night of November 6–7, 1917, the Bolsheviks gained control of Petrograd.</u>

1. The Bolsheviks seized the telephone exchanges, railroad stations, and power plants. A warship shelled the Winter Palace, headquarters of the Provisional Government. Kerensky's government was without an organized defense.

2. Late on November 7, Lenin assembled an "All-Russian Congress of Soviets" and declared the Provisional Government had fallen.

   a. The assembly speedily named a Council of People's Commissars.

   b. Few were surprised to learn that the chief commissar was to be Nicolai Lenin.

   c. This revolution is also known as the "October Revolution" since the Bolshevik seizure of power occurred during October according to the Julian Calendar used in Russia until 1918.

3. On November 25, 1917 the elections for the Constituent Assembly took place.

   a. This election, long sought by Kerensky, was as close to a free election in the Western sense as Russia ever came.

   b. Of approximately thirty-six million votes cast, twenty-one million were for Kerensky and the Social Revolutionaries, nine million favored Lenin and the Bolsheviks, and the remainder favored other parties.

   c. When the elected Constituent Assembly met in January, 1918, the Bolsheviks broke up the meeting with troops.

4. One of the first acts of the Bolsheviks following their seizure of power November 7, 1917 was the creation of the "Extraordinary All-Russian Commission of Struggle Against Counter-Revolution."

   a. The Russian initials for this commission were C.H.E.K.A. The C.H.E.K.A. became the Bolsheviks' secret political police, at least as dreaded as the tsarist police had ever been.

   b. When the C.H.E.K.A.'s reputation became so notorious, a new name and initials were supplied, the O.G.P.U. Later, this became the N.K.V.D., which, in turn, became the M.V.D., still in existence and still notorious.

   c. In January, 1918, the Bolsheviks created the Red Army and placed Leon Trotsky in command.

   d. In March, 1918, the Bolsheviks changed their name to the Communist Party.

F. Lenin's slogans had promised peace, bread, and land; but the Communist seizure of power brought civil war and terror instead.

   1. The Communists did end the war against the Central Powers by signing the Treaty of Brest-Litovsk on March 3, 1918.

      a. By this treaty Russia surrendered Finland, Estonia, Latvia, Lithuania, Poland, Kars, Ardahan, and Batum (the last three areas lie beyond the Caucasus Mountains and were ceded to Turkey). The Ukrainians and Georgians became independent.

b. The Treaty of Brest-Litovsk cost Russia one fourth of
its population, one fourth of its European territories,
and three fourths of its developed coal and iron
mines. The Russians had not signed such a costly
treaty for centuries.

c. The Communists, however, viewed the war as a struggle among capitalists and no affair of theirs, and most
Russians yearned for peace after four years of sacri-
fice and slaughter.

d. The Communists also thought the territories lost
could be recovered easily in the future. Within
twenty-five years, all but Finland had been regained
and included within the Soviet Union.

2. The Communists, in the spring of 1918, were also confronted by the problems of enacting their revolutionary
program and defeating counterrevolutionary forces, both
domestic and foreign.

a. By a series of decrees the Communists confiscated
private bank accounts and all the property of the
Orthodox Church. They nationalized the banks and
established state-controlled labor unions which were
to furnish compulsory labor. All land was to be distributed among the peasants.

b. The disorder created by four years of war plus a
sweeping revolution produced civil war and widespread violence. Workers fought peasants for food,
and peasants and landlords fought for control of the
land.

c. The Communists were a tightly organized minority
trying to keep control. They were opposed by tsar-
ists, liberals, constitutional monarchists, Social Revolutionaries, and many others. The failure of the opposition to the Communists to unite or to cooperate
effectively saved the Communists.

d. The Communists used terror to enforce internal
unity. The Red Terror of 1918–1920 was far more
severe than the Jacobin Terror of 1793. Terror in
the French Revolution had struck at individuals; the
Red Terror carried out wholesale slaughter of any
class or group opposed to the Communists. Thousands of persons were shot merely as hostages, and

thousands more were executed without any trial at all.

e. While disorder and terror racked Russia internally, the Red Army, brilliantly led by Leon Trotsky, saved the regime from foreign intervention. Ukrainian nationalists supported counterrevolution in the south; Poles attacked from the west; a counterrevolutionary army from the Baltic area attacked Petrograd; Japanese and American forces landed in Vladivostok.

f. Poor timing and lack of coordination of these attacks provided the Red Army with the opportunity to meet them one at a time.

II. The Union of Soviet Socialist Republics from 1922 to 1939

A. Late in 1922, after disposing of internal opposition and threats of foreign invasion, the Communist leaders proclaimed the Union of Soviet Socialist Republics.

1. The U.S.S.R. at first included four federated republics; by 1940, changes and conquests increased the number of republics to sixteen, representing a population of about two hundred million.

   a. The Communists chose a federal structure to accommodate the many distinct nationalities within the borders of the U.S.S.R.

   b. Since just one federated republic, the Russian Soviet Federated Socialist Republic, contained over half the population and territory of the U.S.S.R., its influence outweighed the others.

   c. The cultural autonomy permitted each national group in its own republic has been generally considered a wise policy, but critics of the regime point out that cultural activity is dominated by the Communist party policy, which merely produces equal intolerance for all minorities.

2. The government of the U.S.S.R. was based upon the Constitution of 1918 of the Russian Soviet Federated Socialist Republic. The essentials of the 1918 constitution were embodied in the Constitution of 1924 for the entire U.S.S.R.

a. Lenin conceived of the state as an instrument for the control of society by one class.

b. Lenin wanted the bourgeoisie destroyed to clear the way for the "dictatorship of the proletariat."

c. The constitution, therefore, denied the vote to persons who "utilized the work of others for profit," such as "salesmen, wholesalers, and priests."

d. Voting was carried on by a show of hands, and elections were arranged so that the vote of an urban worker counted about twice as much as a peasant's vote.

e. The constitutions of 1918 and 1924 were also characterized by indirect elections, indirect representation, and concentration, rather than separation, of legislative, executive, and judicial powers.

f. There were no primary elections because but one party, the Communist Party, existed. Until 1940, party membership was never over two per cent of the total population, but all the higher offices of government were held by members of the party.

g. The nine member Central Committee of the Communist Party directed all party decisions on organization and policy. The party exercised complete control over the government.

B. Eight years of war, revolution, and civil war had shattered the Russian economy. Economic pressures produced the proclamation of the New Economic Policy (the N.E.P.) in 1921.

1. By 1921, Russian industrial production was only twenty per cent of what it had been in 1913.

2. In the same eight year period, the amount of farm land under cultivation had decreased about forty per cent. About five million people are thought to have starved to death during 1920 and 1921.

3. Prices of 1913 had increased twelvefold by 1921.

4. The N.E.P. was a frank compromise with capitalism.

a. The state kept its control over heavy industry, banking, foreign trade, and transportation; but it permitted private individuals to produce and engage in trade for private profit.

b. Farmers planted more crops and sold the surplus for

profit; the few businessmen who had survived the terror returned to their commercial pursuits.

   c. By 1927, the ruble was stabilized; and the U.S.S.R. had climbed painfully up to the level of national poverty Russians had enjoyed in 1913.

C. Lenin died in 1924, and a power struggle ensued within the party; the major rivals were Leon Trotsky and Josef Stalin.

   1. Trotsky, the brilliant organizer and leader of the Red Army, advocated a more radical program than Stalin.

      a. Trotsky denounced the N.E.P. and demanded complete socialization of the entire economy.

      b. Trotsky also desired the immediate adoption of an aggressive program for world-wide proletarian revolution.

   2. Stalin, secretary of the Communist Party, wanted to concentrate upon the development of the U.S.S.R. He worked steadily to strengthen his position in the party and to undermine Trotsky by conspiracy.

   3. In 1927, at the fifteenth All-Union Congress of the Communist Party, Trotsky and his supporters were outvoted, condemned for deviation from the party line, and expelled from the party.

      a. Trotsky was exiled. He eventually settled in Mexico only to be murdered in 1940, probably by an agent of Stalin's secret police.

      b. Soon after he took power, Stalin adopted part of Trotsky's program to extend socialization of the economy by the initiation of the First Five Year Plan.

D. The Five Year Plans were administered by a supreme planning agency, Gosplan. Within the framework established by the Communist Party line, Gosplan determined how much of every article should be produced, what wages each worker should be paid, how much of the total economic activity should be used to produce articles for daily consumption, how much to lay aside for capital, and so on.

   1. The First Five Year Plan was begun in 1928 with the primary aim of building up heavy industry without the use of foreign loans.

      a. The program involved extreme hardship for the Russian people. In addition to their normal effort to feed themselves, it required the additional work of building a heavy industrial plant.

b. Extremely long hours and terrible working conditions characterized many of the industrial projects. Workers were regimented and could not change jobs.

c. The First Five Year Plan also undertook the collectivization of agriculture, combining small peasant holdings into farms of one thousand or more acres each.

d. The more prosperous peasants, the *kulaks,* resisted collectivization, burning their crops and killing their livestock. Stalin, therefore, ordered the liquidation of the *kulaks.*

e. Hundreds of thousands of *kulaks* and their families were killed or sent to slave labor camps. Even more severe was the subsequent loss of life caused by famine following the execution of the most skilled agricultural producers in Russia.

f. The First Five Year Plan was ended in 1932 with the allegation that its goals had been reached ahead of schedule.

g. While all the goals had not actually been achieved, Soviet industry had made spectacular gains in industrial capacity and output.

h. In agriculture, output in 1932 was still far below the levels of 1913 and 1928, according to official Soviet statistics. Resistance to collectivization had been so severe that only twenty-four per cent of peasant homesteads had been collectivized.

2. The Second Five Year Plan extended from 1933 to 1937; the Third begun in 1938, was interrupted by World War II; and the Fourth, begun in 1946, aimed at post war reconstruction.

a. Both the Second and Third Five Year Plans envisaged slightly slower industrialization and gave more attention to agricultural collectivization and the production of consumer goods.

b. Collectivization of agriculture was changed to allow each worker on the collective a small additional plot of his own. More machinery was used, and peasants began to learn how to use it effectively. By 1939, ninety-nine per cent of the agricultural land was collectivized.

c. Production of consumer goods rose very slightly because of the diversion of effort to military preparation. It is estimated that the U.S.S.R.'s military expenditures in 1939 were thirty times what they had been in 1932.

3. The Five Year Plans, in spite of mistakes and hardships, brought tremendous industrial progress to Russia.

   a. The ability of the Russian people to produce more than they consumed enabled the government to invest the surplus in industrial expansion.

   b. It is unknown whether Soviet industrial growth was more or less rapid than the early industrial growth of Britain, Germany, or the United States.

E. Whatever benefits the Communist regime brought to Russia were purchased by acceptance of an extreme totalitarianism.

   1. Russians could belong to only one party, and it was for the elite. No labor unions, no free press, no freedom of association, no freedom to leave the U.S.S.R., no freedom for skepticism or nonconformist thought were all part of the price.

      a. Religion received at best a grudging tolerance, and those ambitious to succeed carefully avoided any association with any church.

      b. Art, literature, and even science became propaganda vehicles.

   2. The complexities of the Five Year Plans and the Communist struggle for power inevitably produced divergencies of opinion within the Party, and these led to the infamous purges of the 1930's.

      a. In 1933, Stalin guided a purge of the Party resulting in the expulsion of one-third of its members.

      b. In 1934, the assassination of one of Stalin's close associates led to the execution of one hundred three persons before the guilty Party member was apprehended.

      c. In 1936, sixteen important Party members, most of them veterans of the 1917 revolution, were arrested, made astounding "confessions" at their trials, and were executed.

      d. In 1937, another group met the same fate for "conspiracy with Trotsky."

      e. In 1938, Bukharin and many of the more conservative elements of the Party were charged with conspiring with Trotsky (whom the Party line considered "radical") to restore capitalism to Russia. They were executed.

    f. Meanwhile, in 1937 and 1938, severe purges struck at the Party administration, the schools, and the army. Marshall Tukhachevski and seven other ranking generals were tried by a secret court martial and executed for conspiring with the Germans, the Japanese, and the ubiquitous Trotsky.

3. <u>Stalin got rid of his rivals by the purges.</u>

    a. Virtually none of the old Bolsheviks survived to embarrass Stalin by reference to Lenin or to use the ideals of 1917 to belittle the accomplishments of 1937.

    b. A new leadership was emerging. These were practical men of affairs who had grown up in the Party bureaucracy and were ready to operate an established system. Among them, fervently endorsing Josef Stalin's every whim, was the bouncing Nikita Khrushchev.

III. Great Britain and France: 1919–1939

A. <u>The belligerent powers faced staggering problems of conversion from war to a peacetime economy.</u>

    1. Demobilized soldiers had to be integrated into civilian life.

    2. During the war, normal commercial activity had been disrupted; and England and France found it difficult to sell goods to pre-war customers.

    3. Both the British and French were deeply in debt at the end of the war; their hopes for financial aid from war reparations were largely unrealized.

    4. An economic depression from 1920 to 1922 raised serious problems of unemployment and overproduction. In the 1930's, these problems became chronic.

B. <u>The British were particularly plagued with unemployment</u> problems growing out of difficulties in foreign trade.

    1. The National Insurance Act of 1911 provided unemployment insurance, and a large number of citizens had to rely on the "dole" for subsistence.

    2. The government negotiated trade agreements with the U.S.S.R. (1924, 1927) and arranged reciprocal trade treaties with the members of the British Commonwealth

of Nations ("imperial preference," 1932) to stimulate employment.

3. In 1926, a coal strike developed into a general strike in Britain. The economy was temporarily shaken, but no permanent gains resulted for anyone.

4. The world depression beginning in 1929 led many nations to raise tariff barriers still further and reduced British export sales. The British abandoned the gold standard (1931) and their long tradition of free trade.

5. Various political measures did little to solve problems that were basically economic.

   a. Universal manhood suffrage was adopted in Britain in 1918, and women's suffrage was enacted in 1928.

   b. The extension of suffrage and the national concern with unemployment were probably closely related to the displacement of the Liberal Party by the Labour Party as the major opposition to the Conservative Party.

6. The leader of the Conservative Party, Stanley Baldwin, served as Prime Minister in 1923 and from 1924 to 1929.

   a. In 1929 when the effects of the depression were most keenly felt by the British public, Ramsay MacDonald, the Labour Party leader, became Prime Minister with a Liberal-Labour coalition cabinet.

   b. In 1932, another coalition cabinet, called the "National Government," was formed. MacDonald served as its prime minister until he was replaced by Stanley Baldwin in 1935.

   c. In 1937, Baldwin retired; the new coalition leader was Neville Chamberlain, who served until his replacement by Winston Churchill in 1940. Churchill served as Prime Minister until 1945.

7. British preoccupation with economic problems, particularly unemployment and foreign trade, profoundly affected British foreign policy, especially in regard to offering firm resistance to the aggressive policies of Germany and Italy.

C. The French faced many of the same economic problems as the British but, in addition, had to rebuild the areas devastated by the war.

   1. Approximately three hundred thousand homes, twenty thousand factories, and two thousand railway bridges

had been destroyed. Thousands of acres of productive farm land had to be restored to a condition suitable for cultivation. Over a thousand towns were left without a single building standing.

2. France, with a pre-war population of about forty million, suffered over four million casualties in the war.

3. These catastrophic losses compelled the French to concern themselves with material reconstruction and security against another invasion.

4. The French planned that German reparations payments would pay the costs of material reconstruction of war damages.

     a. Germany soon fell behind in her payments, however, and the <u>French and Belgians occupied the Ruhr</u> industrial area to force the Germans to pay.

     b. The British and the United States gave no support to the French occupation, and the Germans first resorted to passive resistance and then inflation.

     c. The French occupation of the Ruhr began in 1923 and ended in 1925 and cost the French more than they gained.

     d. The American, Charles G. Dawes, worked out a new schedule of reparations payments (<u>the Dawes Plan</u>). American money was loaned to and invested in Germany; Germany was to pay reparations at a rate lower than planned by the Versailles settlement; and the French and British were to make payments on their war debts to the United States.

     e. The Dawes Plan and its successor, the <u>Young Plan,</u> and the hope for reparations had largely disappeared by 1932 when the depression was at its worst. The French, meanwhile, had paid most of their material reconstruction costs themselves by issuing government bonds.

5. To secure themselves against another costly invasion, the French relied on a series of alliances, membership in the League of Nations and remilitarization, which took the form of a large army and the construction of a great system of permanent fortifications facing the German frontier, the Maginot Line.

6. <u>The costs of the quest for security and of reconstruction</u>

of the war-torn areas depressed French living standards and postponed social reforms.

   a. Economic and social issues frequently embittered political struggles.

   b. French moderates and conservatives opposed social reforms which would jeopardize private property or traditional economic freedoms.

   c. The Socialists and more radical parties desired fundamental economic changes.

   d. The fundamental cleavage between these groups was responsible for much political bickering and the frequent changes in the cabinets characteristic of French government from 1919 to 1939.

7. By 1929, nevertheless, the French had strengthened agriculture, industry, and commerce. The value of the franc was finally stabilized at about one-fifth its pre-war value.

   a. The effects of the world depression of 1929 were slow in reaching France, probably because its economy was so well balanced between agriculture and industry.

   b. By 1932, however, French exports declined, prices fell, and unemployment became widespread and chronic.

8. In reaction to the depression, the French voters gave more support to the Socialists and Communists.

   a. In 1936, many of the radical parties formed a coalition known as the Popular Front. Leon Blum, a Socialist, became premier; and the Communists in France supported the coalition.

   b. The Popular Front limited the work week to forty hours, fixed grain prices, and attempted to reform the Bank of France.

   c. Blum's program was weakened by waves of strikes as the workers demanded additional reforms.

   d. Blum requested the Senate (the upper house of the legislature) to grant him emergency powers to deal with fiscal problems. The Senate refused, and Blum resigned in 1937.

   e. From 1938 until its fall in World War II the Third French Republic was led by a coalition of center parties. This coalition chose Édouard Daladier as premier.

f. Daladier's government, however, was so pressed by problems of rearmament and German aggression that it achieved little in any attempts at internal reform.

IV. Eastern European States Between the World Wars

A. Immediately following World War I, most of the smaller European states created from the Russian, German, and Austro-Hungarian empires adopted democratic forms of government for various reasons.

1. Most of these states wished to discard the political machinery of previous imperial overlords.
2. States with many nationalities considered democratic government the most feasible way to represent and harmonize the aims of various national groups.
3. Some groups, notably the Czechs and Poles, had long desired democratic institutions.
4. The new states in Baltic and Danubian Europe generally adopted universal male suffrage, proportional representation, and a cabinet responsible to the legislature.
   a. Most of the states adopted a bill of rights similar to those in use in the western democracies.
   b. Some of the states included provisions for health insurance and old age benefits in their bill of rights.
   c. The rights of minorities, a particularly pertinent subject in many Balkan states, had been guaranteed by treaties ending World War I.
   d. The Minorities Commission of the League of Nations provided international supervision for problems involving minority groups.
5. Redistribution of farm lands was a serious and inflammatory issue in most of these newly created states.
   a. Sound agricultural economics often gave way to political, nationalistic, or social pressures in questions of land reform.
   b. Dividing large estates into many small farms frequently reduced a nation's total agricultural output.
   c. Probably Finland experienced the most effective and sensible redistribution of farm lands. Poland and Hungary adopted the fewest land reforms.
   d. Large estates were broken into such small farms in many of the new states that many peasants could

barely subsist on their lands. Their dissatisfaction made them easy prey for Communist propaganda.

e. In the states, such as Finland, where adequate amounts of land were made available to the peasants, the peasants' political parties firmly supported democratic government.

B. The chances that democracy would endure in most of the new Baltic and Danubian states, however, were reduced by conditions inherent in the creation of those states.

1. Before World War I free trade existed within each of the empires that had been broken up to create the "succession states."

   a. After the war each new state was forced to rely on its own resources and markets or to compete with much larger powers in a world market complicated by tariff barriers and economic nationalism.

   b. Economic problems in the succession states were severe even before the world depression began in 1929.

2. Almost every newly created succession state suffered serious problems with national minorities included within their boundaries.

   a. Probably some federal form of government in each state would have been the best way to protect the minorities and their local liberties and, at the same time, make them an integral part of the central government.

   b. Usually, however, the dominant national group tried to create a centralized government with power to exercise economic controls over the whole state.

   c. Minority groups were too large to ignore or to dominate without regard for their wishes. In Poland, about one third of the population was non-Polish. One fifth of the population of Latvia was composed of minorities. Even progressive Czechoslovakia had problems with Slovak and German minorities.

3. These minority problems and economic difficulties put a tremendous strain on new states which lacked a deeply rooted democratic tradition. Many reverted to authoritarian government to solve their problems.

   a. Lithuania turned to a conservative dictatorship in 1923. Marshal Pilsudski established a dictatorship in

Poland in 1926. Latvia and Estonia abandoned democracy in 1934.

b. Austria and Hungary were particularly hard hit by the world depression. Chancellor Dollfuss became virtual dictator of Austria in 1933, and Julius Gömbös assumed dictatorial powers in Hungary in 1932.

c. In Rumania, agricultural and business activity were so impaired by 1928 that King Carol II created a royal dictatorship in 1930.

d. Yugoslavia accepted the sole rule of King Alexander I in 1929, and Boris III of Bulgaria took complete control of his country in 1935. King Zog of Albania established his personal rule in 1925.

e. Among the new Danubian states, only Czechoslovakia maintained a government which was democratic in form and in fact; and Czechoslovakia was crushed by the aggression of Nazi Germany in 1938 and 1939.

V. The Rise of Fascism in Italy

A. World War I left Italy in particularly acute financial distress, and Italians were resentful of the peace terms.

1. The Italian population of forty million could not be fed on Italy's agricultural output; its industry was severely handicapped by Italy's lack of coal.

2. The government was left practically bankrupt by war costs and could purchase coal and food only with great difficulty.

3. Unemployment was rife; discharged soldiers were jobless. Strikes and riots, growing from both economic and political unrest, occurred constantly.

4. The peace settlement failed to award Italy either Albania or any of the German colonies. Italians blamed their government for Italy's slim share in the spoils of war.

5. The elections of 1919 might have provided the government with more vigorous leadership, but the Socialists would not cooperate with the Catholic People's Party.

a. To make matters worse, the left wing of the Socialist Party, apparently inspired by Bolshevik successes in Russia, broke away and formed the Italian Communist Party.

    b. Political differences among the various parties made it impossible for a premier and his cabinet to hold office long enough to get a real reform program started.

    c. To make matters worse, large scale <u>political strikes</u>, seizures of factories by workers, and the violence attending these events stirred up widespread fear of Communism and moved many conservatives to clamor for order, regardless of the cost.

  6. <u>To bring order from chaos, King Victor Emmanuel III asked Benito Mussolini, leader of the Fascist party to form a cabinet.</u> Mussolini responded promptly in October, 1922; he remained in power until July, 1943.

B. <u>Mussolini organized the Fascist party</u> around a nucleus of war veterans and nationalists crusading against the peace treaties and the ineffectiveness of the Italian government.

  1. The Fascist party took its name from the Latin *fasces,* a symbol of authority carried by the ancient Roman lictors. The Fascists constantly harped on the theme of ancient Roman glories.

  2. Party members wore black shirts, were frequently armed, and soon gained a reputation as terrorists by roaming the streets and beating up political opponents.

  3. In the elections of 1921, the Fascists were able to elect only thirty-five members to the Chamber of Deputies.

    a. The Fascists compensated for their numerical inferiority by jingoism, violence, and shrill warnings about the imminence of Communist seizure of power in Italy.

    b. Actually, the Communists were stronger in Italy in 1921 than in 1922, but Fascist propaganda played upon Italians' fear of Communism and gained the support of many important Italian industrialists.

    c. Fewer than half the members of Mussolini's first cabinet were actually Fascists, and most Italian politicians regarded the new government as a temporary expedient.

  4. <u>Once the Fascists gained power, however, Italians were soon introduced to totalitarianism.</u>

    a. Universal suffrage disappeared, the freedom of the press was restricted, and unions lost the right to strike.

b. In 1924, when some dissent was still permitted in parliament, <u>Giacomo Matteotti</u>, a Socialist deputy, publicly exposed many cases of Fascist violence and political corruption. He was almost immediately murdered by the Fascists.

c. A strong wave of public reaction to the Matteotti murder swept through Italy, but the king made no move to dismiss Mussolini.

d. Mussolini dismissed the officials directly responsible for the murder, but restored most of them to office soon after public protest calmed down.

e. The Italian parliment soon ceased to exercise political power. Italian political life was dominated by one party, the Fascists; and Mussolini, in turn, dominated the Fascist party.

5. Mussolini seemed to develop his political theory to meet conditions as they arose; he drew ideas from almost any source that could be used for his practical problems.

a. The Fascists were militant nationalists.

b. <u>The Fascists glorified the state</u> as something above and superior to the individuals who composed it. The state was not only the economic, political, and social organization of the nation; but it also was the eternal spirit of the nation as well, transmitting its ideals to the future.

c. <u>In 1933, Mussolini proclaimed the "corporate state."</u> In each major industry, representatives of management, labor, and government were to meet together to set wages, prices, and working conditions.

d. The agreements reached for each major industry were subject to the approval and control of the "Chamber of Corporations."

e. The "corporate state" was not a new idea, though it had never been tried on anything approaching such a large scale. Theoretically, class conflict, strikes, lockouts, and disorders associated with free capitalism were ended. In practice, it meant the government controlled the economy.

f. <u>Fascism openly repudiated popular sovereignty,</u> praised the leadership of an elite, and promised progress for those who would follow the benevolent dictator.

6. In practice, Mussolini's rule was totalitarian; but it gave the appearance of being vigorous and dramatic.

   a. Mussolini was a skilled public speaker and agitator; he made hundreds of speeches to stir popular feeling in his favor. Frequent parades and pageants were used to glorify the regime.

   b. Mussolini's government carried out an extensive public works program aimed at ending unemployment and achieving economic self-sufficiency for Italy.

   c. Hydroelectric power was developed to reduce the need for coal; agricultural output was increased by reclaiming land; state subsidies were used to protect industries against foreign competition.

   d. In 1929, the Lateran Accord settled the old differences between the Italian government and the papacy. Mussolini's continued interference in education, however, led to friction between his government and the papacy.

7. Mussolini's foreign policy aimed at increasing Italy's international prestige. It was initially successful but finally disastrous.

   a. In the 1920's Mussolini gained prestige by annexation of the port of Fiume and establishing controls over Albania.

   b. Preaching the glories of war and gambling for higher stakes, Mussolini built up the Italian army and brutally crushed Ethiopia (1935–1936). He supported General Franco successfully in the Spanish Civil War (1936–1939).

   c. To achieve these aims, however, Mussolini aligned Italy with Nazi Germany, but Mussolini became the junior partner. During World War II, Italian interests were sacrificed for German strategic considerations.

VI. Germany: the Weimar Republic: 1918–1933

A. In the last few weeks of World War I, the government of the German Empire weakened. A mutiny of sailors at Kiel, a German naval base, triggered a revolutionary movement which spread through many of Germany's major cities.

Kaiser William II abdicated November 9, 1918, two days before the signing of the Armistice.

1. The vacuum left by the collapse of the empire was filled by a Provisional Government dominated by the Social Democratic party.

2. The Social Democrats had been Germany's largest party before the war. By 1918, however, the party was split by factions.

   a. Most party members favored gradual socialization of industry; they opposed revolution and became known as the Majority Socialists.

   b. A second group, known as Independent Socialists, wanted immediate socialization but were unwilling to resort to violent revolution.

   c. The most radical group were the Spartacists, who favored the immediate establishment of the dictatorship of the proletariat like the Bolsheviks in Russia.

3. In January, 1919, the Spartacists attempted a revolution in Berlin.

   a. The Provisional Government used army units and crushed the Spartacist revolt in a few days.

   b. Unlike the Russian army, the German army did not support the cause of violent revolution in 1919.

   c. The army's action in suppressing the Spartacist revolt tended to restore the Germans' esteem for the army even though it had been defeated in the war.

4. In February, 1919, a National Assembly met at Weimar and drafted a constitution. The Weimar Constitution provided the new German Republic with a thoroughly democratic governmental structure.

   a. The president was to be elected by universal suffrage as was the *Reichstag,* the lower house of the legislature.

   b. Parties were to be represented in the *Reichstag* in proportion to party strength in the electorate as a whole.

   c. A chancellor (prime minister) was provided, and he was responsible to both the president and the *Reichstag.*

   d. One article of the constitution gave the president power to set aside laws and rule by decree in an emergency.

e. The president could also force a chancellor to resign regardless of the *Reichstag,* and the *Reichstag* could force a chancellor's resignation even if the president desired to keep him in office.

f. Germany was to be a federal union. Each state was required to have a republican constitution, and each sent representatives to the upper house of the legislature, the *Reichsrat.*

5. The Weimar Republic, having survived the Spartacist revolt and having adopted its new constitution, was soon seriously challenged by another violent uprising, the Kapp *Putsch* (1920).

   a. A group of disaffected army officers began an armed uprising in Berlin, drove the republican government from the city, and tried to put their own creature, Dr. Kapp, at the head of the State.

   b. The Weimar Republic was saved from the Kapp *Putsch* by the Berlin working people, who turned off all the public utilities.

6. Only three years later, another armed uprising occurred under the leadership of the aged Field Marshal von Ludendorff and an upstart fanatic, Adolf Hitler.

   a. Hitler's "Beer Hall *Putsch*" in Munich misfired, but in the 1924 elections, both right wing nationalists and Communists gained strength at the expense of moderates.

   b. Probably the most fateful political event of 1925 was the right wing victory achieved in electing Field Marshal Paul von Hindenburg president.

7. As the Weimar Republic was attacked by extremists from both left and right, its continued existence depended on the moderate parties: the Majority Socialists, the Catholic Center, and the liberal People's party.

   a. These moderate parties were by no means in agreement; very fundamental differences divided the socialists from the Catholic Center.

   b. The Weimar Republic never took very firm measures against extremists who tried to overthrow the government by violence. Consequently, conspirators from both right and left were soon free to try again.

   c. The Weimar Republic also suffered from its association by the Germans with military defeat and the

Versailles Treaty. German national pride made the loss of German territories and colonies hard to bear.

d. Just as galling to the Germans were the "war guilt" clauses of the treaty and the reparations payments. The Weimar Republic was responsible for none of this, but in the "good old days" Germany had been an empire.

e. The "revolution" of 1918 in Germany had produced almost no significant economic or social change. The officials who had served the empire kept their jobs; the army was smaller, but it did not lose its German and Prussian traditions.

B. In addition to its political problems, the Weimar Republic had to face enormous economic difficulties.

1. The imperial government did not pay for World War I as it progressed. Instead, it issued large quantities of paper money; and by 1917, prices were climbing steadily.

2. Germany's defeat did nothing to restore confidence in her currency, and inflation continued.

a. French occupation of the Ruhr industrial area in 1923 disrupted the Germany economy further, and the pressure for payment of reparations made matters worse.

b. In 1923 a runaway inflation occurred. Late in 1923, one dollar, which had been worth about four marks before the war, could be exchanged for over four trillion paper marks.

c. During 1924 and 1925, the Dawes Plan for reparations payments took effect. The currency was stabilized, and industrial expansion began.

3. The inflation had many economic effects.

a. Debtors, and this category included many industries, easily paid off their obligations in inflated currency.

b. Freed of debt, many industries invested in replacing worn out plants and in expanding their facilities. Industrialists prospered, and Germany became increasingly industrialized.

c. The middle class, particularly those who held their savings in banks or insurance or lived on fixed incomes, was financially ruined.

4. The political and social scene was also affected by inflation.

     a. The prosperity of the industrialists meant additional financial resources for the right wing parties. Adolf Hitler received financial support for his party from many industrialists.

     b. The shattered middle class could not bring itself to join the workers or their political parties in class-conscious Germany. Nazi racial theories offered status to this group whose plans and ideals had disappeared with their wealth in the inflation.

  5. The foreign policy of the Weimar Republic was peaceful. Except for French occupation of the Ruhr in 1923, the decade was a period of relative international calm.

     a. In 1922, the Germans signed the treaty of Rapallo providing for the sale of much German equipment to the Russians.

     b. German officers were sent to Russia to instruct the Red Army and used the opportunity to test new tactics, weapons, and training methods which the Versailles treaty forbade them to do in Germany.

     c. In 1925, Germany signed the Locarno agreements guaranteeing the German, French, and Belgian frontiers. The Germans agreed to arbitrate any change in Polish or Czechoslovakian frontiers.

     d. In 1926, Germany joined the League of Nations. International peace appeared secure; democracy seemed to be flourishing; but the world depression shattered the complacency of the twenties.

C. Soon after the depression of 1929 struck highly industrialized Germany, six million people were unemployed.

  1. The political repercussions of unemployment took the form of increasing the support for parties of the right and left at the expense of the moderates who were devoted to the republic.

  2. In the elections of 1930 and 1932, both the Communists and Hitler's National Socialist Party gained strength.

  3. Apparently associated with this development was a widespread tendency among the Germans to feel that the depression had hit them harder than it hit others because of the inequity of the Versailles Treaty.

     a. Germans tended to blame all the problems they had faced since 1918 on the peace treaties, and this attitude favored an extremely nationalistic party like Hitler's.

    b. The middle class never really recovered from the inflation of 1923. They and the industrialists were particularly fearful of the Communists.

    c. Wanting stronger government than the Weimar Republic could offer, these middle class people and industrialists threw their support to Hitler's Nazis.

D. The Nazi, or National Socialist party was an outgrowth of the National Socialist German Workers' Party, which originated in 1920.

    1. Adolf Hitler was born in Austria in 1889. Orphaned at an early age, he drifted to Vienna where he developed a deep hatred for Jews, whom he blamed for his failure to gain either a higher education or recognition as an artist.

        a. He moved to Bavaria two years before the beginning of World War I. There he joined the German army.

        b. Discharged from the army, he returned to Bavaria where he became one of the first members of what eventually became the Nazi party.

        c. "Nazi" is a combination of the first syllable of the German word, *national,* and the second syllable of the German word for socialist, *sozialistische.*

    2. In 1923, the Nazis tried to seize power in Munich by the "Beer Hall *Putsch,*" which was promptly suppressed; Hitler landed in prison.

        a. While imprisoned, he dictated *Mein Kampf (My Struggle),* which combined personal reminiscences with his analysis of Germany's problems and what should be done to solve them.

        b. *Mein Kampf,* Gottfried Feder's *Program of the National Socialist German Workers' Party* (1920), and Alfred Rosenberg's *Myth of the Twentieth Century,* became the bibles of the Nazi movement.

    3. The Nazis' theories centered around a series of myths. One advantage of Nazi idealogy was that it was so fantastic that few took it seriously until it was too late to do anything about it.

        a. One of the most important tenets of Nazi theory was the concept of the superior German race (the *Volk*). Germans were declared to be members of the master race whose members had accomplished every constructive achievement in human history.

b. The destiny of the master race was to rule the world; non-Germans (the inferior races) were fit only to serve as slaves of the master race. Those who were not enslaved would be destroyed to provide "living space" *(lebensraum)* for the master race.

c. The purpose of the party was to rule the state in the interests of the *Volk*.

d. Another central theme was the "encirclement" myth which asserted that Germany was surrounded by foreign powers dominated by inferior races trying to destroy Germany and the master race. This myth was particularly suited for exploiting German attitudes toward the Versailles treaty.

e. The Nazis also stressed their idea of leadership (the *Führer princip*). *Der Führer* ruled the *Volk* through his understanding of the collective soul of the *Volk*.

f. Every member of the *Volk* owed the *Führer* unquestioning obedience; this applied to every German whether he lived in Berlin or Buenos Aires or Milwaukee, Wisconsin. This concept proved useful in creating a Nazi "fifth column."

g. The greatest criminals in human history, according to the Nazis, were the Jews. The Jews provided the Nazis with a scapegoat; everything wrong with the world was the fault of the Jews. Germans who resented Jewish competition in business and professional life supported the Nazis' bid for power.

h. Hitler shifted the Nazi idealogy around to meet temporary political expedients. When Germany and Japan were allied during World War II, for example, Hitler described the Japanese as "honorary Aryans."

4. In the early 1930's, the Nazis formulated a program which they judged would be popular among the Germans. Its main points were:

a. Anti-Communism;

b. Anti-Semitism;

c. Revision of the Versailles Treaty;

d. Reduction of war reparations payments;

e. The recovery of Germany's colonies.

5. Hitler was a spellbinding orator working among people

who were despondent about the depression and who listened uncritically.

6. The Nazis general technique was to promise everything to everybody; all the voter was asked to do was to follow the leader and kill the scapegoat. In the long run, the only promise kept was the one made to the Jews.

E. In the elections of July, 1932, the Nazis won two hundred thirty seats; they were the largest party, but they did not hold a majority of the seats in the *Reichstag*.

1. President von Hindenburg did not want to appoint Hitler chancellor.

   a. The Nazis would not enter a coalition cabinet with Hitler as vice-chancellor under Franz von Papen.

   b. The Communists also refused to join a coalition; so no cabinet could be formed under von Papen, and the *Reichstag* was dissolved pending new elections.

2. Elections in November awarded more seats to the Communists. The Nazis remained the largest party but still did not receive a majority of the votes cast. Von Papen resigned.

3. President von Hindenburg then tried to form a cabinet under General Kurt von Schleicher. Von Schleicher resigned when he could not get support from the center and leftist parties.

4. On January 30, 1933, President von Hindenburg appointed Hitler chancellor.

   a. The cabinet was composed of Nazis and conservative nationalists and militarists.

   b. It was expected that the responsibilities of power would lessen the fanaticism of the Nazis.

   c. Like the Italians in 1922, German politicians expected Hitler to be dominated by the conservatives in the cabinet.

   d. But Hitler would not compromise with anyone. The moderate parties, therefore, would not support him; the *Reichstag* was paralyzed, and new elections were ordered for March 5, 1933.

5. The violent election campaign culminated in the burning of the *Reichstag* building. Hitler denounced the fire as a Communist plot, although the available evidence indicates the Nazis set the fire to stir German fears of Communism.

      a. Von Hindenburg fell into the Nazi trap by issuing emergency decrees suspending freedom of speech and freedom of the press.

      b. With the election only six days away, the Nazis moved quickly. The presidential decrees silenced their opponents, and Nazi storm troopers intimidated and bullied the opposition with impunity.

      c. At the same time the Nazi propaganda machine was going full blast; speeches, parades, demonstrations, and violence were used to get votes.

6. The election gave the Nazis only forty-four per cent of the votes, in spite of all their incendiary labor.

      a. The Nazis' nationalist collaborators won eight per cent of the vote.

      b. The Nazi-nationalist coalition had a majority but not the two-thirds majority necessary to amend the constitution.

7. Hitler then wooed the Catholic Center party by promising to negotiate a concordat with the papacy if the Catholic Center would support passage of the Enabling Act.

      a. The Enabling Act (passed March 23, 1933) granted the government dictatorial powers until April 1, 1937.

      b. Only ninety-four votes were cast against the Enabling Act, and all the opposing votes were cast by socialists.

      c. In January, 1934, Hitler received power to change the constitution by decree.

VII. Nazi Germany: the Third Reich

A. Hitler called the new German state the Third Reich (empire) because he considered the First Reich to have been the Holy Roman Empire and the Second Reich to have been the German Empire from 1871 to 1918. The Third Reich became a totalitarian state which bore very little resemblance to the first two.

1. The Third Reich changed Germany from a federal union to a centralized, unified, national state. The separate states existed but had no power; the *Reichsrat* was abolished in 1934.

2. The Civil Service Law of April, 1933 removed all non-Aryan (Jewish) officials from national, state, and local

government. No opponent of the Nazis had much hope of holding office.

3. The judicial system was completely changed; law was whatever Hitler decreed.

   a. In May, 1934, the People's Court was established to try treason cases. Almost any offense could be declared treason.

   b. People's Court trials were secret, and sentences could be appealed only to the *Führer*.

4. All political parties except the National Socialist party were forbidden (July, 1933).

5. Racial persecution marked the whole duration of the Third Reich.

   a. The Nürnberg Laws (1935) deprived all Jews of citizenship. Intermarriage with Jews was forbidden.

   b. The government did everything possible to drive the Jews from Germany while forbidding them to take any money or property with them.

   c. The height of Nazi persecution of the Jews came during World War II when the Nazis systematically exterminated Jews from Germany and the areas they occupied. About six million Jews died in Nazi death camps such as Auchswitz or Buchenwald.

6. A dreaded secret police, the Gestapo (from *Geheime Staatspolizei*) was established.

   a. Concentration camps, where thousands of suspected opponents of the regime were held without trial, were another feature of the Third Reich.

   b. The Gestapo and the People's Court kept the concentration camps filled and the executioners busy. The concentration camps justifiably earned a reputation for horrifying brutality.

7. The Nazis persecuted both Protestants and Catholics. The strongest resistance came from Protestant clergymen, notably Martin Niemoeller. The Nazis did their best to undermine the churches by requiring children to belong to government sponsored youth movements.

B. At the same time the Nazis were enforcing their political and judicial policies, they made many economic and military changes.

1. The Nazis quickly undertook a vast program of public

works to provide employment and to make Germany as economically self-sufficient as possible.
   a. Programs of housing and road construction, reforestation, swamp drainage, and fortification building employed thousands of workers.
   b. The unemployed were organized into labor batallions and provided with food and shelter while they worked on public projects.
2. All labor organizations were merged into the Labor Front under Dr. Robert Ley.
3. Ownership of industries and land remained in private hands, but the government intervened more and more to dictate industrial policy.
   a. All strikes and lockouts were forbidden. Compulsory arbitration was imposed, and the government made the decisions that mattered in setting wages and hours.
   b. The government told the industries what to produce, the quantity to produce, and the prices at which products would be sold.
4. The Nazis took complete control of Germany's foreign trade. When short of gold or international exchange, they arranged large scale barter agreements with other countries.
5. The Nazis were shrewd and unscrupulous international traders. Political objectives were often more important than economic considerations in their dealings, and Nazi propaganda usually accompanied German goods.
6. Unemployment almost completely disappeared in 1935 when the Nazis restored universal compulsory military service and began large scale rearmament.
7. The tyrannical but vigorous policies of the Nazis at home were accompanied by an extremely aggressive foreign policy.

VIII. The Quest for Security and the Road to War

A. The relative international tranquility of the 1920's disappeared in the next decade. Ushered in by the world depression, the 1930's proved to be a crisis ridden decade which culminated in World War II.
   1. During the 1920's probably no nation had fewer illu-

sions about depending solely on treaties for security than
the French.

    a. When the United States refused to join the League of
Nations or join the British and French in guarantee-
ing the Rhine frontier, the French sought security in
alliances.

    b. France tried to contain Germany by cooperating with
Belgium and Poland and supporting the "Little Entente" (Rumania, Yugoslavia, and Czechoslovakia).

2. So long as Russia and Germany were preoccupied with
recovery from the war, the French network of alliances
was strong enough to stabilize central Europe and provide security for France.

3. The French and British took different attitudes toward
Germany following World War I.

    a. The French wanted Germany kept too weak ever to
invade France again.

    b. The British seemed to think German economic re-
covery could be arranged so that Germany would become a market for English goods.

    c. The British were also fearful that France might be-
come too strong and dominate the continent, exclud-
ing the British from exercising a critical role as the
nation that could shift the European balance of
power.

    d. The French, therefore, had to walk a tightrope be-
tween their own need for continental security and
their desire to maintain strong ties to British power.

B. The depression forced political leaders all over the world
to concentrate on domestic issues.

1. Concerns for large scale international arrangements to
maintain world peace were pushed into positions of priority secondary to the need for domestic survival.

    a. President Roosevelt, for example, scuttled the World
Economic Conference (1933) by his apparent conviction that the United States should avoid world economic commitments at that time.

    b. The World Economic Conference was aimed at stabi-
lizing world currencies and ending suicidal economic
competition.

    c. In the same year, lack of international cooperation

produced the failure of the Disarmament Conference at Geneva.

    d. Both Germany and Japan withdrew from the League of Nations in 1933.

  2. Domestic economic concerns produced by the depression led nations to raise tariffs and juggle currency values to gain advantages in world trade. The intensification of economic nationalism led to a veritable economic war among nations.

C. The spread of dictatorship did little to improve the chances for world peace.

  1. Among the major powers Italy, Soviet Russia, Japan (after 1931), Germany (after 1932), and China were dictatorships, as were many smaller powers in the Baltic and the Balkans.

  2. The dictatorships were generally a greater menace to international cooperation and peace than the democracies.

    a. Few of the dictators had any commitment, either political or ideological, to the League of Nations or its ideals.

    b. Fascists, Nazis, and Communists had become accustomed to using force to settle domestic issues and did not hesitate to apply it to international problems.

    c. Dictators liked quick and dramatic solutions to problems to impress their subjects and the world with their decisiveness and efficiency. These quick solutions frequently produced international crises, bringing the world closer to war.

D. The Japanese conquest of Manchuria was the first of a series of major aggressive actions by the dictatorships.

  1. The Japanese were particularly concerned about China as a market for Japanese goods.

  2. Soon after the Chinese established tariffs to protect their own new industries, the Japanese army conquered Manchuria (1931), changed its name to Manchukuo, and established a Japanese puppet as ruler.

  3. Chiang Kai-shek's Chinese government immediately sought aid from the League of Nations.

    a. The League sent an investigating commission (the Lytton Commission) to China.

    b. The Lytton Commission could find no evidence that

Japan's military action was in self-defense and recommended Manchuria be given autonomy under Chinese sovereignty with recognition given to Japanese economic interests.

   c. When the League adopted the recommendations of the <u>Lytton commission</u>, Japan withdrew from the League (March, 1933).

4. Japanese seizure of Manchuria indicated that aggression could be very profitable and might go unchallenged if it could be carried out while the great powers were preoccupied by other problems of their own.

E. Concern about the weakness of the League and the growing strength of Germany and Italy was increased further in March, 1935, when <u>Hitler denounced the Versailles treaty and announced Germany would rearm.</u>

1. France countered the German announcement by concluding a five year military alliance with Russia.
2. French ratification of the alliance was so hotly contested in the Chamber of Deputies, however, that serious doubts were raised as to the potential effectiveness of the alliance.
3. The alliance gave France the crucial initiative.
   a. If France supported Czechoslovakia against any aggressor, Russia agreed to help.
   b. If France did not support the Czechs, Russia was not bound to do so.

F. <u>In October, 1935, Italian troops marched into Ethiopia.</u>

1. Hitler's remilitarization policy weakened the League and forced the French to improve their relations with Italy. Mussolini recognized this and utilized his advantage.
2. Mussolini was willing to gamble that the League would not take effective action against Italy.
3. The League declared Italy an aggressor and voted for economic sanctions against Italy.
   a. The economic sanctions, however, did not apply to many vital war materials.
   b. More important, United States, Germany, and Japan were outside the League; and the League had no hope of restraining non-members.
4. The British were no great help, either. Neither they nor the French took real action either inside or outside the League.

5. When Ethiopia finally fell in 1936, most of the prestige of the League of Nations fell with it.

G. In March, 1936, even before Ethiopia's conquest was complete, Hitler ordered German troops into the demilitarized Rhineland in violation of the Versailles treaty.

1. At the crucial moment, the British and French were divided. The French wanted to resist; the British did not.

2. Unknown to the French and British, the German military commanders were under orders to retreat if any resistance was encountered. But none was, and Germany took over the Rhineland.

3. The lack of a firm, unified British-French policy was a great asset to the dictators.

   a. The British had favored a stronger stand against Mussolini, but the French feared such a policy would drive Italy completely into the Nazi camp. This opened the way to Ethiopia.

   b. British refusal to take a firm stand in the Rhineland, in effect, awarded that trophy to Hitler.

   c. The policies followed in London and Paris became known as "appeasement," surrendering on one issue after another in the hope the dictators would not demand more.

   d. Had Hitler only desired redress of the Versailles treaty, appeasement might have worked; but the Nazis hoped to embrace the world in their "New Order."

H. The gale of international crises only increased in intensity with the outbreak of the Spanish Civil War in July, 1936.

1. During World War I, neutral Spain prospered from allied orders of iron and munitions.

   a. The Armistice ended such orders, and Spain found itself with a working class interested in socialism and communism.

   b. These ideologies clashed with the military, dynastic, and clerical elements supporting the established regime.

2. Catalonia, the most industrialized area of Spain, demanded independence of or autonomy from the rest of Spain as did Moroccan tribesmen, who usually defeated the military units sent to subdue them.

3. In 1923, King Alphonso XIII agreed to the establishment of a dictatorship run by General Primo de Rivera.

  a. General de Rivera's dictatorship abrogated almost all Spanish civil liberties and vigorously suppressed liberal and socialist opposition.

  b. Liberals and republicans harassed the regime in any way they could, and popular uprisings were common. Discouraged by his failures, Primo de Rivera resigned in 1930.

4. The restoration of civil liberties only opened the floodgates which had restrained criticism of the monarchy.

  a. Agitation against the crown was so severe that Alphonso XIII left the country to give his subjects freedom to decide between his constitutional monarchy and a republic.

  b. A constituent assembly chose a republic and wrote the Constitution of 1931.

  c. The new constitution provided for religious freedom, separation of church and state, secularization of education, and nationalization of ecclesiastical property. To many Spaniards, these were shocking innovations.

  d. Catalonia was granted autonomy in 1932.

5. The Spanish Republic tried to steer a course between conservative and radical extremists, but it was constantly challenged by pressure and violence from both sides.

6. In July, 1936, leaders of the army began a revolt in Spanish Morocco and quickly gained support from the conservatives.

  a. The republicans and radicals united to oppose the rebels. Because the republicans supported the legally established government, they became known as Loyalists.

  b. The Loyalists proved strong enough so that the rebels, known as the Insurgents, could not topple the government quickly; and the struggle turned into a civil war, which lasted for thirty months.

7. The Spanish were not permitted to settle their own problems.

  a. The Insurgents, composed of the army, the conservatives, and the clerical party were aided by Italy and Germany. The leader of the Insurgents was General Francisco Franco, who later became dictator of Spain.

    b. Soviet Russia supported the Loyalists, but the thoughtful Communists first removed the Spanish government's gold reserve to Russia to protect it. It is still receiving protection.

    c. The French and British tried to get all the powers to agree to non-intervention in Spain; but, while the powers discussed the problem, those that wished to intervene did so anyway.

    d. Both the French and British were concerned lest the Spanish Civil War become a general European war. As the Insurgents gained ground, the French grew more willing to risk a showdown; but the British restrained them.

    e. The Spanish Civil War ended in March, 1939 with the victory of Franco's Insurgents. About ten thousand German and seventy-five thousand Italian troops had aided Franco. The Germans and Italians had also used the war to test their new weapons.

    f. It was another victory for the dictators. Spain remained neutral-in-favor-of Germany in World War II.

8. Other international developments, probably due in part to the Spanish Civil War were the formation of the <u>Rome-Berlin Axis (1936)</u> and the <u>Anti-Comintern Pact (1937) of Germany, Italy, and Japan against the Communists.</u>

I. The dictators did not permit their participation in Spain to prevent them from other aggression. <u>The Nazis grabbed Austria in March, 1938.</u>

   1. Combining pressures of the Nazi party within Austria with the threat of German military action, Hitler overawed the Austrians.

   2. <u>This union of Germany and Austria, known as the *Anschluss*,</u> was timed to coincide with a French cabinet crisis. The British, led by Neville Chamberlain, had neither the arms nor a very strong inclination to rescue Austria.

   3. Soviet Russia called for a conference to discuss collective action against Germany.

    a. Two months earlier, President Roosevelt had requested a conference to discuss European problems.

    b. Prime Minister Chamberlain, ignoring both the

American and Russian proposals, chose to negotiate
directly with the dictators.

4. Nazi acquisition of Austria placed Germany in a position which outflanked the Czechoslovakian fortifications
along the previous Czech-German frontier. Germany
could now invade Czechoslovakia from the south.

J. The crisis which produced the partition of Czechoslovakia
was next. Hitler used a method of operation similar to the
one he employed against Austria.

1. Konrad Henlein, leader of the Nazi party in Czechoslovakia, was ordered to demand an autonomous state for
the Sudeten Germans.

   a. The German minority living in Czechoslovakia were
concentrated in the area of Sudetenland.

   b. This area occupied much of the territory along the
Czech-German frontier. It had been heavily fortified
by the Czechs as a defense against the possibility of
German invasion.

   c. If the Germans acquired Sudetenland, the Czechs
would be extremely vulnerable to German invasion.

   d. The foregoing considerations led the Czech president, Eduard Beneš, to refuse Henlein's demands.

   e. Henlein indicated the Sudetens might use force, and
Beneš replied by a partial mobilization of the Czech
army and a call to Russia and France to prepare to
fulfill their treaty obligations.

   f. Beneš' firm action led the Nazis to delay the invasion they had planned for May, 1938.

2. Chamberlain tried to mediate the crisis during the summer of 1938, but Henlein deliberately sabotaged the
negotiations.

3. On September 15, 1938, Chamberlain met with Hitler
at Berchtesgaden (Hitler's estate in the mountains of
southern Germany).

   a. Chamberlain was amazed to learn that Hitler demanded the cession of Sudetenland to Germany.

   b. Chamberlain consulted with the French premier,
Édouard Daladier, and the two agreed war must be
avoided even if Czechoslovakia was partitioned.

   c. The Czechs were handed the big news and decided
not to fight Germany without French and British
support.

4. On September 22, Chamberlain took the news of the Czech decision to Hitler at Godesberg.

    a. Again Hitler jolted Chamberlain by new demands, the principle one being that the Czechs must evacuate the Sudetenland by October 1.

    b. Hitler apparently wanted the Czechs pushed out too quickly to dismantle fortifications or industries in the Sudetenland.

    c. Chamberlain consulted again with Daladier and Beneš, and on September 26 told Hitler they rejected his occupation plans. Another world war appeared likely to begin at any hour.

    d. The next day Chamberlain proposed another conference be held, this time at Munich.

5. On September 29, 1938 representatives of France, Germany, Italy, and Great Britain met at Munich.

    a. The Czechs were sold down the river. Practically everything Hitler demanded at Godesberg was agreed to at Munich.

    b. The Czechs, faced with the alternative of accepting the Munich agreement or fighting Germany by themselves, gave in.

6. The consequences of the Munich pact were extremely serious.

    a. Chamberlain was apparently sincerely convinced he had achieved "peace in our time," as he called it. The English people hailed him like a conquering hero when he returned from Munich.

    b. But others, both in London and Paris, thought differently. Winston Churchill attacked Chamberlain saying that Czechoslovakia had been given to Hitler without cost to the Germans, that Britain had thrown away a valuable ally in Czechoslovakia, that the friendship and respect of Russia had been lost, and that Hitler soon would break the pact and make new demands.

    c. Churchill was, unfortunately, accurate in every assertion.

    d. The Russians took the view that the British and French were concerned about German expansion to the west but not to the east.

    e. The French security system of Balkan alliances

was hopelessly wrecked. In the weeks following Munich, Poland and Hungary each occupied parts of Czechoslovakia.

f. In March, 1939, Hitler showed how much appeasement was worth by occupying all the rest of Czechoslovakia.

g. Following Hitler's seizure of all Czechoslovakia, France and Great Britain began rearming as fast as politics and industrial capacity allowed.

h. Negotiations with the U.S.S.R. were undertaken to prevent further German aggression, but they failed. Mutual distrust between the Russians, on one side, and the Anglo-French combination, on the other, prevented formation of an effective alliance. Once more Churchill, in favoring a strong alliance with Russia, was in the minority among British political leaders.

i. Stalin, however, wanted security for Russia above everything else. After Munich and the failure of further negotiations with Great Britain and France in April, 1939, Stalin turned to Hitler.

j. A German-Russian pact was signed August 23, 1939. It pledged that each party would refrain from attacking the other for ten years.

k. Much more important were the secret clauses of the treaty. The two powers agreed that Russia could occupy Finland, Estonia, Latvia, eastern Poland, Bessarabia, and northeastern Rumania. Hitler received Stalin's blessing for future German occupation of Lithuania and the remainder of Poland.

l. Stalin may have considered Hitler's agreement to a treaty worthless. If so, he still gained time to build up Russia's defenses.

K. Hitler had secured his eastern front by his agreement with Stalin; so he increased the pressure of his diplomatic offensive against Poland.

1. Hitler had already completed the first diplomatic moves in his campaign against Poland.

a. In March, 1939, he began demanding the cession to Germany of the international free city of Danzig.

b. By May, 1939, he had denounced the German-Polish

     non-aggression pact of 1934 and concluded a new military alliance with Italy.

  c. The German army had completed its plans and preparations for war against Poland by August, 1939.

2. Hitler waited a few days after signing the pact with Russia to see if Chamberlain would not rush to him with some new plan of appeasement.

3. The British and French, however, repeatedly warned Hitler they would support Poland.

4. On September 1, 1939 German forces invaded Poland without an official declaration of war.

5. On September 3, Great Britain and France formally declared war on Germany, and World War II had begun. It was to be the biggest, the most widespread, the most costly in blood and treasure, and the most total of any war so far in human history.

BIBLIOGRAPHY

Black, C., and Helmreich, E., *Twentieth century Europe* (New York: Knopf, 1950).

Brogan, D., *France under the Republic* (New York: Harper, 1940).

Deutscher, I., *Stalin: a political biography* (London: Oxford University Press, 1949).

Hirst, F., *The consequences of the war to Great Britain* (New Haven: Yale University Press, 1934).

Hitler, A., *Mein Kampf* (New York: Reynal & Hitchcock, 1939).

Pasternak, B., *Doctor Zhivago* (New York: Pantheon, 1958).

Salvemini, G., *Prelude to World War II* (New York: Doubleday, 1954).

Seton-Watson, H., *Eastern Europe between the wars* (New York: Macmillan, 1945).

Shirer, W. L., *The rise and fall of the Third Reich* (New York: Simon and Schuster, 1960).

Shub, D., *Lenin: a biography* (New York: Doubleday, 1948).

Silone, I., *Bread and wine* (New York: Harper, 1937)

Thomson, D., *Democracy in France,* (2nd ed., London: Oxford University Press, 1952).

Vernadsky, G., *The Russian revolution, 1917–1931* (New York: Henry Holt & Co., 1932).

Wheeler-Bennett, J. W., *The nemesis of power* (New York: St. Martin's, 1954).

Wolff, R. L., *The Balkans in our time* (Cambridge: Harvard University Press, 1956).

Chapter 14

THE MIDDLE AND FAR EAST BETWEEN THE WARS

I. Greece

A. The geographic position of Greece involved the nation in the affairs of the Middle East as well as Europe. Crises and problems growing from the Greeks' struggles with Turkey, the Balkan powers, and Italy seriously influenced internal Greek politics.

  1. At the end of World War I, Greece was a constitutional monarchy under Alexander I.

  2. Almost every power interested in the Middle East was concerned about the control of the Dardanelles and the Straits between the Black Sea and the Mediterranean.

   a. The British and French, seeking to limit Turkey's control of the Straits, encouraged the Greeks to attack Turkey (June, 1920) to force the Turks to sign the Treaty of Sèvres.

   b. After the Turks signed the treaty (August, 1920), the war began to turn against the Greeks.

   c. Greek dissatisfaction with the progress of the war led to the loss of elections by the liberal-republicans, led by Eleutherios Venizelos.

   d. Popular support shifted to King Alexander's successor, King Constantine I. Constantine, however, announced continuation of the war against Turkey.

   e. Almost two more years of war only improved the situation for the Turks, led to an internal uprising of Greek republicans, and forced the abdication of King Constantine (September, 1922).

  3. From 1922 to 1935 Greece endured constant internal turmoil resulting from the struggle between military

leaders, on one side, and the liberal-republicans, on the other.

    a. The monarchy was overthrown and a republic proclaimed (May, 1925); but less than two months later, General Theodore Pangalos seized power and openly declared his dictatorship.

    b. In nine more months, Pangalos was overthrown. A succession of governments, some essentially military dictatorships, some dominated by liberal-republicans, ensued.

    c. The monarchy was restored in 1935 under King George II. At that time the Venizelos faction was the largest in the parliament, but it did not hold a majority of the seats. The premier was General John Metaxas.

4. Internal strife handicapped the successive Greek governments in their conduct of foreign affairs. Failures in foreign policy undermined confidence in the government at home and often increased domestic disorder. The net result of this vicious circle was deterioration of the Greek international position.

    a. The Treaty of Lausanne (1923) revised the Treaty of Sèvres (1920) in favor of Turkey, partly at the expense of Greece.

    b. In 1923, the murder of an Italian general on the Albanian frontier led to Italian occupation of Corfu. The League of Nations settled the incident, and the Greeks were censured for their role in the affair.

    c. In 1925, Greek forces invaded Bulgaria. The League intervened; the invasion was stopped, and Greece was fined.

    d. A controversy with Yugoslavia in 1929 ended in an improvement of Yugoslav privileges in the free zone at Saloniki.

    e. The conclusion of a Balkan pact between Greece, Turkey, Yugoslavia, and Rumania was aimed at resisting encroachment on the Balkans by the great powers. It was a weak arrangement, however, without Bulgaria.

B. On August 4, 1935 General John Metaxas, the premier, seized power and established himself as dictator, though King George II remained on the throne.

1. Metaxas proclaimed martial law, dissolved parliament, instituted rigid censorship, abolished political parties, and persecuted opponents of the regime. The regime rested on military power.
2. On the other hand, Metaxas made a real effort to meet material needs of the Greek people.
   a. Wages were increased, a social security program was put into effect, agricultural debts were cancelled, and low bread prices were enforced.
   b. An extensive public works program was also begun. This increased employment, but it also required heavier taxes.
   c. Metaxas improved Greek foreign trade by arranging to barter goods with Nazi Germany.
   d. At the same time, he maintained good relations with Turkey, France, and England.
   e. Following the Italian conquest of Albania (April, 1939), Metaxas signed a defensive alliance with the French and British by which they guaranteed to maintain Greek independence.

II. Turkey

A. The end of World War I found the Turkish armies defeated, an Allied military administration holding Constantinople, and Greek and Italian forces invading Anatolia.
   1. An ardent nationalist and military hero, Mustapha Kemal Pasha, began organization of a nationalist party to resist further loss of Turkish territory and oppose military occupation.
      a. Mustapha Kemal was dismissed by Sultan Mohammed VI and declared an outlaw
      b. Mustapha Kemal, however, continued to direct the Nationalist Party, which won the parliamentary elections.
      c. The sultan's government, located in Constinople and seeking peace with the allies, denounced the Nationalists, sent many into exile, and dissolved the parliament.
      d. Mustapha Kemal then established a revolutionary government at Ankara (April, 1920).

    e. As president of his new government, Mustapha Kemal concluded a military agreement with Soviet Russia which gave him needed supplies.

  2. The sultan's government protested the terms of the Treaty of Sèvres but signed it because of pressure from the allies.

    a. The Nationalist Party gained increasing popular support from popular reaction against the treaty.

    b. Mustapha Kemal made agreements with both the Italians and the Russians in 1921. The Italians withdrew their forces from Turkey in return for economic concessions, and the Russians agreed to new territorial arrangements along the Russo-Turkish border.

    c. The Greek-Turkish conflict continued, but the Turks won several important battles in 1921. The British and French proclaimed their neutrality, but the British encouraged the Greeks to continue.

    d. Soon after the Turks launched a major offensive against the Greeks, the British intervened, landing a force near the Dardanelles.

    e. In October, 1922, the powers agreed on the return of Eastern Thrace and Adrianople to the Turks who, in turn, agreed to the neutralization of the Straits under international control.

  3. In November, 1922, Mustapha Kemal proclaimed the abolition of the sultanate; and Mohammed VI fled from Constantinople on a British ship.

  4. On July 24, 1923 the powers signed the Treaty of Lausanne, which replaced the Treaty of Sèvres. It was a major victory for Mustapha Kemal and the Turks.

    a. Turkey gave up her claims to non-Turkish territories lost in World War I but regained Eastern Thrace and some of the Aegean Islands.

    b. Turkey paid no reparations, but agreed to protect minorities within her borders.

    c. The Straits were demilitarized. They were to be open to all nations in time of peace and in time of war, if Turkey remained neutral. If Turkey was at war, they would be closed only to Turkey's enemies.

B. With the formal proclamation of the Republic of Turkey on October 29, 1923, a period of vigorous reform began.

  1. The constitution provided for popular sovereignty, uni-

versal manhood suffrage, a parliament, a ministry responsible to the parliament, and a president with extensive powers.

2. <u>Mustapha Kemal, the new president, introduced many reforms.</u>

   a. Religious orders were suppressed because they were the center of some of the strongest opposition to the new government.

   b. Polygamy was abolished; civil marriage was made compulsory; and divorce was legalized. Later, the article of the constitution which declared Islam to be the state religion was abolished.

   c. New civil, criminal, and commercial law codes were introduced.

   d. The Latin alphabet was introduced. It was applied first to newspapers, then to books. The Arabic alphabet was abandoned, and Arabic and Persian words were to be removed from the Turkish language.

   e. An extensive program of road and railroad building, industrialization, development of mining, and agricultural reforms was undertaken.

3. <u>The internal reform program was accompanied by a judicious foreign policy.</u>

   a. At various times the Turks entered agreements with almost every Balkan and Middle Eastern power in addition to the great powers interested in the Middle East.

   b. Mustapha Kemal was willing to enter agreements with the U.S.S.R. and other totalitarian powers, but he was very shrewd in frustrating every attempt they made to exercise undue influence on or inside Turkey.

   c. By means of alliances, the Turks accomplished much toward securing themselves against invasion from both the Balkan and Asiatic frontiers.

4. Mustapha Kemal went so far in his efforts to bring Turkey along the road to political maturity that he encouraged the formation of an opposition party.

   a. The new Liberal Republican Party made a poor showing in the elections, however.

   b. The party never developed much strength, but an independent group of deputies remained in the parliament.

5. Mustapha Kemal, in 1935, introduced family names in Turkey. He adopted the name, Kemal Atatürk (father of the Turks).
   a. Mustapha Kemal was reelected president every four years until his death in 1938.
   b. The assembly unanimously elected Ismet Inönü president the day after Kemal Atatürk's death.
6. In May, 1939, the Turks concluded an agreement of mutual assistance with the British in case of war or aggression in the Mediterranean area.
   a. The next month, the Turks, in return for concessions from France, concluded a non-aggression pact with the French.
   b. Strong economic ties between Turkey and Germany did not prevent the Turks from doing all they could to prevent German expansion in the Balkans.
   c. Turkey was officially neutral in World War II, but used its neutrality to aid France and Great Britain.

III. Arab Nationalism versus Western Control

A. While all the Middle Eastern states were profoundly affected by Arab nationalism, it was particularly influential in the affairs of Syria, Transjordan, and Iraq. Palestine was torn by both Arab and Jewish nationalism.
B. As World War I was drawing to a close, the Syrians proclaimed a Syrian state.
   1. At that time, British troops occupied part of Syria, and the Syrians modified their demands in a few months, requesting either a mandate under British or American supervision or complete independence.
      a. In September, 1919, in spite of Syrian demands, the British withdrew their troops and turned the country over to the French.
      b. By December, 1919, the French and the Syrian Arabs were engaged in open warfare.
   2. In March, 1920, the Syrians proclaimed Faisal king, but the British and French refused to recognize him.
      a. The League of Nations declared Syria a French mandate.
      b. The French took Damascus; Faisal was dethroned and forced to flee.

3. In 1920 and 1921, the French divided Syria into six separate states. The six states were only loosely federated under one French high commissioner.

   a. The French may have intended to weaken the nationalists by appealing to local autonomy.

   b. In fact, the nationalists only became more vehement in their demands for a united and independent Syrian nation.

4. In July, 1925 began the "Great Insurrection of the Druses." The Druses were one of the Arab nationalist groups who accused the French of, among other things, favoritism toward Christians.

   a. The Druses soon controlled much of the countryside and even attacked the major cities.

   b. Arab uprisings in Damascus forced the French to leave the city. The French replied by tank and air attacks on the city.

   c. The French declared Lebanon (formerly a Christian part of Syria) a republic (May, 1926).

   d. The Druse uprising was finally crushed by a major military campaign in June, 1927; but only after a second uprising in Damascus and another French bombardment had embittered the contestants even further.

5. In 1928, the French began efforts to establish a constitutional government for Syria.

   a. The French summoned a constituent assembly, but it was dominated by nationalists who wrote a constitution unsatisfactory to the French. The assembly was prorogued.

   b. The French high commissioner then wrote his own constitution providing for a republic with a parliament.

   c. The French exerted enough pressure in the elections of 1932 to put moderates in office.

6. Not until 1936 did the situation stabilize sufficiently to arrange the French-Syrian Treaty. The treaty specified the French mandate would end in three years and Syria would be admitted to the League of Nations.

   a. Even this inoffensive treaty had been arranged only after prolonged rioting, dissolution of the assembly, proclamation of martial law, and a general strike.

      b. After the treaty was signed, various dissatisfied minorities provoked additional riots.

      c. Syria became a center of insurgent activity devoted to the Arab cause in Palestine.

C. An event of major importance for the future of Palestine occurred on November 2, 1917 when the British government gave its support to the Balfour Declaration.

    1. The Balfour Declaration stated Palestine should be made a national home for the Jewish people insofar as it was possible to do so without prejudice to "the civil and religious rights of existing non-Jewish communities in Palestine."

      a. British army units drove the Turks from Jerusalem November 2, 1917.

      b. The League of Nations made both Palestine and Transjordan British mandates.

      c. The League provided that the terms of the Balfour Declaration would apply to Palestine but not to Transjordan.

    2. By 1921, the Arabs were rioting against the immigration of Jews into Palestine.

      a. The Arab riots were so widespread and violent that the British maintained order only with great difficulty.

      b. The Arabs objected to Jewish immigration and Jewish purchases of land.

      c. The British tried to establish a constitutional government for Palestine, but the Arabs would not take part in any government in which the Jews had a role.

      d. Palestine, therefore, was ruled by the decrees of the British high commissioner.

    3. In 1923, Transjordan was made an autonomous state under Arab rule. It became independent in 1928 except for British retention of military and some financial controls.

    4. In 1929 occurred the first large-scale Arab attacks on the Jews, of whom many were killed.

      a. After investigation attributed the attacks to Arab hatred of the Jews and the frustration of Arab hopes for independence, Jewish immigration was restricted (May, 1930).

      b. Then the Jews struck in protest. The British Parliament debated the matter and slightly relaxed restrictions on Jewish immigration.

c. In 1933, when the British commissioner refused the Arab demand that Jewish immigration be further restricted and all sales of Arab property to Jews be prohibited, the Arabs announced a boycottt of British goods and a policy of non-cooperation with the British.

d. By December, 1933, the Jews were rioting in protest against restrictions on immigration because of the persecution of Jews in Nazi Germany.

5. The British, caught in the Arab-Jewish crossfire, sent additional troops to Palestine in an attempt to keep order.

a. In 1936, the Arab High Committee was formed to unite all Arabs in opposition to the Jews.

b. By this time Arab demonstrations and riots had reached the dimensions of open war against the Jews.

c. The British government appointed the Peel Commission to investigate and advise what could be done in Palestine.

d. In July, 1937, the Peel Commission recommended Palestine be partitioned to separate the Arabs and Jews.

6. The World Zionist Congress voted to accept the Peel recommendations if some provisions were changed in favor of the Jews, although world Jewish opinion denounced the plan as a violation of the Balfour Declaration.

a. The Pan-Arab Congress at Bludan (Syria) flatly refused the Peel plan.

b. The Arabs demanded an independent Palestine allied to Great Britain. The Jews were not to have a national home, and Jewish immigration must stop.

c. Partition was also rejected. The Arabs would concede the Jews nothing but the status of a guaranteed minority within the Arab state.

7. In September, 1937, the Arabs assassinated a British district commissioner; and the next two months witnessed pitched battles between Jews and Arabs in Palestine.

a. The British tried desperately to keep order. They managed to apprehend and exile most of the Arab

High Committee; by early 1938 the British had thirty thousand troops in Palestine.

b. Meanwhile, the British sent another investigating commission to Palestine. The <u>Woodhead Commission</u> abandoned partition plans and recommended a conference of Jews and Arabs.

c. The Palestine Conference (February and March, 1939) was the result, but the Jews and Arabs would not compromise.

d. The British announced an elaborate plan of their own in May, 1939. Both sides denounced it, and before it could be put into effect, World War II began.

D. <u>The British occupied Baghdad at the end of World War I, and Iraq became a British mandate in 1920.</u>

1. Between the World Wars, Iraq abundantly produced two important items: Arab nationalism and oil.

a. Only a few weeks after Iraq had become a British mandate, a serious Arab revolt began.

b. It took the British nearly six months to suppress the uprising. To win popular favor, the British made Emir Faisal King of Iraq after the French had driven him from Syria. King Faisal ruled from 1921 until his death in 1933.

2. From 1922 to 1935, Iraq was involved in a growing tangle of diplomatic negotiations and arrangements with neighboring states and the British and the League of Nations.

a. <u>The British successfully used Arab nationalism for British purposes in this period</u>. They knew Iraq wanted control of the oil-rich Mosul area, which Turkey also claimed.

b. Probably Iraq wanted the Mosul area more for nationalistic than economic reasons. National feeling motivated Iraq's policy in a whole series of frontier disputes with neighbors.

c. The British knew, too, that Iraq wanted independence and membership in the League of Nations; achievement of these goals would gratify Iraq's nationalists.

d. <u>The Iraqi leaders, on the other hand, utilized British desires for Iraq's benefit</u>. They knew the British wanted oil, air bases, and a peace treaty with Turkey that would keep the Straits open to British shipping.

3. By 1935, the mutual exploitation of interests by Britain and Iraq had produced some satisfactory results for both.

    a. In 1927, Iraq was recognized as completely independent and, in return, gave the British permission to build three new air bases and to train the Iraqi army.

    b. In 1932, Iraq was admitted to the League of Nations.

    c. Numerous frontier disputes and tribal uprisings had been successfully handled by Iraq with a bit of British assistance at the proper moment.

    d. The British opened a major oil pipeline from Mosul to Tripoli in 1934 and another to Haifa six months later.

4. In 1935 and 1936, the government of Iraq undertook a serious program of internal development including road and railroad construction and large-scale irrigation projects.

    a. As the situation in Palestine became more serious, Iraq took an active role in defense of the Palestine Arabs.

    b. Iraq also joined Turkey, Iran, and Afghanistan in forming an entente of Moslem states to resist external aggression (1937).

IV. Saudi Arabia

A. During World War I, England, France, and Russia supported the formation of an Arab state on the Arabian peninsula.

1. An Arab state would oppose Turkish domination and weaken Turkey, one of Germany's allies.

2. The British, French, and Russians supported Sherif Hussein and proclaimed him King of the Arabs in 1916.

3. In 1919, however, Hussein's forces were defeated by Abd al-Aziz ibn Saud, leader of the Wahabis of Nejd, a puritanical Moslem sect.

4. From 1920 to 1925, Ibn Saud was engaged in the successful conquest of almost the entire Arabian peninsula. In January, 1926, he was proclaimed King of the Hejaz and Sultan of Nejd; in 1927, he changed his title to King of the Hejaz and Nejd; in 1932, he changed the name of his extensive kingdom to Saudi Arabia.

    a. Ibn Saud is sometimes called "the Bismarck of the peninsula" because of his skill in defeating his enemies and rivals piecemeal.

    b. Like Bismarck, Ibn Saud diplomatically placated potential enemies outside the peninsula while he was engaged in unification. Treaties with Iraq, Iran, Great Britain, and Turkey served his purposes.

B. In 1933, Ibn Saud granted oil leases to the Anglo-American Oil Company. Enormous profits were beneficial to both Ibn Saud and the oil men, and were utilized to begin the modernization of the desert state.

V. Iran and Afghanistan

A. The end of World War I found Iran (then Persia) under the very tenuous control of a small British force sent to northeastern Persia to prevent a Bolshevik invasion.

    1. The British, having driven out the Turks, defeated a Bolshevik naval force on the Caspian Sea.

    2. In August, 1919, the Anglo-Persian agreement was signed.

        a. The agreement recognized Persia's independence and provided that the British would supply munitions and officers for a force to maintain civil order.

        b. The British were also to loan funds to Persia for road and railroad construction.

        c. Since the agreement obviously was intended to maintain British ascendancy in Persia, it caused widespread opposition in Persia and ratification was delayed.

    3. In 1920, the Bolsheviks invaded Persia. The Persian force sent to drive out the Bolsheviks was defeated. Since the Anglo-Persian agreement remained unratified, the British began to withdraw from northern Persia.

B. In February, 1921, control of the government was seized by an army officer, Reza Khan, who made himself minister of war and commander in chief.

    1. Reza Khan's first act was to drop the unratified Anglo-Persian agreement and make a treaty with the Bolsheviks.

        a. The Persian's aim was to destroy British ascendancy in Persia.

        b. The Bolsheviks agreed to evacuate Persia, cancel all

Persian debts to Russia, and cede all Russian property in Persia to the Persian government without compensation.

c. Persian nationalists were, naturally, enthusiastic about the treaty.

2. Reza Khan continued to reorganize and extend the powers of his government. He was particularly zealous in maintaining his control in southwestern Persia where the Anglo-Persian Oil Company was most influential.

C. In 1925, Reza Khan was proclaimed Reza Shah Pahlavi by the national assembly and was given dictatorial powers.

1. Reza Shah Pahlavi followed a policy much like that of Mustapha Kemal in Turkey, but he did not adopt the anti-religious policy of the Turks.

2. He opened Persia to regular air service by both British and German air lines, revised the tariff rates earlier imposed on Persia by European governments, and established a national bank.

3. Reza Shah Pahlavi barred foreigners from owning agricultural land in Persia; and, in 1931, took over the Persian lines of the Indo-European Telegraph Company. In addition, all foreign trade was placed under government control.

4. In 1932, Persia cancelled the oil concession of the Anglo-Persian Oil Company. Prolonged negotiations led to a new contract much more favorable to the Persian government.

5. On March 21, 1935, Persia officially became Iran.

6. The shah conducted a rather cautious foreign policy, taking particular care to maintain close ties with Iraq, Turkey, and Afghanistan.

a. In 1939, the Trans-Iranian railroad, reaching from the Persian Gulf to the Caspian Sea, was opened.

b. The Trans-Iranian, built entirely with Iranian funds, became a vital supply line for sending supplies to Russia during World War II.

D. Afghanistan remained neutral during World War I in spite of considerable Turkish and German agitation and pressure.

1. Afghanistan's ruler was assassinated in 1919 presumably because he was too subservient to the British. His son, Amanullah, succeeded him.

2. Amanullah tried to take advantage of anti-British feeling by calling on the Moslems of Afghanistan and India to join him in a holy war to drive out the British.
    a. The Afghans tried to invade India but were repulsed and threatened by invasion themselves.
    b. The Afghans and the British came to terms in the Treaty of Rawalpindi (1919) in which the British for the first time recognized the complete independence of Afghanistan.
3. In 1921, Amanullah signed a treaty of friendship with Soviet Russia. Like the Turks and Persians, he used the Bolsheviks as a counterweight to the British.
4. In 1923, Amanullah proclaimed the Fundamental Law, a constitution similar to Turkey's and, likewise, intended to modernize the country.
    a. Amanullah, however, was no Mustapha Kemal. He tried to reform his country so fast that his people revolted against him (November, 1928).
    b. As in Turkey, the major oposition to reform came from the Moslem religious leaders.
    c. Amanullah was forced to abdicate, and it was nearly a year until an army officer disposed of his rivals and made himself Mohammed Nadir Shah.
5. Mohammed Nadir Shah continued Amanullah's policies, but he was more cautious and less offensive. He ruled until 1933 when he was assassinated by a servant of one of his victims.
6. His son, Mohamed Zahir Shah, succeeded him and continued his policies.
    a. In 1935, an American oil company was given a concession to search for oil.
    b. In 1937, Afghanistan joined Turkey, Iran, and Iraq in an alliance designed to resist pressure from any of the great European powers interested in the Middle East.

VI. India

A. India provided loyal and generous support to the British during World War I. The British, consequently, passed the Government of India Act (1919) to broaden the base of government in British India.

1. The new government was a dyarchy (government vested in two rulers) with the British and the Indians sharing both administrative and legislative functions.
   a. British and Indian legislators and administrators shared their duties in both the national and provincial governments of British India.
   b. The franchise, however, was limited by rigid property qualifications which excluded many Indians from voting.
   c. British India, to which the new law applied, comprised only about three-fifths of the area of the Indian peninsula.
   d. The remainder of India was composed of about six hundred native states ruled by Indian princes, who recognized British overlordship and accepted supervision by the British viceroy.
2. India's nationalists, organized into the Indian National Congress Party, wanted complete independence from the British.
   a. The Congress Party, therefore, rejected the new government completely.
   b. More moderate Indians, however, formed the National Liberal Federation and took part in the new government. Many of the moderate members of the Congress Party left it to join the National Liberal Federation.
B. Leadership of the Indian nationalists was assumed by Mohandas K. Ghandi (1869–1948), who was called the Mahatma (the Saintly One).
   1. Ghandi worked for complete independence from British rule. In spite of his completely unusual methods, he became one of the most outstanding political leaders of modern times.
      a. Ghandi devised and carried out an amazing policy of passive resistance to British rule. His theory of "nonviolent revolution" proved very effective against the British.
      b. One of Ghandi's most telling weapons was his boycott of British goods. He urged the people of India to weave their own cloth instead of buying British textiles. Partly as a result of his policy, India bought

only half as much cotton cloth from England in 1932 as in 1914.

c. Ghandi's followers sometimes got out of hand and resorted to violence; Ghandi himself was jailed by the British on several occasions. His leadership, nevertheless, created an inexorable pressure for complete independence.

2. Meanwhile, the industrialization of India continued.

   a. Industrialization created a large labor force interested in Marxism and susceptible to Communist propaganda.

   b. India's industrial plant was owned, for the most part, by British capitalists.

   c. On several occasions, India was swept by waves of strikes, often accompanied by violence. Some of the strikes had a distinctly revolutionary flavor and supported the nationalists against the British.

C. In 1931, a series of meetings, called the Round Table Conferences, took place in London.

1. The Round Table Conferences were held to try to solve the economic and political problems of India and were attended by British and Indian leaders, including Ghandi.

2. The major result of the conferences was the Government of India Act of 1935, which proposed a federal system of government giving the Indians greater control.

   a. British India was divided into eleven provinces, each under an appointed governor and an elected legislature.

   b. Each provincial government enjoyed wide powers and a great deal of autonomy.

   c. A central legislature was to meet at Delhi. A British governor-general at Delhi retained control over defense and foreign affairs.

3. When the new government went into effect in 1937, the nationalist party (by then called the All-India Congress Party) won the elections.

   a. The All-India Congress Party was divided internally between Ghandi's moderates and extremists led by Pandit Jawaharlal Nehru, who wanted complete independence and a socialist revolution.

   b. In a party meeting in March, 1937, Ghandi's moderates defeated Nehru's extremists, and this made it possible for the All-India Congress Party to cooperate with the British to put the new government into effective operation.

c. Growing concern in India caused by Japanese aggression in China contributed to greater cooperation between Indian nationalists and the British.

d. The new government made agrarian reform its major concern.

4. The original intent of the 1935 Government of India Act had been to create a federation embracing all India, not just British India.

a. It was hoped that a federation would unify India to prepare it for independence.

b. Fifty Indian princes would not relinquish power to join the federation.

c. Tremendous diversity characterized India; its population was about four hundred million composed of nearly thirty different linguistic groups. Indians were deeply divided on religious matters, and the caste system discouraged unity.

d. The nationalists were by no means satisfied with the 1935 law, and Ghandi's moderates were hard pressed to secure cooperation from the extremists.

e. Plans for immediate unification had to be set aside.

5. In attempting to provide for Indian unification, the British separated Burma and Aden from India in 1935. These two areas became crown colonies.

VII. Japan

A. Japan made great commercial and industrial progress during World War I by supplanting German commerce in Asia and supplying war materials to the Allies.

B. Japanese policy following the war became aggressive and imperialistic as the Japanese sought to extend both their economic and political power in the Far East. Japanese imperialistis policies led to the rise of military dictatorship in Japan and played a major role in causing and enlarging World War II.

1. Japan supported the League of Nations immediately following the war and received as mandates the Pacific is-

lands formerly held by Germany north of the equator.

2. During the decade following the war, the Japanese government was generally dominated by business interests.

   a. A gradual extension of voting privileges was carried on in Japan until universal male suffrage became law in 1925.

   b. Though the Japanese intervened in China and Russia during the war and the Russian revolution, international tensions relaxed somewhat during the early 1920's.

   c. In 1922, the Japanese agreed to the Washington treaties providing for reductions in naval armament.

   d. In 1925, the Russo-Japanese Convention reestablished diplomatic relations between the two countries and settled their disputes over fishing rights and the island of Sakhalin.

   e. From 1924 to 1926, Japanese foreign policy toward China was conciliatory.

3. In the late 1920's, Japanese militarists and imperialists began to play a bigger role in politics. Their rise was accompanied by a revival of older Japanese ideologies of emperor worship and glorification of the military tradition.

   a. The army assumed a major political role and was supported by the peasants in opposition to the urban commercial and industrial interests.

   b. In 1927, General Baron Tanaka became both premier and foreign minister and began what he called a "positive" policy toward China.

   c. Tanaka's policy led to Japanese intervention in the Shantung province of China (1928–1929). Japanese troops seized control of the railways, holding them for a year until the Chinese paid "damages"; only then were Japanese forces withdrawn.

4. Conditions both inside and outside Japan encouraged Japanese imperialism in the 1930's.

   a. The world markets supplied by Japanese producers were flooded with goods during the depression.

   b. Low cost Japanese labor could not overcome the barriers of high tariffs erected against Japanese products.

   c. One form of Chinese resistance to Japanese expansion was an effective boycott of Japanese goods.

    d. Japan's population was growing rapidly. Emigration
could not solve the problem because many areas
barred or limited the entry of Japanese. Those who
stayed home had to be employed, and markets had to
be found for the industries that employed them.

    e. In 1929, twelve nations agreed that China should be
allowed to set its own tariffs. The Chinese wanted
to protect their new industries against Japanese
competition.

5. In September, 1931, Japanese troops began the conquest
of Manchuria by driving out the Chinese forces. In 1932,
the Japanese completed the conquest, renamed the area
Manchukuo, and placed a Japanese puppet ruler in
control.

    a. The League of Nations, in response to China's appeal,
investigated the matter. Japanese refusal to accept
the League's proposal led to the League's declaring
Japan an aggressor.

    b. The Chinese retaliated against Japan by an economic
boycott. The Japanese replied by the seizure and occupation of Shanghai (1932).

    c. In 1933, Japan announced she would withdraw from
the League of Nations; her withdrawal was to take
effect in 1935.

6. Within Japan, meanwhile, the militarists continued to
get more control over the government.

    a. In 1932, most of the important cabinet posts were
taken over by military men.

    b. Military men assassinated the liberal premier (May,
1932), and Admiral Viscount Saito became premier.
This event is generally considered to mark the end of
party government in Japan.

    c. From 1932 to the end of World War II, the govern-
ment was controlled by the militarists. It was not
rare for any official who resisted the militarists to be
assassinated.

7. Japanese military and economic imperialism became
even more aggressive after 1932.

    a. Japan's conquest of Manchuria had produced no seri-
ous action by the great powers which were preoccupied with their own problems.

    b. In 1937, the Japanese began the invasion of China without a declaration of war.

    c. Within a few weeks, the Japanese seized Peking and enforced a naval blockade of most of the Chinese coast.

    d. The Chinese, though desperately short of modern equipment, resisted stubbornly in spite of Japanese atrocities and aerial bombing intended to terrorize the people.

    e. The League of Nations condemned the Japanese invasion, but this had little effect. The Chinese moved their capital from Nanking to the interior city of Chungking.

    f. The invasion of China involved Japan in a struggle which ended only with the conclusion of World War II and Japan's defeat. The Japanese almost completely misjudged their own strength and the Chinese will and capacity to resist.

8. In 1936, Japan joined Nazi Germany in an anti-Communist pact; and the next year, Italy joined them and recognized Manchukuo.

    a. Japanese alignment with the Axis powers and her expansion in the Far East brought a serious clash between Russian and Japanese forces in Mongolia (May, 1939).

    b. The signing of the Nazi-Soviet pact in August, 1939 was a great shock to the Japanese, who immediately scrapped the Anti-Communist pact. The Mongolian situation became an uneasy truce.

9. In 1940, Japan joined a new treaty with Germany and Italy; and in April, 1941 concluded a neutrality treaty with Russia.

    a. These actions freed Japan to concentrate on expansion in the Far East while the European powers fought World War II.

    b. On November 29, 1941, the Japanese premier, General Hideki Tojo, declared that the influence of Great Britain and United States must be eliminated from the Orient.

    c. President Roosevelt requested a definition of Japanese aims in Indo-China and appealed (December 6,

1941) to Japanese Emperor Hirohito to help in preserving peace.
d. The next day, December 7, 1941, the Japanese attacked Hawaii, the Philippines, Guam, Midway Island, Hong Kong, and Malaya.
e. This action brought both United States and Japan
into World War II. It proved to be the last major
error in the foreign policy of the Japanese militarists.

VIII. China

A. The end of World War I found the Chinese struggling to
fulfill the program set forward in the Revolution of 1911
by Dr. Sun Yat-Sen.
1. Dr. Sun's program accepted the doctrine of popular
sovereignty, but he believed China should be governed
by its own elite rather than attempting to rely on universal manhood suffrage and parliamentary government.
a. Dr. Sun believed nationalism would have to be developed to make China a unified state.
b. The traditional basis of Chinese law, government,
and culture had been the family. In Sun's view, the
nation would have to take precedence over the family.
c. Sun's philosophy left no room for concessions to imperial powers.
d. He believed the Chinese could attain a decent standard of living only if the nation's wealth was kept out
of the hands of western (or Japanese) imperialists and
of the old Chinese landlords.
2. By 1919, however, China was still unindustrialized; and
the imperialists remained well entrenched. Chinese living standards were far below those of western nations.
a. China had supported the Allies during World War I,
but felt the Versailles peace conference favored Japan
over China by granting Japan concessions in China
formerly held by Germany instead of returning them
to the Chinese.
b. When other Chinese appeals to the western powers
were not granted, the Chinese turned toward Soviet
Russia for assistance and guidance.
3. In 1924 the leaders of Dr. Sun's party, the Kuomintang
(the Party of the People), decided to invite the Chinese

Communist Party (first organized in Mongolia in 1921) to join the Kuomintang.

 a. The Soviet advisor, Michael Borodin, tried to take over the leadership of the Kuomintang. Radical agitation by the Communists led to their splitting from the Kuomintang in 1927.

 b. When Dr. Sun Yat-sen died in 1925, the moderates in the Kuomintang got control of the party. Their leader was Chiang Kai-shek.

 c. Chiang Kai-shek was a Chinese general who had been trained by the Japanese. From 1920 to 1926, large sections of China had been ruled by local war lords who ignored the central government.

 d. Chiang gained recognition by his many successful campaigns against the war lords and his consequent extension of the authority of the Kuomintang.

 e. Chiang and his followers set up a new government at Nanking; and, in 1927, began a strenuous effort to crush Communist influence in central and southern China. In the same year, he married Mayling Soong, sister-in-law of Sun Yat-sen and a member of a wealthy and powerful commercial family.

4. Chiang continued his policy trying to unify China by military power.

 a. His continuous pressure on the Communists led to their "Long March" (1934) during which Mao Tse-tung guided the Communists from south of the Yangtze River to the northwestern province of Shensi.

 b. From Yenan, capital city of Shensi, Mao Tse-tung directed Communist resistance against Chiang's forces.

 c. Chiang's government, meanwhile, tried to carry forward a reform program to build factories, roads, and railroads and to provide social security and education for the Chinese.

5. But Chiang's government never enjoyed a period of peace when it could concentrate on reform.

 a. The Japanese quickly recognized the threat to their plans posed by a united and modernized China. They did everything in their power to prevent success of Chiang's reforms.

 b. Chiang's government was almost constantly fighting

the Japanese or the Communists, or both at the same time.

c. The reform program was handicapped by Chiang's own followers. Landowners are seldom eager advocates of land reform programs which may deprive them of their lands. Bankers and businessmen are not usually enthusiastic about government control of economic development which may have been China's only hope.

B. The Japanese invasion of China in 1937 forced Chiang to move his government to Chungking where it was isolated from the eastern and coastal cities occupied by the Japanese.

1. Even before the Japanese invasion, Chiang and the Communists agreed to bury the hatchet to fight the Japanese.

a. This agreement never worked out well in practice. Skirmishes between the Nationalists, as Chiang's forces had come to be called, and the Chinese Communists occurred almost every time the two came in contact.

b. The Communists never engaged in anything more serious than guerrilla warfare against the Japanese, although that may have been the limit of their capabilities at that time.

c. Chiang seldom committed all his forces against the Japanese. The Nationalist attitude toward the war seemed to be that they could not decide whether the Japanese or the Communists were their worst enemy.

d. Chiang's judgment of the Communist threat may have been justified. In any case, his war effort was always managed so that he would have a strong force to fight Mao Tse-tung when the war against Japan ended.

2. Equally serious was the effect of the isolation of Chungking on the Kuomintang itself.

a. The eastern and coastal cities of China were the center of the liberal, intellectual, commercial, and industrial elements of the country.

b. Japanese occupation prevented these elements from exercising their usual strong influence in the Nationalist regime.

c. Instead, Chiang was forced to deal with more and

more of the provincial and reactionary war lords of the interior, the very element he had once tried to crush to unify China.

d. The war lords in the regime continued their traditional methods of operation: graft, bribery, corruption, and pillage.

e. The Nationalist regime was seriously weakened by these practices when the struggle with the Communists occurred following World War II.

BIBLIOGRAPHY

Allen, H. E., *The Turkish transformation: a study in social and religious development* (Chicago: University of Chicago Press, 1935).

Chamberlin, W. H., *Japan over Asia*, revised edition (Boston: Little, Brown, 1939).

Chen, S., and Payne, P. S. R., *Sun Yat-sen: a portrait* (New York: The Day Company, 1946).

Clyde, P., *The history of the impact of the west on eastern Asia* (New York: Prentice-Hall, Inc., 1947).

Foster, H. A., *The making of modern Iraq: a product of world forces* (Norman: University of Oklahoma Press, 1935).

Haas, W. S., *Iran* (New York: Columbia University Press, 1946).

Hartog, M., *India in outline* (New York: Macmillan, 1944).

Hitti, P. K., *The Arabs: a short history for Americans* (Princeton: Princeton University Press, 1945).

Jackh, E., *The rising crescent: Turkey* (New York: Farrar and Rinehart, 1944).

Latourette, K. S., *A short history of the Far East* (New York: Macmillan, 1946).

Rosinger, L. K., *China's crisis* (New York: Knopf, 1945).

Smith, S. R., *The Manchurian Crisis, 1931–1932* (New York: Columbia University Press, 1948).

Thompson, V., *French Indo-China* (London: George Allen & Unwin, Ltd., 1937).

Chapter 15

WORLD WAR II AND ITS
AFTERMATH IN THE WEST

I. The Eastern Front: September, 1939 to March, 1940

A. During the first seven months of the war, the world's attention was focused on the conquest and partition of Poland and the Russians' defeat of Finland and seizure of Estonia, Latvia, and Lithuania.

    1. The German armies smashed Poland's military forces and occupied Warsaw in less than a month; the German invasion of Poland began September 1 (without a declaration of war), and Warsaw capitulated September 28.

        a. A horrified western world was introduced to a new concept of war: *blitzkrieg* ("lightning war").

        b. A *blitzkrieg* was characterized by, first, a surprise attack, usually without the traditional declaration of war. The attack was usually begun by air, the first objective being to destroy the victim's air force on the ground.

        c. The attacking air force also struck at communications facilities to prevent effective mobilization for defense and often bombed cities simply to terrorize and confuse the population.

        d. The aggressor's ground forces attacked in coordination with the air strike. The ground attack was usually led by armored units; tanks, self-propelled artillery, and motorized infantry units moved so rapidly the defender was kept off balance.

        e. Often a small country could be completely overrun by a *blitzkrieg* before its defenses were ever completely mobilized.

        f. Either to launch a *blitzkrieg* or to defend an area

against one required careful, detailed planning and training and unprecedented amounts of equipment. In 1939, Germany had the trained forces and the equipment; the British and French did not.

2. The Polish resistance to the Nazi attack was heroic, but the Poles had little equipment, and what they had was obsolete. Their French and English allies could do little to help them. A few Polish ships escaped and later joined British squadrons; and some Polish officials fled to London, establishing a Polish government-in-exile.

3. Germany and Soviet Russia carried out the secret terms of their pact of August, 1939. Poland was divided between them; and Hitler gave Stalin a free hand in the Baltic area.

   a. On November 30, 1939, the Russians invaded Finland. The effectiveness of the Finnish resistance in the winter warfare was amazing, but the numerical superiority of the Russians was overwhelming.

   b. On March 12, 1940, the Finns were forced to accept the harsh terms of a Russian-dictated peace treaty: the Finns ceded the Karelian isthmus, the port of Viborg, and other territories and bases giving the U.S.S.R. complete control of the Gulf of Finland and the Lake Ladoga area.

   c. In June, 1940, Russian forces moved into Estonia, Latvia, and Lithuania. The following August these countries were integrated into the U.S.S.R. as Soviet republics.

II. The Western Front (1940)

A. The Allied strategy in the west was to hold off any German assault by remaining behind the French fortifications (the Maginot Line) while starving Germany into submission by naval blockade.

1. The Allies assumed a Nazi assault on the Maginot line would produce so many German casualties that the attack would fail.

2. Unfortunately, the most powerful fortifications existed only along the French-German border. The French-Belgian border had been only lightly fortified because the

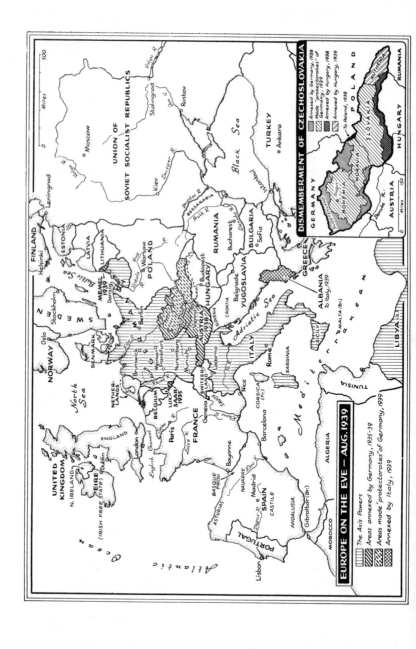

EUROPE ON THE EVE — AUG. 1939

The Axis Powers
Areas annexed by Germany, 1935-39
Areas made protectorates of Germany, 1939
Annexed by Italy, 1939

DISMEMBERMENT OF CZECHOSLOVAKIA

Annexed by Germany, 1938
Made "protectorates" of Germany, 1939
Annexed by Hungary, 1938
Annexed by Hungary, 1939
To Poland, 1938

French had wanted to avoid any diplomatic repercussions from Belgium.

3. The comparative inactivity on the western front from September, 1939 to April, 1940 was derisively referred to as the "sitzkrieg." On the other hand, if Hitler hoped for some sign of appeasement after the conquest of Poland, none was forthcoming.

B. On April 9, 1940, the Germans invaded Denmark and Norway. Denmark was taken so quickly that almost no resistance was offered.

1. Norway was the victim of assault by paratroops and innocent appearing cargo ships actually loaded with German troops and equipment.

2. The German military invasion had been prepared for by an amazing Nazi underground movement in Norway; a large group of spies and saboteurs were poised at vital points to assist the German invaders and hamper the Norwegian defense.

3. The Norwegians rallied from the surprise, driving the Germans from Trondheim and Bergen and sinking four German cruisers and four troop ships.

   a. An Anglo-French expeditionary force landed in southern Norway, but the Germans drove them out May 7.

   b. The British landed another force at Narvik and inflicted considerable losses on the Germans, but were driven out June 9.

   c. On June 10, Norwegian military resistance ended. Meanwhile, King Haakon VII and his cabinet moved to London to continue the resistance.

4. The invasion of Norway emphasized the extreme risk and difficulty of carrying on naval operations without adequate air cover. The *Luftwaffe* (German air force) made it almost impossible for the Anglo-French forces to carry on effective operations in Norway.

5. The Norwegian campaign provided the Germans with better bases to strike at the British Isles and later, when Soviet Russia joined the western allies, enabled the Nazis to attack the communications lines from the west to Russia.

6. In Britain, German successes in Scandanavia led to the replacement of Prime Minister Chamberlain by Winston Churchill (May 10). Daladier, the French premier, had

resigned three weeks earlier. The architects of diplomatic appeasement had turned out to be no more successful in war than in diplomacy.

C. Even before the Scandinavian campaign had ended, the
Nazi juggernaut rolled again. On May 10, without a dec-
laration of war, German armies invaded the Netherlands,
Belgium, and Luxemburg.

1. No one was so surprised that the Germans invaded these
areas, but the shock was that the Dutch were forced to
surrender in just five days. The Belgians, who had successfully resisted the Germans for four years in World
War I, capitulated in eighteen days.

2. As the Germans expected, British and French forces
rushed to aid the Belgians and Dutch.

a. As the Allies advanced into Belgium, the main German thrust struck at Sedan. Breaking through the
lightly fortified line between Belgium and France,
the German forces turned north toward the English
Channel and attacked the Allies from the rear.

b. This meant the Allied armies were cut off from France
and under attack from east and west.

c. To save these forces, the British took them off the
continent at Dunkirk. From May 29 to June 4, the
Royal Air Force beat off the *Luftwaffe* while practically every available British ship shuttled to and fro
across the channel evacuating the Anglo-French
forces.

d. The British saved about three hundred fifty thousand
men at Dunkirk, but all their equipment was lost.

3. The German armies turned toward Paris. Mussolini
jumped on the bandwagon by opening a southern front
against the hard-pressed French on June 10, 1940.

a. French Premier Reynaud was soon urged to surrender
to the Germans. To forestall surrender, Winston
Churchill proposed the formation of an Anglo-French
political union to continue the resistance.

b. Reynaud was replaced by Marshal Pétain, who sought
an armistice rather than moving the government to
North Africa and continuing to resist.

4. The armistice was signed June 22. The Germans occupied three fifths of France including Paris and the entire Atlantic coastline; France had to pay all occupation

costs; French prisoners were to be kept in Germany, and
the French fleet was to be disarmed.

5. In London, the French general, Charles de Gaulle, re-
fused to accept the defeat as final and organized the Free
French (later Fighting French) movement to resist the
Germans by every possible means.

6. At Vichy, where the French government moved from
Paris, Pétain was given the power to establish an authoritarian government. His vice-premier, Pierre Laval, succeeded him on April 18, 1942 and became the virtual dictator of France. On November 11, 1942, German forces
moved into unoccupied France and used Laval as a puppet dictator over the French.

D. The Battle of Britain began in earnest on August 8, 1940
with the *Luftwaffe's* first massive assault on the British
Isles.

1. The initial aim of the German attack was to destroy the
Royal Air Force. If this could have been done, then German air superiority might have served to overcome British naval superiority in the English Channel and made
invasion of England possible.

2. But the British had used their opportunity following
Dunkirk to disperse and camouflage their airfields and
had developed the first radar detection devices.

   a. British fighter aircraft, particularly the "Spitfire" and
   the "Hurricane," were slightly superior to the German planes at that time, although the Germans had
   numerical superiority.

   b. Defending aircraft could stay in the air longer, not
   having to use fuel to make the trip across the channel.

   c. Consequently, the *Luftwaffe,* for the first time, encountered serious opposition and suffered some shocking losses. From August 8 to October 31, 1940, the
   British lost about eight hundred aircraft; but they
   shot down almost two thousand four hundred planes
   of the *Luftwaffe.*

   d. The Nazi high command made a serious error when,
   finding they could not smash the British air force with
   the expected ease, they shifted their attack to British
   industries and cities, hoping to terrorize the English
   into submission.

3. *Luftwaffe* attacks on the British Isles lessened somewhat

during the bad weather of the winter of 1940–41 and resumed in the spring. They lessened in May as the Germans prepared for the invasion of Russia, but German
air raids were continued to some degree for the duration
of the war.

a. The German air attack, however, did not destroy the
   Royal Air Force. The R.A.F. survived and grew to
   deliver gigantic raids on German cities and to play a
   major role in breaking the back of the *Luftwaffe*.

b. German air raids never came close to destroying
   Britain's industrial capacity although they killed
   thousands of British civilians and extensively damaged the cities. Britain's population displayed remarkable courage under air attacks, which only seemed to
   stiffen their will to win the war.

c. As nearly as November, 1940, it appeared no German
   invasion of England would be undertaken. The Battle of Britain was the first serious struggle in which
   the forces of the Third Reich were made to eat the
   bitter dirt of defeat.

III. The Balkan Campaigns: 1940–1941

A. Exactly when Adolf Hitler first decided to invade Russia
   is unknown, but to do so he needed to secure his Balkan
   flank. Stalin's aggression in 1940 denied Hitler the Baltic
   area; probably preoccupation with the attack on England
   led him to leave an African campaign to his Italian ally in
   1940.

B. Hitler wanted the Balkan area as a base for his attack
   against southern Russia; and he wanted Balkan manpower
   and resources, particularly oil.

   1. The Russians had already occupied Bessarabia and
      northern Bukovina (both belonged to Rumania) in
      June, 1940.

   2. On October 8, German troops entered Rumania to "pro-
      tect" the Rumanian oil fields; and the next month both
      Hungary and Rumania joined the Berlin-Rome-Tokyo
      pact.

   3. Actual military operations began October 28 with an
      Italian attack on Greece from Albania.

   4. Only two days later, British troops occupied the Greek

islands to reinforce the Greeks; and one hundred thirty four Russian fighter planes were sent to Greece in accordance with existing agreements between Russia and Greece.

5. During November and December, the British sank or damaged half the Italian fleet anchored at Taranto; and the Greeks took twenty eight thousand Italians prisoner and occupied about one fourth of Albania.

C. In March, 1941, Bulgaria and Yugoslavia joined the Berlin-Rome-Tokyo pact; but the Yugoslavs refused to follow their leader, the regent Prince Paul, and overthrew the government, placing young King Peter on the throne. Yugoslavia then declared its neutrality.

1. In April, German troops, massed along the borders of Hungary, Rumania, and Bulgaria, invaded Yugoslavia and Greece.

2. The Yugoslavian government surrendered in twelve days, although resistance continued in the mountains.

3. The Greeks signed an armistice in seventeen days. The British had put sixty thousand troops into Greece, but they could not stop the German armored divisions.

4. The British evacuated forty eight thousand men to the island of Crete, but German air attacks and a paratroop invasion forced the British to move their forces back to Egypt in May, 1941.

5. German possession of Greece and Crete denied the Aegean Sea to British shipping.

IV. Africa and the Mediterranean: 1940–1941

A. The African theater of the war came to life with the Italian effort to invade Egypt from Libya in September, 1940.

1. The Italian advance moved slowly forward until it encountered a surprising British counterattack under the direction of General Sir Archibald Wavell.

2. The British drive rolled the Italians back almost halfway across Libya during December, 1940 and January, 1941. The British suffered about three thousand casualties, but they took one hundred fourteen thousand Italian prisoners and captured all their equipment.

B. The British, however, could not maintain their position in

Libya because it was necessary to detach troops from their African forces for service elsewhere.

1. In January, 1941, British forces in the Sudan struck at the Italian colonies to the south while, simultaneously, British forces based in Kenya advanced northward toward the same objectives.

2. By April, the Italian colonies in Africa were under British control. Haile Selassi, the Ethiopian ruler dispossessed by Mussolini in 1936, took part in this campaign and ultimately regained his kingdom.

3. Wavell's army furnished the troops who were sent to Greece and others who were used to deny the Axis powers a foothold in Syria, Iraq, and Iran.

4. Taking advantage of Wavell's shortage of troops, the Germans reinforced the Italians in Libya and placed General Erwin Rommel in command.

   a. In April, 1941, Rommel's forces drove the outnumbered British back to the Egyptian frontier.

   b. When the Germans invaded Russia, however, they depleted Rommel's reserves. In December, the British took the offensive again and drove Rommel's forces clear back to Bengasi.

5. By the end of 1941, the British were convinced that desert warfare resembled naval warfare in that territory taken meant little. The primary objective had to be the destruction of the enemy's forces. This task could not be done until their own strength in north Africa could be greatly increased.

V. The Invasion of Russia

A. The actions of both Soviet Russia and Nazi Germany during the latter's Balkan campaign made it clear Stalin and Hitler were uneasy allies.

1. German and Russian interests were in obvious conflict in the Baltic and Balkan areas.

2. Diplomatic negotiations between the two powers led to Hitler's suggestion that the U.S.S.R. expand in Iraq and Iran.

3. Stalin was happy to accept Hitler's advice in that regard, but Stalin also demanded Soviet control of Bulgaria and the Straits.

    4. Hitler would not agree to the additional demands because to grant them would give Russia too much power in the Middle East. By December, 1940, Russo-German negotiations were deadlocked on these issues.

B. On June 22, 1941, German forces invaded Russia, violating the Russo-German nonaggression pact of August 23, 1939. The attack by four-fifths of the *Luftwaffe* and one hundred sixty divisions of the German army was launched on a two thousand mile front from the Black to the White Sea.

    1. The invading force is estimated to have totaled about three million men including Germans, Italians, Finns, Rumanians, and Hungarians.

    2. The Russians apparently had about two million men under arms with an indefinite number in reserve.

    3. By December, 1941, the German armies held Sevastopol, were about thirty miles from Moscow, and were within artillery range of Leningrad.

    4. The Red Army had sustained many casualties, but reserve manpower filled the gaps. In retreat, the Russians had carried out a "scorched earth" policy leaving nothing the invader could use. The Russian winter was well started, and the Germans were not properly equipped for it.

    5. Only a few weeks after the invasion began, Great Britain and Russia signed a mutual aid agreement. In October, the United States granted the U.S.S.R. a billion dollar credit for Lend-Lease supplies for Russia. The United States and Great Britain undertook to deliver war materials to Russia; Nazi sea and air power made delivery extremely difficult and costly.

VI. Early Japanese Victories and the Allied Reaction

A. The preoccupation of the great powers with events in Europe encouraged the Japanese to think they could exploit the situation in the Far East as they had during World War I. Japan had allied itself with Italy and Germany and had signed a neutrality pact with Russia in April, 1941.

    1. During the summer of 1940, the defenseless government of Vichy France had permitted Japan to occupy Indo-China.

    2. United States, Great Britain, and the Netherlands re-

acted by freezing Japanese assets in their countries. Japan needed oil and iron available only in those markets and was willing to go to war to get them.

3. Once the Germans invaded Russia, only the United States and Great Britain stood in the way of the realization of the Japanese imperialists' plan, "The Greater East Asia Co-Prosperity Sphere." And Great Britain had its hands full fighting in Europe, Africa, and the Middle East.

B. <u>Militarily, the Japanese raid on Pearl Harbor, December 7, 1941, combined with the attacks on the Philippines, Guam, Midway, Hong Kong, and Malaya, was a great success.</u> The American forces suffered tremendous damage and began the war in the Pacific handicapped by serious numerical inferiority to the Japanese.

1. The Japanese exploited their opportunity and soon took Siam, Malaya (including Singapore), the Netherlands East Indies, the Philippines, and other islands in the Indian and Pacific Oceans, even including the Aleutian Islands of Attu and Kiska. Many of these places were heroically defended, but no amount of courage could prevail against Japanese air and naval superiority.

2. Within a few days of the initial Japanese attacks, United States and Great Britain had declared war on Japan, and Germany and Italy declared war on the United States.

C. The general war aims of the Anglo-American group of nations were set forward by the subscription to the principles of the <u>Atlantic Charter</u> by representatives of twenty six nations on January 1, 1942.

1. The Atlantic Charter had been drafted August 14, 1941 by Franklin D. Roosevelt and Winston Churchill. The U.S.S.R. was among the nations which endorsed its principles at the beginning of 1942.

2. Among the major principles of the Atlantic Charter were: no territorial aggrandizement, no territorial changes against the wishes of the people concerned, and the guarantee that people must have the right to choose their own form of government.

3. Winston Churchill soon began to refer to the signatories of the Atlantic Charter as the "<u>Grand Alliance.</u>" This term will be used here to refer to those powers opposing

Germany, Italy, Japan, and their allies, who will be
called the "Axis powers."

4. The strength of the Grand Alliance lay in the power of
United States, Great Britain, and the Soviet Union.
These three dominated the planning and furnished the
greater part of the troops and material of the Grand
Alliance.

D. The Grand Alliance was quick to lay down the main lines
of its overall strategy.

1. United States, with its industrial potential beyond the
reach of the Axis powers, was to become the "arsenal of
democracy."

2. All possible defense measures were to be taken to prevent an Axis breakthrough until American industrial
output could bring the Grand Alliance to full offensive
strength.

3. When the United States was ready, the first major offensives would be directed at Germany.

   a. This decision was a blow to the American leaders in
   the Pacific theater of operations which would neces-
   sarily be reduced to secondary priority, but the decision was basically sound.

   b. Germany had much greater military resources and far
   more skilled scientific personnel than Japan.

   c. Russia was already at war with Germany but not with
   Japan. The Red Army could be utilized to bring
   heavier pressure upon Germany than Japan.

   d. Supply lines from the United States to the European
   theater of operations were much shorter than those
   to the Pacific.

   e. Japanese power depended on the retention of scattered islands vulnerable to air and sea blockade.

4. The United States was involved in the Battle of the Atlantic long before Pearl Harbor.

   a. At the beginning of World War II, Americans generally wanted to avoid participation. Before long,
   however, it was realized that refusal to export arms
   to any belligerent was no aid to American security.

   b. In November, 1939, Congress adopted the "cash and
   carry" principle permitting belligerents to purchase
   war supplies in America if they could pay and provide transport for the purchases. This action clearly

     favored France and England because they dominated
the Atlantic shipping routes.

  c. In September, 1940, the Selective Service Act was
    passed, enabling the United States to begin drafting
    and training men; and the United States traded fifty
    destroyers to the British in return for leases on British
    bases in the Atlantic and Caribbean.

  d. In March, 1941, the Lend-Lease Act became law and
    empowered the president to supply materials to any
    country whose defense he deemed essential to the se-
    curity of the United States.

  e. During the spring and summer of 1941, American
    forces, at the invitation of the Danish and Icelandic
    governments, occupied Iceland and Greenland, reliev-
    ing the British units already there.

  f. American naval forces began convoying supplies when
    German submarine attacks threatened to put all the
    lend-lease deliveries on the bottom of the Atlantic.

5. The British and the Americans carried the brunt of the
terrible struggle to convoy supplies from North America
to the theaters of operation.

  a. Nazi submarine "wolf packs" and bombers sank over
    seven million tons of shipping in the first two years of
    the war. Over half the world's shipping afloat in 1939
    had been sunk by 1944.

  b. Possibly the most cruel of the major convoy routes
    was the one to Murmansk via the northern coast of
    Scandinavia because of German bombers, submarines,
    and surface raiders based in occupied Norway.

  c. These losses were overcome by the tremendous out-
    put of American shipyards and improved methods
    and devices for convoy protection.

VII. 1942: The Turn of the Tide

A. During the first half of 1942, the Axis powers took the offensive; and their forces advanced on most of the fronts.

1. The Germans' major offensive was directed toward the
southern sector of the Russian front where a Nazi breakthrough would cut Russia off from Middle Eastern and
Russian oil sources. The Germans reached Stalingrad
(on the Volga River) by September.

2. In Africa, General Rommel launched an attack on the British in May. By the end of June, the Germans had rolled the British back to El Alamein, just seventy miles west of Alexandria, but there the British held firm.

3. The Japanese pushed into Burma, threatening India, and drove south to the approaches of Australia (New Britain, New Ireland, the Solomon Islands, and New Guinea).

B. The tide began to turn in the Pacific even though it was in that theater that the Axis enjoyed the greatest numerical superiority.

1. The United States Navy defeated the Japanese fleet in the Battle of the Coral Sea (May, 1942); and in June, at Midway destroyed the Japanese preponderance in aircraft carriers. These victories stopped the Japanese advances toward Australia and Hawaii.

2. The counterattack by the Grand Alliance began on the Solomon Islands where the Japanese were finally defeated after six months of heavy fighting on Guadalcanal Island.

3. The Battle of Stalingrad turned the tide on the Russian front. The Russians, suffering heavy casualties, killed or captured about three hundred thousand Germans in the Stalingrad sector; and the Germans had to retreat.

4. The campaign that destroyed Axis hopes in North Africa began with the landing of British and American troops on the Atlantic and Mediterranean coasts of North Africa (November 8, 1942).

   a. As the invading force, under the command of General Dwight D. Eisenhower, drove east, the British Eighth Army, commanded by General Bernard L. Montgomery, drove west from Egypt.

   b. The Axis armies were trapped. When they surrendered (May, 1943), the forces of the Grand Alliance took two hundred fifty thousand prisoners.

   c. Final estimates are that the campaigns in North Africa cost the Axis powers almost a million casualties, eight thousand planes, and over two million tons of shipping.

5. The secret "Manhattan Project," supported by a two billion dollar appropriation, was begun and ultimately resulted in the production of the atomic bomb. German

scientists were also trying to produce such a weapon, but apparently they lacked the time or the necessary support to succeed before Germany was defeated.

VIII. The Invasion and Defeat of Italy

A. On July 10, 1943, American, British, and Canadian troops landed in Sicily. King Victor Emmanuel III forced Mussolini and his cabinet to resign July 25. Marshall Pietro Badoglio was appointed to replace Mussolini.

1. Badoglio declared the Fascist Party dissolved and began negotiations for an armistice. Mussolini was imprisoned in Rome.

2. On September 3, an armistice was signed between the Anglo-American forces and those of the Badoglio government.

3. The Germans, however, had no intention of permitting the Italian surrender to expose the southern flank of Nazi-occupied Europe.

   a. German troops rescued Mussolini on September 12, and he proclaimed the establishment of a Republican Fascist Party in alliance with the German army of occupation.

   b. German army units then seized control of all the major Italian cities.

4. The Americans landed at Salerno (September 9) and soon occupied Naples.

   a. The German defense of Italy was stubborn and skillful and was aided by winter weather and the mountainous terrain.

   b. In an attempt to outflank the German defense, American and British forces landed at Anzio (January 22, 1944); but the Germans maneuvered to meet the new offensive. The allies pushed ahead slowly, but they had to fight for every mile.

   c. Rome was taken June 4; by August, the Allies captured Florence. Then the front stabilized as the major action was carried on in France and eastern Europe.

   d. The German divisions in Italy surrendered only in May, 1945, as the Third Reich finally collapsed.

e. As Mussolini tried to escape to Switzerland, he was caught and shot without trial by his captors.

IX. The European Theater of Operations: 1944–1945

A. While American and British forces were slugging it out with the Germans in Italy, the major effort of the Grand Alliance was made on the Russian front and in the invasion and liberation of France.

B. <u>After months of careful preparation, British and American forces landed on Normandy June 6, 1944.</u> The invasion was supported by ten thousand planes and over four thousand ships. Within a week, the Allies held a strip of beach sixty miles long.

1. Early in July, the Allied forces broke through the German defenses at St. Lo and drove east toward Paris, Belgium, and Germany.

2. On August 15, the French First Army and the American Seventh Army landed on the Mediterranean coast of France and advanced northward up the Rhone Valley.

3. By December, the Allied Expeditionary Forces were trying to break through the Germans' fortified line along the Rhine (the Westwall).

   a. December 16th to the 25th witnessed the last major German offensive in the west. General Karl von Rundstedt's forces broke through a lightly held sector of the Allied lines in southern Belgium, planning to swing north to the English Channel.

   b. Aided by severe winter weather which grounded Allied aircraft, the Germans created a bulge in the Allied lines which gave the campaign its name, the Battle of the Bulge.

   c. General Dwight Eisenhower, commanding the Allies, rushed reinforcements to the area and shifted Allied units to attack the sides of the bulge. The German attack was turned back, and the Allies prepared for the final push into Germany.

C. <u>Following the German defeat at Stalingrad, the Russians began to drive the Germans back.</u> Beseiged cities like Leningrad were relieved. A German offensive, using two hundred sixty divisions, pushed the Russians backward only temporarily. By the end of 1943, the Russians had nearly regained their pre-war western boundaries.

1. Russian forces outnumbered the Germans on the Russian front in 1943.
2. By late 1943, United States and Great Britain had delivered seven thousand planes, twenty thousand military vehicles, and thousands of industrial machines to Russia. A hundred thousand tons of supplies each month were reaching Russia via Allied-controlled Iran.
3. British and American air offensives against Germany prevented the Germans from replacing their own equipment lost in battle.
4. Their own strenuous efforts, supplies from the west, and air raids on Germany gave the Russians control of the air over the Russian front and more equipment for war than the Germans had.
5. By May, 1944, the Red Army was ready to advance up the Danube Valley; and by August, the Russians were moving into East Prussia, Poland, and Rumania.
6. The presence of the Allied forces in western Europe prevented the Nazis from reinforcing their eastern front, increasing the Russian preponderance in eastern Europe. The power and the position of the Red Army provided Stalin with rare political opportunities, and he used them skillfully.
   a. In 1944, Russia forced Finland to sign an armistice and reconquered the Baltic states.
   b. Stalin refused to recognize the Polish government-in-exile in London and dealt with the Union of Polish Patriots, a Communist-dominated group organized in Russia and transplanted to Lublin, Poland.
   c. The Polish underground in Warsaw, loyal to the London Poles, was advised to rise against the Nazi occupation troops to aid the Red Army to take Warsaw.
   d. The Warsaw underground attacked the Nazis as planned, but Stalin halted the Red Army's advance and did all he could to prevent British and American aircraft from supplying the Warsaw underground by air.
   e. The Nazis crushed the uprising, killing the Poles loyal to the London government-in-exile. Then the Red Army resumed its advance, placing the Lublin (Com-

munist) Poles in control as it moved westward across
Poland.

   f. In Yugoslavia, Stalin supported Tito's underground
movement against the nationalist underground group
led by Milhailovitch. Tito's forces were Communist,
and Yugoslavia became a Communist state after the
war.

   g. In Rumania, Bulgaria, and Hungary, occupation by
the Red Army was the prelude to Communist domination. Albania, too, dropped into the Communist
basket.

   h. Communism obtained a foothold in Greece as well,
through the action of the Greek underground against
the Nazis. British troops, however, were moved into
Greece and prevented the Communists from getting
control of the country.

   i. The Czechoslovakian government-in-exile was persuaded to sign a twenty year defensive alliance with
Russia in December, 1943. The Communists did not
manage to take over Czechoslovakia, however, until
1949.

D. The Grand Alliance crushed the remaining military power
of Nazi Germany in the first four months of 1945.

   1. In the west, Eisenhower's forces crossed the Rhine March
8 and met the Red Army at Torgau (on the Elbe River)
April 25.

   2. The Red Army took Berlin May 1; Adolf Hitler apparently committed suicide April 30.

   3. A group of German military leaders signed terms of surrender at Reims on May 7. On June 8, an Allied Control Committee including General Eisenhower, Field
Marshal Montgomery, and Marshal Zhukov assumed full
control of Germany, which was divided into zones of
military occupation.

X. Victory in the Pacific

A. The attack against the Japanese Empire was delivered from
three fronts: To the east from Nationalist China, to the
northeast from India and Burma, and north and northeast
along the island groups between the southwestern Pacific
and Japan.

1. The Chinese, the Americans, and the forces of the British Empire were all handicapped by long supply lines; it is fifteen thousand miles by ship from San Francisco to Calcutta.

2. Supplies for China had to be flown in from India or Burma or trucked over a thousand miles of the tortuous Burma Road.

3. The supply problem and the opportunities to utilize air and naval power led the Americans and the British Imperial forces to make their major effort on the southwest Pacific front.

4. The Allies' island hopping strategy made it possible to by-pass and isolate many Japanese strong points and pockets of resistance so long as the Allies could maintain aerial and naval supremacy to keep such Japanese units isolated.

B. Jumping off from the Solomon Islands and New Guinea, the Allies established bases on New Georgia and Bougainville by the summer of 1943.

1. By November, the advance reached the Gilberts, where the Japanese were defeated in the costly invasion of Tarawa.

2. February, 1944 witnessed the conquest of Kwajalein and Eniwetok in the Marshall Islands, five hundred miles northwest of the Gilberts.

3. Another fifteen hundred mile jump gained Saipan and Guam in the Marianas by July. When the Americans smashed the desperate Japanese defense of Saipan, the Japanese Premier Tojo resigned.

   a. The United States had been hard at work building a larger, longer range bombing plane, which could carry twice the bomb load of the B-17 "Flying Fortress." The new bomber was the B-29 "Superfortress."

   b. The B-29's could reach the Japanese home islands from Saipan, and the Americans began an aerial assault on Japan that finally surpassed the intensity of the raids on Germany.

4. In October, 1944, the Americans, commanded by General Douglas MacArthur, made successful landings on Leyte Island in the Philippines.

   a. The Japanese fleet made a tremendous effort to smash

the Leyte invasion in a two day naval engagement, the Battle of the Philippine Seas.

b. The United States navy drove off the Japanese who lost forty ships, had forty-eight more damaged, and lost over four hundred aircraft.

c. The Battle of the Philippine Seas left the Japanese navy too weak to fight a major battle with the American fleet.

5. At the extreme ends of the long battlefront, the war no longer appeared so promising for the Japanese.

a. In August, 1943, American forces drove the Japanese from their positions on the Aleutian Islands.

b. At the other end of the battle line, the Chinese Nationalist forces scored major victories over the Japanese forces in Kiangsi province in July, 1942.

c. In Southeast Asia, the British Imperial Army began a drive against three Japanese armies early in 1944. This offensive, commanded by Admiral Lord Louis Mountbatten, was concluded April 30, 1945 and cost the Japanese an estimated three hundred seventy-five thousand casualties.

6. As 1945 began, American heavy bombers were pounding Japan from Saipan, but bases closer to Japan were needed for fighter planes and as staging areas for the actual invasion of Japan.

a. By mid-March, Iwo Jima in the Vocano Islands had been secured. Iwo Jima is seven hundred fifty miles from Tokyo but only about four hundred miles from the nearest Japanese home islands.

b. The American Tenth Army and Marines fought particularly bitter battles in April and June to take the island of Okinawa in the Ryukyu Islands.

c. Japanese suicide planes (kamikazes) inflicted severe damage on the ships supporting the invasion of Okinawa, but the Allies gained a base three hundred twenty-five miles from Japan.

7. As the American and the British Imperial forces prepared for the invasion of the Japanese homeland, they expected to lose at least a million men in the assault. The necessity of such a costly campaign was avoided by the use of the atomic bomb.

a. One atomic bomb was dropped on the Japanese city

of <u>Hiroshima</u> on August 6, 1945. It killed slightly less than eighty thousand people.

b. On August 8, Soviet Russia declared war on Japan and invaded Manchuria.

c. The next day another bomb was dropped on Nagasaki. The Japanese accepted the terms of surrender set by the Grand Alliance on August 14. American occupation troops arrived August 26, and the formal surrender terms were signed September 2 aboard the U.S.S. *Missouri* in Tokyo Bay.

C. <u>The costs of World War II were staggering</u>. Slightly over seventy million men were mobilized for its battles, and nearly ten million of these were killed. About twelve million civilians died in the war.

1. Exactly how many persons died in concentration camps will probably never be known, but the total is in the millions.

2. How many more died later due to conditions during the war will probably remain unknown. Malnutrition, epidemics, overwork, battle fatigue, and various neuroses were all by-products of war.

3. Monetary costs and property damage caused by the war have been estimated at over three trillion dollars, about ten times the material cost of World War I.

XI. Major Wartime Conferences Affecting the Post War World

A. Perhaps the most important and ominous of the meetings of the "Big Three" during the war was the <u>Yalta Conference, which was a meeting of Churchill, Roosevelt, and Stalin in February, 1945.</u>

1. Because the Red Army occupied so much of eastern Europe and the British and Americans were still concerned with the war against Japan, Stalin's position at Yalta was particularly strong.

2. The Americans were anxious to disentangle themselves from long range European commitments. The United States apparently expected to exercise continued responsibility only in occupying Germany and had no desire nor intent to gain territory.

3. Russia was given a large part of eastern Poland, and Poland was compensated by being given territory in east-

ern Germany. Later, German inhabitants of the territory given to Poland were moved into occupied Germany and Poland's western border was extended to the
Oder River a few miles east of Berlin.

4. Russia received the lion's share of reparations to be
taken from Germany.

5. Germany was divided into zones for military occupation.
    a. Each of the Big Three was to occupy one zone.
    United States demanded that France also be given a
    zone, but Stalin objected.
    b. The Russians finally agreed to a French zone of oc-
    cupation if it were taken from the American zone,
    and this arrangement ultimately was adopted.
    c. Berlin was to be occupied jointly by the Americans,
    the British, the French, and the Russians. In the post
    war power struggle, it, too, was finally divided into
    zones.

6. At Yalta, the Big Three agreed that the populations of
liberated areas would be assisted in organizing democratic interim governments. These provisional governments were to hold free elections to assure the people of
each liberated area the government they desired.
    a. Roosevelt and Churchill hoped this provision would
    mitigate the effect of Russian expansion.
    b. Neither Stalin nor any of his successors, however, has
    permitted elections which were "free" by western
    standards.

7. Concessions made to Stalin at Yalta concerning affairs in
the Far East were as portentous as those in Europe.
    a. Russia was to recover areas of Sakhalin and the
    Kurile Islands and rights she enjoyed in Manchuria
    before 1905. Included were the lease of the Port
    Arthur naval base and a share in the operation of
    Manchurian railroads.
    b. Outer Mongolia was to become permanently autono-
    mous as the Mongolian People's Republic, a Soviet
    satellite state.
    c. All Stalin conceded in return was that the U.S.S.R.
    would declare war upon Japan sixty to ninety days
    after hostilities ended in Europe.
    d. In fact, Russia did not declare war on Japan until
    after the atomic bomb had been dropped. The Rus-

sians disarmed the Japanese army in Manchuria following the surrender of Japan and turned their arms
and equipment over to the Chinese Communists.

B. The United Nations Organizations emerged from a conference of fifty world powers meeting in San Francisco from
April 25 to June 26, 1945.

   1. The San Francisco Conference developed from a series
   of earlier conferences concerned with relief for war
   refugees and international financial and monetary
   problems.

   2. As established by its charter, the United Nations was
   composed of three major parts at the top level: the General Assembly, the Security Council, and the International Court of Justice.

      a. The General Assembly, in which each member na-
      tion of the United Nations holds one vote, acts as the
      major policy making forum.

      b. The Security Council, whose function is to supervise
      action on military and political problems, has eleven
      members. Five members are permanent, and the re-
      maining six members rotate.

      c. Decisions by the Security Council must be supported
      by all permanent members and by two rotating mem-
      bers. In effect, each permanent member of the Se-
      curity Council can veto any action of the council, ex-
      cept procedural matters.

      d. The third major part of the United Nations is the
      International Court of Justice. It is the principal
      judicial body established by the U.N. charter. All
      United Nation members belong to the Court which
      consists of fifteen judges. Sessions are held in the
      Hague.

   3. At the secondary level in the United Nations are the Sec-
   retariat and such agencies as the Relief and Rehabilita-
   tion Administration.

      a. The primary function of the Secretariat is to handle
      administrative work of the U.N.; it is directed by a
      Secretary General.

      b. The Relief and Rehabilitation Administration
      (UNRRA) forestalled starvation for millions in the
      years following the war. Agencies such as the Interna-
      tional Children's Emergency Fund (UNICEF) and the

Educational, Scientific, and Cultural Organization (UNESCO) have carried out many programs seeking to relieve hardship and promote international good will.

4. At the end of 1961, the United Nations embraced one hundred four sovereign states in its membership.

C. In July and August, 1945, occurred the Potsdam Conference. Representing the United States was President Harry Truman (President Roosevelt had died suddenly April 12, 1945). Great Britain at first was represented by Prime Minister Churchill. During the conference, however, the British Labour Party won the elections, and the Labour leader, Clement Atlee, replaced Churchill. Stalin spoke for Russia.

1. The Potsdam Conference was marked by much more extensive disagreement than Yalta had been.

2. Nevertheless, Stalin won recognition for most of the satellite states even though their Communist-dominated governments had not been made more democratic by the admission of non-Communists and had not held free elections.

3. It was also agreed that the U.S.S.R. could occupy Korea north of the thirty-eighth parallel while the Americans would occupy it south of that line.

4. Questions unresolved at Potsdam were left to a conference of foreign ministers. In December, 1945, the Council of Foreign Ministers met. Almost every issue resolved was settled in favor of the demands made by the U.S.S.R. in regard to eastern Europe.

D. One of the first major problems considered by the United Nations was control of atomic energy.

1. The United States and Great Britain proposed a United Nations Atomic Energy Commission in 1945, and the Soviet Union agreed.

2. In March, 1946, Bernard Baruch, the American representative on the UNAEC, presented a plan to control the uses of atomic energy.

   a. To insure effective control, the proposed International Atomic Development Authority was to be given the means to inspect atomic raw materials and production facilities throughout the world.

   b. The Russians, as they have ever since, adamantly refused to accept inspection. When the General As-

sembly voted forty to six in favor of the Baruch proposal, the Soviet Union vetoed the first major attempt
to establish international control of atomic energy.

XII. Communist Expansion and the Defense of the West

A. Soviet military occupation of eastern Europe enabled the
Communists to consolidate their leadership in that
area. In 1948, the Communists executed a *coup d'état* in
Czechoslovakia.
   1. The Communists had obtained about forty per cent of
   the popular vote and gained control of the unions in
   many of the leading industries. One of their members
   held the cabinet position which gave them control of the
   police.
   2. A series of carefully planned strikes and demonstrations
   convinced Beneš and Masaryk, the Czech leaders, that
   they must step aside for Klement Gottwald, the Communist leader, who became dictator.

B. Soviet domination was often maintained, however, only by
violent repression of serious popular uprisings. The power
of the Red Army proved to be almost as indispensable to
the endurance of several of the satellite regimes as it had
been to their establishment.
   1. The Communists promised reforms to the populations
   of the satellite countries. Sometimes the reforms were
   achieved, but often they were not, and living standards
   were frequently very low. But almost everywhere Communist control meant more severe restrictions on individual freedom than satellite populations had previously endured.
   2. Trade treaties between the satellite states and the Soviet
   Union often produced economic hardships for the people of eastern Europe. The Communists restricted and
   sometimes prohibited trade with western European
   countries. This practice led to economic difficulties for
   many of the satellites.
   3. Discontent was manifested in low output from factories
   and farms and by a steady flow of refugees to western
   Europe. The workers of east Germany rose in open revolt in June, 1953. The uprising was so serious that the

East German Communist police lost control, and order was restored by Russian armored divisions.

4. In Poland, the summer and fall of 1956 witnessed a series of strikes and demonstrations which brought promises from the U.S.S.R. that Soviet troops would no longer interfere directly in Poland's internal affairs.

   a. Russia also cancelled Polish debts to the U.S.S.R. and loaned the Poles one hundred seventy-five million dollars.

   b. The Polish government, led by Wladyslaw Gomulka, remained Communist, but was no longer so completely dominated by the U.S.S.R. No longer, for example, was a general of the Russian army to be the Polish Minister of Defense.

5. Encouraged by Polish success, Hungarians demonstrated against Soviet control of their government. Soviet troops and Soviet controlled secret police fired into the crowds and precipitated the bloody and tragic Hungarian uprising which began October 23, 1956.

   a. The Hungarians fought the Soviet puppet regime with such ferocity that the Russian forces were withdrawn from Budapest, the capital city.

   b. Pretending to negotiate with the rebel leaders, the Russians secretly reinforced the Red Army units and treacherously seized the rebel leaders during the negotiations.

   c. The Red Army then opened a full-scale attack on Budapest and finally regained control, putting a new puppet, Janos Kadar, at the head of the government.

   d. Large-scale resistance to the Russians was crushed by mid-November though fighting continued into January. About sixty-five thousand Hungarians are thought to have been killed fighting the Russians. One hundred seventy-five thousand more fled to western Europe, and how many additional thousands were deported to Russia in sealed trains is unknown west of the Iron Curtain.

   e. Several neutral governments denounced Russia's bloody repression of the Hungarians, and the U.N. later censured the Soviet action, but no major power actively interfered to help the Hungarians.

6. The Hungarian uprising presented the Communists with

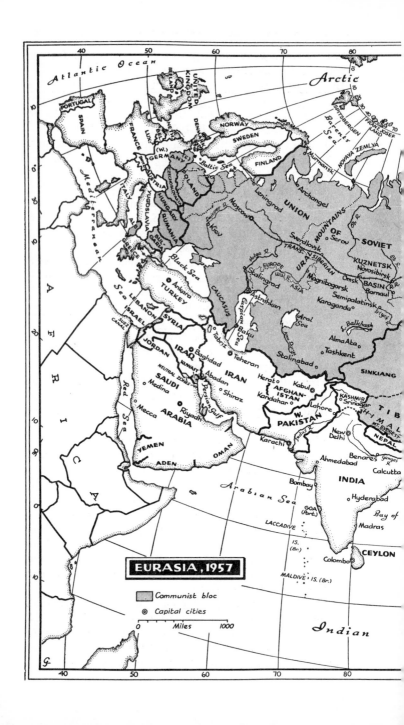

EURASIA, 1957

Communist bloc

◎ Capital cities

0   Miles   1000

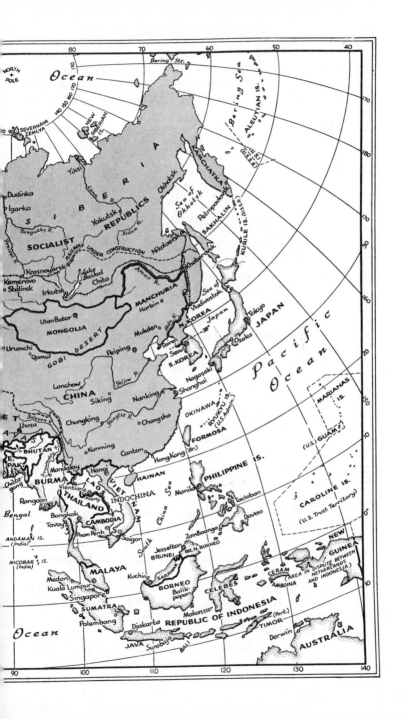

a nasty dilemma. If the U.S.S.R. made serious concessions to the Hungarians, other subject peoples might follow the line taken by Poland and Hungary; and Russia would risk losing control of its satellites. If the uprising was crushed, satellite discontent with Soviet domination would be displayed to all the non-Communist world. The U.S.S.R. chose to maintain its control regardless of the cost.

7. The Russians faced another type of problem in trying to maintain their control of Yugoslavia and Albania.

   a. Russian support had enabled the Communist partisan leader, Josip Broz Tito, to establish his dictatorship over Yugoslavia in 1944.

   b. Rival partisans were executed and a Communist-run election prevented King Peter from returning.

   c. But Tito's resentment of Russian control grew with his strength; and in 1948, he took Yugoslavia out of the Soviet bloc.

   d. Tito strengthened Yugoslavia's position by signing a Mutual Defense Treaty (1953) with Greece and Turkey.

   e. The western nations had been quick to exploit Russia's difficulty, making loans and trading privileges available to Yugoslavia. By 1953, the Russians were seeking to restore some of their influence by reestablishing diplomatic relations with Tito's regime.

   f. Tito was trying to profit from the rivalry of the two power blocs by seeking favors from both sides. Such neutralism usually requires great skill but can be very profitable for a nation which can manage it successfully.

   g. Albania broke with Russia in 1961 when Premier Enver Hoxha forced the pro-Khrushchev elements out of the Albanian Communist Party and announced that Albania henceforth would look to Communist China for leadership.

   h. Hoxha forced the Russians to give up their submarine base (Saseno) on the Albanian coast, and they cancelled their wheat shipments to Albania.

   i. Red China, however, promised to supply the wheat Albania had expected from Russia and granted the Albanians a sizeable five year loan.

j. In December, 1961, Russia and Albania severed diplomatic relations.

8. Since the Russians had made it possible for the Communists to gain control in China and Albania, it was hardly reassuring to Moscow to see China rival Russian leadership and begin to gain followers from the Soviet satellite bloc.

C. The western nations tried to reverse the spread of Communism and Russian influence by political, economic, and military measures. The United States, the only western power with the essential financial resources took the lead.

1. In 1947, the "Truman Doctrine" was set forth. The United States undertook to support peoples who would resist "attempted subjugation." Four hundred million dollars were loaned to Greece and Turkey to aid them in resisting Russian attempts to use them as stepping stones to control of the Straits.

2. The Marshall Plan (European Recovery Program) was approved by Congress in 1948 and authorized the expenditure of about seventeen billion dollars in the period 1948 through 1952.

   a. The European Recovery Program aimed at stimulating production in the countries receiving aid.

   b. It was assumed that increased production would relieve misery and discontent and enable the aided countries to resist Communism.

   c. The Marshall plan was a great success in restoring the European economy. Most nations of western Europe were producing more in 1952 than they had in 1938.

   d. The voting strength of Communist parties in the western European nations, however, did not decline greatly even though unemployment almost ended.

   e. By 1953, few observers were worried about any western European nation joining the Soviet bloc.

D. The western nations soon realized that the Russians respected strength above all. This realization led to extensive action to achieve collective military security.

1. A series of alliances led to the creation in 1949 of the North Atlantic Treaty Organization (NATO).

   a. NATO fused the defense of the United States, Canada, Britain, France, the Netherlands, Belgium, Luxembourg, Italy, Denmark, Norway, Iceland, and

Portugal against any attack on their territories in Europe, North Africa, or North America.

b. To support NATO, the United States enacted the Mutual Defense Assistance Program to grant about one billion dollars per year to members of NATO. When the Korean War began (1950), this amount was quadrupled.

2. The primary purpose of NATO was to create and maintain a force capable of holding back the Red Army, which was estimated to be one hundred seventy-five combat divisions which could quickly be expanded to three hundred divisions.

3. The changing conditions of Germany, however, forced the architects of NATO to remodel their plans.

a. In 1949, the U.S.S.R. changed its occupation zone in Germany to the "German Democratic Republic," usually referred to as East Germany.

b. The western states joined their occupation zones to create the Federal Republic of Germany, ordinarily known as West Germany.

c. West German industrial resources and manpower were needed for NATO, but the French refused to sanction German rearmament.

d. A new plan, the European Defense Community, was worked out and was accepted by the French cabinet; but the National Assembly (including ninety-nine Communist members) refused to ratify the plan.

e. The Nine Power Conference which met in London in the fall of 1954 was ably guided by British Foreign Secretary Anthony Eden and worked out a solution bringing West Germany into NATO under conditions suitable to all the NATO members.

4. By 1961, NATO, under the command of the American General Louis Norstad, included about thirty combat divisions supported by air and naval units. Since the NATO members had never planned a force of over fifty divisions, the units existing in 1961 represented a considerable accomplishment.

5. The concern of each member state of NATO for its own national interests and the constant change of conditions in Europe make the maintenance and command of NATO a difficult task, but the U.S.S.R. has not made a

direct military attack on any NATO member in the fourteen year existence of the alliance.

E. As the western European nations regained economic strength with the aid of the Marshall Plan, they began to move toward <u>integration of the whole west European economy.</u>

1. In 1950, <u>Robert Schuman,</u> the French foreign minister, proposed the establishment of a single authority to manage all the coal and steel production of western Europe.

   a. Schuman hoped that eventually all tariff barriers to European trade would be abolished. His plan was to start toward that goal in the basic coal and iron industries.

   b. By 1953, the plan was ratified by six nations (France, West Germany, Italy, Belgium, the Netherlands, and Luxembourg). These nations formed the <u>European Economic Community (EEC, or Common Market)</u> and adopted a longer range plan to establish a free trade area among themselves.

2. The coal and steel program worked out so well that other western states began to follow suit.

   a. <u>The European Free Trade Association</u> was established by seven nations (Great Britain, Austria, Denmark, Norway, Portugal, Sweden, and Switzerland). These nations each cut their tariffs ten per cent on the products of members of the EFTA.

   b. <u>The members of the EEC came to be known as the "Inner Six" and those of the EFTA as the "Outer Seven."</u>

3. As the EEC and the EFTA began to function with increasing effectiveness, member states of each group found the common tariff policies of the other group interfered with previously established trade.

4. In 1961, it appeared that the "Inner Six" were about to be involved in a trade war with the "Outer Seven."

   a. In August, 1961, however, Great Britain applied for admission to the EEC; and Denmark soon took the same action.

   b. This was an historic step for Britain which had traditionally avoided such economic ties to the continent because of her economic relations with the British Commonwealth of Nations.

      c. Other members of the EFTA were urged to join the EEC, but Switzerland and Sweden feared such a step would endanger their strict neutrality.

  5. So far, the EEC has been a resounding success; and its members enjoy the most prosperous economic conditions in their history. In 1961, they agreed to abolish all tariff barriers within the EEC four years sooner than was originally planned.

  6. The success of the EEC impressed the Russians who, in 1961, began a new program using economic ties to bind the satellites still more tightly to Russia.

      a. The Soviet's Council of Mutual Economic Assistance (COMECON) encouraged each satellite to specialize in producing one commodity not in competition with any other satellite.

      b. The COMECON program aims at keeping all Soviet satellites economically interdependent. All the plans for COMECON and all its marketing arrangements are made in Moscow. Each satellite is told what product to make in what quantities and to whom to sell it at what price.

F. The continued tension between the U.S.S.R. and the west is referred to as the "cold war." Characterized by political, economic, and diplomatic struggles, the risks have increased as new weapons of destruction have been developed without any practical means of controlling their use.

  1. The cold war suddenly became hot when the Communists invaded South Korea (June, 1950) and touched off the Korean War.

      a. At the Potsdam conference it was decided that Russia would occupy Korea north of the thirty-eighth parallel and American units would occupy the country south of that line.

      b. The Russians refused to allow inspectors to enter their zone of Korea at any time before the war. American occupying forces were withdrawn from South Korea at the request of the United Nations. Soviet officials insisted Russia had no troops in North Korea but refused to let any outside agency or individual verify their assertion by actual inspection.

      c. At the time of the invasion, the Russians were boycotting the U.N. The U.N. voted to support South

Korea against North Korean aggression, and the Russians were not present to use their vote.

d. The forces supporting South Korea carried the United Nations flag. Most of the troops were Americans although there were valuable detachments supplied by America's allies in the cold war.

e. The United Nations forces drove the invaders back into North Korea, and then about two million Chinese Communist "volunteers" entered the war and pushed the U.N. forces back to a line close to the thirty-eighth parallel.

f. An armistice signed in July, 1953 did little to change the situation that prevailed before the war. The Communist's aggression had cost thousands of lives and created widespread misery. The gulf between Communists and the anti-Communist bloc only increased.

g. The Republic of Korea (really South Korea) continued under the heavy-handed leadership of President Syngman Rhee. Forced from office by popular protests against coercion in connection with the elections of March, 1960, Rhee left the country four months later.

h. The new government, led by John M. Chang, seemed unable to cope with Korea's economic problems; and a military junta, directed by General Park Chung Hee seized control May 16, 1961.

i. General Park suppressed civil liberties and announced an austerity program to bolster Korea's sagging economy. He promised military rule would end in two years with general elections in May, 1963 and a return to civilian government.

2. With the American announcement in November, 1952, that they had successfully tested a hydrogen bomb, the problem of international control of such powerful weapons became more acute. In August, 1953, the U.S.S.R. announced it had also tested the H-bomb.

a. The United States and the western European nations consistently stipulated that any disarmament program or plan for international control of such weapons be enforced by inspection teams.

b. The U.S.S.R. has constantly harangued the world with various disarmament schemes, but it has always refused any plan which might expose its nuclear activities to international inspection.

c. Negotiations between the western bloc and the Soviet bloc have repeatedly broken down on the inspection issue. The Russians refused the Baruch proposal (1946), the Eisenhower proposal for "open sky" inspection by aerial photography (1957), and every proposal offered at the Geneva conference on methods of detecting nuclear explosions (1958).

d. The problem has been made even more serious by the development of the intercontinental ballistic missile (ICBM) as a means for delivering a hydrogen bomb to its target. So far, no really effective defense against such weapons has appeared.

e. While the United States tried to promote some system of international control, it sought to protect itself by reconnaissance flights of a special type of long range, high altitude plane, the "U-2."

f. On May 1, 1960, a U-2 plane crashed in Russia. The Russians' reaction was to break up the summit conference on disarmament at Paris on May 16. American prestige suffered considerably, and the world was still without international control of atomic and nuclear weapons.

g. Two more conferences in Geneva in 1961 brought neither disarmament nor an end to nuclear testing. The Russians continued to refuse any sort of international inspection.

3. Another aspect of the cold war was the battle between the U.S.A. and the U.S.S.R. to gain prestige and power by successful flights into space.

a. The Russians gained an early lead in this contest by the first successful launching of an earth satellite October 4, 1957. "Sputnik I," as they called it, was large enough to be seen as it orbited the earth.

b. Sputnik I made a tremendous impression on world opinion of Russia's accomplishments. Many promptly assumed the U.S.S.R. was the world's greatest power.

c. America's first attempts to launch a satellite failed; but on January 31, 1958, the United States Army fired the "Explorer" into orbit. It was equipped with instruments to report on cosmic rays, meteorites, and temperatures.

d. In the next three years the Russians and the Americans fired all sorts of hardware into space. The Russians scored another victory by hitting the moon (September, 1959) and photographing the side of the moon opposite the earth (October, 1959).

e. In 1961, both nations succeeded in launching men into space and recovering them apparently unharmed, but the Russians were first again.

f. On April 12, the Russian <u>Yuri Gagarin</u> circled the earth in one hour and forty-eight minutes. Twenty-three days later, the American astronaut Alan B. Shepard successfully completed a sub-orbital flight. In July, the Americans put Virgil I. Grissom through a flight very similar to Shepard's.

g. On August 6, 1961, <u>Gherman Titov</u> circled the earth seventeen times in a Russian space vehicle; and on February 20, 1962, the American <u>John Glenn</u> made three complete orbits of the earth. On May 24, M. Scott Carpenter, Jr., another American astronaut, duplicated Glenn's feat and carried out additional experiments.

h. While the Russians were apparently the first to accomplish these feats, their flights were launched and made secretly. The Americans carried out their flights in a glare of publicity that left no room to doubt their authenticity nor any chance to conceal a failure.

i. Both nations are racing to land a man on the moon. President Kennedy expects the United States to put a man on the moon by 1970 at an estimated cost of forty billion dollars.

G. The internal development of the most important European states since World War II has been largely determined by their efforts to solve internal problems and meet the pressures of the cold war.

1. The victory of the Labour Party in Great Britain in 1945 led to the nationalization of several major industries and the adoption of an austerity program to increase the profits from export trade.

a. In 1951, the Conservative Party, led by Winston

Churchill, returned to power. The Conservatives retained most of the Labour policies and convinced the English voters that their administration was more effective than that of the Labour Party.

b. Sir Anthony Eden succeeded Churchill in 1955 and served as the Conservative leader until 1957, when Harold Macmillan took the post, which he still holds.

c. As of 1962, Great Britain is enjoying an unprecedented prosperity and is probably America's most dependable ally in the struggle with Russia.

2. The West German Federal Republic became a sovereign state in 1955 and a full partner in NATO. Chancellor Konrad Adenauer continued to press for the reunification of Germany. As of 1962, the U.S.S.R. has been able to prevent reunification in spite of British and American support for Adenauer.

a. German rearmament ran into bitter opposition from the German people. The government had to accept a smaller force trained for a shorter period of time than it had anticipated.

b. Germany has been the scene of some of the most serious crises of the cold war. In April, 1948, the Russians tried to force the other occupying powers out of Berlin by closing all the land routes to the city which lay within the Soviet occupation zone in Germany.

c. The Americans organized the Berlin airlift, supplied the city by air for several months, and the Russians ended the blockade.

d. In 1961, the Russians tried to force the western nations to recognize East Germany as a sovereign state by exerting pressure on Berlin again. The western allies prepared to fight for the city, and thousands of refugees fled from East Germany to the western sector of Berlin.

e. To stop the flow of refugees, the Communists built a wall separating the eastern zone of Berlin from the western zone. Soviet pressure was gradually relaxed, and the crisis passed.

f. Chancellor Adenauer has proven to be a staunch friend of the western powers, but he will be eighty-five years old in 1962. The western bloc is concerned about who his successor may be and how West Germany's role may be affected by the change.

3. Following World War II, the Fourth French Republic made a reasonably successful economic recovery; but it fell back into the pattern of constant cabinet change which had so seriously weakened the government of the Third Republic.

   a. General Charles de Gaulle was asked to form a cabinet and took office June 1, 1958. He was given full powers to draft a constitution which would strengthen the government.

   b. De Gaulle's new constitution was presented to the French voters in September, and they voted to adopt it by a four-to-one margin. In elections held in December they chose de Gaulle as the first president of the Fifth French Republic.

   c. The new constitution greatly increased the power of the president and curbed the power of the political parties to delay the work of the National Assembly.

4. Soviet Russia faced a serious internal crisis when Joseph Stalin died in 1953. He was apparently succeeded by Georgi Malenkov, but actually a series of changes at the top level of the government and the Communist Party was just beginning.

   a. Lavrenti Beria, who controlled the secret police under Stalin, was mysteriously executed without trial in December, 1953. Many observers had thought Beria would be the real dictator of Russia when Stalin died.

   b. By July, 1957, Nikita S. Khrushchev, First Secretary of the Communist Party, emerged as the new ruler of the Soviet Union. Those who had opposed him were pushed out of important positions along with some who had supported him but were potential rivals.

   c. As the leader of the Soviet Union, Khrushchev has proven to be at least as able as Stalin. His direction of foreign policy has been more flexible and subtle than Stalin's, and he seems much more skillful in creating and manipulating world opinion than Stalin ever was.

   d. Basically, Russian objectives seem to have changed little since Stalin's death; and the U.S.S.R. still suffers from many of the same internal problems, in particular, the inadequate production of consumer goods.

e. Khrushchev, in 1962, continues to have trouble with the collectivization of agriculture. The Communists have been in power in Russia for forty-five years, and it seems worth considering why the rulers of a nation which can shoot rockets around the moon cannot provide enough for their people to eat.

BIBLIOGRAPHY

Brzezinski, Z. K., *The Soviet bloc: unity and conflict* (Cambridge: Harvard University Press, 1960).

Churchill, W. S., *The Second World War,* 6 vols. (Boston: Houghton Mifflin, 1948–1953).

Dallin, D. J., *The new Soviet empire* (New Haven: Yale University Press, 1951).

Eisenhower, D. D., *Crusade in Europe* (New York: Doubleday, 1948).

Feis, H., *Churchill, Roosevelt and Stalin* (Princeton: Princeton University Press, 1957).

Fuller, J. F. C., *The Second World War* (New York: Duell, Sloane, and Pearce, 1949).

Hersey, J., *Hiroshima* (New York: Knopf, 1946).

Kennan, G. F., *Russia, the atom, and the west* (New York: Harper, 1958).

Lettis, R. and Morris, W. E., *The Hungarian revolt* (New York: Scribner's, 1961).

Monsarrat, N., *The cruel sea* (New York: Knopf, 1951).

Wilmot, C., *The struggle for Europe* (New York: Harper, 1952).

Chapter 16

THE UNDERDEVELOPED AREAS: REVOLT AGAINST IMPERIALISM

I. The Reaction to Imperialism and the West

A. <u>A strong reaction to imperialism has characterized developments in many areas since World War II.</u> This reaction has been both political and economic and has occurred quite peacefully in some areas and as violent revolution in others.

   1. The development of strong national feeling, which occurred in most western countries in the nineteenth century, has taken place in most of the underdeveloped areas in the mid-twentieth century.

      a. This new nationalism very frequently was a reaction against western imperialism of the nineteenth century and was directed particularly against the French and British.

      b. Germany, Italy, and Russia had also been imperialist powers; but Germany and Italy lost their colonies in the two World Wars, and the Russian Revolution enabled the Communists to disassociate themselves with earlier Russian imperialism.

   2. Nationalism in the underdeveloped areas, therefore, gave the Soviet Union an advantage over the western bloc in its relations with the new nations of Asia and Africa.

B. <u>Economic circumstances also favored relations between these areas and the U.S.S.R.</u>

   1. Almost all the new states wanted to industrialize to raise their standards of living. Industrialization requires capital which they lacked. It was possible to borrow foreign capital, but foreign capital was too closely associated in their memories with the imperialism they hated.

2. Almost the only modern nation which had industrialized in the twentieth century without relying on huge foreign investments was Soviet Russia. The Russians had made terrible sacrifices, including the western concept of freedom, but they had made the grade. So, many of the new nations looked at the Soviet example as they laid their economic plans.

II. India and Pakistan

A. When the British Labour Party won the elections at the end of World War II, they promised to grant India independence.

1. As the Hindu Congress Party and the All-India Moslem League tried to draw up a constitution, however, they found themselves in almost complete disagreement.

2. The Moslems had long favored, and the Hindus opposed, the partition of India into separate Hindu and Moslem states.

   a. In 1947, Hindu India and Moslem Pakistan were established as self-governing dominions within the British Commonwealth.

   b. Pakistan is divided into two parts, widely separated by intervening Hindu territory. West Pakistan is the larger, and the smaller East Pakistan is approximately the old territory of East Bengal.

   c. Pakistan has a population of about seventy-five million and far less industry than India. Since Pakistan is much weaker than India, it has tended to maintain closer ties with the Commonwealth and the western bloc than India.

   d. Even the fully independent Republic of India, established in 1950, however, has not tried to break all its ties to Great Britain. India still considers itself a member of what Indians call the "Commonwealth of Nations," but the adjective "British" is carefully omitted.

3. The partition of India was accompanied by fearful violence as Moslems were driven from Hindu India and Hindus from Pakistan. Fighting between communities of different faiths cost thousands of lives.

4. India and Pakistan quarreled over the mountainous re-

gion of <u>Kashmir</u>. The Indian army occupied Kashmir; and, in 1957, Kashmir adopted a constitution as a state of India. By 1962, Pakistan still refused to accept that settlement; and the disagreement continues.

B. <u>India has used a series of "Five Year Plans" in attempting to solve its economic problems.</u> Unlike the Soviet model, however, India has accepted extensive foreign aid from the World Bank and from both the U.S.S.R. and the U.S.A.

1. The government has tried to encourage industrialization and increase agricultural production by irrigation projects and the use of modern agricultural methods.

2. Indian production is trying to run a race with the population explosion, and starvation is nothing rare. Inflation wrecked the second Five Year Plan in 1959, and the country still faces serious economic problems.

C. <u>Prime Minister Jawaharlal Nehru has tried the difficult task of establishing India as a mediator between the Communists and the western bloc.</u> This role is flattering to Indian self-esteem and beneficial to the Indian economy so long as both sides seek Indian support by extending loans and aid.

1. In 1955, Nehru helped to arrange the Bandung African-Asian Conference of twenty-nine states. Nehru and the Chinese Premier, Chou En-lai, hoped to swing the Arab states and the new Asiatic nations away from the western democracies and into closer collaboration with the Communist bloc.

2. Many of the Arab states did not welcome close ties with Russia; and Pakistan, Ceylon, and the Philippines objected so strongly that the plan was dropped.

3. In 1959, Nehru was alarmed by the Chinese conquest of Tibet. To make matters worse, the Chinese claimed several thousand square miles of border territory which India regarded as its own. The border dispute remains unsettled.

4. In 1961, Nehru ordered the Indian army to invade three small Portuguese-held territories in India: Goa, Damao, and Diu. Since there was little justification for India's action, the Indian pose as mediator and moral arbiter of world affairs suffered considerably.

D. While Pakistan has kept closer ties with the western bloc than India, it, too, has worked both sides of the international street, receiving aid from Russia as well as the United States. Like India's, Pakistan's economy is constantly threatened by overpopulation. Political instability led to the establishment of a military government directed by General Mohammed Ayub Khan in 1957. A new constitution has been drafted, substituting a president for the cabinet system originally used. General elections and a return to civilian government are planned for 1962.

III. China

A. At the end of World War II, the United States hoped to see a democratic government established in China, representing both Chiang Kai-shek's Nationalists and the Communists. In such an arrangement the Communists, led by Mao Tse-tung, would have been a large minority party, as in France or Italy.

B. By 1946, however, an American diplomatic mission led by General Marshall reported such hopes could not be realized.

   1. Civil war was breaking out in China, and the Communists were receiving vigorous support from Russia, which supplied them with arms taken from the Japanese.

   2. Chiang's government was losing its popular support and could not restrain a runaway inflation which intensified economic hardships caused by the war with Japan.

   3. The Communist military successes forced Chiang and his supporters to leave the Chinese mainland in 1949. Chiang's group established the capital of the Republic of China on the island of Formosa.

   4. The Communists proclaimed the "People's Republic of China," but some nations, notably the United States, refused to extend diplomatic recognition to the Communist state (Red China). Chiang's Republic of China still represents China in the United Nations although many attempts have been made to give China's seat in the U.N. to the Communists. Chiang's forces remain poised on Formosa, hoping for an opportunity to invade and reconquer the mainland.

C. The Communists were apparently very successful in selling their program to China's vast population.

   1. The Communists convinced the Chinese that soldiers,

formerly considered the scum of the earth in China, were vital to the welfare of the people and were working with the peasants to achieve common goals. Popular acceptance of this idea enabled the Communists to build a very powerful army.

2. The new government told the people that it was the Communists who had liberated China from Japan and that popular support for Communism would bring about the destruction of western imperialism if all the people —peasants, workers, intellectuals, soldiers—would work together to create a new China.

3. The Communists destroyed "extraterritoriality," the right various powers had enjoyed by which an accused foreigner was tried by the laws of his own country for a crime committed in China.

4. The old ties to the west were replaced by new bonds to the U.S.S.R.

5. Another very popular idea the Communists emphasized was land reform. A strenuous effort was made to give every peasant his own plot, even if it was only three or four acres.

    a. This policy was reversed within a few years, but it was very popular when initiated and helped the Communists gain popular support immediately following the revolution.

    b. Since China was only partly industrialized, peasants outnumbered workers. The Chinese Communists changed the party line, temporarily, to insist that peasants, not workers, were the class whose interests must be advanced by the revolution.

D. As Red China developed, it appeared in some respects similar to Soviet Russia's history in the decades following the Russian revolution. Reliable information on China's internal affairs is very scarce.

1. China has had a series of Five Year Plans, but they seem to have been less successful than the Russians were. Chinese economic planning appears to change so rapidly that its efficiency is questionable. In 1958, for example, a tremendous drive was made to increase steel production by using thousands of small "backyard" furnaces; in 1959, the effort was abandoned as "inefficient."

2. Like Stalin, Chairman Mao Tse-tung "purged" undesir-

ables from the ranks in 1955. At times, the Chinese Communists have permitted expression of a variety of views, but any dissent was vigorously crushed in other periods.

3. <u>In 1955, the Chinese Reds began collectivizing agriculture like the Russians had in the 1930's.</u> This was a direct reversal of their earlier land reform program.

   a. The Chinese went further than the Russians by creating "communes." Members of the commune live in barracks, men separated from women; the children of families brought into the commune are separated from their parents because both parents work. Eating is done in large mess halls, and normal family life is almost completely destroyed.

   b. The Chinese government maintained ninety per cent of all residents of rural areas lived in communes in 1958. People who resisted joining communes were sent to slave labor camps. Commune workers receive no wages; they are given a uniform and shoes and four-fifths of the food they need; they get additional food only by working beyond a set minimum standard. The average commune includes the members of seven thousand families.

   c. By 1959, however, the Chinese Communists began breaking up the communes; family life was restored and each family was permitted a garden and livestock.

4. As of 1962, Red China's economy is mysterious to outsiders. The Chinese admitted, in 1959, that their 1958 production figures had been exaggerated to encourage the workers and peasants.

   a. The government has admitted famine is widespread in China; but it is blamed on floods, drought, and insects. Refugees describe famines and cholera epidemics.

   b. Like many Asian countries, China's economy is constantly threatened by overpopulation. Economic assistance from Russia seems to have fallen short of Chinese expectations.

   c. One thing is clear. In 1962, the British erected an elaborate barbed wire entanglement to stem the flow of refugees crowding into Hong Kong; and thousands of Chinese "volunteers" captured in the Korean War refused to return home.

E. <u>Red China's foreign policy has consistently been extremely aggressive.</u>
   1. The Chinese have given strong support to any group resisting western influence in southeast Asia. Chinese power was critical in driving the French from Indo-China.
   2. <u>Red China played a vigorous role in the Korean War</u> although it was not officially among the belligerent powers.
   3. In 1956, the Chinese tried to seize territory from Burma along their common border. China finally withdrew its troops in the face of Burmese resistance probably aided by diplomatic pressure from Russia and India.
   4. <u>In 1959, the Chinese conquered Tibet</u> and occupied about twelve thousand square miles of territory along the Indian border. India claimed the territory as its own and prepared for war. As of 1962, the Chinese still hold the disputed areas.

IV. The Post War Explosion in Southeast Asia

A. <u>During the war the initial successes of the Japanese and their occupation of southeast Asia destroyed the image of white supremacy.</u> The western powers granted outright independence or made substantial political concessions in most southeast Asian states shortly after World War II.
   1. The United States granted complete independence to the Filipinos, who proclaimed their new republic July 4, 1946.
   2. The Dutch were forced to consent to independence for most of their colonies in the East Indies, which formed the Republic of Indonesia in 1949.
   3. Burma became completely free of British control and left the Commonwealth, and the British made substantial concessions to the Malayan Federation.
   4. Vietnam, Cambodia, and Laos gained some liberties from the French after the war; these three states occupied the area formerly known as French Indo-China.
B. <u>Economic problems, however, were at least as serious as political issues in southeast Asia.</u> The major products of the new states are raw materials and food. With growing populations, they need some measure of industrialization to

support their people. They hate to be forced to accept economic aid from their former imperial masters, but the alternative may be economic chaos paving the way to Communist domination, which they also fear.

1. <u>French concessions in Indo-China were too little and too late.</u> In 1954, the French were driven out after a costly war and a humiliating defeat at <u>Dien Bien Phu.</u>

   a. Communist invasion and guerrilla warfare forced the partition of Vietnam.

   b. The northern portion of <u>Vietnam</u> became Communist. South Vietnam emerged as a weak republic supported by France and the United States.

   c. The Kingdom of <u>Laos</u> suffered from internal political division, encouraged, of course, by the Communists. In 1961 and 1962, the Communists exerted heavy military pressure on Laos, which received financial and open military support from the United States. The issue is undecided.

2. <u>Malaya was saved from Communist imperialism only by firm action by the British and the Malayan government.</u> Communist riots in Singapore were kept under control and the Communist guerrillas were driven off the Malayan plantations.

3. The government of <u>Thailand</u> succumbed to military control in 1958 to meet the Communist threat. A new constitution is being considered in 1962, but renewed military threats by the Communists place Thailand's plans in jeopardy.

4. <u>Cambodia</u> is playing the neutral game and receiving aid from both the western and Communist blocs.

5. These nations are located in an area often referred to as the "rice bowl of Asia." Red China wants food for her multiplying millions and is willing to go to extreme measures to get it.

6. <u>The Republic of Indonesia</u> held its first elections in 1955. The Nationalist Party secured the largest vote; the Moslem Masjumi Party was next and the Communists were third.

   a. Indonesia produces oil and rubber, which the U.S.S.R. wants.

   b. Indonesia has been trying to take over the western New Guinea area known as West Irian. When an appeal to the U.N. did not succeed, Indonesia resorted to force. Sporadic fighting was going on in 1962, but the issue remained unresolved.

   c. In 1960, President Sukarno, dissatisfied by resistance in parliament, installed a new government which concentrates the power in his hands and leaves the legislature with little more to do than approve his proposals.

   d. The Republic of Indonesia also seeks to get aid from both power blocs by playing a presumably neutral role; many westerners consider it pro-Soviet, however.

7. The Philippine republic carried out economic and social reforms under President Ramón Magsaysay, who rammed land reforms through the Philippine Congress despite objections from the landlords.

   a. Magsaysay was also largely responsible for defeating the Huk (Communist) guerrillas who terrorized parts of the islands.

   b. Magsaysay was killed in a plane crash in 1957 and was succeeded by Vice President Carlos P. Garcia.

   c. Garcia remained president until 1961 when Liberal Party voters elected Diosdado Macapagal president. Garcia's regime probably owed its defeat to Liberal charges of corruption.

   d. The Philippines have developed foreign trade with the southeast Asian countries to the point that it exceeds Philippine–U.S. trade, and exports exceed imports.

   e. The United States has continued economic support for the Philippine republic, which is one of the foremost leaders of the anti-Communist group of southeast Asian states.

8. While the Philippines and most of the southeast Asian states have their share of economic problems, they are not quite so pressed by overpopulation as India and China.

V. Post War Japan

A. Japan's economy was shattered by the war whose end found the emperor still on the throne with the government's authority in the hands of the occupying powers.

1. When the occupation ended (April, 1952), a new constitution went into effect providing a constitutional monarchy with a bicameral legislature and a bill of rights for
Japanese citizens.

2. The most successful Japanese political group so far, is
the Liberal Democratic Party, which favors the western
powers and rearmament.
   a. The Socialist party is cool to the west and wants nationalization of industry.
   b. The Japanese Communist Party opposes rearmament
   and has gained considerable influence among Japanese workers.

B. Communist aggression in the Far East pushed the Japanese
into a mutual security alliance with the United States in
1953; the alliance was revised and renewed in 1960.

1. Russia blocked Japanese entry into the United Nations
until a Russo-Japanese peace treaty was signed in 1956.

2. The Japanese economy recovered from the war with surprising speed and strength. By 1957, they played an important role in world commerce and were the world's
leaders in shipbuilding.

3. Japanese living standards are far below those of the west
but are the highest in Asia.
   a. Japan's own leaders are currently concerned that the
   country's economy is growing too fast.
   b. If Japanese exports do not increase even faster than
   its economy is growing, an economic crisis leading to
   depression might result.

VI. Australia and New Zealand

A. New Zealand's development since World War II has been
a peaceful and dignified continuation of westernization.

1. New Zealand's economy remains somewhat colonial in
that raw materials such as wool and frozen meats are
exported and most finished goods are imported.

2. The country can support its population easily and the
native Maoris have been gradually and smoothly integrated into the life of the dominion.

3. New Zealand is developing a social program, although
the country is by no means socialistic. A welfare pro-

gram to provide medical care was adopted as early as 1941.

B. Australia has gone farther than New Zealand toward becoming a welfare state, though not so far as Great Britain.
1. The leading political parties are Labor and the Liberals. Each has controlled the cabinet from time to time; and, currently, Australia's Prime Minister is Robert Menzies, the Liberal leader.
2. As of 1961, Australians were deeply concerned by rising unemployment. They have attempted to meet this problem by restricting immigration, which has been limited to Caucasians for many years. They are also trying to attract new industries which will provide jobs.

C. Australia and New Zealand are the west's real defense in depth against Communist expansion in and south of Asia.
1. Both states clearly illustrated their military strength in the two World Wars. Particularly in World War II, the fighting qualities of the "Aussies" and the "Anzacs" earned widespread respect.
2. Together with the Philippine republic, Australia and New Zealand are the backbone of the Southeast Asia Treaty Organization (SEATO).
   a. In addition to those three states, SEATO includes Pakistan, Thailand, France, Great Britain, and the United States.
   b. It was hoped SEATO could be modeled on NATO and operate the same way. So far, SEATO is far less powerful than NATO.
3. Australia and New Zealand are both tempting targets for overpopulated Asian nations which are very interested in those great uncrowded lands with their developing industries and their agricultural resources.

VII. The Middle East Since World War II

A. In the rapidly changing Middle Eastern scene political considerations seem to be the most frequent cause for change, but other factors contributed to the turbulence.
1. The Middle East contains vast oil reserves, and there is constant struggle to determine who will develop it and reap the profits.
2. Hostility between the Jews and Arabs aggravated by the

creation of the new state of Israel, has played a major role in causing several serious crises.

3. The desire to unify the Middle East into one great Arab state has often produced revolution and international crisis in the area.

B. As in southeast Asia, a wave of liberation followed World War II, and new, completely independent states emerged.

1. Syria and Lebanon threw off their French mandates.

2. The British withdrew from Palestine in 1948.

a. The western portion of Palestine became the new state of Israel.

b. The eastern areas were annexed by Transjordan, which changed its name to the Hashemite Kingdom of Jordan ("Hashemite" is the name of Jordan's ruling dynasty).

3. In 1956, Sudan, located in Africa on the upper Nile but tied by interest and language to the Arab world, became independent. It had been jointly ruled by Britain and Egypt for half a century.

4. Egypt had been proclaimed an independent monarchy in 1922, but the British retained the right to station troops in Egypt and foreigners enjoyed special privileges.

a. In 1936, an Anglo-Egyptian agreement provided for an eventual end to foreigners' privileges and withdrawal of British forces.

b. In 1952, Egyptian nationalists, dissatisfied with corruption in the regime of King Farouk and his close ties with the British, carried out a revolution which ultimately placed an Egyptian army officer, Gamal Abdul Nasser, in power.

C. The internal development of some Middle Eastern states has been particularly important for the area since the war.

1. Nasser's regime in Egypt is republican in form but, to a considerable degree, totalitarian in action.

a. Egypt's most pressing problems seem to be economic. About twenty-two million Egyptians try to live in a land which is ninety-five per cent desert; in terms of its productive resources, Egypt is probably the most overpopulated nation on earth.

b. The government has planned vast new irrigation projects, including the Aswan Dam across the Nile.

It has promoted birth control to try to reduce overpopulation.

c. Nasser has made bartering arrangements with foreign powers, trading Egyptian cotton for foreign goods. Unfortunately, purchases of armaments from satellite Czechoslovakia appeal to Egyptian nationalists but do little to increase the standard of living.

d. Oil was discovered in the Sinai Peninsula, and construction of a large refinery to process it began in 1955.

e. Nasser has had some success utilizing a neutral pose to get aid from both the east and west.

f. In 1958, Egypt joined Syria in forming the United Arab Republic. Each retained autonomy over its own "province," but Egypt clearly dominated the new joint cabinet and parliament.

g. The United Arab Republic was formed partly from fear of Communist penetration of Syria. Relations between the U.A.R. and the Soviet Union became very strained in 1959, and western aid and influence increased.

h. In 1961, Syria revolted and left the U.A.R., but Egypt continued to call itself the United Arab Republic.

i. During the past year, the United Arab Republic has continued a program of nationalizing commerce and industry, limiting individual incomes and ownership of stocks and land. Nasser has asserted that these steps will produce an "Arab, socialist, cooperative" state.

2. Turkey, supported by American military and economic aid, is probably the most reliable of America's allies in the Middle East.

a. The Turks are clearly aware that the centuries-old Russian desire to control the Straits is still a real threat.

b. Turkey has been trying to achieve the goals established by Kemal Ataturk before World War II.

c. The government has built roads and schools and is building more; it has completed several extensive hydroelectric projects and has plans for increasing industrialization.

d. Some of the earlier religious reforms have been dropped to overcome conservative opposition.

e. The first free post war elections occurred in 1950. By 1956, however, the government of <u>Premier Adam Menderes</u> curbed the opposition parties by muzzling the press and banning public meetings.

f. By 1957, the Turkish economy was in trouble from mismanagement and inflation, which created difficulties in the search for more foreign aid to extend industrialization.

g. In 1960, the army toppled the Menderes regime, placing Menderes and many of his party leaders under arrest.

h. A new constitution was approved in May, 1961. Elections the following October resulted in a coalition government headed by <u>General Cemal Gursel.</u>

i. The new government has adopted an austerity program to combat inflation and reduce the public debt.

3. <u>The new state of Israel quickly secured recognition from the United Nations</u> but found itself at war with the Arabs (the Palestinian War of 1948).

a. The Jews were greatly outnumbered, but the Arabs never put a united army in the field nor matched Israeli morale and technical equipment.

b. An uneasy truce was concluded with the Jews holding most of Palestine and part of Jerusalem.

c. The refugee problem is a continued source of trouble. Arab refugees, displaced by Jewish immigration, refuse to accept resettlement because they regarded the state of Israel as temporary.

d. Internally, the Jews face a rugged task in trying to support a population of slightly over two million on a rocky, semi-desert land about the size of the state of Connecticut.

e. The application of the most advanced techniques has so far not enabled Israel to balance imports by exports.

f. The existence of Israel depends on outside support, particularly from sympathizers in the United States. Arabs view Israel as a western creation, deliberately established by American Jewish voters and financiers to thwart Arab economic development.

    g. Israeli development of oil discovered in the Gaza Strip and the continued realization of long range plans for economic development considerably improve Israel's economic position by 1960. As more recent plans materialize, the nation may win its fight to support itself.

    h. The world's attention was fixed on Israel by the trial of <u>Adolf Eichmann</u> in 1961. Eichmann had been chief of the Nazi Gestapo's "Jewish Affairs" section and had sent millions to their death. He was hanged May 31, 1962.

D. <u>Middle Eastern oil has enriched some states, notably Iraq and Saudi Arabia,</u> and has created trouble over its development, its transportation to world markets, and the division of profits it produces.

    1. In Iran, the government, led by <u>Premier Mohammed Mossadegh,</u> seized the Anglo-Iranian oil Company in 1951.

        a. Mossadegh was fervently supported by Iranian nationalists.

        b. In 1953, after the failure of prolonged negotiations, a political upheaval drove Mossadegh from office to prison.

        c. Iran oil remains nationalized, but the government of Iran receives half of the profit; and the remainder is divided among several oil companies.

    2. <u>The Arab states seem to vary in their utilization of oil profits.</u>

        a. Iraq apparently has been the most effective in using oil revenue to carry out long range economic projects likely to contribute substantially to the future Iraqi standard of living.

        b. Such projects, however, are no guarantee of popularity in the turbulent world of Arab politics. In 1958 Iraq's king, crown prince, and premier were killed in a revolt led by the army.

        c. Iraq's internal affairs were chaotic in 1959 and 1960 as the army, Iraqi nationalists, conservative landowners, and Communists fought for ascendancy.

        d. By 1961, <u>Premier Abdel Karim el-Kassem,</u> an Iraqi nationalist, seemed to have consolidated his control.

Iraq presently leans more toward the U.S.S.R. than toward the west.

e. The Saudi Arabian government is frequently criticized for using too little of its oil profits for long range economic enterprise, but it is still in power. Greater efforts have been made in the last three years to provide the economic basis for education, industrialization, and modernization of Saudi Arabia.

3. Oil pipelines are among the most vital arteries of the Middle East.

a. The bulk of Middle Eastern oil goes to Europe, and British and French concern over the threat to their oil supply posed by Egyptian seizure of the Suez Canal contributed to their action in the Suez crisis of 1956.

b. During the Suez crisis, every Middle Eastern pipeline except one owned by the United States, was seized or blown up by Arab nationalists.

c. Iraq, Kuwait, and Saudi Arabia agreed, in 1959, to cooperate to build a pipeline from the Mediterranean to the Persian Gulf. They plan to exchange information on oil development and production and to insist that foreign oil companies use more native employees and technicians.

E. The deep hostility between Arabs and Jews and the possibility of Arab unity have contributed heavily to Middle Eastern turbulence.

1. Arab leaders such as Nasser have dreamed of a united Arab nation reaching from Morocco to the eastern tip of Arabia.

a. The "pan-Arab" advocates see a modern state occupying much of the same territory the Ottoman Empire held for ages.

b. But the term "Arab" is fairly exact only in reference to the Arabic language. No Arab race exists, and the Moslem faith by no means coincides with the Arab world.

c. Each Arab state is reluctant to accept the leadership of others. The United Arab Republic seems the natural leader with its developed nationalism and the modern capital of Cairo. But Iraq, oil-rich and without a serious population problem, contests U.A.R. leadership.

2. Even the <u>Suez crisis of 1956,</u> the greatest crisis in the Middle East since the Palestinian War of 1948, failed to produce effective or lasting Arab unity.

3. <u>Nasser ordered the nationalization of the Suez Canal Company in July, 1956,</u> and stated he would use its revenues to build the Aswan Dam since the Americans and British had refused him funds to build it.

   a. The British and French saw their Suez oil lifeline threatened by Nasser's action.

   b. International conferences through the summer and fall achieved nothing. On October 29, Israeli forces, in retaliation for repeated Egyptian border attacks, advanced into Egypt.

   c. Great Britain and France sent an ultimatum to Israel and Egypt demanding their forces remain ten miles from the canal. Egypt refused.

   d. On October 31, British and French forces attacked the canal zone. In the ensuing battles, the canal was blocked by sunken ships, precisely the contingency the French and British hoped to prevent by their intervention.

   e. It was not fear of Arab unity which caused the invasion forces to be withdrawn from the canal zone but pressure from the United States and Soviet Russia.

   f. To make matters worse, western preoccupation with the Suez crisis provided the U.S.S.R. with the needed opportunity to crush the Hungarian uprising (see chapter 15, part XII).

   g. In Great Britain, the Suez fiasco brought the resignation of Prime Minister Anthony Eden, who was succeeded by Harold Macmillan.

   h. Only prolonged negotiations and a United Nations occupying force led to Israeli evacuation of the Sinai Peninsula, and the canal was closed until late spring while a U.N. commission cleared it of sunken ships.

F. <u>The turmoil of the Middle East makes it vulnerable to Communist penetration</u> aimed at capturing its resources and realizing traditional Russian territorial ambitions.

1. The west has tried to counter Soviet imperialism by economic assistance and military alliances.

2. In 1955, the Baghdad Pact was signed by Great Britain, Iran, Iraq, Turkey, and Pakistan. The United States

did not sign the alliance to avoid antagonizing Israel and the U.S.S.R.

    a. This mutual security alliance created the "northern tier" of states as a barrier to Soviet aggression from Istanbul to India's northwest border.

    b. The Baghdad Pact was shattered by the Iraqi revolt of 1958 because the new government of Iraq dropped out of the Alliance.

    c. The remaining members then formed the Central Treaty Organization (CENTO). To strengthen CENTO, of which it is not a member, the United States signed separate defense treaties with Iran, Turkey, and Pakistan.

  3. In January, 1957, the United States proclaimed the "Eisenhower Doctrine."

    a. This doctrine offered assistance by American armed forces to any Middle Eastern nation threatened by Communist or Communist-inspired aggression if the nation requested help from the United States.

    b. The Communists denounced the Eisenhower Doctrine, but Turkey, Israel, and Lebanon approved it.

    c. In July, 1958, Lebanon requested American troops to establish order. The Lebanese feared election riots were being used by agents of the United Arab Republic to gain control of the country.

    d. American forces landed in July and August, restored order, and withdrew in October. The elections, meanwhile, proceeded peacefully; General Fouad Chehab was elected president.

G. Algeria was incorporated into France by the Constitution of 1946, which established the Fourth French Republic. Algeria sends deputies to the National Assembly and is administered by a Governor General appointed in Paris.

  1. A rebellion of Algerian nationalists against French rule began in 1951.

    a. About five thousand rebels (fellegha) used guerrilla warfare and terrorist tactics against the French.

    b. In 1955, the French began enacting legislation to provide social benefits in Algeria, but it was too late.

    c. By 1956, the French had half a million soldiers in Algeria. They refused to assent to discussion of the Algerian situation by the United Nations because Algeria was technically a part of France, and the rebellion was an "internal matter."

d. The discovery of oil in Algeria in 1957 only increased the value of the prize to be exploited by the victor. To make matters worse, a split in the rebel forces led to fighting between rebel factions.

2. <u>1958 was a critical year for France and Algeria.</u> General Jacques Massu, commanding the French forces in Algeria, led the formation of a "Committee of Public Safety" which took control of Algeria and demanded that Charles De Gaulle become premier.

a. This action precipitated a political crisis in France that ended the Fourth Republic bringing a new constitution and the Fifth Republic led by De Gaulle (see Chapter 15, part XII, G).

b. It also became clear that the headquarters of the rebels was Cairo and that the leader of the <u>Algerian National Liberation Front (F.L.N.)</u> was <u>Ferhat Abbas.</u>

c. For two more years the fighting continued inconclusively; but in 1961, the French and the F.L.N. began to talk in terms of full independence for Algeria.

d. Before formal peace negotiations began, some of the French paratroop units in Algeria mutinied and formed the <u>Secret Army Organization (O.A.S.)</u> to keep Algeria French. The O.A.S. used terrorism against anyone supporting Algerian independence, and loyal French units fought the O.A.S. terrorists.

e. Peace negotiations between the French and the F.L.N. (May–July, 1961) broke down over control of Algeria's new oil wells. Talks were resumed in 1962, and a peace settlement was signed March 18, 1962.

f. The settlement provides for Algerian independence. French troops will be gradually withdrawn over a three year period. All citizens are guaranteed full civil rights.

g. The French colonists *(colons)* have three years to decide if they wish to become Algerian or return to France. Algerian oil will be developed jointly by the French and Algerians.

h. The voters of France approved the Algerian settlement by referendum April 8, 1962; and the rebel parliament has also ratified its terms.

    i. The O.A.S. has extended its terrorist activities to metropolitan France, and the French government is pursuing a relentless campaign against them. The government's objective is to achieve a cease-fire by stopping the activity of the O.A.S.

    j. The Algerian struggle has had other repercussions. France, normally not the most cooperative member of NATO, has been hard pressed to support both NATO and the French forces in Algeria. Assuming her geographical position makes her indispensable to NATO, France has given her NATO commitments secondary priority.

H. <u>Tunisia and Morocco have both won their independence since World War II.</u> Pressures similar to those operating in Algeria dominated the scene in both countries: French *colons* fighting nationalists; both sides resorting to violence; and the French government, anxious to protect French interests but recognizing the inevitable, trying to find a dignified way out.

    1. In 1951, the Tunisians were given a greater share in running their own affairs than they had enjoyed previously; and in 1954, the French granted them complete control of internal affairs.

        a. Violence erupted in February, 1956, as Tunisian nationalists demanded full independence and French *colons* fought for continued French control.

        b. The French government, nevertheless, granted Tunisia complete independence on March 20, 1956. The Tunisian government was led by Premier Habib Bourguiba, and Tunisia joined the United Nations the following November.

        c. In 1957, the traditional ruler, the Bey of Tunisia, was deposed; and Bourguiba became the first president of the Republic of Tunisia. Bourguiba is the leader of the pro-western Neo-Destour Party.

        d. In 1958, accusing Nasser of trying to overthrow Bourguiba, Tunisia broke diplomatic relations with the United Arab Republic.

        e. Tunisia, in spite of its ties to the Arab world, has quite consistently supported the west against the Communist bloc and is receiving American aid.

        f. A clash with the French at Bizerte in 1961 resulted in

the agreement that the French would give up their base in Bizerte when the Berlin crisis ended.

2. The French Constitution of 1946 included Morocco as an "associated state" of the French Union. Moroccan nationalists wanted complete independence.

   a. Again, violence and terror grew out of the clash between *colons* and nationalists; and, in 1956, the French formally recognized the nationalist leader, Sidi Mohammed ben Youssef, as Sultan Mohammed V:

   b. Later, Moroccan demands led to the addition of part of Spanish Morocco to the new state, which also joined the United Nations in 1956.

   c. Morocco has received American aid and has permitted the United States to maintain air bases in the country; the United States has promised to give up its Moroccan bases by 1963, however.

   d. A fairly extensive land reform program has been undertaken in Morocco, involving, in part, the evacuation and compensation of French *colons*.

   e. Sultan Mohammed V died in February, 1961 and has been succeeded by his son, Hassan II.

VIII. Sub-Saharan Africa

A. In the last century white settlers have pushed northward from the Cape of Good Hope and have created an area often called "White" Africa.

1. The settlers have always been outnumbered by the natives, who frequently have been used as cheap labor on ranches and plantations and in factories and in mines.

2. In spite of bad living and working conditions, the native population has increased; and the natives want their lands back.

3. In the cities, the natives want to share in or, better yet, to control the government. They wish to repeal laws that tell them where they may live, work, and travel.

4. The situation is complicated further by divisions within the European and non-European groups.

   a. The non-European group embraces the native "black" Africans, the "Colored" persons of mixed Europeans and non-European blood, and Asians who are mostly from India.

b. The Europeans are divided into "Afrikaners," who are descendants of Dutch "Boer" settlers, and the British colonists.

c. Non-Europeans outnumber Europeans by a ratio of about four to one. Afrikaners outnumber the British.

d. Each of the five groups—native Africans, Colored, Asian, Afrikaner, British—exist as self-conscious, propagandizing factions, frequently mutually exclusive in their aims.

5. Kenya, a British crown colony of "White" Africa, has furnished an example in the mid-twentieth century of the tensions in Africa.

a. The major African tribe in Kenya is the Kikuyu. Some of the Kikuyu developed a secret terrorist society, the Mau Mau.

b. The Mau Mau fanatics struck at both the whites and the more peaceful and conservative members of their own tribe.

c. By late 1952, the Mau Mau terror had reached such dimensions that, at the request of the colonial government, help was flown from Britain and the rebellion was finally crushed.

d. Jomo Kenyatta, leader of the Mau Mau, was imprisoned, and measures leading to self-government for Kenya were undertaken.

e. By 1962, Kenyans had elected their first legislative council. Kenyatta was released. The Legislative council is dominated by African parties, and the British have agreed that a constitutional conference be held in London in 1962.

f. The basic land problem is unresolved, and serious tensions remain. How to find an arrangement meeting the needs of both white settlers and land-hungry natives is an unsolved problem.

6. The Republic of South Africa is probably the most important political unit of "White" Africa.

a. The government is dominated by the Nationalist Afrikaner Party. The British and Afrikaners are mutually hostile, though neither group intends to drive out or exterminate the Africans in the Republic.

b. Afrikaners regard the British as too liberal toward non-Europeans, although the British have little desire to turn the government over to a black majority.

c. The dominant Afrikaners' policy is *Apartheid* (apartness). *Apartheid* advocates assert the whites should govern, and the non-whites will receive some of the benefits of modern economics and technology.

d. *Apartheid* involves separate jobs, living quarters, and

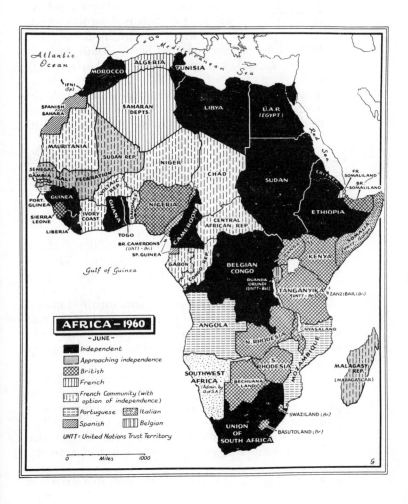

education for each separate non-European group. Naturally, the non-Europeans refuse to accept this situation as final, and their programs aim at driving the whites out of Africa.

e. The Republic of South Africa replaced the self-governing Union of South Africa within the British Commonwealth of Nations in 1961 as a result of the Commonwealth nations' condemnation of South African racial policy.

f. *Apartheid* has drawn the censure of the United Nations twice and has led to economic boycott of South African products by many other African states.

g. 1961 witnessed economic decline in South Africa as private capital was withdrawn and boycotts took effect.

h. The Afrikaners, led by Prime Minister Hendrik Verwoerd, won the elections in 1961 and are still in control. But the situation within the Republic of South Africa is potentially explosive.

B. The west and central African region reaching from the Sahara Desert, to the north, into Angola, to the south, is sometimes referred to as "Black" Africa. It straddles the equator and embraces the area from the west coast to the Mitumbi Mountains and the highlands at the western edge of the basin of the Nile.

1. The population of about seventy-five million includes hundreds of tribes and a variety of religions. The economy is largely devoted to agricultural and tropical products.

2. European colonial control of the area usually followed the "indirect rule" formula: natives governed those matters where traditional tribal custom was binding, and whites applied the economic, technical, and legal apparatus of the modern world.

3. Since World War II, the Africans have demanded, with great success, that they govern themselves; and completely independent African states have appeared in rapid succession.

4. In most of the new states there is a real danger that political reform will get hopelessly ahead of economic growth.

a. Strong tensions exist between the educated natives of

the cities and their fellows in the tribal villages.

b. Political independence, *per se,* does not produce wealth nor the technical skill necessary to create it. The emancipated but unsophisticated natives, naturally dissatisfied with their low standard of living, may prove to be easy targets for political agitation.

5. Ghana, formed from the British colony of the Gold Coast, was the first of the west central African states to be freed since World War II.

   a. Ghana's formal independence was recognized March 6, 1957. It remained within the British Commonwealth of Nations and is led by President Kwame Nkrumah.

   b. Ghana's economy faltered in spite of massive aid from the Communist bloc, and Nkrumah imposed an austerity program in July, 1961.

   c. Nkrumah has moved toward changing Ghana from a republic to his personal Socialist dictatorship in spite of internal oposition marked by violence. Admitted to the U.N. in 1957, Ghana tends to support the Communist bloc.

6. In the one year of 1960, seventeen African states became independent; fifteen of them are in the west central African area.

7. The experience of the Republic of the Congo (formerly Belgian Congo) provides an unhappy example of the conflicting tensions affecting some of the newly independent states.

   a. It was hoped the Congo would progress peacefully under the presidency of Joseph Kasavubu, whose government was located in Leopoldville.

   b. The mineral-rich province of Katanga, led by Moise Tshombe and supported by foreign investors, wanted to be independent from the rest of the Congo.

   c. Antoine Gizenga, in Stanleyville, supported by the Communists, declared Orientale province should be independent of the Leopoldville government.

   d. The situation was complicated further by the role of pro-Communist Patrice Lumumba, who had been deposed from his position as prime minister in Kasavubu's government. Lumumba was, however, popular among the Congolese. When he was imprisoned in Katanga and later murdered, pro-Lumumba and anti-Lumumba factions within the Congo went to war.

    e. The United Nations resolved to use force to end the civil war in the Congo. After a series of conferences produced little more than defiance from Tshombe, U.N. troops went into action against Katanga, and an uneasy truce was arranged after eight days of fighting.

    f. The truce (September 21, 1961) followed by only a few hours the death of the United Nations Secretary-General, Dag Hammarskjöld, who had flown to the Congo seeking a peaceful solution to its problems.

    g. Fighting was renewed in October; and, in December, the U.N. forces hit Katanga again and restored peace.

    h. As 1962 opened, the Congolese factions were meeting in Leopoldville to draw up a new constitution to re-unite the Congo. Thousands had died needlessly in an area which, however much it deserved freedom, was unprepared for it.

8. Violence in the Congo had other repercussions. The death of Hammarskjöld provided the Soviet Union with another opportunity to try to change the structure of the United Nations.

    a. The U.S.S.R. proposed to replace the single Secretary-General with a three man Secretariat, each member having a veto over the others' actions.

    b. Other members, ably led by Adlai Stevenson, the United States ambassador to the U.N., defeated the Russian attempt.

    c. U Thant of Burma was unanimously chosen by the Security Council as the new Acting Secretary-General.

BIBLIOGRAPHY

Antonius, G., *The Arab awakening* (Beirut: Khayat's College Book Cooperative, 1955).

Clark, M. K., *Algeria in turmoil* (New York: Praeger, 1959).

Dean, V. M., *The Nature of the non-western world* (New York: New American Library, 1957).

Feis, H., *The China tangle* (Princeton: Princeton University Press, 1953).

Fisher, S. N., *The Middle East* (New York: Knopf, 1959).

Laqueur, W. Z., *The Soviet Union and the Middle East* (New York: Praeger, 1959).

Low, F., *The struggle for Asia* (New York: Praeger, 1955).

Marquard, L., *The peoples and policies of South Africa* (New York Oxford University Press, 1952).

Paton, A., *Cry, the beloved country* (New York: Scribner's, 1948).

Reischauer, E. O., *The United States and Japan* (Cambridge: Harvard University Press, 1957).

Spear, T. G., *India, Pakistan and the west,* (2nd ed., New York: Oxford University Press, Home University Library, 1952).

Tillon, G., *Algeria: the realities* (New York: Knopf, 1958).

INDEX

Abbas, Ferhat, leader of Algerian National Liberation Front, 483

Abdel Karim el-Kassem, Premier of Iraq, 479

Abdul Aziz (Sultan of Turkey 1861-1876), 317-318

Abdul Hamid II (Sultan of Turkey 1876-1909), 318-322

Abdul Mejid (Sultan of Turkey 1839-1861), 313-317

Aberdeen, George, 4th Earl of, 256

Aboukir Bay, battle of, 132

Academic Legion, 171

Act of Union (of 1707), 14; (of 1800), 16

Action Française, 291

Adenauer, Konrad, Chancellor of West German Federal Republic, 462-463

Adowa, Battle of, and influence on India, 71; and resignation of Crispi, 247-248

Adrianople, Treaty of (1829), 154, 312

Afghan War, of 1839-1842, 69; of 1878-1879, 260

Afghanistan, 1918 to 1939, 414-415

Africa, theatre of military operations (1940-1941), 433-434; Allied conquest of (1942), 439

Afrikaner, 486-488

Agadir, 347

Aix-la-Chapelle, Peace of (1668), 31; Treaty of (1748), 58, 67; conference (1818), 152

Aksakov, Ivan, 296, 302

Alchemy, 95

Alexander I, King of Greece, 402

Alexander I, King of Yugoslavia, 378

Alexander I, tsar (1801-1825), 138, 140-141; and Congress of Vienna, 149-150; Holy Alliance, 151-153; internal policy, 293-294

Alexander II, tsar (1855-1881), 297-301, 327, 340-341

Alexander III, tsar (1881-1894), 301-304

Alexandra, tsarina, 360

Algeciras conference (1906), 346

Algeria, 230, 273-274

Allenby, General Edmund, 353

All-India Congress Party, 417-418, 466

All-India Moslem League, 466

Alphonso XIII, King of Spain, 396

Alsace-Lorraine, 281

Amanullah, ruler of Afghanistan, 415

Amiens, Peace of, 136

Amritsar massacre (1919), 72

Anarchism, 195

Anatomical Exercise on the Motion of the Heart and Blood in Animals, 94-95

Andrássy, Julius, 328-329, 341

Anglo-American Oil Company, 413

Anglo-German Treaty of 1890, 337